ALSO BY RONALD HINGLEY

Nightingale Fever: Russian Poets in Revolution

Russian Writers and Soviet Society: 1917–1978

A New Life of Anton Chekhov

Chekhov: A Biographical and Critical Study

Dostoyevsky: His Life and Work

The Undiscovered Dostoyevsky

Russian Writers and Society: 1825–1904

Nihilists

The Tsars: Russian Autocrats, 1533–1917

A People in Turmoil: Revolutions in Russia

The Russian Secret Police

A Concise History of Russia

Joseph Stalin: Man and Legend

EDITOR AND TRANSLATOR OF

The Oxford Chekhov:
Volumes 1–3 *(plays)*; Volumes 4–9 *(stories)*

TRANSLATOR OF

Alexander Solzhenitsyn:
One Day in the Life of Ivan Denisovich
(with Max Hayward)

PASTERNAK

RONALD HINGLEY

PASTERNAK

A BIOGRAPHY

ALFRED A. KNOPF   NEW YORK   1983

THIS IS A BORZOI BOOK

PUBLISHED BY ALFRED A. KNOPF, INC.

Copyright © 1983 by Ronald Hingley
All rights reserved under International and Pan-American
Copyright Conventions. Published in the United States by
Alfred A. Knopf, Inc., New York. Distributed by Random House,
Inc., New York. Originally published in Great Britain
by George Weidenfeld & Nicolson Limited.

Library of Congress Cataloging in Publication Data

Hingley, Ronald.
Pasternak: a biography.

Bibliography: p.
Includes index.
1. Pasternak, Boris Leonidovich, 1890–1960—
Biography. 2. Poets, Russian—20th century—Biography.
I. Title.
PG3476.P27Z68   1983   891.71'42 [B]   83-48114
ISBN 0-394-51595-1

Manufactured in the United States of America
First American Edition

Воспоминание о полувеке
Пронесшейся грозой уходит вспять.
Столетье вышло из его опеки.
Пора дорогу будущему дать.

Не потрясенья и перевороты
Для новой жизни очищают путь,
А откровенья, бури и щедроты
Души воспламененной чьей-нибудь.

Fifty years' memories recede.
The tumult of their thunder dies.
This century has come of age.
It's time to let the future happen.

Catastrophes and revolutions
Don't clear the path to life's renewal
As do the insights, squalls and bounties
In one man's incandescent soul.

BORIS PASTERNAK, JULY 1958

CONTENTS

ILLUSTRATIONS

following page 178

Rozaliya and Leonid Pasternak, 1896
Pasternak Family Collection

Boris Pasternak, aged eight
Ashmolean Museum, Oxford

Pasternak as a youth
Courtesy of Ardis Publishers

The Pasternak family at Molodi
Pasternak Family Collection

Pasternak, 1913
Pasternak Family Collection

Pasternak with his first wife Yevgeniya and son Yevgeny, 1924
Pasternak Family Collection

Marina Tsvetayeva
Courtesy of Ardis Publishers

Vladimir Mayakovsky
Society for Cultural Relations with the USSR

Anna Akhmatova
Novosti Press Agency

Osip Mandelstam
Novosti Press Agency

Nina and Titsian Tabidze, 1933
Einaudi

Boris and Zinaida Pasternak, 1934
Pasternak Family Collection

PASTERNAK

INTRODUCTION

Towards the end of his three score years and ten (1890–1960) the Russian poet Boris Leonidovich Pasternak emerged as the author of a renowned novel with a poet as its hero: *Doctor Zhivago*. He also became an important figure on the international political stage.

These activities or experiences were not equally consistent with Pasternak's temperament and skills. He was one of nature's poets, no one can deny that. But he was never one of nature's novelists. Still less had he any natural leaning towards politics. Yet his very distaste for public affairs was prominent among the factors which, given the peculiar tensions of his period, helped to make him so significant a public figure. To study his life and work is to examine over forty years of interaction between art and society in the political ultra-low-temperature laboratory which was Russia.

Boris Leonidovich found his own unique solution – courageous, ingenious and sometimes undignified – to the problem of fitting his life to his age, and that aspect of his development is fascinating. But an enquiry into his activities is more rewarding still for what it reveals of an outstandingly gifted individual who discovered a new way to wield words, images and ideas. No one, before Pasternak wrote, could have suspected the enormous range of potentialities still open to the Russian language.

The present study of Pasternak's life and works attempts a more detailed exploration of an author who has already been discussed in my previously published *Nightingale Fever: Russian Poets in Revolution* (1982) alongside three other Russian poets of comparable talent (Akhmatova, Mandelstam and Tsvetayeva). In this later volume Pasternak occupies the centre of attention on his own. To this it must be added that the important last two decades of his life, from 1940 onwards, are here considered in far greater detail. In *Nightingale Fever*, which effectively ends with the death of Tsvetayeva in 1941, Pasternak's later period could be no more than briefly summarized.

Pasternak is still chiefly known to the world at large for his novel, and for the world-wide repercussions which it provoked. *Doctor Zhivago* was first published in Milan in 1957, and it helped to earn its author the offer, which came from Stockholm in the following year, of the Nobel Prize for Literature. The announcement of the award, followed in quick succession by Pasternak's enthusiastic acceptance and sudden renunciation of it, provoked a global drama in which he figured as the hero and the Kremlin (except in its own version) as the villain. On so grand a scale did the international reactions develop that a contemporary observer could, without danger of exaggeration, speak of *Doctor Zhivago* as follows. 'It is hard to think of another literary work in the whole history of literature that has aroused such a world-wide public stir.'[1] Now, more than a quarter of a century after the novel's first appearance, this claim still seems as valid as it was when it was originally put forward.

Yet Pasternak remains faceless. In 1980 he could be described, in a detailed study of his work, as 'one of the most enigmatic authors of the twentieth century'.[2] Not until 1981 did the first comprehensive biography appear, by Guy de Mallac. The work is a labour of love and the product of many years' application, but here too Boris Leonidovich tends to emerge as a man without qualities. What of his loves, his marriages, his living conditions, his temperament? Where is the 'human interest' which some publishers and editors believe to be an obsessive concern of the reading public? Can it be that this figure, so vivid when projected on to the world stage in his seventh decade, was dull and featureless in private life?

Most certainly not, but his essence is difficult to grasp. He is a most elusive man, if only because the material on his life is sparse and tends to be inaccessible, much of it still being buried in closed archives in his native country. This helps to explain the fact that a recent authority on the subject has even denied the right of any specialist to put forward a new hypothesis about Pasternak's work while so much evidence remains unavailable.[3] The unsatisfactory nature of the sources is further confirmed if the material on Pasternak is compared with that which is to be had on other leading Russian poets among his contemporaries. Vladimir Mayakovsky and Marina Tsvetayeva are both extensively covered in sources far more substantial than are available in Pasternak's case. Those on Osip Mandelstam include the two superb chronicles by his widow Nadezhda, while Anna Akhmatova has been admirably served by her devoted amanuensis Lidiya Chukovskaya. It is a measure of the poverty of the Pasternak material that the memoirs of Chukovskaya and Nadezhda Mandelstam provide a fair proportion of the most valuable information on him too – and this despite the fact that he represented a topic of only secondary importance to these two memoirists.

The dearth of documentation derives in part from the delay with which Pasternak received recognition. Only in his thirty-third year, and with the publication of his verse collection *My Sister Life*, did he begin to become widely known. Even then his was the reputation of a brilliant pioneering poet chiefly honoured in his own country, and with such limitations as that implies. Not until the publication of *Doctor Zhivago* in 1957 did the name Pasternak begin to become a household word in the world at large. He was then aged sixty-seven – an old man, almost, in years if not in spirit. By that time he had given the authorities of his native country every reason to suppress information about him, and they have shown no lack of zeal in doing so. The material on his early decades is in particularly short supply. As his life progresses, so too do the sources become more ample and useful. But they never become lavish.

The man himself would have welcomed this lack of documentation. He repeatedly asserted that he did not wish to be the centre of attention. He was so far from seeking to smooth the path of future thesis-writers and biographers that he actually went out of his way to boast of his success in destroying evidence about himself. 'I don't have any establishment, library, archive, sanctum or collection of this, that or the other. I don't keep my correspondence or my drafts. I don't let anything pile up. My room's easier to tidy than a hotel room. I live like a student.'[4]

This policy accords with his belief that a poet's work is all-important, whereas his life and personality matter not a jot. He makes the point explicit in a famous lyric of the 1950s.

> There's ugliness in being famous.
> That's not what elevates a man.
> No need to institute an archive
> Or dither over manuscripts.

The poem goes on to concede that biographers may have the duty of assessing a poet's life and work, but claims that the poet himself must be more modest.

> Let others, hot upon your trail,
> Pace out your life's span inch by inch.
> But *you* your failures from your triumphs
> Must never differentiate.[5]

Though Pasternak was eager to dismiss enquiry into his life as an activity suitable only for others, he nevertheless did contribute two sizeable autobiographical studies in prose, *Safe Conduct* (1929–31) and *Autobiographical Sketch* (1959). The former was written around his fortieth birthday, and the latter when he was approaching his seventieth. Despite the dates at which they were written, he virtually confines himself in both to charting his experiences during his first thirty years – that is, up to the year 1920 or thereabouts. On the following decade they are unrevealing, having more to say about other poets than about the author himself. After that the narrative, such as it is, breaks off – in each case at the beginning of the 1930s.

These two autocommentaries have other points in common besides an insistence on concentrating on the subject's early decades. Both are sketchy, quirky and of suspect reliability, while at the same time being stimulating and admirable guides to their author's nature. Both are highly selective, and perversely insist on omitting virtually all reference to what is known in Russian as *byt* – that is, to such topics as his income, children and wives, together with everything else bearing on the material conditions of his domestic and working life. But the two works also differ radically from each other. The earlier, *Safe Conduct*, is by far the more self-indulgent, the more obscure and the more offhand in its treatment of the reader, whereas *Autobiographical Sketch* conforms with the cult of simplicity followed by Pasternak in later life by imparting information more directly and comprehensibly. Still, even *Autobiographical Sketch* is far from being a conventional autobiography.

In *Safe Conduct* Pasternak explicitly abjures any intention of giving an orderly account of his life. He baldly states that 'I am not writing my autobiography', and he goes on to explain that only a hero deserves to have his doings properly described. But the poet (by implication an inverted hero) 'imparts so deliberately steep a slant to his whole life that it cannot exist in the biographical vertical where we expect to find it'. Pasternak also boasts that the account of his own life given in *Safe Conduct* is 'deliberately arbitrary'. He has picked certain details at random. But he might just as well have decided to give more of them or to have substituted others. As if repenting of such high-handedness, he begins his second account of his own life, *Autobiographical Sketch*, by denouncing its predecessor for being unnecessarily pretentious.[6] *Autobiographical Sketch* consists, in effect, of a translation of the mannered *Safe Conduct* into plain man's Russian. But it still omits virtually everything in the way of *byt*, 'human interest' and the like, while remaining capriciously selective in many other areas of its author's activity.

Another salient feature of the autocommentaries is that Pasternak does not deploy his life in systematic and orderly progression, but offers a series of blinding flashes against a featureless background. Existence chugs along uneventfully, but now and again the lightning strikes as the author takes up musical composition, gives up musical composition, has a marriage proposal rejected, abandons the study of philosophy, falls under the spell of Mayakovsky's poetic personality, frees himself from Mayakovsky's spell and so on. He often spoke – not so much in the autocommentaries as in other remarks which he let fall over the years – of the chief crises in his life as moments of rebirth. Death and resurrection were fairly commonplace experiences for him, and his entire career consists, in his own presentation, of a chain of such episodes. He had a tendency to dramatize them, exaggerating the suddenness of the successive crises and the abruptness of the changes of direction.

With all their deficiences as evidence, many of which are literary virtues, the two autocommentaries remain the most important source material on Pasternak up to the age of thirty. Still, given the nature of these writings and the lack of adequate corroborative sources, the biographer must experience some relief as he enters, from about 1920 onwards, the period of the poet's life which he himself has tended to ignore in his autobiographical studies. From now on certain other authorities become particularly valuable for the acuteness of their observations. Pasternak's cousin Olga Freydenberg, Nadezhda Mandelstam and Lidiya Chukovskaya are among them. With each successive decade the information becomes more adequate. This is partly because Pasternak's activities became more and more a matter of public record as his life proceeded, and partly because he was increasingly attracting the attention of memoirists, critics and correspondents. The testimony of Mandelstam's widow and Lidiya Chukovskaya is reinforced, from the Second World War onwards, by the reminiscences of another friend, the playwright Aleksandr Gladkov. The post-war period is also covered by Olga Ivinskaya, the intimate companion of Pasternak's last years, whose book *V plenu vremeni* (*A Captive of Time;* 1978) provides the most revealing account of the poet to be found in any of the primary sources other than his own writings.

All these sources have come to light only in the last few years, and some of them (the correspondence with Freydenberg and the long concluding section of Chukovskaya's memoirs) were not yet available when I was writing the pages on Pasternak in *Nightingale Fever*. The same is true of three important, recently published scholarly studies: de Mallac's biography, Lazar Fleishman's *Boris Pasternak v*

dvadtsatyye gody ('Boris Pasternak in the Nineteen-Twenties'; 1980)
and the extensive symposium of critical and memoir material brought
out in Paris under the title *Boris Pasternak* (1979). These works have
considerably clarified my view of the subject. But I have rarely been
forced into outright contradiction of my earlier study, except perhaps
in the interpretation of Pasternak's period as an apprentice poet. When
discussing that phase previously I had not yet had the opportunity to
examine Dr Christopher Barnes's D.Phil. thesis, 'The Poetry of Boris
Pasternak, 1913–1917'. I have now done so – and with immense
benefit to my account of the poet's formative years in Chapter 2.

The prominence given to literary matters in Chapters 2, 3 and 4 is
the inevitable outcome of Pasternak's intensive concentration on
literary creativity during the period concerned. Then, from Chapter 5
onwards, his increasing deviation into politics and public affairs
becomes evident. Yet the political theme never comes near to
superseding the literary. Rather are the two intertwined, and so
intimately that it has been no easy task to trace their combined
evolution in the body of the text. In attempting to do so I have also
sought to pay tribute to a man of great courage who possessed the still
rarer characteristic of being an outstanding pioneer in the exploitation
of his native language's hidden resources. Pasternak was constantly
shifting the angle of his creative vision. He showed a pathological
horror of clichés except when he deliberately exploited them. He
believed, even as he so adroitly or infuriatingly mixed them, that
metaphors are 'the shorthand of the big personality'. He is always
liable to leave his admirers treading on a step which isn't there, and the
critic who has attributed to him 'the power of inevitably right
comparison' has done less than justice to the obsessive and inspired
persistence with which Pasternak so often pursued the inevitably
wrong comparison.[7]

Pasternak flings out his words in a great spray of sizzling poly-
syllables. Or he abruptly cuts off the supply, on the grounds that

> Silence, you're the best
> Thing I ever heard.
> Some ears are agonized
> Even by bat flight.[8]

Will he go straight for the jugular? Will he trip over his own feet? One
can rarely anticipate, half-way through his lines and sentences, what
will happen next.

All one knows with certainty is that he will astonish.

All translations in this book are by myself except where contrary indications are given in the Reference Notes. For the versions of Pasternak's poetry, which are extremely numerous, only one claim is made: that much time and trouble have been devoted to them. Though I have tried to avoid requoting material already presented in *Nightingale Fever*, some overlapping was inevitable. In such cases there has been no mechanical reproduction of the previously published versions. What this means is that, wherever a given rendering of the verse has seemed open to improvement, I have changed it. In one instance this urge to improve has affected the translation of a title: the work termed, in my previous book, *Lofty Malady* figures here as *High Fever*. But the general principles of translation remain unchanged. They are as set out in the Appendix to *Nightingale Fever*, except that stanzaic breaks have been treated in a more cavalier fashion, and that a little more metrical initiative has been admitted.

In the translations of extracts from Pasternak's prose, as in the renderings of his verse, fidelity to the original has been the target. My translations of passages from his critical articles and correspondence are, however, sometimes apt to nudge the sense in the direction of greater intelligibility than the original seems to offer. Pasternak was endowed with many talents. But he signally lacked one humble gift which has been shared by such eminent and varied predecessors as Julius Caesar, Martin Luther, Oliver Cromwell, Anton Chekhov, Joseph Stalin and Little Jack Horner – that of making a plain statement in plain words. He could hardly express anything without complicating it. This trait is especially marked on the occasions when he discusses the virtues of simplicity. It is, in its way, one of his most endearing features, but it does not ease his biographer's task.

An attempt has been made to tell Pasternak's story in plain language very different from that which he himself habitually used. He was, let the fact be faced, a man who liked to muddle things – a process to which he brought the creative flair of genius. One is right, surely, to suspect those of his interpreters who imply that they understand every word he wrote. Nor is it easy to feel much sympathy with those Pasternakologists who – stung, presumably, by the master's own penchant for artistic obfuscation – have patently set themselves to outdo him in an area which he has made so much his own. Some of them may be congratulated on having succeeded.

The awesome textual problems presented by modern Russian poets are discussed at length in the Appendix to *Nightingale Fever*, and that discussion need not be repeated here. It must, however, be pointed out that, since no complete critical edition of Pasternak's works and letters has ever been published, recourse has inevitably been made to a wide variety of editions, as listed in the Bibliography. The general policy has been to refer wherever possible to the Moscow-Leningrad (Biblioteka poeta, bolshaya seriya) edition of 1965 whenever a given passage is to be found there. Though that edition contains only the verse, it is at least comprehensively represented; true, some politically sensitive material has been omitted, but the fact remains that such material is surprisingly rare in Pasternak's *belles-lettres* outside *Doctor Zhivago*. My second recourse has been to an earlier and in many ways superior edition, that of Struve and Filipoff, in three volumes (Ann Arbor, 1961). References to the text of *Doctor Zhivago* are to the first Russian edition (Milan, 1957).

Russian names are transliterated as in *The Oxford Chekhov* (London, 1964–80), edited by myself; see especially vol. 3, pages xi–xii. With Ehrenburg, Khrushchev, Mandelstam, Skriabin, Tchaikovsky and certain other names, common usage is followed in defiance of transliterational consistency. For the capital of the USSR's Georgian Republic I sometimes use the form 'Tiflis' (as Pasternak himself often did) rather than 'Tbilisi', which is now correct. In printing the translated titles of Russian works in the text normal practice has been abjured to the extent that designations of short stories, articles, cycles of lyrics and *poemy* (long poems) are italicized. The purpose is to differentiate what are relatively substantial items from the *stikhotvoreniya* (short poems or lyrics), which are a major subject of study; for the titles of those the usual convention (roman in quotation marks) is followed. Sequences of three dots (four, if a full stop is involved) will be found only in quotations, where they are used to indicate that material has been omitted by myself; they do not reflect any indication of omissions – or any other punctuation device – to be found in the originals. Some of the officially encouraged homiletic formulae of Pasternak's native country, of the type 'Full Speed Ahead' and 'Radiant Faith in the Glorious Future', are occasionally distinguished by initial capitals in order to emphasize their liturgical function and lack of any essential conceptual connection with speed, radiance, faith, the future or anything else. Dates preceding 1 February 1918 are given according to the Old Style calendar current in Russia. This lagged behind the Western European calendar by twelve days in the nineteenth century and by thirteen days in the twentieth century. After 1 February 1918 there is no conflict in dating. Bracketed dates following the titles of works – for example, *Childhood of Lyuvers* (1922) – refer to the year of first publication in complete form, except where other indications are given.

For his skilled advice, many times solicited and received, for the generous loan of his unpublished D.Phil. thesis ('The Poetry of Boris Pasternak, 1913–1917'), as also for his numerous helpful published writings on the subject, I am more grateful than I can easily say to Christopher Barnes. My warmest thanks also go to Angela Livingstone and Guy de Mallac for sending me their much appreciated published contributions to the study of Pasternak. I am most grateful to Melvin Lasky, Editor of *Encounter* (London), for permitting me to draw on my article 'Pasternak's Shakespeare', which appeared in October 1980. I am also grateful for many an informal but informed comment to Barbara Heldt, Catriona Kelly, Michael Makin, Clare Powell, Gerry Smith, Isia Tlusty and Harry Willetts; and to Léontine Cookson and Jackie Willcox for secretarial and editorial help. My wife and Jeremy Newton, whose help has so often been acknowledged in previous books of mine, have continued to give detailed editorial and critical support, so that I am more in their debt than ever. Finally, I am most particularly grateful to Pasternak's sisters Josephine (Mrs Pasternak) and Lydia (Mrs Pasternak-Slater) for their graciousness in discussing with me aspects of their family history, and of their brother's life and work. I hope that they, and others, will forgive this book's many imperfections. That there are not far more of them is due to the sensitivity and patience of the publisher's editor, Linden Lawson.

Frilford, 1983   RONALD HINGLEY

PART ONE

MAZE OF MELODIES

1890–1923

1

INSPIRATION IN SEARCH OF A POET

'Moscow belonged to Pasternak from the time of his birth.'[1] This claim by the foremost Russian literary memoirist of his era, Nadezhda Mandelstam, is amply borne out by the facts.

Moscow and its close environs were the chosen place of residence of the poet, novelist and political delinquent during seventy years of life. He was born in the city, and he died a few miles away, after rarely quitting the area for more than a few months at a time. Moscow provided the background for his idyllic family life in childhood, and acclaimed him as one of its most brilliant creative artists in his early thirties. It accorded him in old age the greatest honour which can be bestowed on any Russian writer – promotion to the rank of the state's internal Public Enemy Number One. By then, however, it was less a matter of Moscow belonging to Pasternak than of Pasternak belonging to the world.

At the date of his birth the infant, whose surname means 'parsnip' in Russian, did not seem likely to inherit his native city or very much else. His father, Leonid Osipovich Pasternak, was still a struggling artist dependent on erratic commissions and lacking regular employment when Boris became the first child born to his wife Rozaliya Isidorovna (Roza) on 29 January 1890. The Pasternak parents were then living in Oruzheyny Street in the north of central Moscow, a district which presented considerable variety. Opposite their home was an Orthodox seminary where future priests received their education, though it is true that many of the pupils had a tendency to deviate into revolutionary terrorism. Other, less exalted, professions were also represented in this thoroughly seedy area where the side-streets were slums. Church, revolutionaries, slums: all made their impact on the future poet.

Boris's parents were not so poor that they failed to equip him with a succession of wet-nurses and nannies who would convey him about this dubious neighbourhood, unable to resist gossiping with its inhabitants while yet seeking to preserve the infant from polluting contact with the squalor around him. They were constantly tugging at his sleeve because 'You weren't supposed to know this, you'd better not hear that.' But the little boy knew and heard enough 'from the yarns and hysterics' of beggars, ladies of the streets and other undesirables to acquire, so early in life, what he has termed 'a heart-breakingly terrifying compassion for woman'.[2] This tender concern for the female lot, together with an urge to attribute transcendental significance to woman the darner of socks and the ironer of trousers, was never to desert him. It inspired much of his poetry, and supplied his novel *Doctor Zhivago* with a major theme.

Contact with the Orthodox Church was provided less by the seminary in Oruzheyny Street than by the boy's pious nanny, Akulina Gavrilovna, who joined the Pasternak household when Boris was three years old. Besides filling his head with folksy speech and lore, she took him to church services, and also – according to his evidence – had him baptized a Christian on her own initiative. Towards the end of his life Pasternak was to hail his adherence to Christianity as one of the principal inspirations of his poetry and his novel. He even called his christening 'the source of my originality', and described it as a semi-secret and intimate event.[3] So secret was it, indeed, that it may not have taken place at all. Pasternak's sisters Josephine and Lydia have both told me most emphatically that they do not accept their brother's story about his baptism – a salutary warning not to believe, literally, everything that he chose to tell the world about himself. In any case the boy's religious status, or lack of status, was conditioned by the position of his parents. Both were of Jewish descent, and they were registered in law as adherents of the Jewish religion. But neither of them practised it. Pasternak's father has been quoted as stating that he believed in God while belonging to no specific religious denomination.[4]

Leonid Pasternak retained sufficient independence to reject conversion to Christianity, even though this could easily have been arranged and seemed likely to assist his career. In practice, however, his Jewish affiliations proved no obstacle to his appointment, in 1894, to the teaching staff of Moscow's School of Painting, Sculpture and Architecture. The school provided him and his family with an apartment on its premises at 21 Myasnitsky Street in central Moscow, about a mile north-east of the Kremlin. This impressive edifice, with its imposing balcony, had been built in the eighteenth century as the residence of a noble family; it now stood opposite Moscow's chief post office in what had become the city's flourishing business district. Pasternak's father was to remain on the staff for over a quarter of a century, and the two flats which the family successively occupied in the School building were to be Boris's home as an infant, adolescent and young man until, in 1911, they moved out to a flat in Volkhonka Street.

The Moscow of Pasternak's childhood was a picturesque city, and his father has briefly evoked some of those aspects which most appealed to his painter's eye. They included 'the innumerable old cloisters, towers and churches with gold-crowned cupolas, the golden-white Kremlin towering over the city and gleaming in the sun'. As Russia's former capital (up to 1712), Moscow still remained the centre of traditional state pageantry. The four-year-old Boris was able to observe from the balcony of the School of Painting the funeral procession of the Emperor Alexander III in 1894, and he also saw part of the ceremonial attending the coronation of his successor Nicholas II two years later.[5]

In these surroundings the child Boris experienced an event which was to become a significant theme in his writings – the dawn of consciousness in the infant psyche. In his prose story *Childhood of Lyuvers* (1922) he gives a haunting picture of the process as experienced by a little girl. Still more impressively, he describes in a lyric of 1921 the birth of creative sensibility in a generalized infant poet.

> One strains, aged two, away from nurse
> To misty maze of melodies.
> One twitters, whistles – until words
> Appear when one is three years old.

This is the age at which, according to the lyric, poets begin to doubt their mothers' and their own identities, to feel their home as alien. That bough of lilac, drooping over a garden bench – can it have any other aim in life than the kidnapping of children? A Faust, a fantasist, a budding gypsy – the infant poet is all these things as he imagines an ocean suddenly rearing up over his garden fence and hastily converts it into iambics. As these superb verses indicate, Boris was a hypersensitive child, a prey to fears and imaginings. 'How often I came near to suicide at the ages of six, seven, eight. I suspected myself to be surrounded by all sorts of mysteries and deceits. There was no nonsense I didn't believe.' The nonsense included the conviction that he had once been a girl, and a determination to resume that delightful status. At other times the boy persuaded himself that he was not his parents' son, but a foster-child.[6]

The words lisped by the three-year-old Boris may not yet have been those of a poet, but they were already those of a Muscovite. Nadezhda Mandelstam, herself Jewish, points out that 'Jewish children who grew up in Moscow picked up the city's accent pretty smartly'. She adds that Pasternak spoke wonderful Muscovite Russian, even though he did not so much speak as 'sing, moo, roar and boom'.[7]

After musing on the birth of an infant poet's consciousness in his lyric of 1921, Pasternak was more precise when he came to his own experience of the same event in *Autobiographical Sketch*, written towards the end of his life. The moment of revelation had occurred on 23 November 1894, he then explained, and the occasion had been a chamber music concert in the drawing-room of the Pasternaks' newly occupied flat in the School of Painting. A trio, probably by Tchaikovsky, was being performed by the poet's mother at the piano and by two professors from the Moscow Conservatory who played the violin and cello. As the trio proceeded the infant poet, who was asleep behind a curtain, was awakened by an unaccustomed sensation – 'a sweet, nagging torment'. He started up in panic and anguish, bursting into tears which only became audible when the music ended. While his mother comforted him he was aware of a glittering scene with flickering candles and billowing tobacco smoke in which he discerned a well-known friend of the family, the painter N. N. Ge. There was also another, more portentous vision, whose spirit was to dominate the Pasternak home. It was the great novelist Lev Nikolayevich Tolstoy.[8]

This moment was important to Pasternak as his first conscious memory. But the scene is also significant because its literary, musical and pictorial components so eloquently emphasize the extent to which the future poet sprang out of an artistic milieu. No other Russian writer has been born with such a rich legacy of genetic and environmental predisposition to artistic creativity.

Pasternak adored his mother and father, and he said that he owed them everything in life.[9] They both came from Odessa. His mother was born there in 1867, and fully lived up to her native city's tradition of generating musical infant prodigies by giving widely acclaimed public piano performances in Russia and abroad from the age of eight. She became a protégée of Anton Rubinstein and potentially one of the great pianists of her age, but sacrificed her art to the demands of domesticity when she married Pasternak's father. He was born in 1862 as the son of an innkeeper, and moved to Moscow in 1887. His close association with Tolstoy began shortly after his appointment to the School of Painting, with a commission to illustrate the great novelist's *War and Peace*. The two men first met in 1893, and the link became particularly close when Leonid Pasternak accepted Tolstoy's invitation to illustrate his last novel, *Resurrection*, as it was serialized in 1899.

Leonid Pasternak was a versatile artist who by no means limited himself to illustrating novels. He also painted landscapes, still lifes, interiors and above all portraits. They included many notables of the age. Tolstoy was one of his subjects; so too were Tchaikovsky, Gorky and Rilke, while Lenin and Einstein were to be added in course of time. Leonid Osipovich also did portraits of his own family; they brought out his special gift for capturing childhood and early adulthood on canvas. His style is vivid and original, and his work has continued to command admiration at exhibitions staged since his death in 1945. He is renowned for capturing fleeting movements of light, in which respect his canvases may be said to rival his son's verse. But his originality did not lead him far into the sphere of the non-representational and the avant-garde. His son, a 'modern' poet as only a poet of the 1910s could be modern, was to strike out in a very different direction from his father.

Self-portraits by Pasternak's father show a handsome, stylish, bearded figure. Leonid Osipovich was elegant, with a touch of Bohemianism, and usually looked as if he had just prepared himself to be auditioned for the part of Mephistopheles. But he was not as flamboyant as he may have seemed: his younger daughter Lydia has described him to me as outstandingly gentle and retiring in manner. Not Leonid, but Roza and Boris were the fiery elements in a family whose idyllic happiness was not so insipid as to exclude occasional displays of temperament.

To Boris, the Pasternaks' first-born, were added a brother and two sisters. Aleksandr, the second son, was born in 1893; the two daughters Josephine and Lydia were born in 1900 and 1902 respectively; and all three siblings have long survived their famous brother. There is no suggestion in the record that family life was ever anything but harmonious, and the mother's ill health (she suffered from heart trouble) is the only cloud which ever hovers over their annals. All six Pasternaks were unusually gifted. But three of them were superlatively endowed. According to Josephine Pasternak, they consisted of 'three suns or stars, and three minor bodies related to them. The minor bodies were: Aleksandr, Lydia and myself. The suns were: father, mother and Boris.'[10]

Such was the Pasternak ménage – a very temple of the arts, but also a workshop. The boy saw his father's canvases take shape in his studio; he became familiar with the work of other painters, including Repin, Serov and Vrubel; he watched the unpacking and installation of the numerous exhibitions held at the School of Painting. Meanwhile

Boris's mother was regularly playing the piano at home long after she had suspended public performances. Music it was that most captured the child's fancy. After the night on which he had been awakened by the trio playing in the presence of Tolstoy, music 'swamped my whole horizon for more than fifteen years'.[11] He was to be a grown man before he turned to writing poetry.

With the advent of the twentieth century Pasternak's native city seemed transformed 'by a magic wand', as Pasternak himself has commented. 'Moscow was seized by the commercial frenzy of the world's major capital cities. . . . Brick giants, sprouting unnoticed, reared to heaven on all the streets.'[12] It was against this background that the boy underwent his second shattering experience of rebirth – six years after his collision with Tolstoy and music. The midwife was the Austrian poet Rainer Maria Rilke.

This momentous encounter took place on a hot summer day in 1900 at the Kursk Railway Station in Moscow as the Pasternak family was about to depart for Odessa. A mysterious stranger in a black Tyrolean cloak, later to be identified as Rilke, approached their compartment window from outside and engaged Leonid Osipovich in conversation. The stranger spoke in German, a language which the ten-year-old Boris already knew 'perfectly', according to his own account. But he had never heard it spoken as the stranger spoke it, though it was only to discuss his travel arrangements. The cloaked apparition struck the boy as 'a silhouette among bodies, a fiction in the midst of the unfictitious'.[13] Boris knew nothing of Rilke's work at the time, but was captivated by the visiting poet's charismatic aura.

In spring of the following year, and in the Moscow zoo, the infant poet's imagination received a further jolt when he witnessed a riding display by a troupe of horsewomen from Dahomey whose costume, it seems, was not designed for concealment. He has described this, his 'first awareness of woman', as 'linked with a sense of naked ranks, of serried anguish, of a tropical parade to the sound of drums'. The result was that the boy 'became a premature slave of shapes earlier than I should have done because, in these women, I had too early seen the shape of slaves'.[14] A slave of shapes! The words sound like those of a seasoned sensualist or philanderer such as he was never to become, though he did not lack the opportunity.

Boris received his earliest tuition at home. He was taught by his mother, and by various tutors from whom he acquired French and German at an early age. He was later to add a reading knowledge of English subtle enough to make him an outstanding translator of

Shakespeare into Russian verse.

At the age of eleven he began to attend the Moscow Fifth Gymnasium. It belonged to the network of state schools in which rigorous training in Greek and Latin formed the basis of the syllabus, though the study of scientific subjects had recently been added. Boris quickly developed an interest in botany, later to be reflected in the varied flora of his verse and prose. But he appears, like Chekhov before him, to have derived little permanent intellectual sustenance from the study of the classics as purveyed by a Russian Gymnasium. His childhood love Ida Vysotskaya was later to remember him 'conceiving a sudden passion for Greek' and seeking to impart it to her.[15] Sudden the passion may indeed have been, but it seems to have been equally transitory. Though occasional classical allusions flicker in Pasternak's writings, Greek and Latin literature did little to fire his ultra-combustible imagination. It was chiefly kindled by poets of his own age, but with exceptions notable enough to include Shakespeare, Goethe and Pushkin. Never was Pasternak to express for Aeschylus, Homer, Horace or Virgil the fierce enthusiasm, the almost mystical exaltation, which a Rilke, a Blok, a Mayakovsky, a Tsvetayeva could ignite in him.

Pasternak was a strange mixture of opposites, according to one of his schoolmates. He was awkward and clumsy. He made a poor showing at gymnastics. Yet there was also a certain meticulousness or fastidiousness about him. As for schoolboy larks, he was character-istically eccentric in avoiding them altogether, except for a habit of joining in at the last moment whenever a group of pranksters seemed threatened with punishment by authority. Such he was as he entered adolescence, a period of life to which he has attributed transcending significance in a sequence of images which is all his own. 'How infinite a thing youth is, everyone knows that. However many decades may pile up on us later, they can never fill this hangar into which they fly to tank up with memories, separately and *en masse*, day and night, like trainer aircraft coming in for fuel. In other words, these years form that part of our lives which is greater than the whole. Faust, who experienced them twice, lived through something mind-boggling and measurable only in terms of mathematical paradox.'[16]

The Pasternaks frequently visited Boris's grandparents at Odessa during their summer holidays. They also took to holidaying nearer home, and the summer of 1903 finds them renting a cottage at Obolenskoye, about seventy miles south-west of Moscow. It was to prove an eventful stay. A young neighbour perished in the local river while saving a drowning girl who afterwards became insane as a result of the incident, and tried to commit suicide. Boris himself fell off a bolting horse while jumping a brook and broke his leg. Then, while he lay immobilized in plaster, a nearby dacha happened to catch fire and was blazing furiously at a time when the boy's father chanced to be returning home from some expedition. From a distance Leonid Osipovich assumed that the flaming cottage was his own and feared for his beloved wife and children, sustaining a shock so profound that his hair turned white. As for Boris's leg injury, that was eventually to prove a blessing in disguise: the injured limb healed imperfectly, leaving him with the slight limp which was to disqualify him from military service in three wars.[17]

Pasternak dismissed all these disasters as insignificant, and with elaborately paraded contempt for his reader. 'I'm not going to describe it because the reader will do that for me. He loves plots and alarms, he looks on history as a never-ending serial story. He likes localities within the ambit of his own strolls. While he's wallowing in prefaces and introductions, for me life's perspectives have opened out just at the point where he's inclined to sum things up.'[18]

If the mundane catastrophes of Obolenskoye were not worth describing, what was? Why, Pasternak's next great cultural collision, naturally. Successively overwhelmed at previous rebirths by Tolstoy, Rilke and the black beauties of Dahomey, the thirteen-year-old boy was now ready to move into a different intellectual habitat, and embarked on his adolescent love affair with music. Such a passion had to have a human focus, and the role was played by the eminent and flamboyant Russian composer Aleksandr Skriabin.

Skriabin happened to be living at Obolenskoye, next door to the Pasternaks' dacha, where he was busy composing his Third Symphony. As he thumped out its themes on the piano, the music 'kept collapsing and falling in ruins like a city under artillery fire'. Skriabin was also fond of philosophical argument with Pasternak's father. The composer denounced Tolstoy, whom Leonid Osipovich revered, while advocating Nietzsche's spectacularly un-Tolstoyan concept of the Superman. Skriabin bewitched the future poet. 'The infatuation smote me more savagely and blatantly than any fever. Seeing him, I would turn pale – only to blush deeply just because I had turned pale. When he addressed me I would lose all power of thought.'[19]

In December 1903 Skriabin left Russia to spend six years in Western Europe while his protégé embarked on the study of musical composition in Moscow. It was no passing whim, but serious preparation for what was commonly assumed to be Boris's future career. His teachers included Reinhold Glière, who was later – unlike his pupil – to become a successful composer. Meanwhile the youth was neglecting his school work for music. During Greek and mathematics lessons he was often detected deep in problems of fugue and counterpoint. But his teachers were always willing to forgive him.

While Pasternak was in the middle of his schooling Russia was overtaken by two overlapping disasters – the unsuccessful war of 1904–5 against Japan and the equally unsuccessful revolution which broke out early in 1905 and which had virtually collapsed by the end of the year. Boris was swept up in the revolution to the extent that the School of Painting, where he lived and where his father worked, became a centre for demonstrating students. From time to time these zealots took over the building, and were on one occasion persuaded to leave it only by the threat of full-scale artillery bombardment. Like most educated young Russians of his generation, Pasternak had vague revolutionary sympathies, even though he was later to qualify his social milieu (and himself by implication) as essentially 'apolitical'. He also describes himself as holding cheap revolutionary sentiments which went no further than braving the whips of mounted Cossacks sent to restore order in the streets of the city, and receiving a lash on the back of his quilted greatcoat.[20]

In his long poem *Nineteen Hundred and Five*, written some twenty years after the event, Pasternak was to commemorate the failed revolution in a sequence of brilliant verse snapshots. He describes the massed workers' demonstration of 9 January, led by the priest Gapon, which was mown down by gunfire, leaving hundreds dead in the streets of St Petersburg; the mutiny on the battleship *Potyomkin* in the Black Sea; the funeral, in Moscow, of the revolutionary student Nikolay Bauman, killed by an agent of the Tsar's political police; the armed uprising in Moscow's Presnya District. He commemorates – and with a display of satisfaction – the assassination in February 1905 of the Grand Duke Sergey Aleksandrovich, official Visitor to the School of Painting and Governor General of Moscow. He also refers, almost in the same breath, to such trivial events as snowball fights in the school playground; the holding of a mock parliament in the classroom; the opportunity, sanctioned by the general collapse of authority, to cheek the Greek master with impunity.[21]

Wearying of revolutionary turmoil in December 1905, Leonid Pasternak took his family to Berlin, where – apart from a summer holiday on the Baltic coast – they spent the whole of the following year, surrounded by Russian *émigrés* and visitors. One was Maksim Gorky, whose portrait Leonid Osipovich drew. Boris quickly grew accustomed to Berlin. He strolled, as he was later to record, along its innumerable streets and in its limitless parks, and he delighted in speaking German with a Berlin accent. He returned to school in Moscow in early 1907 with his head full of gas fumes, beer foam, Wagner and the smoke of locomotives.[22]

Moscow offered special facilities to a youth fascinated by railways. His uncle Aleksandr, manager of a large goods yard, made him welcome there, and he absorbed some of the rich railway lore with which he was later to embellish *Doctor Zhivago*. Uncle Aleksandr also gave his nephew a free travel pass enabling him to visit St Petersburg during one of the Christmas holidays. The historical associations of the Russian capital overpowered him. 'I felt as if I were devouring, with my feet and my eyes, a stone book, a work of genius.' According to his own evidence, his first serious interest in literature may date from this trip to St Petersburg. 'I was poisoned by the most modern literature, raved about Andrey Bely, Hamsun and Przybyszewski.'[23]

During Pasternak's last years at school his imagination was captured by the works of two major poets. One was Aleksandr Blok, the leading Russian Symbolist poet, whom Pasternak has described as an integral part of his youth. Blok was, to his young reader, 'everything that goes to make up a great poet: fire, tenderness, insight. He had his own image of the world, his own special, all-transforming touch, his own restrained, insidious, all-absorbing fate.'[24] It was now, too, that Pasternak first met Rilke on the printed page after stumbling on two volumes by the Austrian poet among his father's books: *Mir zur Feier* ('To Celebrate Myself') and *Das Stunden-Buch* ('The Book of Hours'). The experience affected the youth more profoundly than any previous cultural collision of his life, and he was soon introducing Rilke's poetry to others. This came about naturally owing to the sudden proliferation of groups, usually called 'circles', interested in the arts. They were part of a general artistic ferment. 'From about 1907 publishing concerns mushroomed. There were many concerts of modern music, and there was a succession of picture exhibitions.'[25]

While still a schoolboy Pasternak began to participate in a circle called Serdarda, a name of unknown derivation. It consisted of 'a drunken fraternity founded by a dozen poets, musicians and artists'. Pasternak first became known to this salon in his musical capacity, for he would improvise flourishes on the piano to greet and characterize each new arrival. But he was soon giving readings from Rilke to Serdarda, and with such effect that the poet Yuliyan Anisimov, the group's leading spirit, embarked on the systematic translation of the Austrian's work into Russian. Meanwhile Pasternak was starting to translate and imitate Rilke in fragments of his own as part of the early experiments with verse which were soon to lead him to his main vocation in life.[26]

Pasternak finished his schooling in May 1908, receiving a gold medal from the Gymnasium in token of his success. He proceeded to enrol as a student in the Law Faculty of Moscow University, while also continuing his musical studies. But then, in January 1909, Skriabin at last returned from abroad, and Boris Leonidovich naturally took the first opportunity to play some of his own piano compositions to his adored mentor in the hope of receiving an authoritative verdict on his musical potential.

The outcome was quintessentially Pasternakian. Far from being told that he was wasting his time, the young man was solemnly informed that he possessed something incomparably greater than mere musical talent, and that he had the ability to make original musical statements of his own. Skriabin, who was carried away by his own enthusiasm, sat down and strummed a remembered phrase from one of Pasternak's compositions for the piano. Unfortunately, though, the composer chose the wrong key, and it was this seemingly trivial detail which precipitated a sudden decision by Pasternak to abandon music at the moment of his greatest musical triumph. From Skriabin's choice of the wrong key Pasternak concluded that the composer did not have the gift of absolute pitch. Nor did Pasternak himself, as it happened. But Pasternak was horrified, not so much by the discovery that Skriabin suffered from this professional disability, as by the older man's trite attempt to disparage the talent in question. For Skriabin insisted on putting forward what Pasternak believed to be the hoariest of musical clichés: to the effect that such great composers as Wagner and Tchaikovsky had laboured under the same disadvantage, whereas there were hundreds of humble piano tuners who did not.[27]

What really ended Pasternak's musical career was less his lack of perfect pitch, and still less his touchy reaction to Skriabin's irritating ruminations on the subject, than a failure to master basic musical technique. The fact was that he had not learnt to play the piano adequately, in his own opinion, and could not read music with true fluency. And so the study of music had become 'a constant torment which, in the end, I could not endure'.[28] But it was not Pasternak's way to turn against his cultural idols even when they failed to measure up to his high expectations. Throughout life he continued to make ecstatic references to Skriabin's inspirational impact on himself. He also took Skriabin's advice on a practical point by transferring his studies at Moscow University from law, which bored him, to philosophy. He was to remain a philosophy student until graduating in 1913.

In November 1910 Pasternak's philosophical studies were interrupted by yet another cultural collision. After running away from home at the age of eighty-two, Lev Tolstoy had died in the small rural railway station of Astapovo. Leonid Osipovich was overwhelmed with grief for his illustrious friend and hastened to the scene, with Boris Leonidovich in tow, in order to compose a portrait of Tolstoy in death. Tolstoy's body seemed gigantic, Pasternak has recorded; it was like the Caucasian Mount Elbrus, its summit capped by thunderclouds. Meanwhile the weeping widow was annoying the young man by unleashing a tirade of petty complaints at his father.[29]

Tolstoy's system of beliefs contrasted strongly with Pasternak's concerns of the period, particularly his growing interest in avant-garde poetry. Yet Tolstoy was to remain a long and much valued influence. It was now, and perhaps through the impact of Tolstoy the expounder of Christianity, that the young Pasternak purportedly went through an intense religious phase. He has written of it as follows in a letter of 2 May 1959. 'It was in the years 1910–12, more than at any other period of my life, that I lived inside Christian thought. It was then that my originality's roots and principal bases were formed, together with my vision of things, of the world, of life.'[30] The statement is especially valuable, or suspect, in that there appears to be no other evidence whatever to suggest that the years 1910–12 represented so intense a phase of religious involvement. It may be noted, moreover, that nearly half a century passed between the alleged phase of intense Christianity and Pasternak's own recorded recollection of it. One wonders, not for the first time, how severely he may have edited his past experiences to suit his current purposes.

It is natural to enquire what part the love of women may have played in the young Pasternak's life, especially since later developments were to present the sexagenarian poet–novelist to the popular imagination as a very Romeo of the cupolas and steppes.

Pasternak was a man of striking appearance, whom many regarded as devastatingly handsome. He had deep, lustrous, hollow-set eyes, a strangely elongated face and head, and an alarming jut of jaw, together with an air of intelligence, profound sensitivity, nervous tension and physical energy. It was a formidable combination, and the poet Marina Tsvetayeva, who first met him in his late twenties, has spoken of his magnificent presence. She remarked that there was something in his face both of the Arab and the Arab's steed. It was a watchfulness, a tenseness, an alertness as of one perpetually poised for flight. Like a horse, Pasternak was apt to shoot out glances, wild and timid, from the side of his eyes. And those eyes! They were orbs, not ordinary optic organs.[31]

His cousin Olga, who was about the same age as he, has put it more conventionally. Boris 'had a handsome, spiritually animated face. No mortal being resembled him either in appearance or spirit. He always seemed perfection to me.' Boris and Olga shared a romantic attitude to life, and when they went for walks together the young man would talk for hours on end while the young woman remained silent. One reason for this, as she later confessed, was that 'I understood almost nothing of what he said.' Perhaps the student's conversation with his cousin resembled those rambling letters from him to her which have survived and have recently been published. If so her lack of comprehension must be excused. It certainly proved no barrier to affection, for she adored her handsome cousin. But she could only love him as a brother, while he (according to her account) had fallen in love with her as a woman. This she found hard to cope with, disagreeable and even somehow repulsive.[32]

According to his cousin Olga, Boris 'retained a maidenly purity until comparatively late years'. 'Comparatively' with what or whom? And did Olga really know enough about his life to pronounce him so committed to virginity? It is typical of the Pasternak material that this vague information should be all that is available on so intimate a side of his nature. But his cousin's suggestion is at least tentatively confirmed, in so far as fiction can serve as evidence, by Pasternak's description, at the beginning of *Doctor Zhivago*, of his hero Yury (a character based partly on himself) and of Yury's two closest friends. Their triple alliance was, the novel tells us, devoted to preaching chastity, and they had been deeply influenced by Tolstoy's notorious fictional sermon on the subject, *The Kreutzer Sonata*. 'The world of sensuality which so perturbed them – for some reason they called it *vulgarity*. . . . For them, *vulgarity* embraced the voice of instinct, pornographic literature, the exploitation of women and practically the entire world of physical sensation.'[33]

Against these indications may be set a claim made in Guy de Mallac's biography. 'That the young Pasternak – no less than the young Tolstoy – was at times not above calling on ladies of easy virtue will be documented by some later, less bashful biographer.'[34] Alas, no trace of this documentation has come to light during the preparation of the present study. Celibate or libertine? We do not know. Perhaps, like many another young man, he had tendencies in both directions.

Another of Pasternak's early loves was Ida Vysotskaya, the daughter of a prosperous Muscovite tea wholesaler. She was slightly younger than he, and they first met when he was fourteen. A few years later he was engaged by her family to coach her for her school examinations. The subjects included mathematics. But it quickly became obvious, according to Pasternak's later recollections, that the geometry insinuated into the Vysotsky household by the young tutor owed far less to Euclid than to Abélard. In later life Ida was to remember Boris with affection, but as a youth inadequately endowed with social instincts and graces. 'As a young man Boris Leonidovich did not like going out. He did not dance because of his stiff leg. He was a timid lad who could be very brusque. Yet he was generally popular.'[35]

Pasternak's reputed shyness calls to mind his lifelong habit of belittling himself through a modesty so profound that it sometimes impressed acute observers as being a mere hair's breadth removed from profound immodesty. This is what Olga Freydenburg had in mind when chiding him, in her letter to him of 26 June 1912, with the habit of self-flagellation. 'Your fondness for disparaging yourself – I call it vanity disguised as modesty.'[36]

Pasternak's allegedly long-preserved virginity – if accurately attested – must have proceeded from an idealization of love and women rather than from any rejection of them. Certainly he did not remain an advocate, if he ever was one, of sexual abstinence as remorselessly preached, and sporadically practised, by the elderly author of *The Kreutzer Sonata*. This emerges from his fascinating discussion of 'sex education' in *Safe Conduct*. All the efforts of pedagogues devoted to making it easier for the young to be natural: they are doomed to have the opposite effect, says Pasternak. But he adds that the erection of such barriers to sexual activity is only to be welcomed, for it gives passion a challenge – never mind how nasty or nonsensical – which simply has to be overcome. Pasternak continues the argument with one of the most magnificent tributes ever paid to lust. 'The urge leading to conception is the purest thing in the universe. And this purity, which has triumphed so often throughout the ages, would be sufficient on its own to render everything other than itself infinitely smutty by contrast.'[37]

Though Pasternak is reported as less than diligent in attending lectures, he studied philosophy 'with profound enthusiasm', according to his own account, for he sensed that somewhere in its ambience lay the rudiments of material relevant to his life's work. Perhaps his enthusiasm was excessive. 'I took scholarship more violently to heart than the activity requires.'[38] But such was his way with non-philosophical activities too.

Bypassing Bergsonism and Husserlianism, both of which had their advocates at Moscow University, Pasternak the philosopher became an adherent of neo-Kantianism as expounded by the illustrious Professor Hermann Cohen in the lecture halls of Marburg in western Germany. The Marburg school was well entrenched in Moscow, and it had become customary to send the best Muscovite philosophy students to receive part of their education in Marburg itself. Pasternak had heard so much about the German city's intellectual and topographical charms that he could not wait to go west. His European expedition of 1912 was made possible by a gift of two hundred roubles from his mother, saved through domestic economies and earned by piano lessons. Having received the money, Boris Leonidovich decided to mount as Spartan an excursion as possible: first, because he much appreciated his mother's gift; second, because he wanted to extend his trip to Italy; and, third, because he was committed on principle to austerity and self-denial. Influenced, perhaps, by that eminent simple-lifer Tolstoy to travel third – or even fourth – class, he has explained that 'My tolerance of amenities and need for comfort emerged only after the war.'[39]

The visit to Marburg was indeed a crucial episode to Pasternak, as is attested by the attention given to it in *Safe Conduct*, which is not so much the saga of his life as of his evolving creative sensibilities. This period of only a month or two in Germany and Italy takes up almost one half of a narrative which purports to span four decades in all, and the emphasis placed on the excursion derives from the fact that it marks the end of Pasternak's life as a non-poet.

Describing Marburg in detail, Pasternak has recorded the charms of one of Germany's smallest and most picturesque university cities – of its *Rathaus*, its eight-hundred-year-old castle, its streets clinging to steep slopes like Gothic dwarfs. He evokes historical figures associated with the town: the twelfth-century St Elizabeth of Hungary; Martin Luther; the eighteenth-century Russian scholar–poet Mikhail Lomonosov; the brothers Grimm. Suitably cheap lodgings were rented, and the young man's philosophical studies were soon flourishing to the point where he was asked to deliver two papers at Professor Cohen's seminar; one of them is possibly to be identified with the 'Paper on Psychology' which survives in the Pasternak family archive. He was soon writing to tell his cousin Olga that 'The philosophy situation is just fine. Cohen was pleasantly surprised by my work.'[40] But Pasternak somewhat understated Cohen's enthusiasm, for the Professor actively encouraged the young man to read for a doctorate in philosophy at Marburg, and that before he had even completed his studies at Moscow. An even greater triumph was signalized when the eminent savant invited the young Russian scholar to dinner, for Cohen's dinner invitations were not lightly issued. They were famous in the academic world as constituting an unofficial licence to practise as a professional philosopher. It came to this: that Pasternak the philosophy student had impressed the illustrious German thinker as much as Pasternak the student of music had once impressed one of Russia's leading composers.

Need one say that Pasternak the philosophy student stood on the verge of another grand renunciation?

Pasternak found himself facing problems of a non-philosophical nature when Ida Vysotskaya and her younger sister arrived in Marburg. Having long been in love with Ida, he seized the opportunity of her visit to make a formal, if somewhat distraught, proposal of marriage. The girl already knew of his feelings for her. But she was flabbergasted, he reports, by the 'conspicuousness of my agitation', and backed away from a suitor so ardent. Then, 'As she reached the wall, she suddenly remembered that there existed a way to stop all this straight off. She refused me.'[41]

The rejection of this marriage proposal made an enormous and, it seems, exhilarating emotional impact on the unpredictable Pasternak. It is recorded in his famous lyric 'Marburg' (which was many times rewritten) – even though there are hardly any recognizable direct references to the incident in the first version, as published in 1917. Only in later versions does the poet explicitly refer to the marriage proposal, to its rejection and to the joyous emotions which that rejection had, however paradoxically, released. Feeling 'more blessed than any saint', the scorned suitor debouched on to the town square 'like one born for the second time'. Not only did the episode impart to Marburg's familiar townscape a new and unfamiliar look, but the re-born poet even found that he had to learn to walk all over again. Soon, according to one of his most memorable quatrains, he was stumbling or toddling through the town, his mind still on the Ida whose absence seemed so much more capable of inspiring him than her presence.

> All day your lines from crest to toe –
> Like touring actor conning Shakespeare –
> I carried with me, knew by rote,
> As I lurched round town rehearsing you.[42]

After being rejected by Ida Vysotskaya, Pasternak was more than ready to stage a rejection of his own. He failed to turn up at Professor Cohen's dinner, an outrageously clear indication that he had abandoned the notion of a career in philosophy. Somehow, he wrote to a friend, he felt insulted by Cohen's encouragement, and even by Cohen's flattering suggestion that he should study for a doctorate at Marburg. He was not offended by the Professor himself, to whom he admiringly referred as 'that superman', but by the 'general order of things'. He himself could not say why he had suddenly 'epileptically leapt away' from philosophy just as he was beginning to achieve unexpected success. Perhaps his attitude is partly explained by Lara's words in *Doctor Zhivago*. 'I dislike works devoted exclusively to philosophy. In my view philosophy should be just a meagre seasoning to art and life. To study it exclusively is as odd as eating nothing but horse-radish.'[43]

Purged of his ambitions to become a philosopher and a husband, Pasternak at last found himself embracing what was to be his life's work. 'I tackled verse systematically. Day and night and whenever the occasion occurred I wrote of sea, dawn, southern rain, Harz coal.' With all this running through his head, and none too well equipped with funds, the young poet left Marburg in August 1912 to tour Italy. He stopped at Milan, Venice and Florence before joining his parents at Pisa. His cousin Olga was there too, and at once noticed that he was going through a phase of profound spiritual development. Its symptoms included having nothing to say to her any more, and improvising away on the piano in the family's rented villa while his mother, 'that great and subtle musician', sat by the window shivering all over.[44] She evidently did not share Skriabin's high opinion of her son's musical talents.

From his encounters with Italian art Pasternak was moved to reflect on the 'palpable unity of our culture'. It was in Italy that he first understood the history of culture 'as a chain of equations in images linking in pairs the next unknown thing with something already known'. That he sought to convey this unity of world culture in his own work has been maintained by more than one critic, and with good reason.[45] However, so far as the Mediterranean springs of European culture are concerned, it must be admitted that Osip Mandelstam – student of Dante, translator of Ariosto, inspired exploiter of classical themes in his own verse – went considerably further towards becoming the Russian Ezra Pound.

2

POET IN SEARCH OF A VOICE

Once Pasternak had fully discovered his vocation as a lyric poet he launched himself on a literary career with all the fervour of his impetuous nature, passing rapidly through literary apprenticeship to an explosion of mature creativity. Many of his poems of these early years were first published in periodicals, and were then gathered together in collections which came out in book form: *Twin in Clouds* (1914); *Over Barriers* (1917); *My Sister Life* (1922); *Themes and Variations* (1923). The publication dates of the two last-mentioned collections are a poor guide to their dates of composition since their appearance was delayed by revolution and civil war, most of the material having been written four or five years earlier.

Twin in Clouds and *Over Barriers* were largely experimental and imitative, the former reflecting the influence of Russian Symbolism, while the latter represented a response to the impact of Russian Futurism. Then, with *My Sister Life* and *Themes and Variations*, Pasternak threw off the tutelage of other poets and the burden of 'isms' to emerge as the fully developed master of a mature and original lyrical technique.

While publishing over 170 short poems – roughly half the lyrical output of his entire life – during this phase of intensive activity, Pasternak was also experimenting with longer verse forms and writing several notable works of prose fiction and literary criticism. This outstanding achievement was made possible by a single-minded dedication to the vocation of creative artist. The First World War raged, Russian revolutions erupted in February and October 1917 – all without halting the flow of poetry, and without even seeming to engage the poet's attention. It was now, if ever in his life, that he resembled what he would have denied himself to be: an intellectually self-sufficient aesthete and devotee of Art for Art's Sake. Only with the development of a full-scale Russian Civil War in 1918 was he to lapse into virtual creative inactivity while attempting to adapt his posture to a rapidly changing society.

Even before his momentous visit to Marburg of summer 1912 Pasternak had begun to experiment with writing verse, at first seeing it less as a vocation than as an 'unfortunate weakness' which boded no good. In later life he came to review his earliest poetic efforts in the context of his adolescent apprenticeship to music. With his usual flair for the benumbing comparison he commented that 'My fifteen-year-long abstention from words, which I had sacrificed to sounds, doomed me to eccentricity as certain forms of mutilation impose a predisposition to acrobatics.'[1]

His first surviving verse consists of the posthumously published rough drafts of some seventy poems or scraps of poems from 1911 to 1913. They include echoes – imitative fragments, translated snatches – of Rilke, the poet whose personality had so impressed him as a ten-year-old boy and whose verse he had avidly read while still at school. It is a relief to have concrete evidence of this impact, for Rilke represents one of the most elusive chapters in his Russian disciple's saga. Boris Leonidovich was to pay sporadic tributes to the older poet throughout his life until, in the year before his death, he claimed that he had never done anything but translate or diversify the Austrian's themes during his entire creative career. He had 'always swum' in Rilke's waters.[2] Yet the drafts of 1911–13 are the only works by Pasternak in which the influence is so clearly demonstrable.

In the Russia of this period there was infinitely more to being a poet than writing verse. There was also the responsibility of joining and leaving, preferably in as ostentatious and petulant a manner as possible, various lively, quarrelsome and ephemeral literary or cultural groups. Pasternak had already belonged to one, Serdarda, and he was now about to move on to a succession of three others, each of which operated its own small publishing concern: Musagetes, Lirika and Centrifuge. The first of these was named after one of the titles of Apollo, and Pasternak delivered a paper, *Symbolism and Immortality*, at one of its conclaves in February 1913. The text has been lost, but enough is known of it to show the speaker echoing the Symbolist notion of the poet as a high priest articulating, through his own special form of utterance, the collective subjective impressions of humanity as a whole.[3] The young Pasternak further confirmed his adherence to Symbolism with his first work of prose fiction, also written in 1913: *Story of a Contraoctave*, which remained unpublished until after his death. It is a Symbolist allegory designed to affirm the all-conquering power of art as it depicts a nineteenth-century German organist pounding away at his instrument in such a frenzy of inspiration that he somehow contrives to crush his son to death in the mechanism.[4]

Symbolism had first arisen in Russia in the mid-1890s. By the beginning of the twentieth century it had superseded Realism as Russia's main literary movement, helping to transform and revive literature – prose as well as verse – and exercising considerable influence on the other arts. The new movement threw up half a dozen outstanding poets, among whom Blok was the most notable. Several of them, including Blok, were still active when Pasternak was making his poetic début. But, however much individual Symbolists might continue to flourish, Symbolism as a cohesive movement was virtually defunct by that time. It may have been just as well for the new recruit. An apprentice writer usually begins by imitating something. And if that something turns out to be moribund, so much the better; it can be cast aside the more easily when the time comes.

In early 1913 Pasternak moved on from Musagetes to a breakaway circle with a stronger Symbolist orientation, Lirika. Several other aspiring poets joined him in founding the new group: Yuliyan Anisimov, Nikolay Aseyev, Sergey Bobrov. Their small publishing house was soon bringing out symposia and books under the Lirika imprint, and it was their almanac of early 1913 which carried Pasternak's first published work. It consists of five short lyrics.

Pasternak's Lirika quintet is far from bringing nature to life, which was shortly to become his speciality. Some of the material contrives to do the exact opposite, since it painstakingly robs animate objects of their vitality. One lyric, outstandingly lacking in resonance, portrays that most animated of all animate objects, the poet himself, subsiding into 'the muffled notion of my ego' as into the plaster of a death mask. Even when the early Pasternak does animate the inanimate, he tends to do so lugubriously, as in the invocation of his native city occasioned by what appears to be the funeral of a friend.

> O city mine – all day, all day today
> My grief is on your lips.

Another of the Lirika items equates the composition of poetry with the process of weeping, and in the context of the dismal weather conditions described in the first stanza.

> It's February. Get ink. Shed tears.
> Write sobbingly of February,
> While bombinating slush doth smoulder
> With promise of spring's sunlessness.[5]

Such melancholy characterizes the earliest verses. But it was foreign to the poet's ebullient nature, and he probably derived it from his Symbolist models. On finding his true voice a few years later he was to emerge as a very different writer – the creator of Russia's most radiantly affirmative verse.

Besides flirting with melancholy the Lirika verses toy with themes characteristic of Russian Symbolism: night, secrecy, a mysterious 'creed unheard-of' and the like. They also contain the first reference in Pasternak's work to the candle which was to serve him as a pervasive emblem for creative inspiration long after he had jettisoned Symbolism with a capital S.

Pasternak wrote his Lirika poems while he was completing his degree course in philosophy at Moscow University. Then, after graduating in the early summer of 1913, he was at last able to give himself unstintingly to his new vocation. He did so while staying with his parents at their holiday cottage at Molodi, south of Moscow, where he established a suitably romantic working place in a natural arbour formed by a fallen birch tree leaning over a stream. 'Writing verses, crossing them out and restoring my deletions was a profound need, giving me incomparable pleasure which reduced me to tears.'[6] At Molodi he wrote the lyrics of his first book, *Twin in Clouds*. It was published in early 1914 and bore the Lirika imprint.

The very title reeks of Symbolism. Twins were part of the movement's stock-in-trade, whether they were lifted from the zodiac or invoked as tokens of the contrast between reality and the still more real world of trans-reality. So too were clouds. And so were constellations, stars, moons and anything else in the upper atmosphere or those remoter celestial orbits into which the Symbolist poet's imagination was permanently poised to rocket. Sensitized in later life to the staleness of Symbolist clichés, Pasternak came to deride the title of his first collection as 'idiotically pretentious'. He said that *Twin in Clouds* had been chosen 'in imitation of the cosmological profundities which distinguished the Symbolists' book titles and the names of their publishing houses'. He often regretted that he had ever permitted so immature a work to appear in print.[7]

His flirtation with Symbolism went deeper than the choice of a fashionable title for his first published collection. In several items, which include the individual dualism-obsessed lyrics 'Twins' and 'Twin Astern', he develops the concept of his own *alter ego* along Symbolist lines. He speaks of himself as a double entity. One of his manifestations is physical and belongs to the real world. The other is spiritual. It belongs to the transcendental, still more real world, and is accordingly portrayed as soaring into the heavens.

> A kinsman of escorting stars,
> I shall depart once and for all,

proclaims the poet's spiritual twin, who is soon looking down at his earthly double from on high.

> Through malignant tenebrosities' trans-Lethean miasmas
> I espy my poop-based twin inopportunely asthma-stricken.

A similar soaring is found in the lyric which begins

> I swelled. I was, like Ganymede,
> Swept off by dreams and rainstorms.
> My troubles sprouted, wing-like,
> And cut me off from earth.[8]

Greek mythology, Biblical tradition, signs of the zodiac, constellations, the atmosphere, the stratosphere, outer space – these and similar Symbolist concepts are faithfully paraded in Pasternak's first collection. Its reader strides, floats or soars among Harpies, Argonauts, Gemini, Aquariuses, Phaetons, Ariels, Adams, Prodigal Sons and Gardens of Eden. He hobnobs with Scorpions and Goliaths, he rubs shoulders or wings with Castors and Polluxes. Into this medley the young poet has also injected a dose of Gnosticism as known to him through his philosophical studies at Moscow University. He several times refers to the entities termed Aeons which make up the Gnostic deity. And he is apt to portray the world, Gnostic fashion, as the product of a cosmic tussle between Dark and Light.[9]

Much of this material makes a tired, flat, dead impression, and so it is not surprising that the poet decided to prune many of the Symbolist elements when he came to consider his early efforts for republication in 1929. This reworking of his virgin verses, fifteen years after their first publication, was to be so drastic a process that it cannot be called mere revision. It was re-creation. Out of more than thirty published poems of the *Twin in Clouds* period he discarded over half, including those most larded with Symbolist clichés. He retained fourteen items only, restyling them almost to the point of unrecognizability. But it is also true that he preserved many of the first lines, not a few of the first stanzas, and occasionally more substantial sections of the original versions. The result was to offer a set of virtually new, considerably improved, poems from which much of the Symbolist paraphernalia had been summarily ejected.

Another result of the revision has been to consign the original *Twin in Clouds* to near-oblivion. Without access to the original volume,

which has long been out of print, students of Pasternak can only
familiarize themselves with its text by collating various appendixes and
commentaries scattered about later editions of the poet. Critics have
accordingly tended to ignore the *Twin in Clouds* lyrics in the form in
which they were first published, as they have also tended to ignore the
original versions of the lyrics in Pasternak's second collection, *Over
Barriers*. An admirable and full analysis of both collections has,
however, been made by Christopher Barnes in his study of Pasternak's
early verse.[10]

Though the young Pasternak was not one to introduce personal
reminiscences into his work, the verses of 1913–14 do contain a few
muffled autobiographical echoes. 'Venice' was inspired by his visit of
1912 to that city, but makes no attempt to reproduce the Venetian
scene in detail. No literary Canaletto, the poet is less concerned to
paint the lagoon-girt city than to convey the impact on his psyche of a
mysterious sound, seemingly proceeding from a guitar, which has
awoken him before dawn in what only his title identifies as taking place
anywhere near the Adriatic. The main effect of the experience is that

> The secret of existence in the abstract
> I grasped at daybirth's hour.

In 1929 Pasternak was to throw the Symbolism-reeking secret of
existence out of 'Venice', while infusing a few tangible details. The city
is now described as 'floating like a sodden stone ring-roll', and its
Grand Canal 'looks backwards with a sidelong grin'.[11]

Something similar has happened to 'Railway Station', one of the best
among the earliest lyrics, and the first to evoke the locomotive – that
perennial theme of Pasternak's later writings. The railway is associated
with emotional crises from the start.

> O station, fireproof safe
> Of my partings, meetings, partings.

The poet's 'lovelorn nerve is racked / By smoking Harpies' timetable'. His station beats its wings 'like death's head moth'; the frontier
between his two worlds is as clearly delineated as the permanent
way.[12]

When rewriting the poem for publication in 1929, Pasternak
retained his fireproof safe and even his Harpies. But he jettisoned the
death's head moth and the Symbolism-impregnated two worlds,
substituting concrete details which make the scene easier to visualize.
Still, neither the rewritten 'Railway Station' nor the rewritten 'Venice'
even begins to measure up to the astonishing claim which Pasternak

himself has made for them in his *Autobiographical Sketch* of 1957. He asserts there that his attention had been unremittingly devoted, during these apprentice years, to the content of his verse. A precise picture of the city of Venice, a precise picture of a specific Moscow railway station had been before his mind's eye as he was writing. 'I needed nothing from myself, from my readers, from the theory of art.' All he needed was for one lyric to 'contain' the town of Venice and for the other to 'consist of' a railway terminus in Moscow, the Brest Station.[13]

The reference in 'Railway Station' to the poet's 'lovelorn nerve' is one of several points in *Twin in Clouds* at which he appears to evoke the distant echo of an unhappy romance. Another instance is 'Winter Night'. When first published it was dedicated to 'I.V.' – that is, to Ida Vysotskaya. The poet writes that he is as powerless to throw off his past as is the earth to shrug off winter's frozen incrustations. 'What am I but an encounter's brief arrow?' he asks poignantly and rhetorically.[14] The lyric's melancholy tone offers a strong contrast to the dynamic briskness with which Pasternak focuses on his rejected marriage proposal in the celebrated lyric 'Marburg', as that came to be rewritten for publication in the late 1920s.

Love recollected with melancholy also permeates 'Yesterday, Like a God's Statuette'. Beneath an epigraph from Sappho ('Maidenhood, ah, maidenhood, / Whither goest thou, having forsaken me?') loss of virginity is evoked with profound post-coital gloom. The poet predicts that 'They who last night as children fell asleep / Shall rise at dawn today'; and they shall rise, it soon turns out, in a world shrouded in 'northland's blue-grey, orphaned, dirty rain'.[15]

The lyrics of 1913–14 offer a pointer to the future Pasternak in the prevalence of original images, including comparisons. Not a few are ornithological, as was appropriate to this Symbolist phase.

> Like blood-gorged hawk from sky
> My heart swooped on your hand.

> Space preens itself like smoky-breasted owl.

Nor are earth-bound zoological comparisons despised.

> I press my cheek to winter's snail
> All convoluted round itself.[16]

But the poet's earliest images are less effective than those of his later work. They are also less numerous and obtrusive, even if one particular short lyric does its best to compensate. Within a mere

sixteen lines the poet compares his grief to a captive Serbian girl; his eye
to a cornered weathercock; the outline of his unidentified addressee to
a frisky eel in pursuit of which the same eye drowns; his sigh to the
bellows of an organ; the senselessness of his existence to a burdock and
the 'sweep' of a well.[17]

Twin in Clouds was barely noticed by reviewers at the time of its
appearance, and it has been neglected by critics. After provoking a
few, mostly unfavourable, notices at the time of its first appearance it
was largely forgotten until it became widely known – together with
Pasternak's other published lyrics from the same period – in the
substantially changed and considerably improved versions represented
by the fourteen items reworked for publication in 1929. Vladimir
Markov has claimed that 'Talent and originality of the first rank are
visible in practically every poem' of the collection.[18] But it is hard to
accept this judgement if it is intended to apply to the poems as they first
appeared. The chief interest of those versions does not lie in what they
were or are, but in what they eventually led to.

Unfailingly original and talented or not, the young Pasternak had
unquestionably staked his claim to be a writer of daunting obscurity.
He was to fight a long rearguard action against his obfuscatory urges
throughout the years as he pursued what was to become, for him, the
most elusive and desirable of all qualities: simplicity. But his readers
should be warned that simplicity – like realism, history and many
another abstraction – had, for Pasternak, layers of submerged
significance imperfectly discernible to intellects less adventurous.

In early 1914 Pasternak and two other poets, Aseyev and Bobrov,
decided to leave Lirika. One reason for the decision was the
bankruptcy of Symbolism, the larger movement to which Lirika
looked for guidance, and Pasternak's own motives for departing must
have included his rapidly dawning awareness that Symbolist technique
had nothing more to offer him. There were also personal disagreements so acute that Pasternak is even reported to have challenged
Anisimov, the leading spirit of Lirika, to a duel; but there is no record
that it took place.[19]

After contributing to the break-up of Lirika, Pasternak, Aseyev and
Bobrov helped to set up Centrifuge, a new group with its own
associated publishing concern. Centrifuge soon came to be regarded as
a branch of Futurism, a highly self-conscious artistic movement which
had arisen in the early 1910s, and which presented even less of a united
front than Symbolism. What was there to unite the Futurists? Some
wanted to jettison all humanity's pre-Futurist cultural achievements

lock, stock and barrel. Some were more intent on shocking the bourgeoisie with their weird clothes and antics. Others were deep in linguistic experiment, coining harsh neologisms and promoting deliberate typographical eccentricities. Still others – the so-called *Nichevoki* or 'Nothingists' – had made the startling discovery that the most effective mode of literary expression was to refrain from writing altogether; in certain cases they even carried versatility to the extreme point of abstaining from painting and musical composition as well, as if they had taken as their motto Pasternak's couplet: 'Silence, you're the best / Thing I ever heard.'[20]

If the Futurists had anything in common, other than a dedication to modernism in the arts, it was their passion for denouncing rival Futurists. Bickering was, it seems, nine-tenths of the fun. And so the newly formed Centrifugists were soon challenging their competitors, among whom the Ego-Futurist Vadim Shershenevich and the Cubo-Futurist Vladimir Mayakovsky were prominent.

The clash occurred in the spring of 1914 after Centrifuge had issued its first publication, the almanac *Rukonog*; the title is a typical trans-sensical Futurist coinage, and may be rendered *Handfoot*. This almanac contained three striking lyrics by Pasternak, all in a vein which he had never previously attempted and was never to attempt again: 'Cupro-Nickel', 'On Ivan the Great' and 'Gypsies'. On the first few readings they may appear to offer a broth of aggressively rough-textured phonetic mush rather than anything approaching coherent articulation. But close study shows the theme of 'Cupro-Nickel' to be the bells of the Moscow Kremlin, near which Pasternak was occupying a temporary room at the time of writing. Having sound as its main theme, the poem itself offers a medley of ingenious sound patterns. So too does the companion piece, 'On Ivan the Great', the title of which refers to the well-known Kremlin bell-tower. The third item of the trio, 'Gypsies', is set far from Moscow in the Moldavian steppes, and vaguely echoes Pushkin's poem with the same title.[21] All three *Rukonog* lyrics are crammed with harsh consonantal repetitions, thus typifying the Futurist revolt against the relative smoothness of much Symbolist verse. Here is a reminder that Futurism had, so to speak, rediscovered the Russian consonant, which Symbolism had tended to neglect while pampering the vowel. In a splurge of hissings, splutters and raspings Pasternak piles his *ch*s and *ts*s on his *sh*s and *zh*s, while also revealing himself (in his creative use of cumbrous diction) as one of those Russian Futurist poets who were, unknown to themselves, trying to play Browning to the Symbolists' Tennyson. As for native models, Pasternak's three *Rukonog* lyrics tend to derive from Velimir Khlebnikov, who was renowned for the ingenuity with which his verse subordinated sense to sound.

Pasternak also contributed to *Rukonog* a critical article on poetry, *Wassermann Reaction*; reference is to the diagnostic test for syphilis associated with the German doctor August von Wassermann. Much of the text is a polemical denunciation of Shershenevich, whom Centrifuge regarded as the fount of all evil, and whom Pasternak identified as the main literary disease-carrier. He censures the doyen of Ego-Futurists for writing in an excessively popular manner while allowing his style to be dictated by readers' convenience. Readers ought not to be spoilt like this, Pasternak avers, bracing himself for yet another splurge of ingenious imagery. Poetry is, he says, a lock to which the poet alone holds the key, and all readers can hope for is to peep through the keyhole at the poetic vista beyond. The crime committed by facile poets like Shershenevich is that of gratuitously throwing all the keys of their art to 'amateurs in the crowd'. A true poet would have kept them to himself.[22]

The article stresses Pasternak's rejection of the traditional poetic image based on similarity. Ordinary imagery makes things too easy for the reader, he contends. And so he propounds a more difficult principle for the poetic trope, that of contiguity. The device is sometimes termed 'metonymy', a word which Pasternak does not use in his article despite its considerable credentials as a thought-inhibitor.[23] Whatever terminology may be employed, he is asserting the poet's right to develop his images along 'stream-of-consciousness' lines. Hence the plethora in his work of associations militantly random, casual and arbitrary. He believed in tossing the raw material of poetry – centrifugally – to his readers. It was then up to them to construct in their heads, from an inspired flurry of assorted hints, the finished poem which a lesser artist would meekly – and centripetally – have presented to them on a platter.

Bitter as the attack on Shershenevich is, *Wassermann Reaction* is not a blanket condemnation of all the non-Centrifuge Futurists, for Pasternak goes out of his way to praise Khlebnikov and Mayakovsky. He describes them as true Futurists, and implies that the Wassermann Reaction of his title has given them a clean bill of health.

Pasternak's third contribution to *Rukonog* was to sign, with Aseyev and Bobrov, a scurrilous Charter denouncing rival Futurists: they are an impudent 'gang'; they have thrown off all self-control; they have impudently staked a claim to the future while remaining slaves to the past. They have organized a trust of pan-Russian mediocrities; they are traitors, renegades, impostors and cowards; they are spreading malicious rumours about poets outside their faction. The charter goes on to challenge its rivals to defend themselves if they can,[24] and a counter-challenge was not slow to follow. It bore the signatures of Mayakovsky and Shershenevich, and it demanded confrontation with their assailants within the next four days. It particularly specified that Boris Pasternak must come and give an account of himself. Should the Centrifugists shun a meeting, should they fail to reply within seventy-two hours, 'We shall consider ourselves entitled to solve the dispute by any of the procedures commonly applied to cowards.'[25] These devices were left to the imagination; perhaps they were to have included that traditional expression of Russian literary displeasure, the slap on the face.

The meeting was to take place in a Moscow café in May 1914, and Pasternak approached it with mixed feelings – particularly where Mayakovsky was concerned. Though he admired what little he knew of Mayakovsky's verse, his Centrifuge colleagues had told him that Mayakovsky was an enemy. And so Pasternak felt honour bound to muster what truculence he could.[26]

Mayakovsky was three years younger than Pasternak, but was further advanced in the careers of poet and public figure. His first verse had appeared in the famous Futurist almanac of 1912 characteristically entitled *Slap in the Face of Public Taste*. The following year had seen the publication of his first verse collection, which bore the no less characteristic title *Ego*. Then Mayakovsky and his Futurist colleagues had toured Russia, outraging the staid burghers of Kazan, Kharkov, Odessa, Minsk and other provincial centres into a delicious state of shock with their unconventional attire and public clowning. But Mayakovsky was not only a cultural rebel; he was a political rebel too – an out-and-out revolutionary. He had joined the Bolsheviks at the age of fourteen, though he was later to allow his Party membership to lapse. While still in his teens he already had three arrests and six months' imprisonment for political misconduct to his credit. He had attended the same Moscow Gymnasium as Pasternak, but in a lower form, and he had then become a student at the Moscow School of Painting where Pasternak's father was employed. From both these seats of learning the mutinous Mayakovsky had contrived to get himself expelled with ridiculous ease.

With such a *curriculum vitae* he was indeed an enemy worthy of the name on the hot day in May 1914 when he and his associates strode into the Moscow café designated for the settling of accounts between the anti-Centrifuge Futurists and the Centrifuge Futurists. The atmosphere was tense, if not quite that of the saloon in a traditional

Western film just before the 'shoot-out'.

Pasternak has given his own account of this meeting. He was already seated when the enemy marched in, and it was the first occasion on which he had been close to Mayakovsky. He saw a tall young man, twenty years old, who spoke with an actor's affected voice. There was a reckless look about him. It was not so much the air of one playing a game as of one playing every possible game simultaneously while staking his life on the outcome. Mayakovsky mounted his chair like a motor-cycle's saddle. He seemed (continues Pasternak the inveterate image-switcher) like a skater racing full speed ahead. 'Far more than other people he was contained in the manifestation of himself.' But Pasternak was also quick to detect the sensitivity and insecurity concealed by Mayakovsky's surface flamboyancy: the mainspring of his brazen confidence was wild shyness. All this reduced Pasternak to an uncharacteristically listless mood. Far from assailing Mayakovsky with tongue or fist, he found himself 'betraying those I had not intended to betray' – his Centrifuge colleagues. Infatuated with Mayakovsky, he opted out of the proposed feud on the spot.[27]

On the following day Pasternak chanced to meet his new idol in a different Moscow café, where Mayakovsky recited passages from a recent work of his, the poetical tragedy entitled – no less typically than many of his other works – *Vladimir Mayakovsky*. The recital confirmed Pasternak in a view which he was to express many times, and which the posture-conscious Mayakovsky might have seemed the last person on earth competent to convey: that the artist is nothing, that his art is all. Hidden in Mayakovsky's title was a discovery which (said Pasternak) had the simplicity of genius. The poet was not the author of his poem, he was its subject. Nor was the title the author's name. It was the surname of the contents.[28]

Of his first meeting with Mayakovsky, Pasternak has said that 'I carried all of him from the boulevard into my life. But he was huge. . . . I kept losing him.'[29] During the remainder of Pasternak's life his obsession with Mayakovsky was to ebb and flow against a background of progressive disillusionment with an idol worshipped in youth.

The summer of 1914 found Pasternak living in a dacha on the River Oka, south of Moscow, with the family of the poet Baltrushaytis, whose son he was tutoring. He was no longer writing poetry himself, but was translating Kleist's play *Der zerbrochene Krug* ('The Broken Jug') from German into Russian. Then, with the shadow of war with Germany looming over Russia, he went back to Moscow in July and tried to join the army – only to be rejected because of his leg injury.

War with Germany left the tenor of his life largely unaffected. Unlike the Second World War, it did little to stimulate his latent patriotic urges or to turn his thoughts to his fellow countrymen's sufferings. In *Safe Conduct* (1931) he salutes the outbreak of the conflict with characteristic meteorological information, dignifying the hostilities with no more than a subordinate clause. 'When war was declared, foul weather began and the rains came.' He made further attempts to enlist after hostilities had begun in July 1914, but then gave them up after meeting an ensign on leave. 'He entreated me to abandon the idea. . . . Soberly and emphatically he told me about the front, warning me that I should find nothing there that was not the opposite of what I expected.' Shortly after performing this service to Russian literature the ensign was himself killed in action.[30]

Pasternak spent part of the war – two spells adding up to a year in all – as resident tutor to the son of a German businessman living in Moscow. On one occasion, early in the war, the house was attacked and looted by an anti-German mob, an occurrence characteristic of the period in that the pogrom was planned in advance and took place with police connivance. Pasternak's underclothes remained intact, he has recorded. But he lost some books and manuscripts, which prompted him to reflect forty years later that 'Losing things is more necessary in life than acquiring them. The grain yields no shoot unless it dies.'[31]

Pasternak's output of lyrics temporarily declined after his first meetings with Mayakovsky. But then he began writing verse in which the other poet's influence is easily detectable. His first two Mayakovsky-inspired poems both chance to touch on a theme which he otherwise barely invokes – the war. One of them, 'Gunner at Helm', might almost be Mayakovsky's work. There is a similar strong but metrically elusive rhythmical beat; there is a similar recourse to hyperbole as the earth is pictured hurtling past under the pressure of a milliard atmospheres. Mayakovskian too are the anti-war sentiment and the artilleryman of the title, a modest figure who yet dominates the universe. The last six lines contain material which the authorities considered liable to spread alarm and despondency – references to 'clouds begging for disarmament', and to the 'universe groaning from vertigo' after being 'hastily billeted in smashed heads'. When the poem appeared for the second time, as part of the collection *Over Barriers* (1917), the offending lines had been expunged by the Tsarist censorship as one of its last acts before it disappeared for ever.[32]

Pasternak's second anti-war poem, 'Bad Dream', is swamped by a macabre image: the world turns out to consist of a huge mouthful of decaying teeth, a foretaste of the 'dead mountain mouth of carious teeth' in T. S. Eliot's *Waste Land*. But it is Mayakovsky, not Eliot, whom Pasternak resembles in his imagery and cult of hyperbole. This new influence was more favourable to his muse than Symbolism had been, for Mayakovsky tended to bring Pasternak to life, as a poet, whereas Symbolism had cramped and devitalized him. For example, the Mayakovsky-dominated Pasternak no longer invokes the various heavenly bodies with bated breath, as he had in his Symbolist phase, but treats them with the familiarity or contempt accorded to them by his new mentor. Pasternak does not go so far as inviting the sun to tea, as Mayakovsky does in one of his most celebrated poems, but he is certainly no longer in a mood to stand on ceremony with the cosmos. This deliberate descent into bathos lends vigour to his verse – not least in the comparison (in 'Bad Dream') of the moon over a battlefield to a rotting vegetable from a 'madman's melon-plot'.

> Pale, bloated, puffy pumpkin-moon
> Flopped into near-by rut from stalk.
> Then, battle-ripped and battle-whipped,
> Moon lolloped downhill into ditch
> Through trees' gums, through hedgerows' black
> Gums, twixt gat-toothed scrubwood's gums.[33]

Mayakovsky's influence can also be traced in several of Pasternak's other lyrics of the period, including 'Anguish', '*Materia Prima*' and 'Like Last Planet's Treasurer'. They help to confirm that Pasternak was evolving during these years from a dull and uninspired Symbolism-dominated phase through a dynamic and exciting, albeit still derivative, Mayakovsky-dominated phase into what was soon to be a phase – still more dynamic and strikingly non-derivative – of poetic maturity.

Pasternak spent the second and third winter of the war in the Urals. In 1915–16 he was in the north of Perm Province at the town of Vsevolodo-Vilva, memorable only for having once been visited by Chekhov. The following winter finds him at Tikhiye Gory on the River Kama, where he worked in a chemical factory as a clerk processing exemptions from military service for workers in what had been classified as a reserve occupation.

Residence in the Urals loosened Mayakovsky's hold over Pasternak's imagination, as is evident from his critical article of 1916, *Black Goblet*. Even by the standards of his own aesthetic formulations *Black Goblet* is obscure. He is 'allusive and metaphorical to an extreme, and every sentence of his leaves a reader puzzled as to whom he actually has in mind and what he actually means'. Yet one uncompromising statement, bearing on the perennial Russian problem of the competing claims of art and politics, may be fished out of the swirl of imagery. Art is art; politics is politics; and never the twain shall, or should, meet. Such was Pasternak's message to Mayakovsky as the latter increasingly committed himself to the politics of revolution. But Pasternak does not put his point so crisply. What is here called art he terms lyricism; what is here called politics he terms history. Lyricism and history are portrayed as two opposite poles, 'equally a priori and absolute' and incompatible with each other.[34] In other words, art must not seek to influence life, for it is not the artist's job to 'prepare tomorrow's history' – the role which Mayakovsky was in the process of assuming. There is a sense in which Pasternak was to spend the whole of the rest of his life unlearning this lesson so militantly, yet obscurely, propounded in his article of 1916.

In the short story *Apelles' Mark* (1918), also written during the war, Pasternak again takes issue with Mayakovsky without naming him. Here is a complex allegory in which a romantic poet challenges a non-romantic poet to defend his integrity as an artist. The romantic poet is called 'Relinquimini' in the story, but is crudely identifiable with Mayakovsky; the non-romantic poet is called 'Heinrich Heine' in the story, lacks any obvious connection with his German namesake, and is crudely identifiable with Pasternak himself. The purpose of Relinquimini's challenge is to establish which of the two poets, he or Heine, is the more authentic. Once challenged, Heine–Pasternak decides to respond immediately, and with a strikingly non-literary act: he implements the lightning seduction of Relinquimini–Mayakovsky's beautiful mistress. As this allegory suggests, Pasternak now tended to regard himself as a 'realist' proud of having rejected Mayakovsky's 'romantic' approach. And even though Pasternak characteristically infuses both concepts with many an unspecified buried implication, *Apelles' Mark* implies that Heine's apparent frivolity is, however paradoxically, to be taken as a sign of seriousness and down-to-earth realism contrasting with Relinquimini's ponderous make-believe.[35]

Pasternak disliked Mayakovsky's habit of seeing the poet, by which Mayakovsky always meant himself, as the centre of the universe. As one Mayakovsky-watcher has put it, 'The poet himself is the theme of his poetry. The poet has dealt himself out on to the stage like a card player. Mayakovsky is the two, the three, the jack and the king. The stake is love. The game is lost.'[36] Mayakovsky might equate the whole of life with the poet's life, he might feel doomed to pay for this position with his death, but Pasternak firmly rejected the notion that a poet's biography must be one long bout of spectacular posturing. Did Mayakovsky insist on making himself conspicuous? Very well then. Pasternak would be inconspicuous. The eventual result was, of course, that he made himself still more conspicuous than Mayakovsky. Here is one of the many paradoxes of Pasternak's career. And it would be naïve to assume that his persistent claim to avoid publicity was not, in however slight a degree, a highly successful device for seeking publicity.

Besides rejecting Mayakovsky the flamboyant role-player, Pasternak also came to reject Mayakovsky the poet – a form of self-denial dictated by his innate drive towards absolute originality. The young Pasternak might copy the Symbolists. He might mimic Igor Severyanin, Khlebnikov and other Futurists as well as Mayakovsky. But that was mere experiment. He knew that he had to be his own man in the end. Brooding on the close similarities, including habits of imagery and rhyme, between his own immature verse and the model of Mayakovsky, he decided on a clear-cut break. 'To avoid repeating him and appearing to mimic him, I began suppressing those elements that corresponded to his – the heroic tone, which in my case would have been false, and the cult of flamboyancy. This narrowed and refined my style.'[37]

Occasional references to the Urals, Pasternak's place of residence during two successive wartime winters, appear in his second verse collection, *Over Barriers*. In one lyric dawn assaults the sierras on a crest of brutal obstetrical imagery.

> Midwifeless, in gloom and swoon,
> Groping at night, Urals'
> Stronghold bellowed; slumped in faint,
> Anguish-blinded; spawned dawn.

Another, quieter daybreak surprises the poet in transit, as

> Bluer than drake's plumage
> Dawn sparkled over Kama.[38]

There are also passages alluding, however exceptionally, to actual events and personages. The poet commemorates the founding of St Petersburg by Peter the Great in the early eighteenth century, and the fighting which took place in the Moscow suburb of Presnya during the 1905 Revolution.

He commemorates himself too – however distantly – with the first among many varied drafts of the famous lyric 'Marburg', inspired by the occasion on which he had unsuccessfully proposed marriage to Ida

Vysotskaya in that ancient university town in the summer of 1912. The poem is characteristic of his grudging attitude towards autobiographical detail in that virtually none of the circumstances are communicated to the reader in the first published draft. That contains little more than oracular invocations of an unexplained 'pain' which had made the poet feel as if he had been reborn. Not only is the setting clearer in the later versions, particularly if read in the context of Pasternak's prose account of the Marburg incident in *Safe Conduct*, but the tone has changed too. The later versions are exultant. They suggest what can barely be deduced from the first version, that the episode liberated springs of creative vitality in the young poet. But it took him about sixteen years to discover that this had been the case – if, that is, the successive extant drafts of 'Marburg' are to be taken as evidence.

In *Over Barriers*, as everywhere else in the early Pasternak, references to actual episodes and localities are oblique, sparse and exceptional. His main concern is to record the natural world as it impinges, fleetingly but indelibly, on his consciousness. While doing so he contrives, in not a few lyrics, stanzas and isolated lines of the collection, to unleash language and imagery of awesome brilliance and power. No longer sullen, petrified and static, his landscapes and townscapes whirl past in vivid sequence, embellished by his customary emergency weather bulletins in which winds, blizzards, snowstorms and floods predominate over nature's gentler manifestations. Transitions are much favoured – the points at which town melts into country, night into day, one season into its successor.

A hurried, impressionistic review of this hurried, impressionistic verse, as it trips through the calendar from summer through autumn and winter to spring, may possibly indicate – even through the prism of translation – the quality which eventually inspired other Russian poets, and many discriminating readers, to hail Pasternak's work as a revelation. It may also suggest why some have found parts of the material cumbrous, inarticulate, perverse and obscure.

Attacking summer in 'July Storm', the poet employs multiple simultaneous flashlight photography to create a brilliant, electrifying picture.

> Thundercrack at gate! In yard!
> Self-transfiguring, bemused,
> Darkling, rumbling, silvery,
> Storm swoops to porch up gallery
> In three swift strides. Blindfold my eyes!
> Five mirrors all flash back the face –
> The storm's that snatched her mask off.[39]

Moving through to late autumn, Pasternak begins one lyric with a
'yard meticulously scrawled with sleet', where 'October's frozen
abscess is picked open / By skies' senile nail' as winter prepares to levy
tribute from the street like a medieval Tatar tax collector.[40] Another
seasonal poem, 'Winter Sky', is as richly extravagant an invocation of
cold as may be found in literature. The poet imagines 'the stream of
stars' as having been extracted, frozen stiff, from their misty setting in
the form of an 'integral ice block' and hoisted into position as an
inverted celestial skating club. 'Rink clinks against night's counter-
clink'. Anything is possible here, even that a permanent mark may be
left on the universe by the careless blade of some upside-down skater

> Whose scrunching swerve shall etch
> New constellation into Norway's sky.

The moon – less happily, perhaps – resembles a game dog's tongue
frozen stiff against a metal rivet, while mouths are choked with ice like
those of coiners punished in days of yore by having molten lead poured
into them.[41]

With 'Ice on the Move' Pasternak tosses out a spatter of weird
images to describe the break-up of a frozen river in spring. His earth
pokes its black adam's apple out of the snow, his creek has fastened on
to his meadows 'like a tick'. So firmly is evening locked into the fen's
gums that it cannot be torn out without leaving flesh behind; the river
banks are precise, baleful, charcoal-like; the rising sun on the flat
horizon resembles

> Salmon slivers sliced
> By ice and waters' glint.[42]

Moving further through the calendar, the poet describes the month
of April in 'Spring', a lyric so successful in its original version that he
did not feel the need to rewrite it in later life. He launches the poem
with a characteristic invocation of leaf buds.

> Viscous, slobbered candle-stubs
> Affixed to boughs.

He invokes bird song in the weird setting of

> Woods like buffalo lassoed
> In lariat of feathered gullets.

He then astonishes by making an important comment about the nature
of his art.

Poetic art! Become a sponge,
Sucker-festooned. I'll spread you
Mid gluey foliage on green
Garden bench's sodden plank.

Sprout florid ruffs and farthingales,
Ingest yon clouds and canyons.
And nightly, poetry, I'll wring you out
For thirsty paper's good.[43]

This is one of the most delightfully ingenious among Pasternak's many statements about the essential passivity of the poet and his product. As it suggests, he was beginning to conclude that he should stop writing poetry. The time had come to let poetry write him.

He recognized the superiority of *Over Barriers* to the earlier *Twin in Clouds* by varying his approach to the two collections when he came to process them for republication in 1929. By comparison with his radical transformation of the earlier material, which he gutted and reconstructed, his treatment of *Over Barriers* was respectful. He preserved a higher proportion of the lyrics. Even so he discarded over a third of them, spurning the material which bore the clearest signs of Mayakovsky's influence. Among the poems which were retained he rewrote some to the point of unrecognizability, but kept others virtually intact.

Despite the progress registered in *Over Barriers*, the book's quality has gone largely unnoticed. It appeared while its author was still resident in the Urals in early 1917, and reached him full of misprints which he had not been able to correct in proof. The volume seems to have been ignored by critics and reviewers of that period, as is not surprising in view of Russia's other preoccupations of 1917.[44] In later years the character of *Over Barriers*, as published in 1917, has been obscured by Pasternak's extensive revisions, published in 1929 and subsequently.

The collection has provoked conflicting responses from the few critics who appear to have examined it carefully in its original form. Markov has sought to rescue it from neglect, assessing it as 'the beginning of the Pasternak we know. . . . All basic elements of his style and poetic vision are present here in developed and unmistakable form.' But Christopher Barnes, who has written the fullest and best study of Pasternak's first two collections, takes a less enthusiastic view. Speaking of *Twin in Clouds* and *Over Barriers* in conjunction, he claims that 'The obviously derivative nature of most of these early lyrics precludes them from being considered among Pasternak's best work.' He adds that the years during which they were written 'were really a period of trial in which Pasternak readily assumed a whole series of differing styles in search of the brilliance and novelty which were the touchstone of success at that time'.[45] This summing up is judicious in so far as it concerns the original collections as a whole, but surely errs in underrating the finest lyrics of *Over Barriers*: those in which Markov has detected 'the Pasternak we know'.

3

CLOUDBURST OF LIGHT

In February 1917 the Russian monarchy was suddenly eliminated by the first of the year's two Revolutions. It took the form of riots in Petrograd (as St Petersburg had been renamed in 1914) which precipitated the abdication of the Emperor Nicholas II at a time when few were expecting anything of the sort. To a poet such as Pasternak, for whom the railway held so much significance and who was also apt to associate the march of history with the raging of blizzards, the scene of the last Tsar's impending abdication was bound to appeal – a train from which the doomed monarch vainly sought to sway events in the capital at the last moment as he steamed up and down the provincial permanent way in the snows of winter. Pasternak refers to the episode and to the imperial Russian emblem in a poem of the 1920s.

> Cruising the Pskov vicinity,
> Two-headed Eagle grew fatigued
> By huntsmen's cordon closing in
> From mutiny beyond its ken.[1]

When news of the February Revolution reached the poet he was still at Tikhiye Gory in the remote Urals. He left for Moscow at once with a friend from the locality – Boris Zbarsky, engineer and revolutionary. Their hazardous sleigh ride of over a hundred miles through the snowdrifts to the nearest railway station at Kazan, the upsets, the screech of runners, the many wayside crises, have been vividly described in Pasternak's *Autobiographical Sketch*.[2] They also form a prominent theme in *Loveless*, a fragmentary short story which was written and brought out in 1918 as his first work of prose fiction to achieve publication.

Loveless itself amounts to little, but is significant for the contrast drawn between its two chief characters: the impractical dreamer Goltsev and the fanatical revolutionary Kovalevsky. Here is a conflict which recurs again and again in Pasternak's work. He likes to set some lover of poetry and women alongside a dedicated political activist, and then to indicate that it is the bumbling, dreamy poetry-lover who understands the secret of existence which remains concealed from the revolutionary man of action. The contrast between Goltsev and Kovalevsky thus anticipates the contrast between Yury Zhivago and Antipov-Strelnikov in *Doctor Zhivago*.

In *Loveless* this clash of personalities is conveyed in a single sentence which could have had little significance for its first readers, but is important to those who know Pasternak's work as a whole. 'Kovalevsky thought Goltsev was asleep. He did not suspect that Goltsev was awake, and that it was he himself who was asleep. He lurched from doze to doze, from bump to bump, he and his thoughts on revolution, which had once again become dearer to him than his fur coat and his luggage, dearer than his wife and child, dearer than his own life or anyone else's.' Sleep is used here, as elsewhere in Pasternak, to denote insensitivity to life's finer potentialities as they are to be found in nature, poetry and love rather than in politics. A similar tentative contrast between a dreamer and a revolutionary fanatic has been culled from *Dramatic Fragments*, Pasternak's uncompleted attempt at a verse play about the French Revolution, written in summer 1917. Both the principal figures – Saint-Just and Robespierre – are historical personages and dedicated professional revolutionaries. But the former is contrasted with the latter as one who has the true, non-political issues of life – including love – nearer to his heart.[3]

Pasternak was no ardent revolutionary. But he had never been a supporter of the Tsarist system, and he shared the general enthusiasm provoked by its collapse in February 1917. On reaching Moscow from the Urals shortly afterwards he delved into his stock of imagery to comment on the great upheaval to a literary friend. 'Just fancy! When a sea of blood and mud starts secreting light –'. The poet then broke off the half-uttered sentence with an eloquent gesture; perhaps he felt that it was too good to finish in words.[4]

After the momentous events of February 1917 had taken place, almost absent-mindedly and without significant loss of life, Russia embarked on a period of eight months of ineffectual rule by the self-styled Provisional Government before undergoing its second revolution of the year in October. Forty years later Pasternak was to remember the interval between the two upheavals of 1917 for the enthusiastic aspirations expressed at impromptu political meetings which went on in the open air all round the clock. It was a time when everyone thought aloud in unison, when the common people 'let themselves go, when they discussed the things that really matter – how to live, what to live for, how to build the only conceivable and worthy form of existence'. The borderline between man and nature had been erased by the infectiousness of the universal excitement. 'In that famous summer of 1917 – in the lull between the two revolutionary crises – roads, trees and stars seemed to be holding meetings and delivering orations along with human beings.' In so doing, nature of the revolutionary year was behaving exactly like nature in Pasternak's verse, where it so often seems to speak in place of the silent poet. The same concept is put forward in the important passage of *Doctor Zhivago* where the hero discusses the condition of Russia in July 1917. 'Mother Russia is on the move. . . . Stars and trees have come together to converse, the flowers talk philosophy at night, brick buildings hold political meetings.'[5]

There is a characteristic resemblance between Pasternak's own words on revolution and those which he has attributed to the hero of his novel. Wherever Yury Zhivago discourses on life, history, Russia and kindred topics he is always an exact mouthpiece of his creator. All Zhivago's remarks on revolution may be taken as expressing Pasternak's own opinion, but with this important reservation – that it is Pasternak's opinion as it had crystallized in his mind after an interval of some four decades, and by no means necessarily the opinion which he held at the time when the events occurred.

Writing of the post-February months of 1917 in *Doctor Zhivago*, Pasternak stresses the general sensation of freedom. 'The lid has been snatched off the whole of Russia and we have found ourselves out in the open air with the whole people. . . . Freedom! Genuine freedom, not a matter of words and demands, but something come down from the skies and exceeding all our expectations!' The revolution has burst out involuntarily like a sigh too long held back. Everyone has come to life, has been transformed, has experienced two revolutions – the one in his personal life, the other the experience common to all.[6]

The bracing wind of change helped to precipitate the young poet into the most intensive period of creativity in his life. There came from him, in the course of 1917, a lyrical avalanche. It included all the items which were to be grouped together in his third volume of collected poems, *My Sister Life*, and much else besides.

My Sister Life has been called 'a novel with love as its main theme',[7] but the text contains few rudiments of coherent narrative, whether erotic or non-erotic, fictional or autobiographical. The poet seems to spend some of his time with a beloved woman or with a succession of two such women, each cryptically invoked as 'thou'. They appear to tour the Saratov Province, a few hundred miles south-east of Moscow – so much may be inferred from several place names. For the first edition of the work Pasternak also provided a brief and enigmatic prose commentary to some of the individual lyrics. 'That summer they went there from Pavelets Station.' 'They left again from Pavelets that autumn.' 'These entertainments ended when she went away and handed over her mission to her lady replacement.' This does not take us very far. Who were 'they' and 'she'? Who was 'her' female substitute? Was 'her' mission the solace of the lovelorn poet? Was the mysterious Ye. A. Dorodnova, to whom the first poem in the collection was dedicated on first publication, one of the ladies in question? Did Pasternak actually go to the Saratov area in the difficult summer of 1917? Was a fructifying 'liberation of his spiritual energies' indeed brought about by the marriage of the long-adored Ida Vysotskaya to a Kiev banker in the course of the same eventful year, as she herself was to assert in later life?[8]

The obscurity and rarity of Pasternak's references to his female companion, or companions, is consistent with his policy of keeping human beings to a minimum in his early poems. It has been said, with only slight exaggeration, that 'His verse was written before the sixth day, when God created man. . . . It lacks human beings. He has everything else – storms, forests, chaos – but no people.' There is also 'a striking absence of the animal kingdom . . . no tusk, no horn. . . . Even birds are rare.'[9]

If other animate beings are conspicuous by their absence, what of the poet himself? He is of course present in every line, for what are the lyrics but a record of his own impressions? Yet he seems determined to suppress himself as much as possible. 'The poet is everywhere and nowhere. Instead of viewing the far-flung panorama from without he is its double, becoming now the sea, now the forest.'[10] And so he has dissolved himself, so to speak, in his own verse. Here was his answer to Mayakovsky, the poet who turned his life into a heroic spectacle while simultaneously exploiting that spectacle as the chief subject of his verse.

In 'About these Verses', one of the first lyrics of *My Sister Life*, Pasternak departs as much as anyone could from the poetic posturings of a Mayakovsky. He is so far from seeking to dominate an auditorium that he has buried himself in a remote cottage with a stock of tobacco, alcohol and books by Byron and Poe. His one contact with the outside world is a fleeting enquiry.

> Mufflered, palming my face, through window-slit
> I'll shout to children out in yard: 'My dears,
> What's the millennium out there these days?'[11]

These notorious lines tended to compromise Pasternak politically because they seemed to flaunt his total indifference to his age and to a society which increasingly required from all its members a parade of unremitting, ecstatic and agonized concern for its numerous problems and troubles.

The reader who ransacks *My Sister Life* for references to the events of 1917 will find a bald allusion to peasants burning down manor houses, and even a fleeting mention of the Russian Prime Minister of the era, Aleksandr Kerensky. But he will not find much else in the way of topical material, though he may be struck by the fact that the only noun to be qualified by the age's most hallowed adjective, 'revolutionary', is not the vanguard of a proletariat in arms, but – how typically of the author! – a humble rural haystack.[12]

Despite what may seem to be Pasternak's determined flight from actuality, it has been argued that *My Sister Life* yet carries a distinct revolutionary tang, and not only in the restricted sense of being technically innovative. Valery Bryusov, the only poet prominent in pre-revolutionary years who was also a member of the Russian Communist Party, wrote of the collection as follows in 1922. 'Pasternak has no individual lyrics on revolution. Yet his verse is, perhaps without its author's knowledge, saturated with modernity. Pasternak's psychology isn't borrowed from old books. It expresses the poet's essence, and could have crystallized only in our conditions.'[13] This was not far from Pasternak's own view, as expressed on one occasion when he was discussing *My Sister Life*. 'I saw on earth a summer that seemed not to recognize itself – natural, prehistoric, as in a revelation. I left a book about it. In it I expressed all that can possibly be learnt of the most unprecedented, the most elusive aspects of the Revolution.' This was a time when people's lofty moral requirements, which remain buried in more stagnant eras, had forced themselves to the surface. 'Bright columns of hidden moral deposits miraculously erupt from the earth. People seem a head taller. . . . People you see in the street are no longer mere anonymous passers-by, but indexes and expressions, as it were, of the human race as a whole. That sense of the everyday, observable at every step and simultaneously becoming history; that feeling of eternity having come down to earth and popping up all over the place; that fairy-tale mood I sought to convey in . . . *My Sister Life*.'[14]

In Tsvetayeva's opinion Pasternak indeed had succeeded in conveying such a mood, and 'without hiding from the Revolution in any of the available intellectual cellars'. She quotes half a dozen fragments from the collection in which he vaguely alludes to the revolutionary events of 1917, and she describes him as spending that summer keeping step with the Revolution while carefully listening. She also claims, with prophetic insight, that 'What Pasternak has to say about the Revolution, no less than what the Revolution has to say about itself – it all lies in the future.'[15]

Though the lyrics of *My Sister Life* were composed in 1917 they were barely noticed during the Civil War which followed. But when it eventually became possible to publish the collection as a whole, in 1922, the effect was to establish the author's reputation almost immediately. The poems were eagerly welcomed by critics, reviewers and readers as new, exciting and breath-takingly fresh. Above all, they disclosed what every great poet's work discloses, that his native language had all along possessed resources which might have remained for ever untapped if he had not taken up his pen.

My Sister Life was received with particularly ecstatic praise by other poets, of whom Anna Akhmatova was one. She was a year older than Pasternak, and she often spoke of him as a sister or mother might speak of a refractory but adored small boy. She also believed that he was one of the twentieth century's great creative artists, and she has singled out one lyric from *My Sister Life* as the very 'apex' of Russian poetry. Its title, 'Weeping Garden', brings to mind certain features of Pasternak's earliest work. The 'weeping' recalls his fondness for damp environments, the 'garden' is one of his favourite poetic habitats. And that garden is naturally of the animated variety, a 'he' rather than an 'it'.

> Horrible! He drips, cocks ear:
> Is he alone on earth,
> Crumpling lacelike bough at window?
> Or is there any witness?
>
> Spongy soil's succinctly crushed
> By swellings' burden.
> Midnight is heard afar,
> Ripening in August's fields.
>
> No sound. No witness.
> Convinced he is abandoned,
> He reverts to rolling
> Down roof; into, over gutter.
>   .   .   .
> Silence. No leaf stirs.
> No glimmer glints, save eerie
> Gulps, slipper-shufflings,
> Tear-broken sighs.[16]

Mayakovsky too adored Pasternak's verse, despite the uneasy relations between the two poets, for Pasternak had returned from the Urals in no mood to tolerate the other's tutelage. He disliked Mayakovsky's tendency to take him for granted, and they had quarrelled over the telephone in early 1917 because Pasternak over-reacted to what he considered Mayakovsky's casualness in including his name, without consultation, among the participants listed in the announcement of a forthcoming poetry reading.[17] But Mayakovsky was not the man to resent, or even to remember, such a tiff. When, at a verse reading of the period, a member of the audience began to disparage Pasternak's achievements, Mayakovsky raised himself to his impressive height and praised his colleague's verse 'with loving frenzy' at the top of his still more impressive voice. Surprisingly, too, the militantly political Mayakovsky preferred these lyrics of early maturity to Pasternak's later attempts, in his long poems of the 1920s, to put his art at the service of the Soviet state. Mayakovsky was doing just that himself. Yet he thought little of Pasternak's political verse, while reputedly knowing the lyrics of *My Sister Life* and *Themes and Variations* by heart – works lacking the political dimension which he had come to regard as essential to his own work.[18]

Osip Mandelstam was another major Russian poet of the period to acclaim Pasternak. He wrote that *My Sister Life* contained harmony more original, more mature than had resounded in Russian poetry for many a year. Pasternak was 'no inventor or conjuror, but the initiator of a new mode, of a new Russian verse structure adequate to the maturity and virility attained by the language'. To read Pasternak was 'to clear the throat, strengthen the breath, renew the lungs. Such verse must be a cure for tuberculosis. We possess no healthier poetry nowadays. This is fermented mare's milk after the American canned variety. *My Sister Life* strikes me as a set of first-rate breathing exercises.'[19]

These and all other eulogies of *My Sister Life* are eclipsed by the essay *Cloudburst of Light* which Marina Tsvetayeva wrote immediately after reading the collection in 1922. She records its cataclysmic effect on herself, and proceeds to a frantic analysis of its qualities. The first to attract her is Pasternak's dynamic ebullience. His verse has the exultancy of an explosion, an avalanche, a blow, the sheerest discharging of all vital veins and forces, a sort of white heat which, from a distance, might be taken for a white page. Everything in his work is alight. He is the poet of light as others are poets of darkness. And he knows how to weave mundane everyday detail into verse, as in his famous lines hymning the poetic qualities of a provincial railway timetable.

> While conning in Maytime your timetable's listings
> And riding the local Kamyshin line,
> You'll find it sublimer than Holy Scripture
> Even when studied a second time.

Tsvetayeva also quotes Pasternak's famous comparison of a thunder-cloud to a laundered apron drying and babbling on a clothes line. Everyday things are more of a springboard to him than an end in themselves, says Tsvetayeva. 'They are like earth to foot. A moment's pause, a spring. With Pasternak everything, even sleep, is on the move.'[20] It may be added that none of Pasternak's gardens is static. In 'Mirror' the garden and the looking glass inside a house keep careering into each other, and the wonder is that the glass remains intact. As such passages illustrate, he made up for the virtual exclusion of animate beings from his verse by the extreme degree of animation attributed to personified inanimate objects.

Must Pasternak inevitably have embraced some third 'ism' after shuffling off Symbolism and Futurism in the course of attaining maturity? If so the term most favoured by critics is Impressionism. It has been said that his images recall the paintings of Monet, Renoir, Pissarro and Vuillard. 'Like these painters, he often seeks to set down his momentary impression of objects, and he lays aside his previous knowledge of the world to depict it as it presents itself to his eyes at a given moment.' It has also been said that Pasternak's detail is visualized 'with a painter's eye, with an eye trained in the impressionist school to see not objects, but the space before the eye in which objects and their surroundings mingle in light, shape and colour before separating into their individual terms'.[21]

Pasternak's art is impressionistic to this extent, that he hardly ever seeks to convey his awareness of the world by compiling systematic descriptive structures. Nor do his lyrics build up to an emotional orgasm and then fall away into post-coital sadness like a Verdi aria. No lover of the *crescendo* and *diminuendo*, he casually tosses out arbitrary handfuls of loosely connected, briefly glimpsed manifestations such as his

> Thoughts whipped into white froth
> Of woodpeckers, clouds, heat, firs, cones.[22]

Similarly, in his oft-quoted lyric 'Poetry Defined', he once again broadcasts a scatter of seemingly random associations in an attempt to convey the essence of his art.

> It is tautly bulging whistle.
> It is crushed ice-floes' crunch.
> It is night icing leaves.
> It is nightingales' duel.
> It is sweet-pea pods cradling
> All the cosmos's tears.

Finally, poetry is

> All that night's keen to trap
> In pool's deepest crannies
> And bring to creel as star
> On trembling wet palms.

Such passages, including the characteristic plunge into a liquid environment at the end, recall a couplet inserted by Pasternak during the rewriting of one of his earliest poems.

> The more haphazardly one's sobbing verse
> Is rigged, the more authentic is its ring.[23]

It is perhaps worth looking more closely at the analogy between Pasternak's early work and impressionist painting. Christopher Barnes discusses the equation helpfully, accepting it up to a point. But he also goes on to doubt, in a poem of 1918, 'whether the unrealistic distortion of the landscape could be properly explained in terms of an analogy with French Impressionism'. In the following quatrain the reader is, Barnes suggests, 'more in the realm of van Gogh or the Expressionist work of Munch – or at least in some sphere of art post-dating French Impressionism'.

> I come from the street of the wonderstruck poplar,
> Where the skyline is scared, where that house fears to slump,
> Where the air is as blue as a bundle of clothing
> In the arms of a patient discharged from a clinic.

Barnes goes on to pursue the painting analogues further, also invoking Kandinsky, the 'Blaue Reiter' school and 'perhaps Chagall'.[24]

If Pasternak's art may be termed impressionistic, however reservedly, it must also be added that there was no school of Russian contemporary Impressionist poets for him to belong to. Nor did he found one, since, despite the profound impact which his work made on poets of his own age, attempts to ape his techniques never attained significant proportions. On the other hand his work has been claimed to possess affinities with certain Russian poets, active from the late nineteenth century, who have been classified as Impressionists but who are more commonly classified as Symbolists – Balmont, Annensky and the early Bryusov.[25]

Respectability is also conferred on the term Impressionism, as applied to Pasternak, by the fact that he is known to have applied it to himself. In his essay *Black Goblet* (1916) he alludes to his artistic technique as 'Impressionism of the eternal'. But however eternal the fixing of Pasternak's impressions may seem, they also convey the air of having been glimpsed with total clarity, and for the first time, at the very instant of being put down on paper. Indeed, it has been well said of his lyrics that, just as one is called 'Urals for the First Time', so too all his books could be called 'The World for the First Time'.[26] His speciality is the permanent fixing of a fleetingly descried vision. He can even bring this off in the title of one lyric, 'Momentarily Permanent Thunderstorm'. In that poem, as in many others, he has fulfilled the dream of Goethe's Faust by compelling the fleeting moment to 'Tarry awhile, thou art so fair.'

Though he had already achieved success with this technique in numerous passages of *Over Barriers*, he was later inclined to stress the difference between his verse of 1917–18 and that which preceded and followed it. 'In 1917 and 1918 I was anxious to bring my poems as near as possible to extemporization.' It was more than a matter of trying to finish a poem at a sitting or avoiding the reworking of his drafts. 'In 1917 and 1918 I wrote down only what by the character of the language or by the turn of phrase seemed to escape me entirely of its own accord.'[27] In conversation with Andrey Sinyavsky in 1957, Pasternak said that he had deliberately excluded many lyrics of the prolific summer of 1917 from *My Sister Life* because he wished the book to be 'light' in character. And he spoke of the collection with enthusiasm utterly at variance with other comments of his later years, those in which he renounced his consolidated writings of the pre-1940 period as unworthy of republication.[28]

In *Safe Conduct* Pasternak characteristically says that *My Sister Life* had not been written by himself but by some mysterious outside 'force'. He also indicates his indifference to whatever critical 'isms', including Impressionism, might be associated with his methods. 'I didn't care at all what name was given to the force which produced the book, since that force was immeasurably greater than I and the notions of poetry around me.'[29] An even more eloquent affirmation of his faith in *My Sister Life* was his failure ever to subject the work to radical revision on the scale applied to *Twin in Clouds* and *Over Barriers* in the late 1920s. *My Sister Life* was to be reprinted again and again, virtually unchanged, in the course of its author's lifetime, and many of his admirers still regard it as his supreme achievement.

In October 1917 the second of the year's two Revolutions took place through the *coup d'état* launched in Petrograd by Lenin and the Bolsheviks. There is even less direct information on Pasternak's immediate reaction to this upheaval than is to be had on his response to the events of February. But it at least seems clear that his first instinct was to welcome the second of these two great crises, just as he had welcomed the first.

Indications to this effect are supplied by an undated fragment of autobiography in which he refers to Lenin's sudden appearance from abroad in Petrograd in April 1917. Pasternak salutes the Bolshevik leader's 'inflammatory speeches, striking directness, insistency and drive'. Lenin was, says he, 'unprecedentedly bold in his attitude to elementary popular upheaval. . . . His impatience, his refusal to compromise, combined with the acuteness of his devastating and contemptuous denunciations, overwhelmed those who disagreed with him, forced his opponents to submit, and struck enthusiasm even from his foes. . . . Lenin was . . . the embodiment, the voice of the great Russian typhoon. . . . With the fervour of genius he unhesitatingly assumed responsibility for bloodshed and destruction such as the world had never seen before. . . . He permitted the ocean to rampage. With his blessing did the hurricane surge past.'[30]

Pasternak's enthusiasm for the main architect of the October Revolution is further reflected in *Doctor Zhivago*, where the hurricane has been transformed into a surgeon's knife. 'What superb surgery! To excise all the old, stinking sores with such artistry at one fell swoop! A straightforward, no-nonsense guilty verdict on age-old injustice accustomed to having people bowing, scraping and curtsying to it!' There was something essentially Russian, dear to the heart and long familiar – 'something of Pushkin's sheer luminescence and of Tolstoy's unswerving fidelity to the facts' – about the fearless way in which the whole business had been dispatched. The October Revolution was a stroke of genius, a very miracle of history, precisely because of the suddenness and inappropriateness of its timing. It was 'a revelation belched into the very bowels of everyday life without taking account of its evolution'. And that at a time when mundane 'trams were still coursing the city in full swing'! Yet no sooner has the hero of Pasternak's novel hailed October's events as a stroke of genius than he is already disillusioned. 'Such things exist in their pristine purity only in the heads of those who bring them about, and that solely on the day of their proclamation. On the morrow political chicanery turns them inside out.'[31]

The passage reflects Pasternak's tendency to see history as he saw his own life. Each presented itself to his consciousness as a sequence of isolated piercing instants of colossal significance separated by long, flat periods of dreary uneventfulness. In this spirit, and in his own name, Pasternak wrote to Bryusov in a letter of August 1922 that 'the stage of revolution closest to the heart and to poetry is its *morning*, its explosion'.[32]

The swiftness of Yury Zhivago's disillusionment with the October Revolution furnishes a striking instance of the novel cleaving more faithfully to the facts of its author's evolution than to their timing. Pasternak's novel telescopes into a matter of days a development which its author required nearly two decades of mingled sympathy and antipathy for Russia's October Revolution to live through. Barely has the Bolshevik *coup* proved victorious than Zhivago has already concluded that his country has been taken over to its lasting detriment by a conspiracy of sterile, blinkered fanatics. That conclusion the Boris Pasternak of real life did not form with any degree of finality before 1936, or even (arguably) 1946. His was to be no gradual and progressive transformation, for he was vulnerable to competing political pressures the resolution of which – being the man he was – he postponed again and again. The eventual lesson of *Doctor Zhivago*, that private life is more important than politics, had to be relearnt many times after first being tentatively propounded in *Loveless* and *Dramatic Fragments* – both written before the October Revolution had even taken place.

Between 1917 and 1936 Pasternak was often to express enthusiasm for the October Revolution, and for the new society to which it had given rise. He was to write further paeans of praise to Lenin, he was to publish verses hailing Stalin as a genius. Yet such was at no time the dominant current of his thinking. Neither on this nor on much else will consistency be found in his record. Many of his pronouncements on the first two decades of Soviet society are ironical, ambivalent, violently favourable, violently hostile – and, of course, unrelentingly meshed in images of merciless originality.

During the Russian Civil War, which flared up in 1918 and ended within three years with the victory of the Moscow-based Reds over the anti-Bolshevik Whites, Pasternak remained in Moscow and continued to make his parents' flat in Volkhonka Street his operational centre. He shared the acute privations of the period, and especially of the Civil War's three bitter winters, when desperate fuel shortage combined with disease, famine and overcrowding to create appalling conditions. 'There were three of these terrible winters in a row', Pasternak writes as the narrator of *Doctor Zhivago*. The triumph of materialism, so widely proclaimed by the Revolution's promoters, has (he claims) converted material into an abstract concept. The provision problem and the fuel shortage have replaced food and firewood.[33]

In the winter of 1918–19 Tsvetayeva met Pasternak when he was on his way to sell books from his library because there was no bread in the house. The same atrocious winter also figures in two of his rare lyrics of the period: 'Kremlin in Blizzard, End of 1918' and 'January 1919'. He pictures the Kremlin as a ship ripped from its moorings by a raging sea. The Old Year had often whispered that he should commit suicide by jumping out of his window, and he has every reason to dread the impending New Year as it threatens to 'Take me, shattered as I am / And tackle my re-education'.[34] But Pasternak underestimated, for the shattering and the re-education were both to continue over another forty years.

It proved impossible to earn a living from creative literary work in revolutionary Moscow. 'In spring 1918 I had to abandon original writing and tackle commissioned translations.' By June 1920, when he claimed to be near starvation, he was reputedly calculating that he had translated a total of twelve thousand lines of verse in a single year – intensive hard labour incompatible (he asserted) with conscientious craftsmanship, let alone with art.[35] But, complain though he might, it is possible that he was rescued from starving by commissions from Vsemirnaya literatura ('World Literature'), the huge publishing concern set up under Gorky's sponsorship after the Revolution with the dual purpose of bringing books of the past to the masses and keeping authors of the present alive. And Pasternak was, like it or not, to depend on literary translation as his basic means of livelihood throughout much of his life.

Pasternak's version of Kleist's play *Der zerbrochene Krug* had been completed early in the war, and had appeared in a journal of 1916. During his wartime residence in the Urals he had translated Swinburne's play *Chastelard*, but the text was never published and has been lost. After the Revolution he began a translation of Ben Jonson's *The Alchemist*, which was not to appear until 1933, and his version of Goethe's *Die Geheimnisse* ('The Secrets') appeared in 1922 – but only after it had been severely criticized by his eminent editor, Aleksandr Blok. Blok called Pasternak's translation 'cumbersome, contrived, artificial, stilted, finicky and devoid of talent'. Pasternak accepted this 'contemptuous and devastating comment' as fully justified.[36]

Despite the need to earn his living by translation, he was also writing prose fiction. In the spring of 1918 he told Tsvetayeva that he wanted to write a long novel 'with love and a heroine, like Balzac',[37] and much or all of the work was completed in that year. He then lost the manuscript (under circumstances which remain obscure), except for the opening chapter. That came out in 1922 as the short story *Childhood of Lyuvers* and is one of his most admired prose works, partly for passages subtly evoking the dawn of consciousness in the infant heroine's mind. The work offers little in the way of plot or action, thus conforming with the assumption, characteristic of all the author's fiction, that events do not matter and that sensations are all-important.

Letters from Tula, his other short fictional work written in 1918 – but not published until 1922 – consists of correspondence addressed by its hero to his beloved and is a study of the false and the genuine in art. False art is represented by a group of film actors who spend all their lives play-acting. Even when they are not in front of the cameras they 'posture as geniuses, they pontificate, they bandy phrases with each other, theatrically tossing down their napkins on the table'. With these Bohemian show-offs the story contrasts an elderly retired actor who is perturbed by their theatrical antics and retires to the privacy of his room to stage an inspired histrionic performance in the absence of any audience. Here is fidelity to art as Pasternak understood it. 'The true actor does not find his ultimate standard in himself, but in the role he incarnates.'[38] *Letters from Tula* is particularly significant as the first of many occasions on which Pasternak reflected on the similarity between the roles of the poet and the actor, a theme which was to find its most complex and moving expression in the lyric 'Hamlet' in *Doctor Zhivago*.

Pasternak's fourth verse collection, *Themes and Variations*, was first published in Berlin in 1923. It contains some three score lyrics written during the previous seven years. About half of them are dated 1918, the year in which his muse began subsiding into relative inactivity after the creative eruption of 1917. Pasternak later told Andrey Sinyavsky that much of *Themes and Variations* consisted of material rejected from *My Sister Life*,[39] which may help to explain why the new collection did not make an impact comparable to its predecessor's. Here was less of the daunting shock of novelty. But it by no means follows that the poet was mechanically repeating a well-tried formula.

His greatest admirer, Tsvetayeva, did not consider *Themes and Variations* to be a tired repeat performance of *My Sister Life*, and she went out of her way to stress the very different and no less potent impression made on her by the new collection. Whereas its predecessor had been a cloudburst, the new book was a burning. She had scorched herself on it, and she had scorned to blow on the spot or palliate the burn with cold cream. She went on to list some of the new lyrics which 'passionately' appealed to her. One of them contains what may be the most vibrant among many invocations of the nightingale's song in Russian poetry.

> Nightingale thrashed, trilled, reigned and beamed;
> Swooped down from herbs like fragrance; dangled
> Like crazed showers' mercury mid cherries;
> Befuddled tree-bark; moved towards
> Mouth, palpitating; swung on plait.[40]

Themes and Variations is less of a self-contained unit than *My Sister Life*, and offers a sequence of separate units corresponding to the six cycles into which it is divided. The longest and last of these Pasternak himself called 'second-rate',[41] but it is far from being so. But it is the least technically adventurous section of the book. It contains four sub-cycles in which the poet follows the unrolling of the seasons, allotting a quintet to winter, spring, summer and autumn in turn. The arrangement makes this part of the collection the most formally coherent among the many successions of poems devoted to the seasons which are to be found in his work of all periods.

In contrast with these seasonal poems – impressive, but holding few surprises for keen students of Pasternak's development – the nine-lyric cycle *The Breach* breaks entirely new ground. It fires a barrage of incoherent reproaches at a faithless mistress whose real-life counterpart, if she had one, has not been identified. The rhythms are, for Pasternak, unusually adventurous, not to say breathless – and startlingly so in the work of one who usually tends to follow conventional metrics, however creatively. The mood, too, is unusual in that bitterness has replaced the customary affirmative jauntiness. Another poet, Nikolay Aseyev, has called the cycle a unique and unsurpassable poem of emotion, 'a magnificent speech of indictment, amplified, as through a megaphone by a grief and irony such as no poetry of the last decade has even come close to'. The London-based Russian literary historian D. S. Mirsky wrote that 'For emotional and lyrical force, these nine lyrics have no rivals in modern Russian poetry.'[42] Yet *The Breach*, with all its virtues, does not quite measure up to so extravagant a billing – as Pasternak himself would surely have agreed, for he wrote no more verse in this particular breathless vein.

Aleksey Surkov – a minor poet, who was one day to become a major literary functionary and Pasternak's bitterest enemy – has complained that Pasternak's comparisons 'have no attributes in common with that to which they refer'. To illustrate his point he fastened on a phrase ('Beer flowing from crags' whiskers') from the sequence on Pushkin which forms one of *Themes and Variations'* six cycles. But it is not only from crags' whiskers that Pasternak's beer flows. He gives fuller measure than that.

> Ports, anchors, jetsam, drowned and sodden
> Cadavers, grizzled plankways have
> Ears stuffed with Pilsen's tufty smoke.[43]

This beery image is surely clear enough. It is by no means one of those admittedly numerous Pasternakian elusive comparisons which indeed do seem to have little in common with what they purportedly evoke, and which seem designed to bamboozle and generally confuse the reader. Such was also the complaint of Maksim Gorky, who, after reading *My Sister Life* and *Themes and Variations*, wrote to their author as follows. 'A lot of it is stunning, but one often has difficulty in grasping the links between your images, and one is fatigued by your struggle with language and words.'[44]

The comparison, derided by Surkov, of majestic sea foam with homely beer foam is a reminder of Pasternak's wide range as a versifier. He is a master of the crashing line, a very Milton when he chooses to conjure up – as he does in his Pushkin cycle – the spumy, fuming, foaming-at-the-mouth squalls of Trebizond, the snoring of snow-bound Archangel, the wafting of Morocco's breezes, the glimmering of dawn over the Ganges. But he is also prone to swoop suddenly from the most grandiose into the most mundane of contexts, relying – as Pushkin and many other Russian poets have also relied in a myriad different ways – on the ever-present tension between the Russian high style and the Russian low style to electrify and vary their prosody.

That poetry need not be perpetually trumpeting about the squalls of Trebizond, but can also concern itself with homelier topics, is magnificently asserted in the best-known lyric of *Themes and Variations*. It is entitled 'Poetry', and proceeds to define itself as

> Not euphuist's pomposity,
> But summer with a third-class seat.

Poetry is 'suburb, not refrain'. And poetry can be as stark and spare as the lines with which, through Pasternak, it concludes its excursion into self-definition.

When under tap stands platitude
Empty as bucket's zinc, the jet
Spurts unimpeded even then
With notebook poised below. Stream on![45]

Though Pasternak had radically reduced the composition of new lyric verse by the end of 1918, his work did not become widely known or acclaimed until the two collections *My Sister Life* and *Themes and Variations* were published in 1922 and 1923 respectively, thus making the best of his early poetry easily available in bulk for the first time. It is therefore natural to think of his first lyrical period as continuing into 1923 while falling into the three phases of apprenticeship (1913–17), maturity (1917–18) and decline (1918–23). To the period 1913–23 as a whole belong about half of the lyrics – nearly four hundred in all – which he was to write in the course of a creative life spanning nearly fifty years. As for the distribution of lyrics within the first lyrical period, roughly a half of them were composed during the great spurt of creativity in 1917–18.

The obscurities, the adventurousness and eccentricities of Pasternak's first poetical decade all help to place him firmly in the vanguard of the flourishing Russian modernist movement. His is a modernism of shattering originality in the areas of theme, language and imagery. Only in considerably lesser degree is it a modernism of verse technique. In that area he cleaves (like many other important Russian poets contemporary to him) more closely to tradition than might be expected by readers familiar only with avant-garde verse written in other languages.

Four-line stanzas; rhymes or semi-rhymes on the pattern *a-b-a-b*; familiar, time-hallowed metres which by no means exclude iambics and trochees – these, rather than aggressively emancipated techniques, are Pasternak's basic framework. Such was from the start – such was always to remain – his position, even though he also contrived to introduce many a variation within his self-imposed limits. This passion for variety is especially typical of his first, pyrotechnically dazzling decade, enlivened as it is by the subtleties of ingenious syncopation – by the shock of grotesque, near-miss rhymes and other echoes; by the clash of spluttering phonetic collisions; by the impact of weird resonances and by the crunch of cunningly deployed discord.

By early 1921 the Civil War had ended with the rout of the Whites and the firm establishment of Soviet rule over most of the former Russian Empire. The country lay in ruins after seven years of foreign and civil war, but the onset of peace did at least bring considerable relaxation as extreme wartime privations were somewhat eased by the temporary restoration of small-scale capitalism under the system termed NEP (New Economic Policy). There was also a temporary decline in the activities of the security police. But cultural regimentation had begun, even though its impact during the 1920s did not approach the extreme oppressions ordained in the following decade by Stalin. Already, in August 1921, the execution of an important poet on a charge of treason – Akhmatova's ex-husband Nikolay Gumilyov – suggested that peace on the battlefronts was no guarantee of serenity in the literary world.

Pasternak's parents emigrated from the Soviet Union to Germany in 1921. They took their daughters Josephine and Lydia with them, and they left their sons Boris and Aleksandr behind. The decision to emigrate was not dictated by political disaffection, but by the need to seek medical care and improved living conditions for Pasternak's mother, who had long suffered from heart trouble. Though the emigration of the parents and daughters was to prove permanent, there are indications that Leonid Osipovich would have been glad to return to his native land at any time if his native land had been able to ensure him adequate living and working conditions.

Meanwhile, back in Moscow, Leonid Osipovich's elder son was still subject to surges of enthusiasm for Russia's greatest revolutionary. In December 1921 he chanced to see and hear Lenin in person at the Ninth Congress of Soviets – one of the last public functions attended by the Soviet leader before ill health removed him from active politics. Pasternak has left a vivid verse portrait of Lenin as he appeared on this occasion.

> As I recall, his speech's burr did pierce
> With sparks my withers like ball-lightning's rustle.
> All rose, eyes vainly scouring distant table,
> When suddenly he loomed on rostrum – loomed
> Before he entered; slipped in tracelessly
> Through serried aids and hindrances, like globule
> Of thunder floating smokeless into room.
> Applause's roar erupted, and relief
> Exploded like a shell that cannot *not* burst.
>
> .   .   .
>
> He was like rapier's lunge in follow-through
> To his own words. He made his jacket bulge,
> He stuck his boot toes out, hewed his own line.
> His words might be of oil, but his frame's twist
> Breathed the stark quiddity of naked soaring
> That split husks' oafish crust as he directed
> The flow of thought – his only way to govern.

These inspiring lines are among the finest poetic eulogies ever addressed to Lenin. But they end on a sinister note, for the deceased Lenin – the genius who had arrived as 'harbinger of bounties' – is portrayed in the final line of the description as 'avenging his departure with oppression'.[46]

In summer 1922 Pasternak met Trotsky – still the world's second most famous Bolshevik, though already poised for decline. Trotsky was himself a connoisseur of literature, and had sent for the poet after trying, as he explained, to force his way 'through the dense under-growth' of *My Sister Life*. He asked Pasternak what he was trying to express in the book, and Pasternak adroitly replied that Trotsky would have to ask its readers. Trotsky then went on to enquire why Pasternak was so determined to avoid 'civic' themes in his verse. The question conveyed a wish to induce the poet to write in praise of the new order. But Pasternak brushed any such notion aside. Never one to miss an opportunity for slipping in a daunting image, he replied by defending 'authentic individualism'; he claimed that it constituted a 'new social cell in the new social organism'. This took the great revolutionary orator's breath away, as well it might, and Pasternak later regretted having so monopolized the conversation that he prevented Trotsky – whom he found highly sympathetic – from expressing his opinions more fully.[47] And the silencing of a Trotsky is no mean feat.

'Starvation', one of Pasternak's few lyrics of 1922, shows how far he still was from attempting to write 'civic' verse of the buoyant and ebullient type envisaged by Trotsky and his ilk. In these verses the poet does, however, at least address himself to a theme of immediate social relevance such as he had hitherto shunned – the great famine which had broken out on the lower Volga and elsewhere in the previous year – even though his manner is dispirited and his treatment character-istically oblique. He complains that his attempt to portray the sufferings of Russia's starving peasants has made him feel con-taminated, that his polluted ink needs to be poured away, and that his verbs all need rinsing out with carbolic.[48]

'Starvation' is not the work of a poet fired by enthusiasm for the new society in Russia or for anything else, and it comes from the period of some four years (1919–23) in which he wrote little in the way of original work, whether in verse or in prose. He himself was painfully aware of this production gap, but it was obscured from the world at large by the spate of his works which, after being delayed by Civil War conditions, erupted into print in 1922. *My Sister Life*, *Letters from Tula*, *Childhood of Lyuvers* all came out in that year, though all had been written at least four years earlier. To them were added, also in 1922, the fragmentary *Three Chapters from a Story*, which vaguely anticipates the later verse novel *Spektorsky* (1924–31) and the prose story *A Tale* (1929). In the short essay *Some Propositions* (1922) Pasternak repeats points from his aesthetic philosophy which he has made elsewhere. It is wrong, he argues, to regard art as a fountain which is obliged to gush forth. On the contrary, art is a receptive and absorptive agency: 'Its task is to be a spectator.' And he goes on to add yet another unavowed dig at Mayakovsky by deploring, not for the first time, the current tendency for art to display itself from a stage.[49]

In the spring of 1922 Pasternak married Yevgeniya Vladimirovna Lurye, an artist. She was beautiful, blue-eyed, well-educated. She spoke fluent French, she was of Jewish descent like her husband, and she was more placid than the mercurial Pasternak. Entranced by her Renaissance profile reminiscent of Ghirlandaio's paintings, he bore her off in August by sea to Germany, pausing in the Gulf of Finland to celebrate the journey with a wind-swept lyric, 'Sailing Away'.

Pasternak was reunited with his parents and sisters in Berlin, where they had already spent a year together in 1906. At about this time the tally of Russians living in the city swelled to six figures, and it became the cultural capital of the Russian emigration – the role later to be taken over by Paris. But Berlin's thronging Russian residents had not all decided to remain permanently exiled from their native land. Return to Russia, officially styled the USSR in December 1922, was still relatively easy to accomplish, and it was still possible for writers to participate in Berlin's thriving Russian literary circles without feeling committed to the expatriate life for ever.

War-devastated Germany held few attractions for Pasternak, and his scattered references to his residence there show him generally low-spirited. His morale gained little from renewed contact with his old love Ida Vysotskaya, now married and living in Berlin with her husband the banker; all that she could later remember of the poet's few visits was that he seemed 'very unhappy'. And Pasternak was further demoralized by the brief excursion which he and his wife made to Marburg in February 1923; Professor Cohen had died and the ancient university city seemed to have lost all its charm. The idea of remaining in emigration did not appeal, and Pasternak took to avoiding contact with those Russian expatriates who were committed to permanent self-exile, preferring to cultivate those who intended to return to their motherland sooner or later.[50]

His depression may have been chiefly due to homesickness, for he was deeply attached to his native land. Here, as so often, *Doctor Zhivago* provides a clue to the working of its author's mind. The novel's hero reflects as follows in the context of the disasters threatening Russia in the immediate post-revolutionary period. 'Some people are thinking of escaping south, to the Caucasus, and are trying to make their way further still. That's against my principles. A grown man must clench his teeth and share his country's fate.'[51] Evidently Pasternak thought so too, and he returned to Moscow with his wife in March 1923. Having achieved little during his seven months in Germany, he had decided to go home and try to establish himself as a writer under Soviet conditions. This meant that he must now address himself to a major theme which had so far lain outside his compass: that of Revolution and of the new society to which it had given rise.

PART TWO

FLIRTING WITH HISTORY

1923–1946

4

KEEPING STEP WITH REVOLUTION

After travelling from Berlin to Moscow in March 1923 the Pasternaks quickly discovered that the return to their native land was unlikely to be justified in terms of creature comforts. It had been hard for Boris Leonidovich to keep himself in Moscow as a bachelor, and it was still more difficult to support his new wife and the son, Yevgeny, who was born to them six months after their retreat from Berlin. Earnings from original literary work were inadequate; translation commissions were elusive; hard-won translation contracts were sometimes repudiated with impunity by editors or publishers. All in all the year following the poet's return from Berlin proved 'one of the most difficult' in his life.[1]

He had retained a single room in the Volkhonka Street apartment which had been occupied by Pasternaks since 1911, but had now been converted into a 'communal flat' – as had similar dwellings all over the country. The result was that premises designed for a single family were swamped by strangers who had set up house in the bathroom, hall and corridor as well as in the living-rooms. The communized lavatory was 'under perpetual siege' by assorted lodgers who mustered fifteen primus stoves among them. They treated the poet and his dependants with scant ceremony.[2]

Boris Leonidovich's marriage partner was not one of nature's housewives, having little interest in the management of primuses and infants. Cramped though conditions were in the one room, a child nurse whom they could ill afford was engaged to care for their son. The poet had to fit his literary work into the screaming, the jostling, the queuing at the ablutions. He sometimes took refuge in the adjoining room occupied by his brother Aleksandr and wife. He also resorted to working through the night, keeping himself awake with strong tea and cigarettes.[3]

The marriage also had the disadvantage of bringing two creative artists into excessively close proximity. The husband needed a study, the wife needed a studio; but there was no chance of acquiring either in a country so starved of living space. Then again, Pasternak's cousin

Olga says that Yevgeniya's natural ambience was that of Puccini's *La Bohème*, whereas her husband craved something established and patriarchal along the lines of Tolstoy's *War and Peace*. It is no wonder that the marriage went into decline under these circumstances. Akhmatova has made some typically tart observations on it. 'Boris never understood anything about women. Perhaps he had bad luck with them. His first wife, Yevgeniya Vladimirovna, was a nice intellectual person. But, but, but! She considered herself a great artist, and so Boris had to make soup for all the family.'[4]

Pasternak's cousin says that husband and wife had become estranged by 1927. An extra strain was put on marital harmony when Yevgeniya Vladimirovna's mother turned out to be dying of a brain tumour – a source of desperate distress to the daughter, who was herself in poor health. When Pasternak's mother-in-law died in 1928 he was provoked by her funeral to utter one of his many remarks stressing an extreme degree of alienation from his Jewish origins. 'It's the first time I ever saw a Jewish burial. It was horrible.'[5]

Despite some vague sympathy for the abortive Revolution of 1905, and despite an instinctive dislike of the Tsarist order, the Pasternak of the pre-1923 period had come almost as near as an intelligent and educated man can to absolute non-involvement with his society and its problems. He had preached such non-involvement – militantly, but obscurely – in the article *Black Goblet* of 1916, while his refusal to commit himself and his art to politics and public posturing had formed an important item in the catalogue of his many disagreements with Mayakovsky.

In 1923 Pasternak's phase of political non-involvement comes to an end. From that year onwards he is to behave – with intervals of absent-mindedness – as if he considers himself bound up with the politics of his country, and later of the world. His attitude, as it develops during the remaining years of his life, falls into two main phases. For twenty-three years, between 1923 and 1946, his political stance vacillates. It is hesitant, experimental, uncertain. Phases of enthusiasm for the Soviet system and its leaders alternate with other phases – of apathy, of outright or disguised hostility. His attempts to advertise the regime's virtues in verse alternate with attempts to disparage it by implication in verse. Lenin is eulogized, but with reservations. Stalin too is eulogized, and a determined attempt is made to strike up a dialogue with that dictator, whose worst oppressions eventually help to reduce the poet to silence in the late 1930s; after that, wartime patriotism briefly reconciles him in very limited degree, once again, to the Stalinist order. Not until the post-war period does he experience his most 'powerful and categorical' feeling of 'shocked revulsion against the existing dispensation',[6] and from 1946 onwards his political attitudes are no longer so unstable. He has become an uncompromising opponent of the Soviet system in his mind, if not always in his actions. He is now clear on what he thinks of it. In that spirit he is to live out his days, fighting the system by the extremely restricted but astonishingly effective non-political means available to him.

Such, briefly, is a foretaste of the whole of Pasternak's further evolution as an apolitical animal who was to become deeply involved, against most of his natural instincts, in the politics of his era. The process will be charted in detail in due course. Meanwhile it seems worth stressing again what has been said before – that, for Pasternak, art always remained paramount. He was never a politician – he was a poet sporadically forced, against his instinctive inclinations, into what amounted to political postures. He might show occasional streaks of enthusiasm for the newly established community. But he was unable to maintain the stance for long, however sincerely his fleeting sympathies may have been held.

In a society less fraught with political tension than that of Soviet Russia – that is, in almost any other society known to recorded history – Pasternak's political attitudes would have attracted no notice whatever. It was the special pressures of his age and country which eventually made a political symbol out of a man who, under conditions less extreme, would have remained remarkable for his art alone.

The trouble with such a man as Pasternak, from the point of view of his would-be manipulators, is that he rarely has the faintest idea what he is going to say next, and that his expressions of revolutionary enthusiasm are always liable to veer off into paradox, irony or sheer incomprehensibility. What use was it to the authorities, as they sought writers willing to boost the new regime, to hear Boris Leonidovich boasting that he too was a Communist – but then immediately making nonsense of this profession of faith by adding that Peter the Great and Pushkin had been Communists too?[7] Such self-indulgent impishness made it unlikely that the poet would ever contribute effectively to the simple litanies of political affirmation which Soviet authority was increasingly to require from writers as the price of their survival.

Pasternak is first found attempting to accommodate himself to these new pressures after his return to Moscow from Germany in the spring of 1923. Soviet Russia was just entering the third year of Lenin's New Economic Policy, but Lenin himself was now an invalid and a mere figurehead. His death on 21 January 1924 was important as a historical landmark. But it had little practical effect on the course of events, including the leadership struggle in which Stalin was gradually ousting Trotsky and other rivals.

As Lenin's body lay in state in the Hall of Columns in Moscow's House of Unions long queues of Muscovites formed to pay their last respects. Nadezhda Mandelstam has described the scene as 'ancient Muscovy burying its Tsar', adding that Lenin's obsequies represented 'the last splutter of the Revolution as a popular movement'. She and her husband took their places among 'the usual drab, glum folk' waiting patiently in the streets by the bonfires which protected them against the bitter cold. Near the Bolshoy Theatre the Mandelstams were joined in the queue by Pasternak, whose admiration for Lenin somewhat exceeded theirs.[8]

Soon after this occasion Pasternak was able to put his wavering enthusiasm for the dead leader to practical use when he was employed by the Commissariat for Foreign Affairs to compile a bibliography of references to Lenin in the foreign press. The pay was miserable, but the poet was not so rigorously supervised that he was prevented from browsing at will on the world's periodicals.[9] He has recorded some of the details in the verse novel *Spektorsky*, revealing a genially sardonic attitude strongly at variance with the admiration of Lenin which he has also been known to express. Nor, to put it mildly, does he pay lip service to the sanctity of labour on behalf of the State, that keystone of the Communist work ethic.

> Having got used to prying out
> Melodies' currants from life's bun,
> I once was forced to drop the role
> Of know-all surfeited with rhymes.
>
> I was in need. Our son was born.
> I had to put off childish things.
> Gauging my age with sidelong glance,
> I saw the first glint of grey hair.
>
> But I did not sit idly by.
> A keen, responsive friend was found
> To help, and I was straightway set
> To process foreign stuff on Lenin.
>
> My job? To fish out sentences
> About him. So I kept alert,
> Teasing the stuff out, diver-like,
> With lots of plunging through the press.

He goes on to boast that this new employment has taught him about clothes fashions, Conrad and Proust, and implies that he is more concerned with such trivialities than with the main architect of the October Revolution. No wonder that

> At Christmas I was booted out,
> Which curtly cut off my research.[10]

Soon after Pasternak's return from Berlin he came out with a somewhat eccentric profession of loyalty to the new political order by publishing a lyric, 'May Day', in Mayakovsky's journal *Lef*, which was outstandingly active in commending the new way of life. 'May Day' has been described as 'pretty well Pasternak's first purpose-directed work'; it was commissioned by Mayakovsky himself, and it represents 'an unprecedented demonstration of Pasternak's poetic solidarity with Mayakovsky's literary group'.[11]

'May Day' harnesses breathless ardour and mixed meteorological metaphors to a paean of enthusiasm for the revolutionary cause. It calls on Moscow to take a nip of boiled wind, and then shoos the city off in search of grass with which to wipe off the fungus of corpse-meat banquets before the first trams start up. The blue sky is to rave deliriously about the disappearing snow while scattering disconnected words above the mud. There is to be no turning back, and there are to be no fences and boundary lines between human beings. Today's bond of solidarity between City and Worker is 'neither partial nor incidental'.

> We've ganged up to make humanity the equal of the gods.
> It's the crucial last engagement we must fight.[12]

At this point the jaunty poet almost seems to be feeling for the 'full-speed-ahead' jargon of Communist cliché. But 'May Day' was only one of four lyrics which he submitted to Mayakovsky in early 1923. Mayakovsky rejected the other three – all examples of private, non-political verse.[13]

Evidence of an attitude unsympathetic to Mayakovsky, as also to the Soviet system so enthusiastically supported by Mayakovsky, is to be found in certain posthumously published verses by Pasternak which he inscribed in a copy of *My Sister Life* presented to the other poet in 1923. He rebukes Mayakovsky for prostituting his art to politics, and mocks him for fussing over budgetary and economic problems while writing 'slogans about oil'. Pasternak also compares Mayakovsky the purveyor of versified propaganda to a grounded Flying Dutchman, and adds

> I'm yearning for that therapist
> Who might restore your wrath.[14]

Pasternak had a meeting with Stalin in the winter of 1924–5, according to an account 'more than once' given by the former to Olga Ivinskaya after an interval of over twenty years. This was, if the story can be believed, the only face-to-face encounter ever to take place between two men whom many might regard as the USSR's two most remarkable citizens. By now Stalin was already well on the way to succeeding Lenin as the dominant leader of the revolutionary State, but had found time to concern himself with a minor literary matter. He questioned three leading poets – Pasternak, Yesenin and Mayakovsky – on the problem of translating verse into Russian from Georgian, his mother tongue. When Pasternak recalled the episode in later years, he described Stalin as the 'most terrifying' person he had ever seen – a crab-like dwarf with a yellow, pockmarked face and a bristling moustache. And yet the Pasternak of this period regarded Stalin as 'a true leader', according to Ivinskaya.[15] If Pasternak's recollection of the episode, and Ivinskaya's account of it, are both correct, it may mark the beginning of the obsession with Stalin which was to haunt the poet in the 1930s.

The Pasternak of the mid-1920s was to be heard expressing flashes of approval for the political system in process of being taken over by Stalin. Nadezhda Mandelstam recalls an occasion on which Boris Leonidovich fired off a loyalist political harangue at herself and her husband. 'Cloaking his ideas in his usual illustrations and images', Pasternak maintained that 'What's happened is here to stay, the People is behind it, we're in the thick of it, and there's no other way out because every worker – '. Nadezhda Mandelstam broke in at this point to retort that Soviet Russia was the only country in the world which had 'got the upper hand of its workers' movement'. Her contention flagrantly contradicts official Soviet dogma, whereby the interests of the workers, of the Communist Party and of the State are deemed to coincide. Pasternak was horrified to hear such a remark, and Mandelstam's widow was even convinced that the episode provoked the 'wary and distant' attitude which he was to display towards her during their sporadic meetings of the next thirty-five years.[16]

He may well have taken an orthodox political line on this and other occasions, but he clung to it less steadfastly than Nadezhda Mandelstam has implied. At about the time of lecturing her on the popularity and historical inevitability of the Revolution, he was revealing an attitude markedly less loyalist in his reaction to the Party Decree on Literature of 18 June 1925. The background to this document must be sought in the rift which developed in the 1920s between those writers who offered active loyalty to the new regime and those who sought to preserve some degree of independence. The loyalists tended to call themselves Proletarians and to belong to various associations of Proletarian writers, though many were in fact of genteel origin. The more independent-minded came to be known as Fellow Travellers, a term popularized by Trotsky. They were neither Communist Party members nor sympathizers, but politically unaffiliated authors who were still free to write as they pleased on whatever topic they liked, provided always that they did not directly attack the new political system. Pasternak was, in effect, a Fellow Traveller – but one who occasionally uttered Proletarian sentiments.

In the course of the 1920s the Proletarian writers mounted increasingly vicious attacks on the Fellow Travellers. They were trying to silence a group more talented than their own, and thereby to gain control over literature and the associated perquisites. The campaign developed less as a literary debate than as a political witch hunt, and it was unwelcome to the Party leadership, which was in any case more concerned with present economic disasters than with the future of something as useless as literature. The Proletarians' bland assumption that they were entitled to speak in the Party's name was especially unwelcome to authority, and this was the chief reason why the decision was taken to protect the Fellow Travellers by sanctioning the continued existence of conflicting literary movements. Such was the main provision of the Decree on Literature of 1925 – a decree less liberal in its implications than appeared at first sight. The Party had, it is true, decided to legislate in favour of tolerance. But the crucial point was that the Party had decided to legislate at all. If freedom could so easily be conceded, could it not be withdrawn with equal ease? The Fellow Travellers as a whole chose to ignore so sinister a prospect. It was enough for them that they had been granted permission, however easily retractable, to carry on writing as they wished, and they greeted the new decree with enthusiasm.

The one dissenting voice in the applauding chorus was Pasternak's. His statement on the Party Decree was contributed to a Moscow periodical of October 1925, and is a masterpiece of corrosive sarcasm. He flatly denies that the country is undergoing any cultural revolution, as the decree had maintained; he claims that this is, on the contrary, a period of cultural reaction. Then again, the decree had proclaimed that a literary style 'appropriate to the epoch' was just on the point of emerging – a style grand enough (it was implied) for an age so majestic. Pasternak sourly dismisses this proposition. A style appropriate to the epoch already *has* been discovered, says he. It is officialese; it is the language of nonentities and statisticians; it has been distilled from all that was most mediocre in pre-revolutionary and post-revolutionary writing; it is the traditional style of official literary censorship, which now happens to have been taken over by writers as well.[17]

This is the only occasion on which Pasternak ever responded in full and in print to a Party ruling on literature, and publication of his blistering response in a Soviet periodical shows that the freedom conceded to the literary fraternity by the Party was, for the time being, anything but illusory.

In a letter to Rilke of 12 April 1926 Pasternak stresses the self-contradictory features of the Revolution. The Revolution is grand, but it is petty. It is dynamic, but it is inert. It is, in sum, 'a sinister, noble historical curiosity'.[18]

His ambivalence towards revolution is amply reflected in the four long poems *High Fever*, *Nineteen Hundred and Five*, *Lieutenant Shmidt* and *Spektorsky*. They were composed roughly in that order, except that their periods of composition tended to overlap. All four were published piecemeal in a variety of periodicals, and each was substantially rewritten before assuming its final form. They were written and first published between 1923 and 1931, forming a self-contained block within the poet's work as a whole. Here are the only long poems which he ever completed, the shortest being *High Fever* (about 300 lines) and the longest *Spektorsky* (about four times that length).

As is indicated by Pasternak's choice of revolutionary themes, he had at last abandoned his original view of the poet's task. He no longer saw art and politics as diametrically opposed concepts forbidden to intermingle, as he had maintained in his essay *Black Goblet* of 1916. On the contrary, his long poems of the twenties represent a determined attempt to bring the two together.

In turning from short poems to long poems, and from material independent of politics to material reflecting politics, he was responding to an atmosphere grown acutely hostile to the lyric muse. According to the notions of the day, post-revolutionary Russia was an epoch of unparalleled heroism which had been ushered in by the noblest, the greatest upheaval in human history. Here was a time for greatness, for spaciousness, for grandiose artistic structures, not for the delicate sensibilities of personal poetry. Lyric bards had twittered away about their private sensations long enough, and they were due to go out of production. Akhmatova and Mandelstam, two of the most sensitive, indeed did lapse into protracted periods of silence, while

Pasternak – being more in sympathy with the new regime than they – was able to react by exchanging one kind of poetry for another.

He has referred to his new form as 'epic', contrasting it with his previous 'lyric' mode. He has also claimed that the new form was imposed by the new age. 'That is why I am moving from lyrical thinking to epic, difficult though the transition is.' He further claimed that *Nineteen Hundred and Five* consisted of 'separate epic fragments',[19] though one might be forgiven for assuming the concepts 'epic' and 'fragmentary' to be mutually exclusive; an epic may *survive* in fragments, but what kind of an epic poet is it who proclaims in advance that he intends to write in fragments? Need it be said that by 'epic' Pasternak implied, as he usually did when using literary terminology, something elusively different from the stale conceptions that lurk in less original minds?

Pasternak's long poems are not epics in any traditional sense. They offer neither the 'continuous narrative' nor the 'heroic personages' which the pedestrian *Oxford English Dictionary* requires from the genre. The narrative consists of impressionist glimpses flashed on the screen by an author who assumes that his plot must already be known to his readers through some such procedure as osmosis or telepathy. There is only one remotely heroic character: Lenin, as he appears – so memorably, but so briefly – in *High Fever*. The more prominent leading figures – Lieutenant Shmidt, Spektorsky, the poet himself – are all, in their not so different ways, anti-heroes and accentuators of the negative.

High Fever, on which Pasternak began work in 1923, is not only the shortest item in his quartet of long poems; it is also the most obscure and the least favoured in criticism. 'From its very inception it broke into pieces which could not be stuck together again.' It has been called 'a long-drawn-out lyrical digression', and 'the unhappy utterance of a poet who cannot see that he matters to the new dispensation'.[20] It is still less of an epic than the other three long poems, for it contains no narrative at all – not so much as the hazy untold tale that lurks in the background of *Lieutenant Shmidt* and *Spektorsky*. Even the main theme, Revolution, is concealed to the extent that the word 'revolution' does not figure in the text.

Far from deploying *High Fever* as the epic poem of his ruminations, Pasternak begins the work by mocking the very notion of epic. His first sixteen lines facetiously dismiss the Trojan War as a series of fussy comings and goings which spawned 'the Trojan Epic'. The subject of the *Iliad* thus disposed of in about one thousandth of that sublime work's length, he proceeds to suggest that poetry (the 'High Fever' of

his title) is embarrassingly out of place in a world that has 'flounced off
from books / To pikes and bayonets'. But poetry which mindlessly
praises the new order is more out of place still.

> Hell's paved with good intentions, and
> The view's become established now
> That if you pave your verse with them
> You'll be absolved from every sin.[21]

The poet is a mere visitor to the world at the best of times; he is never
its true citizen.

> I am a guest. In every world
> High fever is a transient.

And the poet is naturally an anachronism in the Soviet age. He and his
milieu, that of the pre-revolutionary Russian intelligentsia, have no
place in the new society.

> All that we were was icebound music.
> I speak of that whole social set
> With which I have made up my mind
> To leave the stage, as leave I shall.[22]

In the modern era the intellectual has become pathetic. Pasternak
depicts him as follows, and with a further incidental tilt against
Mayakovsky, who was now heavily engaged in 'selling' the new order
to the masses through posters of his own devising. Mayakovsky is to
be identified with Pasternak's

> Foolhardy intellectual
> Back there in legends' afterglow,
> Printing and painting placards that
> Depict his glee at his own doom.[23]

The poem's basic theme is not revolution as a great and glorious
event, but revolution as the forerunner of the destruction and
privations of the early post-revolutionary years. It is typical of the
author that these are not explicitly described, but conveyed in
meteorological guise as a storm which first spits a few scattered
snowflakes. And then, suddenly,

> Like cooper thumping barrel, blizzard smites;
> Holds off a little; then smites harder still,
> Till panic lets the tempest burst indoors.[24]

This invocation of revolution as a terrible storm runs to over sixty lines
of considerable power, but they were removed by Pasternak when he

gave *High Fever* its final shape.

Toward the end of the poem brief allusion is made to two historic events. The first is that with which Russia's February Revolution began: the abdication of the Emperor Nicholas II in a railway train on 2 March 1917. The second represents the end of the period of upheaval and the beginning of the consolidation of the revolutionary State: the Ninth Congress of Soviets, addressed by Lenin in Moscow in December 1921. With the heroic description of the great revolutionary, much of which was added in the course of later revisions, Pasternak supplied some of *High Fever*'s finest lines and the only passage which achieves a little of the epic quality so misleadingly attributed by him to his long poems as a whole. But even here the poet cannot bring himself to offer an unrelievedly stirring, positive revolutionary message, as witness his ominous concluding lines.

> The genius who harbingered good fortune
> Is avenging his departure with oppression.[25]

In spite of Pasternak's inability or deliberate refusal to build *High Fever* as a harmonious literary structure, the poem has been too easily dismissed in criticism. Its superb half-lines, lines and sequences, its haunting opacities do much to redeem any architectural defects.

Pasternak compensated for *High Fever*'s lack of revolutionary zeal with *Nineteen Hundred and Five*, which was first published in 1926. It is not a eulogy of the Communist Party or of Lenin, but a hymn to early Russian revolutionary history as a whole, and it is almost bloodthirsty in gloating over the attacks launched against the Tsarist regime by disaffected citizens up to and including the year of the title.

The poem starts by addressing the Spirit of Revolution as a reckless girl who loathes everything mean and petty.

> Gaolbird turned Joan of Arc, sprung from
> Siberia's stockades, you are
> The sort to dive into life's well
> Too fast to regulate your run-up.[26]

Pasternak then parades the forerunners of 1905. He presents the young Dostoyevsky as an early revolutionary, reminding the reader that the great novelist had served a prison sentence for political disaffection in the 1850s. He then goes on to praise revolutionary terrorism of the succeeding decades, describing the conspiratorial cells of 'nihilists in smocks' and 'students in pince-nez'. He also invokes the secret bomb-manufacturing laboratories set up by heroic, fiery-souled 'dynamiters and daguerrotypes' who include the ever-prominent and ultra-dangerous female of the species.

> If we'd been born thirty years sooner
> We would have found, going indoors,
> That these laboratory girls
> Amid their glimmering retorts,
> In paraffin lamps' murkiness,
> Were our own mothers or their friends.[27]

The poem then speaks of Stepan Khalturin, who had made an unsuccessful attempt to blow up the Emperor Alexander II in St Petersburg's Winter Palace on 5 September 1880, causing extensive casualties among soldiers of the guard. Allusion is also made to the terrorist movement People's Will, to its leader Sofya Perovskaya and to its supreme achievement – the fatal bombing of the same Emperor on the Catherine Quay in St Petersburg on 1 March 1881. It is here, too, that gleeful reference is made to the assassination, on 4 February 1905, of the Grand Duke Sergey Aleksandrovich, official Visitor to the School of Painting where the author had lived as a boy, and where his father had long been a member of the staff.

In his portrayal of the revolutionary year the poet displays rioting peasants, demonstrating workers, mutineering sailors and student protesters – all at some length and in considerable detail. This abundance of factual historical reference is without precedent in the work of an author hitherto shy of real-life material. Yet even here he avoids descriptive narrative. Rather than tell the story of 1905, he deploys his theme allusively as if in disconnected film 'clips'. He explains nothing. He assumes that his reader must already be familiar, as most of his Russian readers in fact were, with such persons and places as Father Gapon, the Grand Duke Sergey, the battleship *Potyomkin*, the Presnya District of Moscow.

Nineteen Hundred and Five is an impressive poem. It has been acclaimed as containing the finest lines yet to have come from Pasternak's pen at the time when it appeared,[28] and it was welcomed by supporters of the new order as a successful revolutionary study.

Lieutenant Shmidt was first published in 1926–7. It is similar in content and spirit to *Nineteen Hundred and Five*, it is of comparable length, it treats the same historical period. But, whereas the earlier poem spans the full range of revolutionary events in 1905, *Lieutenant Shmidt* concentrates on a single minor episode. Its theme is the naval mutiny which took place in the Russian Black Sea fleet in November and was led by Lieutenant Pyotr Petrovich Shmidt.

The poem has the ghost of a plot. It flicks at the love affair in which the hero becomes involved during the revolutionary year and at his rejection of private happiness when chosen to lead the mutiny. There are glimpses of the failure of that mutiny, of the hero's trial and of his execution by firing squad on 6 March 1906. Pasternak had studied the episode in the historical sources, and characteristically treats his readers as if they have done the same. He gives no systematic description of Shmidt's personal tragedy, or of his contribution to history, any more than he had given a consecutive account of the 1905 Revolution in the earlier poem. He offers only an array of glosses on events. Abrupt transitions, a seemingly perverse refusal to identify individual characters and authors of speeches except as 'he' or 'she' – these are staple features of a technique which has retained many of its impressionist features despite the move from short to long poems. As the bard of revolution, Pasternak shows little more patience with impatient readers than he had shown in *Twin in Clouds*.

Such features have led Vladimir Weidlé to dismiss the poem as inferior to *Nineteen Hundred and Five*, and as 'extremely strained and contrived, written to order unwillingly – whether to his own order or to another's makes no difference'. Boris Thomson expresses a contrary view, assessing *Lieutenant Shmidt* as undoubtedly the most successful of Pasternak's long poems of the late 1920s.[29] There is something to be said for both judgements. *Nineteen Hundred and Five* is the more brilliant, the more clear-cut, the more structurally impressive of the two poems. It is also, for what that may matter, the more impeccably revolutionary in its sentiments. And yet, muddled and even exasperating though some of *Lieutenant Shmidt* may seem, and even more so after repeated re-reading, the poem penetrates deeper into Pasternak's particular territory. It also does more to foreshadow the chief work of his maturity, *Doctor Zhivago*.

Nothing could be further from the rugged, violent, self-confident revolutionary sailor–hero of conventional Soviet literature than Pyotr Petrovich Shmidt. This Shmidt is no more a man of action than his creator. Far from fomenting mutiny in the fleet, he accepts leadership only when leadership is thrust upon him. He does so without expecting a successful outcome, and because he believes it his duty. Marina Tsvetayeva, who was always looking for a hero to worship, found such passivity distasteful. She told Pasternak that Shmidt was no true sailor, but a typical pince-nez-wearing Russian intellectual, a fount of pretentious jargon, a kind of 'sea-faring Chekhov'.[30]

Pasternak had not only failed to project a revolutionary man of action. He had also rejected by implication the official Soviet view of the Russian October upheaval as a revolution destined to end all revolutions by creating a permanent social and political Utopia. Far from accepting this contention, the poet uses powerful figurative language to suggest that history does not come to a stop whenever a revolution occurs, since history's fundamental rhythm consists of an endlessly repeated cycle. It is that of oppression followed by revolution followed by oppression. The State created by revolution may seem to promise freedom, but the promise is never fulfilled. All that follows is institutionalized dogma.

> Thou monstrous idol of the State,
> Freedom's eternal ante-room!
> The centuries slink from their cells.
> The wild beasts scour the Coliseum.
> The preacher's hand boldly confers
> On the damp cage his benediction,
> Seeking by faith to tame the panther.
> Eternal is the cycle's swing
> To Roman church from Roman circus.
> We too live by the self-same law,
> We from the catacombs and mines.[31]

Thirty years after writing the poem, Pasternak himself was to become the Shmidt of a later generation. Just as Shmidt had accepted leadership of a naval mutiny against the Empire of the Tsars in 1905, so his creator was to sponsor a one-man literary mutiny against the Soviet State fifty years later. Pasternak, like Shmidt, never sought the martyr's role. It was thrust upon him by God, history or destiny, and he accepted it only as a matter of duty – a point made with awesome resonance in his lyric 'Hamlet'. And so Pasternak himself was one day to become 'part of time's great dislocation', the phrase by which he causes Shmidt to describe himself in the speech addressed to the judges at his trial. The passage closely follows the transcript of the original, as preserved in the records, but the message is no less poignant for that. Like Shmidt, the Pasternak of 1958 was to feel that his accusers were just as much the 'victims of the time' as he himself was. He too felt 'Lifted from throng / By elemental surge'. He too had no regret over having trodden so fateful a path. And he too could say of himself, as Shmidt does,

> I know this stake I stand by
> Shall prove to be the frontier
> Of two historic epochs.
> Glad am I to be chosen.[32]

Lieutenant Shmidt is a subtler poem than *Nineteen Hundred and*

Five. As such it was less fitted to commend its author to the custodians of Soviet opinion. The author was further courting official disapproval when he prefaced the work, as it began to be published in the journal *Novy mir* in 1926, with a verse dedication to Marina Tsvetayeva. Its fifteen lines are lightly encoded to the extent that their initial letters form an acrostic of her name. To honour a self-expatriated refugee from the Soviet Union in this way did not yet rate as high treason, but it was more than a minor misdemeanour. Nor was Pasternak's guilt mitigated by the text of the dedication, in which – through the blur of characteristic obscurities – looms the spectre of the poet as a creature hunted throughout the centuries by hostile forces.[33]

Pasternak called *Spektorsky* a 'novel in verse'. It is the longest of his four long poems, and the most perversely tortuous of them, 'astounding contemporaries by its opacity and by the obscurity of its plot structure'.[34] It also has the most complex publication history of the four.

The poem first appeared in various almanacs and periodicals as a sequence of fragments – parts of cantos, complete cantos, groups of two or three cantos. The first seven are set in the years 1912–13, and they stuttered into print in 1924–8. But Pasternak then suspended work in order to write a short piece of prose fiction, *A Tale*. This is set in 1914–16, and it continues the plot of *Spektorsky* to the extent that either *Spektorsky* or *A Tale* possesses anything so definite as a plot. *A Tale* has the same hero as the poem, Sergey Spektorsky; and it brings in some of the poem's other characters, including the hero's sister Natasha. Only after the publication of *A Tale* did its author go on to complete *Spektorsky* by adding Cantos Eight and Nine, which are set in 1919. He then concluded the issue of piecemeal drafts by publishing an Introduction separately in 1930. Finally, he rounded up *Spektorsky* as a whole and brought it out as a self-contained work in 1931.

Spektorsky is, as its publication history suggests, a work of fiendish deviousness. In its Introduction, consisting of twenty-six four-line stanzas, the poet begins by speaking in his own name about his employment in 1924 by the Commissariat for Foreign Affairs to ransack the foreign press for allusions to Lenin. He then describes how these same researches chanced to throw up references to an expatriate Russian woman author whose writings have made her famous abroad. She is called Mariya Ilyina, and is later to develop into one of the poem's three shadowy heroines. But is Ilyina fact or fiction? Though her name will not be found in the annals of *émigré* Russian literature, she yet emerges as a distorted portrait of a real Russian expatriate writer – the poet Marina Tsvetayeva, with whom Pasternak had been corresponding since 1922. Having introduced the quasi-fictional Ilyina–Tsvetayeva in the Introduction to *Spektorsky*, Pasternak goes on to explain that it was the references to her which had originally suggested to him the idea of writing a work on Sergey Spektorsky; for Sergey Spektorsky had, as it turns out, been a friend of Ilyina.

So far Pasternak has introduced: first, an individual from real life who speaks as 'I' and is clearly intended to be identified as himself; second, the quasi-fictional character, Ilyina; and, third, what purports to be a wholly fictional character, Sergey Spektorsky. But what of Spektorsky's characteristics, in so far as they can be elicited from the skimpy and scattered references to him which lurk in long passages of townscape description and extended weather bulletins? He turns out, if the material of *A Tale* is also collated, to be a young writer. He has worked as a private tutor just before the First World War. He has spent part of the war in the Urals. He also seems to have suffered a leg injury, since surprise is expressed at the fact that he does not walk with a limp.[35] These are all traits of Pasternak himself. His lengthy Introduction to *Spektorsky* is thus a perversely involved statement to the effect that he intends to write about himself. Indeed, it would be surprising if such were not the case. Nearly all Pasternak's fiction – from *Apelles' Mark* to *Doctor Zhivago*, and with the sole significant exception of *Childhood of Lyuvers* – turns on the experiences of a hero who is himself an author or artist, and who is broadly identifiable as his creator's *alter ego*.

The identification receives further confirmation from the temperamental passivity with which Pasternak endows Spektorsky – like many of his other author–protagonists, including Yury Zhivago. This feature accords with aspects of Pasternak's own nature, and also with his conception of the poet as a medium or sponge through which nature and art express themselves. But Spektorsky is not only a man without qualities. He is also, says his creator, a 'person without merits'. He is not there for his own sake; he is a peg on which to hang a description of his age.

> I think but little of my hero
> And might have jibbed at such a subject,
> Did I not wish to show the cage
> Of rays in which he vaguely loomed.[36]

Pasternak went out of his way to confirm that the subject of his poem was a way of life rather than an individual. In a comment on *Spektorsky* published by a newspaper in March 1931 he claimed to have tried to depict 'the crisis in the world before our eyes while giving a general composite picture of the age, the natural history of its life style'. And since this was an age of revolutionary ferment, *Spektorsky* was specifically designed to portray the Revolution. 'I shall stick to it that I've said far more about the recent Revolution here..., and said it far more aptly, than what I said about the 1905 Revolution in my factual and chronological book *Nineteen Hundred and Five*.'[37]

It is lucky that Pasternak has so uncompromisingly defined *Spektorsky*'s theme as revolutionary, for without this plain statement many readers of the poem might never have suspected anything of the sort. Nowhere in the text is either Revolution of 1917, nowhere are the ensuing changes of government so much as mentioned, still less described. It would be possible to read the entire work without realizing that a major political crisis was the main object of study, or even that such momentous events as two wars and two changes of government occur in the course of the narrative. In contrast with *Nineteen Hundred and Five* and *Lieutenant Shmidt*, where revolution is unmistakably the chief burden, *Spektorsky* is all background, and by no means obviously revolutionary background at that. The greater part of the poem, consisting of its first seven cantos (set in the period 1912–13) antedates by five years the Revolution which purportedly forms the chief subject. But this was ever Pasternak's way. When he set himself to describe something he was apt to proceed by describing something entirely different.

This is as true of private as of public affairs. For example, a prominent theme of Canto Two is the love affair of Sergey Spektorsky and Olga Bukhteyeva, the wife of an acquaintance. Yet most of the stanzas are devoted to the setting, a woodland cottage during the Christmas of 1912 as it is celebrated by a rout of revellers who arrive by train from Moscow for a combined skiing and drinking holiday. The general hubbub 'favours the stormy secret of two individuals' – the lovers Sergey and Olga; but by the time of the final draft, as published in 1931, Pasternak had so castrated their liaison that readers may even have failed to notice that a love affair of any kind had been part of the thematic material at all. In the first version of the poem the matter had been made starkly explicit by a passage which surely represents the nearest that Boris Leonidovich ever came to dabbling in pornography.

> Two wrists' hot wind stripped quivering female. Dimple
> To dimple two hearts clashed. In breast-bones' broadsides
> Grappled twin maddened hulks. Her gasping bosom,
> Straining to rick her lover's neck, came near
> To self-decapitation. When lust wearied

Of mane-tossing, concupiscence's potent
Effusion swept away on rigid spindle
The mattress's shagged out equestrienne.[38]

A far cry, this, from the soupy strains of 'Lara's Song', the theme melody to the film *Doctor Zhivago*!

Spektorsky is revealed as less potent in the political than in the sexual area by Cantos Three and Four, which invoke a visit paid to him at his Moscow home in 1913 by a female whom ultra-careful reading will identify as his sister Natasha. She also turns out, after still more pernickety collation with the material of *A Tale*, to be married to a doctor called Pasha with whom she normally resides in the Urals. And she further emerges, from the verbal onslaught which she launches against her brother during her Moscow visit, as a revolutionary sympathizer. She is, in fact, one of those young women (Russia has long possessed them in unlimited quantity) who are blessed with a vocation for reprimanding their menfolk as insufficiently collect-ive-minded and ideology-geared. She addresses the vacillating Sergey as follows.

'Look here, your being young's a plus.
Your being odd-man-out's a minus.
You've got no sense of mission, to my shame.
In what camp are you? What a nuisance too,
That, what with coming here, I'm going to miss
The May Day do with Pasha and his comrades.'

Sergey replies like a true Pasternak hero confronted by a political activist – with an adroit side-step. He curtly tells his sister that

'A meal of silence is enough for me
Without your salad dressing.'[39]

The scene is echoed in Canto Nine, set in the Moscow of 1919, where Spektorsky is accidentally reunited with Olga Bukhteyeva. But the mattress's equestrienne of Christmas 1912 is far indeed from seeking any repetition of her earlier rough-riding exploits. Merely throwing her former lover a glance that says 'you miserable little squirt',

She jokingly adjusted her revolver:
A gesture that was Olga to a tee.[40]

Olga turns out to be another revolutionary activist and claims herself 'a daughter of People's Will', that gang of political terrorists of the late 1870s which Pasternak had approvingly invoked in *Nineteen Hundred and Five.* But Sergey is no more impressed by his ex-mistress's revolutionary sentiments than he had earlier been impressed by his sister's homily, and he again makes an evasive reply. Both revolutionary women – sister Natasha of 1913 and ex-mistress Olga of 1919 – are presented as farcical rather than menacing, while the dithering, slippery Spektorsky clearly enjoys the author's approval and sympathy. And so *Spektorsky* is by no means the hymn to 1917 which might have been expected from the author of *Nineteen Hundred and Five.* It is, on the contrary, an early statement of a major thesis of *Doctor Zhivago,* that revolution and its claims are too insignificant to be worth wasting time on. The best way to describe them is to describe something altogether different. But that, of course, was the best way of describing anything, according to Pasternak. He was permanently poised to proceed to Paradise by way of Moscow's equivalent of Kensal Green.

This attitude helps to explain the emphasis on the chaotic building operations outside the tenement where Mariya Ilyina resides in 1913. The 'hail' of beams, stones, sweat, the 'ocean of earthworks sowing rubble everywhere like subversion' – all symbolize the coming revolutionary upheaval. And the accomplishment of that upheaval only creates an even more depressing form of chaos. Moscow of 1919 is portrayed as a scene of desolation. Wooden fences have been torn down for fuel and replaced by all-night food queues. Derelict trains, dead horses and freezing cold combine to lower the spirits.

> All around is frost's ungobbled fodder.
> Jammed in blizzard's wan jaws,
> Slump locomotives' black cruppers
> And horses, shied full length.

Here is no vibrant new society, but an 'age of cave-dwellers on pitted waste plots'. Moscow is, in short, 'a farewell souvenir of the war'. It is anything but the capital of a proletariat triumphant.[41]

The more one reads *Spektorsky* the more one is impressed by its effectiveness as a challenge – a challenge so oblique that the work has been sanctioned for repeated publication in the Soviet Union – to the official view of the October Revolution as the most inspiring event in history, and of Soviet society as the basis for a future glorious beyond conception. Pasternak resembles Spektorsky in failing to meet his opponent head on. He uses, rather, the method whereby one wrestler allows another to defeat himself through his own strength. His answer to the Revolution's claims is not to deny or denounce them, but to side-step into a different topic altogether – usually the weather.

As these considerations suggest, the Pasternak of *Doctor Zhivago* is more in evidence in *Spektorsky* than in any previous work. *Spektorsky* is a maze of absurdities and evasions which help to make it the most challenging, the most rewarding and the most Pasternakian of the four long poems. Its style also raises it above the other items in the group to which it belongs. All the four long poems are crisp, epigrammatic, laconic, sardonic, ironical and self-mocking in their texture and tone. They stand in much the same relationship to Pasternak's lyrical work as Horace's *Epistles* and *Satires* to his *Odes*.

As analysis of these four 'revolutionary' poems has attempted to show, only one of them (*Nineteen Hundred and Five*) fails to project – however obscurely and indirectly – what was in effect a politically subversive message. It may therefore seem surprising that *High Fever*, *Lieutenant Shmidt* and *Spektorsky* all achieved prompt publication without any serious attempt being made by authority to suppress them. This was partly due to the relatively lax standards of Soviet literary censorship in the 1920s, as opposed to the rigours which lay in wait in the 1930s and beyond. It was also due to Pasternak's oblique and elusive method of expressing himself. He had not, of course, devised this method specifically in order to circumvent the censorship: such procedures came naturally to him, and he employed them in almost everything that he wrote. But his innate deviousness did in practice have the fortunate effect of making his work less vulnerable to interference by the censors than it might otherwise have been. He was to remain a publishable writer long after the relatively easy-going 1920s had given way to the harsher 1930s. And publishable he was still to be (with a few unimportant reservations) right up to the late 1950s, when *Doctor Zhivago* and the accompanying scandal suddenly put him beyond the pale.

Since the *Zhivago* affair was eventually to present Pasternak to the world as a spectacular lone outlaw defying the Soviet political and literary establishment, it is natural to assume that he had been something of the sort all along. He had not. True, he never purveyed, in his pre-*Zhivago* years, the pious platitudes which authority increasingly tried to elicit from its supposedly imaginative writers. But neither did he, in the pre-*Zhivago* years, openly offend by offering for publication material of a blatantly unacceptable character. Though much of what he wrote might seem calculated to dismay custodians of political orthodoxy, the point must be borne in mind that his underlying meaning could only be apparent to the hypersensitive reader. Such readers were indeed to be found among the custodians of political orthodoxy. But they were decidedly in the minority. There is also the point that authority was for many years disposed to give the benefit of the doubt to an author as illustrious as Pasternak, while for his part Pasternak chose to adapt himself to his times and to write little or nothing in particularly sensitive periods.

Hence the contrast between Pasternak on the one hand and Akhmatova and Mandelstam on the other. Virtually everything written by Pasternak before he began work on *Doctor Zhivago* (in the late 1940s) has appeared under a Soviet imprint. There is not, in his *œuvre*, any corpus (such as the bibliographies of Akhmatova and Mandelstam contain) of Soviet-banned writings going back to the early post-revolutionary years. Pasternak's Soviet-banned writings –*Doctor Zhivago* itself and certain other works of his last few years – are important and extensive indeed. But it is worth stressing that they belong almost exclusively to the last phase of a long and complicated career.

The Pasternak of the period under review showed so little interest in continuing his earlier experiments with prose fiction that he published only one new short story during the NEP years: *Aerial Ways* (1924). It leads up to a young man's execution for counter-revolutionary activity despite an appeal made by his mother to an influential Cheka officer – her former lover, whom she claims to be the condemned youth's father. Once again, as in *Spektorsky* and elsewhere in Pasternak's work, a slender plot line is carried on dimly discerned and flickering allusions. *Aerial Ways* has been acclaimed for its 'wholly original linguistic tissue', and as the point at which 'the theme of revolution's tragic consequences in the modern age' enters Pasternak's work for the first time.[42]

Pasternak's output of lyric poetry, like that of his prose fiction, went through a period of decline after 1918. But he by no means abandoned the genre entirely, and wrote some thirty new short poems between his return from Germany in 1923 and the end of the decade. Many of them first appeared in periodicals and were then gathered together and published as *Verses of Various Years* in a collection of 1929. The verses themselves are various, not to say miscellaneous, both in their style and subject matter. They include impressionistic weather reports reminiscent of *My Sister Life*. There is the usual Pasternakian arboretum of sodden, dripping willows and poplars. And there are many botanical references – to cow-wheat and heart's-ease, to spadixes and rhizomes – together with a spattering of gadflies, cocoons, larvae and other entomological fry.

To this material reminiscent of the 1910s must be added other material more typical of the Pasternak who was now increasingly permitting identifiable individuals to peep into his panoramas. There is an address to the French novelist Balzac, whose fist is said to have the weight of a mason's sledgehammer. The beautiful and tempestuous Bolshevik journalist and author Larisa Reysner, dead of typhus in 1926, is invoked as one 'gloriously whipped together by struggles, / Bursting like compressed salvo of charm'. Another lyric is addressed to the poet Valery Bryusov, on the occasion of his fiftieth birthday. Pasternak also commemorates Russia's two most important women poets, Akhmatova and Tsvetayeva, each of whom had become an embarrassment to the new dispensation.

His verses to Tsvetayeva, an addressee compromised by self-exile from Russia, include one of his most successful lyrics of the period; an account of it will be given when an examination is made of the friendship of the two poets as it developed by correspondence in the 1920s. As for Akhmatova, she had remained in Russia, but was out of favour as the unrepentant author of lyrics about her private emotional experiences. That did not prevent Pasternak from addressing her with a congratulatory poem. He refers to the primordial simplicity of her verse, and says that it contains 'grains of intent prose': a reflection of the assertion to which he was given, that poetry actually *was* prose. Pasternak also claims to hear the 'babble of wet roofs' in Akhmatova's verse,[43] but the image suggests that his inner ear was more attuned to his own verse than to hers when he coined the line.

Besides writing some thirty new lyrics between his return from Berlin and the end of the decade, Pasternak also undertook the reworking of his early verse as originally published in *Twin in Clouds* and *Over Barriers*. About two-fifths of this material was rejected as unworthy of republication, and the rest was subjected to drastic surgery.

As earlier discussions of *Twin in Clouds* and *Over Barriers* have indicated, the chief aim of the revision was to eliminate or reduce the traces of apprenticeship to various poetic schools. Lyrics bearing the stamp of Symbolism were removed entirely or substantially rewritten with the Symbolist elements toned down. The same was done with items bearing obvious signs of Futurist influence – of Khlebnikov, Mayakovsky and others. The effect was to abbreviate and tauten the lyrics, and to spike them with a good measure of Impressionism in the manner associated with *My Sister Life*. It was now that the poet sharpened the detail of 'Venice' and 'Railway Station', making his scenes less difficult to visualize, while 'Marburg' – the most frequently revised of all the lyrics – acquired what it had previously lacked in the way of specific biographical, topographical and cultural references. 'Ice on the Move' was shortened, but the image of the fen as a ravenous beast preying on the sun was expanded, clarified and rendered still more effectively grotesque.

> Dire northern waste! Thou carnivore,
> Throttled by half-gulped sun, that lugs
> Sun's carcass over moss; then slaps it
> On ice, slashing the rosy salmon.[44]

Though these procedures suggest that Pasternak had set himself to simplify his earlier verse, a contrary view has been expressed by Lazar Fleishman. He believes that some of the later versions are significantly harder to decipher than the earlier. He maintains, for example, that 'Winter Night' has become more, not less, obscure in the reconstituted version of 1929 than it had been as first published in 1914. He even argues that it was the express intention of Pasternak the reshaper of his own work to force his readers to collate the refurbished lyrics, as published in the 1929 version, with their earlier variants.[45] Now, it is true that such a process of collation is not only fascinating, but absolutely indispensable to the full understanding of both sets of texts. It is also true that Pasternak often seems to have written for Pasternakologists rather than for the general reader. But was he really capable of consciously crediting his admirers as a whole with this extreme degree of addiction to literary detective work? To literary scholars the process is meat and drink. But literary scholars are few, and readers of poetry are comparatively numerous. Back in 1929 they would not have found it easy to carry out the assignment allegedly imposed on them by the poet. Apart from anything else, they would have had difficulty in laying their hands on many of his early lyrics in their original form. Is it really conceivable that Pasternak deliberately rendered such a lyric as 'Today they'll Rise with First Snow' more difficult on revision (as Fleishman suggests), expressly in order to send his readers scuttling back to the – virtually unobtainable – first version?[46] The interpretation surely exaggerates the poet's deep-laid guile, if not his confusion of purpose. But it is an index of Pasternak's deviousness of approach that a scholar so profoundly versed in the material can put the suggestion forward in all seriousness.

It is typical of Pasternak, that incarnation of self-disparagement, to have deprecated the verses under discussion, both in their original drafts and as they appeared in revised form. In a letter to Osip Mandelstam of 14 September 1928 he condemns his first versions as barbarous, poverty-stricken, frigid and pretentious, and as the products of an attempt to suit the fashions of a bygone age. He was no more complimentary about his new versions, calling them 'an unpretentious heap' of revisions which had horrified everyone who had so far seen them.[47]

Pasternak's assessment is unjust to the skilled work on which he was engaged. It transformed his earliest verse, and so raised its poetic level that it is not possible to regard the first two collections, in their reconstituted form, as part and parcel of the immature early period in which they were originally written, or as forming a mere lead-in to the triumph of *My Sister Life*. Though the immaturities have by no means all been purged, and though strong residual associations with Pasternak's earliest versions do remain, the rewritten lyrics are perhaps better regarded as belonging, with *Second Birth* (1932), to Pasternak's middle period as a lyric poet. They certainly do not deserve to be classified with his juvenilia.

So much for Pasternak's poetic activities of the 1920s. The time has now come to consider his personal relations with certain poets during the same period.

After his brief *rapprochement* with Mayakovsky in 1923, which had been marked by the publication of the lyric 'May Day' in Maya-kovsky's journal *Lef*, the two men drifted apart, and their love-hate relationship gave way to indifference. Pasternak has summed up its evolution as follows. 'Many years passed during which we met each other at home and abroad, tried to be friends, tried to work together. But all the time I understood him less and less.' In 1927 Pasternak broke with *Lef*, which he disliked for its commitment to militant politics, and what he called its 'excessive Sovietism – meaning its oppressive servility and habit of throwing its weight about while brandishing an official licence to do so'.[48]

Meanwhile he had found another major Russian poet to dote on, but at a greater distance and through correspondence. He was inspired to write to Marina Tsvetayeva on 14 June 1922 by *Mileposts*, a newly published collection of her verse. He had previously been indifferent to what he knew of her work, but he was now 'knocked sideways by a wave of sobbing that brought a lump to my throat'. He wrote and told her so, greeting her as 'my dear, golden, incomparable poet'.[49] He was never to deviate from this high opinion, which few connoisseurs of Tsvetayeva's verse would challenge, and seems to have preferred her to all other poets – Russian and non-Russian, dead and living.

Tsvetayeva was herself no stranger to being 'knocked sideways', and Pasternak could not complain of any lack of fervour in her lengthy reply. She began by describing the five occasions on which they had met in Russia during the previous five years, but without yet suspecting that they were potential soul-mates. The encounters had included a poetry recital by Pasternak, of which she could only remember that he had mumbled his lines in a monotonous voice and kept forgetting them.[50] This was, of course, his normal mode of delivery – that of an inverted Mayakovsky. At another of their meetings, in autumn 1921, Tsvetayeva had inquired into Pasternak's general well-being and had received the following oracular reply. 'River . . . ferry . . . shore approaching me, or me approaching shore . . . or perhaps there are no shores. . . . Or perhaps. . . .' Tsvetayeva has called this style of discourse 'the inarticulacy of the truly great',[51] and the remark has often been quoted as an apt description of Boris Leonidovich's method of expressing himself. But it is tempting to argue that there were also occasions on which he projected the inarticulacy of the truly inarticulate.

Soon after writing her first letter to Pasternak, Tsvetayeva laid hands on *My Sister Life*. She took it along Unter den Linden and into the Tiergarten; she ate and slept with it. 'For ten days I lived it, on the crest of a high wave.'[52] It was in this exalted mood that she sat down to write her article *Cloudburst of Light*, which contains one of the most eloquent tributes ever paid by one poet to another.

Despite the fever of mutual esteem the two poets did not contrive to meet during the months of 1922–3 when both were in Central Europe. Tsvetayeva's departure from Berlin to Prague, before Pasternak had arrived in the German capital, has been compared by her daughter to that of a nymph fleeing from Apollo. The two were kept apart less by their marital attachments – by Tsvetayeva's decision to be reunited with her husband and to live with him in Czechoslovakia, by the presence of Pasternak's new bride in Berlin – than by Tsvetayeva's belief that what she called non-meetings were more significant and satisfying than the kind of vulgar, mundane encounter which actually takes place in time and space. 'I don't like meetings, those clashings of foreheads. . . . I could not live with you, Boris. Not because we don't understand each other, but because we do. Meeting you, I meet myself with all my own sharp points turned against me.' Tsvetayeva also claimed that, should she ever encounter Pasternak again in the flesh, she would be 'cured of' him in a flash, 'just as I would be cured of Goethe and Heine if I saw them'. Tsvetayeva goes on to lament, somewhat prematurely, her alleged loss of sex appeal, complaining that no man has ever shot himself for love of her. She also proclaims her failure to comprehend or recognize the demands of carnal love.[53]

Such being Tsvetayeva's attitude, she was presumably relieved when Pasternak left Germany early in 1923 and put himself beyond temptation by returning to Russia. After his departure she reflected how little she knew of him, in terms which his biographers may feel inclined to echo. 'I know nothing of Pasternak, and there's a lot I'd like to know. What's his wife like? What did he do in Berlin? What are his reasons and aims in leaving, who were his friends and so on?' But at least his departure for Russia left her free to develop her myth of the transcendental compatibility of herself and Boris Leonidovich as two heroic spirits irrevocably separated by destiny. She does so in some of her most splendid lyrics of 1923–5, later published in her collection *After Russia*. Pasternak's name does not appear in the published collection, but eighteen of the lyrics are known to have been written with him in mind, and a draft dedication of one of them has survived in her archive: 'To my brother in the fifth season, the sixth sense and the fourth dimension – Boris Pasternak'.[54] Tsvetayeva also dedicated her long folk poem *The Swain* (1922) to Pasternak, while another of her long poems, *From the Sea* (1926), is known to have been written with him in mind. Besides *Cloudburst of Light* she also devoted two further critical articles to his writings.

Tsvetayeva's verse tributes to Pasternak abound in classical and other cultural references. She is, respectively, a Euridice, a Helen and an Ariadne to his Orpheus, Achilles and Theseus. She is also Brünnhilde to his Siegfried, and she uses all these comparisons to point up the heroic significance of the enforced separation of Boris and Marina.

> It is not fated in this world that strength with strength be matched.
> Thus sword-spliced Siegfried and Brünhilde lost each other's love.

Pasternak is the unnamed 'thou' of another poem, whom Tsvetayeva describes as her 'only equal in strength' in a world where everyone else is 'hunched and lathered'.[55]

Pasternak's tributes to Tsvetayeva of the 1920s are less extensive and effusive. They include two items already mentioned (his acrostic dedication of *Lieutenant Shmidt*, his distorted portrait of her as the elusive Mariya Ilyina of *Spektorsky*) and also the lyric entitled 'To Marina Tsvetayeva'. This last item begins by paying tribute to her habit of baring her innermost soul in her works. But then Pasternak seems to forget her as he goes on to characterize a generalized poet's overriding importance as an emblem of stability independent of passing fashions. True, the poet may seem an ephemeral phenomenon, and there are times when he appears to have vanished.

Wreathing in many conduits, he'll
Drift underground like smoke
Through fateful epoch's apertures
On into blank dead end.

But then, just as the smouldering bard seems irretrievably lost for ever, behold!

Fuming, he'll burst from crevices
Of fates squashed pancake-flat.
His sons' sons, as of peat, shall say:
'That's So-and-so's age burning.'[56]

Despite much mutual esteem fervently expressed, Pasternak and Tsvetayeva remained independent in their verse techniques; each could be inspired by the other without feeling impelled to translate that inspiration into anything approaching mimicry.

In 1925 Tsvetayeva moved from Prague to Paris, where she was plagued by increasing poverty, and where she failed to sustain her initial popularity with her Russian *émigré* readers. Pasternak was informed of her privations by correspondence, and sought to relieve them by interesting the influential Maksim Gorky in her welfare. In October 1927 Pasternak wrote to Gorky as follows. 'The vast talent of Marina Tsvetayeva is crucial and dear to me, as is her fate – so unhappy, so complex, so much beyond her power to cope with. Should you ask me what I'm about to write or do, I should answer: "Anything whatever to help her, and to sustain and restore to Russia this great woman who has not managed to bring her gifts into balance with her destiny, or – more likely – vice versa." '[57] But there was little that Gorky, Pasternak or anyone else could do for the demoralized Tsvetayeva.

By the end of the 1920s Tsvetayeva's correspondence with Pasternak was in decline. It was not broken off, however, and the links between them were to continue until her death in 1941. Many of her letters have survived, and have been published. Meanwhile his letters to her have been consigned to the memory hole of the Soviet State Archives, flung into that oubliette by her daughter Ariadna Efron many years after the death of the poet.[58]

After Pasternak had translated and imitated Rilke in fragments of his earliest experimental verse, the older poet's influence over the younger proceeded to plumb depths of the human psyche far beyond the mere investigator's reach. Only in 1925 do specific traces of interaction between the two re-emerge. Rilke chanced to read some of Pasternak's verses in that year, and praised them in a letter to Pasternak's father.

When Pasternak was informed of this he immediately burst into tears. For the first time in his life it was borne in on him that Rilke was a real person. Now at last he could tell the other poet how enormous his influence had been. Pasternak wrote a long letter to Rilke in German which is certainly eccentric, but not notably more so than his Russian. He wrote of the 'electrical short circuit between souls' that had shattered him when he first learnt that Rilke had noticed his work. The possibility of making a poet's confession to Rilke was as exciting as if such contact had suddenly become possible with Aeschylus or Pushkin. Not for the first or last time, Pasternak proclaimed himself 'born again'. He also took the opportunity to draw Rilke's attention to Marina Tsvetayeva, 'a born poet and a great talent . . . my greatest and perhaps my only friend'.[59]

Rilke replied briefly, saying that Pasternak's letter had 'shaken me by the extent and force of its devotion'. But then, before Pasternak could respond or attempt to arrange a meeting, Rilke suddenly died. A few years later Pasternak dedicated *Safe Conduct* to him.[60] The work insistently emphasizes Rilke's impact as the paramount influence on its author's evolution, but it makes no attempt whatever to define the nature of that influence. Pasternak also paid a farewell tribute to Rilke by translating two of the latter's obituary poems.

Safe Conduct is Pasternak's longest and most important prose work apart from *Doctor Zhivago*. It is in three parts, of which the first came out in 1929 and the last two in 1931. The writing and publication accordingly coincided with the beginning of a new decade, and also with an important turning-point in Soviet history – Stalin's achievement of full dictatorial power. Stalin celebrated his eminence, so patiently achieved during the 1920s, by instituting drastic measures: cancellation of the relatively mild economic system known as NEP; industrialization imposed at high pressure through the First Five Year Plan; enforced collectivization of agriculture. As Stalin used his vast power to impose totalitarianism on the USSR, certain Soviet institutions already prominent in the 1920s began to expand and flourish as never before: concentration camps, show trials, executions of alleged saboteurs and wreckers, political security activity in general.

The literary world did not escape, though it was less under physical than verbal attack for the time being. In 1929 two prominent authors of prose fiction, Pilnyak and Zamyatin, were pilloried through a vicious and prolonged publicity campaign for having allowed certain of their works of fiction to be brought out abroad. This was now retroactively treated as a crime against the State, though it had involved no contravention of Soviet law. In 1923 Pasternak himself had published his *Themes and Variations* with impunity in Berlin. But that did not contain material offensive to Soviet orthodoxy, as did *Mahogany* and *We*, the works which formed the basis for persecuting Pilnyak and Zamyatin respectively. Nor had Pasternak, fortunately for him, turned out to possess the special qualities sought by those who selected the era's literary scapegoats. But he could not fail to notice that the persecution of Pilnyak and Zamyatin was designed to render writers as a whole more amenable to regimentation.

It was in this atmosphere that Pasternak wrote *Safe Conduct*. It is the first of his two autobiographical studies in prose, and he was later to repudiate it as 'unfortunately vitiated by otiose preciosity, a common sin of those years'.[61] But it is hard to accept his view. Precious or affected some passages of *Safe Conduct* undoubtedly are. But the work as a whole is a far more impressive contribution to literature than *Autobiographical Sketch*, the simplified version of the same story which he was to write many years later. The admirers of *Safe Conduct* have included Aleksandr Gladkov. 'I consider the chapters on childhood, on the genesis of poetry, on first love, on Skriabin, Rilke and Mayakovsky equal to the best Russian prose.' But even Gladkov has admitted that the work contains obscurities which defeated him.[62]

Safe Conduct's defects as autobiography have already been touched on in the Introduction to the present study. They spring from the poet's tendency to over-dramatize the successive cultural crises through which he passed, and from his practice of selecting his material on a deliberately arbitrary basis – as he openly boasts in the text. He has little or nothing to say of his parents, his siblings, his studies, his friendships, his love affairs, his living conditions and his sources of income. Historical developments, too, are largely ignored. One world war, one civil war and Russia's two Revolutions of 1917 barely earn a nod as they flit past. As for the rise and fall of NEP, the death of Lenin, the decline of Trotsky, the ascent of Stalin, the collectivization of agriculture, the First Five Year Plan, the victimization of Pilnyak and Zamyatin – readers will search the text of *Safe Conduct* in vain for enlightenment on these topics. Embarking on the work in his late thirties, Pasternak has also virtually ignored the last decade of his own life. One fifth of his text is taken up by impressionistic sketches of certain aspects of his first twenty-two years. He then plunges into the exhaustive description of his summer excursion of 1912 to Germany and Italy which takes up almost a half of the work. The final section – one third of the whole – is less an account of Pasternak himself than of another poet, Mayakovsky, as seen through his eyes.

Instead of telling the story of his life, Pasternak has chosen to log the genesis of his artistic and poetic sensibilities by concentrating heavily on specific episodes which possessed overriding significance for his cultural development. Each involved the abrupt renunciation of one activity and associated individual in favour of another activity and associated individual. Part One accordingly relates his abandonment of music and Skriabin. Part Two records his rejection of philosophy and the eminent Marburger Hermann Cohen while being simultaneously turned down as a potential husband by Ida Vysotskaya. Part Three records the rise and fall of Pasternak's infatuation with Mayakovsky in considerable detail, but without analysing the technical impact of Mayakovsky on Pasternak's early verse. Then, after Pasternak has assigned the completion of his disillusionment with the other poet to an occasion (probably in 1920) when Mayakovsky had recited his poem *150,000,000*, the text suddenly leaps ten years to Mayakovsky's suicide, while also vaulting from disillusionment to ecstatic admiration.

The renunciation of life by Mayakovsky thus forms the last link in the chain of grand rejections recorded in *Safe Conduct*. But Pasternak has nothing to say of the motives for the suicide, which appear to have included disappointment in love as well as disappointment with the literary politics of the day. Instead of discussing such matters, Pasternak begins his account of the tragedy with a report on the attendant weather conditions (but then, Pasternak would most certainly have made an eyewitness description of the end of the world into a dependent clause subordinated to a vivid evocation of the meteorological context). 'The beginning of April caught Moscow in the white stupor of a return of winter. On the seventh of the month it started to thaw for the second time. On the fourteenth, when Mayakovsky shot himself, not everyone was used to the novelty of spring's return.' In the ensuing description of the poet's death Pasternak deploys some of his most moving prose to suggest that nothing in Mayakovsky's life became him like the taking of it. His final epitaph describes his old friend and enemy as spoilt since childhood by a future that yielded to him quite easily, and obviously without much effort on his part.[63]

Pasternak is characteristically paradoxical when he suggests that the dead Mayakovsky is more alive than the zombies who have survived him. 'Even in sleep he was stubbornly straining to get away.' The same effective conceit is repeated in Pasternak's obituary elegy to the suicide, 'Poet's Death', written shortly after the event.

> With pillowed cheek you slept as hard
> As leg and ankle power could speed you.
> Headlong you did repeatedly
> Slice into newborn legends' ranks.
> To foothills' cravens of both sexes
> Your shot was as the blast of Etna.[64]

As the last two lines illustrate, Pasternak sharply contrasted the vital and independent figure of the dead poet with the moribund and increasingly regimented literary world around him. Was Maya-kovsky's suicide chiefly important to Pasternak as an outstanding example of an individual's personal revolution against the impositions of the oppressive State? The suggestion is consistent with indications that Pasternak wrote the later sections of *Safe Conduct* in a mood of disillusionment with current political trends, spiking the text with cryptic indications calculated to express his dissatisfaction without provoking the intervention of the censor. Such an enigmatic hint – a tilt at the literary persecutions of the day – is found at the point where Pasternak describes himself as viewing Mayakovsky's body in the company of a person designated by the initials 'O.S.'. Recent investigation has shown that his allusion was to a certain Olga Sillova, and that she was the widow of a minor writer who had been arrested and who was probably shot in 1930.[65] Even as early as 1931 a more cautious scribe would have refrained from providing evidence, however disguised, of his association with the relict of an Enemy of the People. A more obvious example of submerged political criticism is the passage in which Pasternak makes his visit of 1912 to Venice an excuse for denouncing the political oppressions of the Venetian State, especially as imposed on the world of Venetian art. That 'Venetian' was meant to be read as 'Soviet' is self-evident; this kind of subversive political comment through encoded symbols had long been hallowed in Russian tradition, and was termed 'Aesopian language' under the Tsars.

Perhaps the presence of such ingredients helps to explain the work's otherwise mysterious title. As one authority on Pasternak has put it, *Safe Conduct* represents an attempt to defend art 'against the encroachments of an age of enslavement and to ensure its route to eternity'.[66] The explanation is attractive, for the work can hardly have been intended to ensure the safety of its author. Indeed, certain aspects of it might have contributed to ensuring the very opposite.

5

DUET FOR ONE

Pasternak entered the early summer of 1930 in a state of gloom which the memory of Mayakovsky's suicide and the horrors of intensified political oppression did nothing to diminish. He was in an almost suicidal mood himself when he wrote to his cousin on 11 June to say that he was 'increasingly haunted by the feeling that it's all over'. He felt that his work was rooted in the past, and that he was powerless to move it along. 'I've taken no part in creating the present, and I have no active love for it.'[1]

He was not cheered by the prospect, which now faced him, of spending the summer in a dacha at Irpen, near Kiev. Yevgeniya Vladimirovna had gone on ahead with their son, but family life had long lost its charms for Boris Leonidovich, and he was not looking forward to joining them. Yet Irpen turned out a great success. 'My work suddenly recovered in the sunlight. It's ages since I worked so well.'[2] The little holiday colony offered isolation combined with congenial company consisting of four friends from Moscow – the philosopher Valentin Asmus, the pianist Genrikh Neygauz and their wives.

Pasternak was soon commemorating these experiences in verse published in literary journals. In one lyric he refers to the 'union of six hearts' represented by the friendship of the Asmuses, Neygauzes and Pasternaks. He alludes to their walks and bathing expeditions. A lyric dedicated to Irina Asmus sums up Irpen in one of the catalogues common in Pasternak's poetry.

> Memory of people, summer,
> Freedom and escape from thraldom,
> Torrid conifers, grey stocks.

'Ballad' commemorates a recital given in Kiev by Genrikh Neygauz, from whose piano a mournful phrase of Chopin's floats over the befuddled monkey-puzzle trees 'like a sick eagle'. In other verse of the period Pasternak's wife Yevgeniya appears as 'the artist', and he refers to her innocent, wide, 'gulping' smile, 'huge and bright as a terrestrial globe'. But it was to Zinaida Nikolayevna Neygauz that his thoughts were now more and more turning. In 'Second Ballad' he refers to the peaceful sleep of her two small sons, contrasting it with his own fitful slumbers during which he has contrived to dream of their mother five times in succession. The poem was openly dedicated to Zinaida Nikolayevna Neygauz when it first appeared, though she is not named in the body of the text.[3] Clearly the 'six-heart union' was coming under new pressures.

When Pasternak returned to Moscow after his working holiday in the south he experienced such happiness that one hundredth part of it could, he said, 'be set in rings and used to cut glass'. Meanwhile his semi-estranged wife was suffering from profound depression following the death of her mother, and had also contracted tuberculosis. Despite the difficulty of obtaining Soviet exit visas, arrangements were made for her to go to Germany, where she was treated in a sanatorium while their son Yevgeny stayed with his grandparents in Munich. These dispositions had two advantages: Yevgeniya Vladimirovna recovered her health and Boris Leonidovich was free to pursue the courtship of Zinaida Nikolayevna. He did so with such effect that he and his new mistress are found touring the Northern Caucasus and Georgia together in summer 1931. The visit came about by chance after a meeting with the leading Georgian poet Paolo Yashvili in Moscow. On learning that Pasternak had become estranged from his wife, but had nowhere to live with his mistress, Yashvili offered them refuge in the Georgian capital, Tiflis (Tbilisi). The result was, as Pasternak wrote in the early draft of a lyric, that

> We reached Tiflis at crack
> Of July's fourteenth dawn.
> Three dream-like months flashed past.[4]

He was soon almost as infatuated with the southern mountains as with Zinaida Nikolayevna, for the Caucasus came as a revelation. The awesome sierras and lively café life of Tiflis enthralled him. He long remembered the picturesque nooks and alleys, the thrum of tambourines beating out Caucasian folk tunes, the goat-like bleating of Georgia's bagpipes and other instruments, the onset of the southern evening. The region was Stalin's birthplace, but it had not escaped the general hardships of the period. 'There was nothing to eat; there was nothing to wear. There was nothing tangible around, only ideas.'[5]

Pasternak was never to learn the Georgian language, but acquired a profound admiration for Georgian culture and Georgian poets. He became a particularly close friend of Paolo Yashvili, as also of Titsian Tabidze, another renowned Tiflis poet. The literary world of Tiflis as a whole took Pasternak to its heart, and he was able to eke out his life there on advances from local publishing concerns.

One by-product of these excitements was that he briefly re-emerged as a productive lyric poet, suddenly turning out two score new lyrics in 1931. Not since 1918 had he written so many in a year. The new poems were published in 1932 as part of the significantly entitled small volume *Second Birth*. His tendency to proclaim himself born anew persisted throughout his life, and the renaissance of the early 1930s may well have been his twenty-second rather than the second of the title. But this was an especially vivid occasion. *Second Birth* charts its creator's resurrection as poet, lover and connoisseur of landscape. It also bears the scars of attempts to hymn the devastating social changes introduced through Stalin's latest measures.

The poet responded ardently to the grandeur of the Caucasus. He logged its vistas in some of his most majestic lines, and triumphantly demonstrated that even Pushkin and Lermontov had by no means exhausted the region when they had drawn inspiration from it in the early nineteenth century. Pasternak's Caucasian verse is full of local references. He praises the crystal-clear five-mile beach at Kobulety between Batum and Poti on the Black Sea. He speaks of storm clouds above Vladikavkaz which the swaggering peaks try to toss away like irksome horse-collars. Other scenic glimpses include the postal station of Lars on the famous Georgian Military Highway, along which the poet travelled with his mistress; Daghestan Gorge smoking like a mess of poisoned pottage inside a cauldron of peaks which, colossus piled on colossus, choke the exit from the great ravine; dawn over Mlety where the River Terek, seen far below as if at the bottom of a mine shaft, is

> Poisoned by caustic soda, as its ore
> Makes the whole amphitheatre resound
> With howls of terror, agony and shame.

Meanwhile, as if to assert the poet's capacity for minting new images, the glacier of Devdorakh on the north-east slopes of Mount Kazbek

> Like puling, nurse-scared infant mooed and thawed.[6]

Smoke, poison, noxious chemicals, chokings, beheadings, rivers, mountain, forest – all are united in 'When Clambering in Caucasus', which is the finest of these invocations. It describes the mist-enshrouded River Kura carrying out a creeping gas attack on the mountain-choked River Aragve while, far above, the silhouettes of executed ruined castles heave up their adam's apples like the throats of men decapitated. From this Gothic setting the poet calls on the Caucasus to help him solve his marital problems, and invokes his absent wife Yevgeniya without naming her.

> When summits make hearts flutter
> And mountains swing their censers,
> Do you suppose, my far one,
> That you've somehow let me down?
> Carousing Alps in distant Germany
> May be clinking crags as ours do,
> But the echoes are yet fainter.
> Do you think, out there, that you've failed me?

The poet goes on to offer what, if his estranged wife ever received the message, must have seemed to her cold comfort.

> Don't fear your dreams, don't fret, calm down.
> I love you, think of you and know you.[7]

Another, more outspoken, poetical address of 1931 to his wife was even more calculated to puzzle the poet's readers and to dismay the unnamed addressee. 'It's not linked souls, it's mutual deception / That we are chopping down', he tells the unnamed Yevgeniya Vladimirovna, adding that the time has come for them to abandon 'palliasse's typhoidal torment'. Who but Pasternak could have publicly referred to his deserted marriage bed through such an image? Scarcely more tactful towards his estranged wife is the lyric, addressed to his new love Zinaida Nikolayevna, in which he contrasts their uncomplicated relations with those which had existed between him and her predecessor.

> Some women's love's a cross to bear,
> But you are charm unconvoluted.
> Your beauty's simple secret is
> The clue to life's complexities.[8]

Alas, it was to prove nothing of the sort.

To match his new mistress's unconvoluted beauty a style without convolutions seemed appropriate, and it is in verse unavowedly addressed to Zinaida Neygauz that Pasternak most intensively culti- vates his new and simpler manner. It appears at its most impressive in the lyric, also written with his new love in mind, which begins 'There won't be anyone at home / Except the twilight.' The poet is alone in his dwelling in winter, menaced by snow, frost and anticipated depression, when he suddenly imagines his beloved's arrival.

> Through curtain, unawaited,
> Shall flit intrusion's quiver.
> With steps that pace the silence
> You'll enter like the future,
> Appearing at my threshold
> In something white and simple
> Cut straight from the material
> They use to tailor snowflakes.[9]

Soon after the lovers arrived back in Moscow, the domestic drama distantly invoked in *Second Birth* was acted out on a less poetic level when Yevgeniya Pasternak returned from a successful convalescence in Germany to discover that her husband considered their marriage terminated. The acute housing shortage complicated the mechanics of separation. Having decided to treat his wife as generously as possible, the poet vacated the room in the Volkhonka Street flat which they had occupied together. He pressed money on her which she was reluctant to accept, and also conceded to her the privileged shopping facilities enjoyed by those registered as writers. Domestic discomforts and worries, including scarlet fever and other ailments contracted by the small sons of the two marriages, created additional complications under conditions inconvenient enough to depress even a lovesick poet.[10]

Pasternak's unconventional expectations in terms of human behaviour were revealed in his attitude to the discarded Yevgeniya. Why, he kept asking himself, did she accept her new situation grudgingly when it offered so splendid an opportunity to display magnanimity by forgiving him completely and by accepting her new status cheerfully? He simply could not understand it until he reflected on the 'blinding egoism' instilled in her by her upbringing. But Pasternak's own conduct was hardly a model of unselfishness. That his 'naïve' charm did not always exclude downright cruelty was to be the opinion of the companion of his last years, Olga Ivinskaya,[11] though she found these qualities so spontaneous and childlike that she always forgave him in the end. So too, it appears, did Yevgeniya, for they remained on friendly terms. The divorce went through, and she eventually remarried. The marriage of Pasternak and his new wife Zinaida was also formalized, probably in 1934.

Pasternak's second partner in life was better adapted to his needs than the first. Zinaida Nikolayevna was closer to what he seemed to need most in a wife – a woman to make a home for him, and to create tolerable working conditions. When they moved into an undecorated two-room flat allotted to them by one of the writers' organizations in 1932, she was soon running up curtains and scrubbing floors until she had made the place properly habitable. She was a competent mother too, well able to look after the two sons of her previous marriage.

These skills helped to create a home for the poet during the period of nearly thirty years which he was to spend with her between their Georgian trip and his death. But she also had her disadvantages as a companion in life. Pasternak was later to insist that his second marriage had been unhappy from the start, and he said that he had only made up to Zinaida in the first place because he had taken a liking to her husband the pianist; this in turn had somehow obliged him, through a Pasternakian twist of logic, to become intimate with the unfortunate man's wife! His remark need not be taken seriously. Nor, perhaps, need the comment which he made about his cuckolded friend many years afterwards: 'When Zinaida left him the ass even wanted to kill me. Later on, though, he was very grateful to me.' And it is true that, impressive as the beauty and charm of the young matron were, she was not ideally equipped to be the spiritual partner of a gifted man. There is no evidence that she cared a fig for poetry, and there are abundant indications that she feared its power to upset the equilibrium of her well-managed household by provoking official disfavour. Perhaps her tendency to side with authority was inherited; Pasternak himself once pointed out that one of her close relatives was a colonel in the Gendarmes, the uniformed branch of the Tsars' political police.[12]

Akhmatova, who always kept a watchful eye on Pasternak and his doings, readily admitted Zinaida Nikolayevna's competence as a housewife and mother. But Akhmatova also regarded her as an 'eight-pawed dragon'; she thought of her as coarse, as lacking in resonance, and as anti-art incarnate. Akhmatova once said that she disliked Pasternak's *Second Birth* because Zinaida figured in it with Pasternak hovering round her in the role of 'distraught suitor'. When he relapsed into lyrical silence after the publication of that collection, Akhmatova believed that it was Zinaida Nikolayevna's fault, her nature being such as to prevent him from functioning as a poet.[13] That a form of polygamy offered the true solution he was only to discover in the evening of his days.

The rich subject matter of *Second Birth* is not exhausted by Pasternak's two wives and the Caucasian mountains, for the collection also possesses an important political dimension. In this respect it resembles his long poems of the 1920s, and differs from the lyrical collections which preceded and followed it. *Second Birth* is, in fact, the only one of Pasternak's lyrical sequences to offer such a wealth of specific political references.

With the drastic intensification of totalitarian controls from the late 1920s onwards, imaginative writers could no longer hope to stay out of trouble by the mere avoidance of implied slurs on the Soviet system. After the introduction of the First Five Year Plan a more active approach was imposed. Official disfavour was no longer limited to works – in so far as there still were any – which abused the regime, but was now extended to those which failed to offer their positive support. Pasternak did his best to meet this requirement in *Second Birth*, assisted by the fact that he had become a genuine, if eccentric, supporter of Stalin and his methods. Hence one significant change in the political attitudes expressed in his verse of the 1930s, as opposed to his verse of the preceding decade. The revolutionary poems of the 1920s had been retrospectively orientated, consisting largely of sidelong glances back at the past and barely acknowledging the existence of post-1917 Russia. How different are the political references of *Second Birth*, where the poet makes a particular point of looking forward into a new era. For example, several passages allude to the First Five Year Plan instituted by Stalin in 1928. One lyric salutes the start of the plan's fourth year. Another sees the plan as symbolized by the Caucasian mountains. It looms ahead as a great barrier challenging its would-be conquerors, just as the Caucasus had itself challenged conquest by Russian soldiers a hundred years earlier. In each context Pasternak links the system's political goals with his own marital position. The country is destined to become an earthly paradise in which his two wives will be able to live side by side, while 'lust's hooks creak not'. All three of them are part of the future, says the poet. Never mind if they can only hope to live on as cripples run over by the new man. They need not grieve, for Pasternak swears 'by all my weakness' to remain a part of them both. Meanwhile

> The strong have promised to abolish
> All the last traumas that have vanquished us.[14]

Here is the resurrection of a notion previously mooted in *High Fever*: the poet and his kin have been left far behind by the Revolution; but that matters not at all if only others can reap the benefit.

The same idea figures in a lyric of 1931, 'To a Friend', which begins by stressing the poet's awareness that the Revolution has led the masses out of darkness. He does not care if it has inconvenienced himself and the small élite to which he belongs.

> Ogre-like, do I rate the bliss of millions
> Below the futile welfare of the few?
> Do I not make the Five Year Plan my measure?
> Do I not fall and rise along with it?

Still, what the poet renders unto Stalin and Stalinism in one breath he is
apt to take away with the next, and the lines continue with a blurred
reference to the era's cultural regimentation.

> But what am I to do about my chest cage?
> And what about stagnation outstagnated?

Pasternak concludes by asserting, ominously, that the poet is a
superfluous figure dangerous to the new society.[15]

In a similar spirit he penned the paradoxical line 'Thou art my
neighbour, distant Socialism.' And what could be more typical of
Pasternak the paradox-monger than his decision to hymn the Thirtieth
of April just when all other poets were celebrating the First of May?
On the one hand he announces that his country will one day blossom
like the rose. On the other hand he emphasizes the remoteness of that
desirable prospect, asserting that the First of May has not even dawned
yet, and that its eve is

> Long to remain a time of reconstruction,
> Pre-carnival spring-cleanings and emprises.[16]

Only in one respect does the poet salute the aims of Soviet society as
already attained – in the freeing of women from their subordinate
position. Poised since infancy to pity and idealize the eternal feminine,
he had persuaded himself that women had been accorded equal rights
under the Soviet system, and commemorated the achievement in the
following eight lines.

> And since I have from infancy
> Been galled by woman's lot;
> Since poets' steps are but the trace
> Of her paths and no more;
> Since only she can touch me
> And since we've set her free,
> Glad am I to be cancelled out
> At revolution's will.[17]

Pasternak might cheerfully announce his willingness to step aside in
the supposed interests of woman or the masses, but the same idea is
very differently expressed in the lyric 'Had I but Known the Way of
It'. These famous lines on the tragic side of the poet's destiny were
eventually to evoke the tears of mourners when declaimed at his

graveside. Sincerely as Pasternak may have accepted aspects of Stalinism at this stage, he was also aware of the dangers inherent in his profession as practised in Russia, and this is his first lyric to show so acute a consciousness of impending doom. It is also the first occasion on which he fully equates the poet with an actor reluctantly playing the part which can only end with his own destruction.

> Had I but known the way of it
> When launching my career:
> That verse is spurting haemorrhage
> From throat, bloody and slaughterous –
>
> All frolics with such pitfalls
> Would I have turned down flat.
> My début was so long ago,
> So slight my first concern.
>
> Old age, though, claims from actor
> No Roman circus tricks,
> No Thespian recitals.
> It wants him killed stone dead.
>
> When passion lays the line down,
> It sends its slave on stage.
> This is the place where art ends.
> Here soil and fate draw breath.[18]

Well might Pasternak choose to allude to his own future in such sombre terms. He had done his best, in *Second Birth*, to hymn the glorious perspectives allegedly opened up by Stalinism. But he had not gone nearly far enough in that direction to conciliate authority, as he himself must have been well aware. Above all, he had shown insufficient zeal in cultivating the tired cadences of the era's official jargon in a period which increasingly demanded the repetition of approved formulae of the 'full speed ahead' type from all its citizens, poets and non-poets alike.

The frequent references to actual persons, places and occurrences in *Second Birth*, the presence of so much political and biographical material – here are features which help to distinguish these poems from the four lyrical collections by Pasternak which had preceded them in 1914–23. Another difference lies in the forebodings of impending doom, which are by no means confined to 'Had I but Known the Way of It', even though high sprits comparable to those expressed in *My Sister Life* are also abundant in the later collection. But the most striking difference lies in this: that the new verse is less obscure, less open to ambiguous interpretation, more easily elucidated than the old. Here is a foretaste of the simple style which the poet was to cultivate most intensively from 1940 onwards. In the chart of Pasternak's evolution from complexity to simplicity *Second Birth* comes near to representing a half-way stage between the volume of collected lyrics which immediately preceded it in 1923 (*Themes and Variations*) and that which immediately followed it in 1943 (*In Early Trains*).

The same topic is discussed in a passage of *Second Birth* where Pasternak – never loath to write poems about poems – considers the competing claims of complexity and simplicity, while opting for the latter in oracular terms more appropriate to the former and suggesting that the two conceptual antipodes have jammed into a permanent amalgam inside his head. Never one to coddle his reader, he was (it seems) proposing to embrace simplicity only because it would make the task of comprehension even more difficult than it had been in his earlier, obscurer phase.

> Great poets practise usages so artless
> That those who savour them can but end dumbstruck.
> To be confident of kinship with the cosmos,
> While on terms of easy friendship with the future,
> Is unfailingly to end by falling prey to
> The heresy of unique clarity.
> If we can't hide this trend we'll suffer:
> Simplicity is what men chiefly need;
> Complexity is what their minds best grasp.[19]

For eight years after publishing the lyrics of *Second Birth* Pasternak ceased to write original poetry and prose, apart from a few scattered items of negligible aesthetic value. It is for his collisions with politics, not for his literary achievements, that his evolution of the 1930s is most significant. During the decade's early and middle years he did his best to come to terms with Stalinism, mystified and intimidated though he was – along with the population as a whole – by developments lacking any close precedent even in a history as turbulent as Russia's. The Soviet professional classes were already exposed to severe persecution in the early 1930s, but the main onslaught of advancing totalitarianism continued for a time to be directed against the peasants. They were executed, imprisoned, driven into exile and starved by the million through the drive to collectivize agriculture, while town-dwellers were encouraged to avert their eyes from a spectacle so indecorous. It was the safest and most comfortable course, but it required insensitivity and a strong instinct for self-preservation.

The hypersensitive, sporadically indiscreet Pasternak was ill-equipped by temperament to protect himself by pretending to ignore the horrors of the new decade. Olga Freydenberg writes of 'a sight that Boris once witnessed with revulsion – long echelons of dispossessed kulaks, consisting of peasant families driven into exile by the trainload'.[20] It is not clear when or how often he witnessed this distressing spectacle. But he may have done so in summer 1932, when he and Zinaida Nikolayevna visited the Urals with a delegation of intellectuals and writers charged with composing eulogies on intensified industrialization and agriculture. He was horrified by the contrast between the squalid misery around him and the relative comfort enjoyed by himself and his family, who were housed in the local OGPU (security police) headquarters. He described the trip as a 'depressing and atrocious saga'. When pressed for copy by *Pravda*, he asked how he could possibly be expected to describe such desolation – but was told that he, as an intelligent man, should know that tendencies were required, not facts.[21] He produced neither.

However depressed Pasternak might be by the sufferings of his age, he was still given to occasional expressions of enthusiasm for the new order. He had oscillated in similar fashion in the 1920s – now enthusiastic, now disillusioned. But in the 1930s a new factor emerged: he made repeated attempts to establish a dialogue with Stalin, whom he had met in person (if Olga Ivinskaya's account is correct) in the winter of 1924–5. His motive in trying to attract Stalin's attention was, presumably, a hope of acquiring some influence over events.

The first evidence of such a bid is the lyric 'A Century and More' of 1931.[22] It is a public appeal to the Leader to change his policies by showing clemency to their many victims. Such a message inevitably had to be buried deep in oblique allusions, but that process came naturally to Pasternak even when contemplating a primrose by the river's brim. He begins the poem by saying that he wants 'to view the world without fear', and by expressing a hankering for 'law and order'. Both were compromising wishes since, according to official doctrine which it was perilous to contradict, law and order had already been established, while none but the admittedly numerous 'enemies' of the Soviet system could possibly have cause for fear. The poem is written on the assumption that its reader knows the famous lyric 'Stanzas', composed by Pushkin in 1826 in the hope of inducing the Emperor Nicholas I to show mercy to the opponents of his regime. Writing a century and more before Pasternak's day, Pushkin had pointed out to the Emperor that his (Nicholas's) famous predecessor Peter the Great had been accustomed to pardon his (Peter's) enemies a century and more before his (Nicholas's) day. Pushkin's appeal had borne little fruit, but Pasternak now invokes it in an attempt to influence Stalin. In other words, he is asking Stalin to treat his political enemies with the same degree of clemency that Pushkin had vainly hoped to obtain from the Emperor Nicholas. Did Stalin ever read the poem? That is not known. His mind was sharp and devious enough to have seized its implications, and to have discerned through the veil of obliquities the outline of a poet who was trying to tell him how to run the country. But Stalin already knew all about that. He was not looking to Pasternak or anyone else for guidance in the matter.

Pasternak's next signal to Stalin followed the suicide by shooting of the Leader's second wife Nadezhda Alliluyeva on 7 November 1932, the fifteenth anniversary of the Bolshevik October Revolution. The occurrence was handled with extreme delicacy in the press, where the cause of death was cited as peritonitis. Obituary condolences duly followed, and included a letter published in *Literaturnaya gazeta* of 17 November. It was signed by thirty-three authors and couched in familiar stereotyped idiom. For instance, it referred to the deceased as one who 'had devoted all her strength to the cause of the liberation of the millions of oppressed humanity . . . the cause for which we are ready to sacrifice our lives'. Pasternak's astonishing achievement was to abstain from appending his signature to this gobbledygook while contriving to add a separate message which appeared under his name alone, and which – more recklessly still – ostentatiously avoided the era's jargon. Instead of prating about his Readiness to Sacrifice his Life, instead of any other form of routine claptrap, he baldly stated that he shared his colleagues' feelings. He added that, on the day before Alliluyeva's death, he had 'thought deeply and intensively about Stalin . . . for the first time. Next morning I read the news. I was shaken, as though I had been there, living by his side, and had seen it.'[23]

The gesture was risky. To dissociate oneself from a ritual collective act, thereby emphasizing one's individuality, was to court disgrace and persecution in any context, and to do so in a matter touching the Leader's private life was the rankest folly. Another indiscretion was Pasternak's admission that he had never thought deeply and intensively about Stalin before November 1932 – and this despite the fact that the entire population was, by now, officially presumed to have been thinking non-stop, deeply and intensively, awake and asleep, about little except Stalin ever since the October Revolution! Here was a supplementary heresy which could only aggravate the poet's basic offence of flaunting a departure from officially sanctified phraseology.

Pasternak's obituary postscript was a second attempt to establish contact with the Leader by drawing attention to himself as an individual. There is no evidence that he succeeded. But it was Stalin's habit to monitor events in detail, and the bizarre gesture is unlikely to have escaped his keen eye. It is even possible that the unpredictable dictator was impressed – either by Pasternak's expression of personal sympathy or by the suggestion, conveyed in the text of the postscript, that its author possessed occult powers. The episode may, accordingly, have helped to confer on the poet the otherwise surprising degree of immunity which he was to enjoy when the persecution of intellectuals was drastically intensified from 1936 onwards.

The arrest of Osip Mandelstam in May 1934 imparted a new twist to Stalin–Pasternak relations. Mandelstam was a poet of comparable distinction to Pasternak, and almost his exact contemporary. But Mandelstam was in disgrace, and had long been unable to publish with any degree of freedom. He had composed neither eulogies to Lenin nor verses praising Stalin as ushering in a paradise on earth. He did not so much defy authority as suffer from a temperamental inability to conform with its requirements, and he took risks far greater than Pasternak ever incurred. His most magnificent act of self-destructive folly was the composition of a short poem abusing Stalin and his entourage. The dictator is called 'the Kremlin Highlander', a reference to his origin in mountainous Georgia. His fingers are 'fat as worms'. His 'cockroach whiskers leer'. He is surrounded by fawning humanoids, he issues savage laws, he delights in executions.[24]

Mandelstam was discreet enough not to commit his poem to paper, but contrived to recite it to friends and acquaintances who eventually came to number about a score. That was inconsiderate of him: to be reported as having heard the poem, and without having gone on to denounce the author–reciter, was to become liable to arrest and imprisonment. Pasternak was well aware of this on the evening in April 1934 when Mandelstam accosted him on the Tver Boulevard in Moscow and whispered the Stalin poem to him. His response was the height of prudence and good sense. 'I didn't hear this; you didn't tell me it.' Shortly afterwards Mandelstam was arrested and taken to OGPU headquarters at the Lubyanka after someone had informed the authorities of the offending lines. Pasternak then went round Moscow frantically explaining to anyone who would listen that it was not he who had reported the matter to the authorities.[25]

Pasternak was not one to turn his back on a poet in distress. Immediately after the arrest he interceded on Mandelstam's behalf with Nikolay Bukharin, a leading political figure of the era. Bukharin was already in decline, as it happens, but it seems likely that it was he who brought Pasternak's concern to Stalin's attention. In any case Pasternak received a telephone call from Stalin, who rang up in person to discuss the Mandelstam affair. This conversation has become the subject of an entire folklore, and many versions of it exist. They differ considerably from each other – inevitably, since they all stem from Boris Leonidovich's own accounts retailed by a variety of witnesses.

Whether Stalin's telephone call took him by surprise or not, on which accounts disagree, the gist of their discussion was as follows. Stalin began with an assurance: Mandelstam was going to be 'all right'. But Stalin then reproached Pasternak for failing to stand up for his 'friend' (though in fact no close friendship was involved). Why had he not taken the matter up with Stalin personally or approached the official writers' organizations? The poet replied, all too accurately, that the writers' organizations had stopped defending persecuted members back in 1927. As for his own failure to do anything about Mandelstam, he had done something: he had spoken to Bukharin, otherwise Stalin would probably never have heard of the matter. Stalin then asked whether Pasternak considered Mandelstam a genius, to which an evasive reply was given. This was wise, since a leader himself so widely acclaimed as a genius was not disposed to tolerate rival prodigies in the society over which he presided. Pasternak went on to request an opportunity to meet Stalin in person in order to have a talk 'about life and death', whereupon Stalin hung up. Attempts by Pasternak to have himself reconnected were rebuffed, but word was passed from on high that no objection would be raised to him recounting the contents of the conversation. Hence the numerous occasions on which he told the tale, and the wide variety of versions which have circulated.[26]

The consensus of informed opinion was that Pasternak came out of the ordeal well, in the sense that he did nothing to increase the dangers threatening Mandelstam. He may have helped to ensure that the sentence imposed on the erring poet – three years' exile – was unexpectedly mild. Even so, Pasternak himself considered the conversation a defeat. Once again he had tried and failed to establish a dialogue with the dictator. The failure preyed on his mind, and he told Nadezhda Mandelstam that it was responsible for his continued inability to write poetry.[27]

Nadezhda Mandelstam has stressed Pasternak's morbid curiosity about the Kremlin recluse, claiming that the poet's chief motive for requesting an interview was sheer admiration. 'At that time, I think, Pasternak believed that Stalin was the incarnation of the age, of history, and of the future; he simply wanted a close look at this living, breathing prodigy.'[28] Mandelstam's widow may be forgiven this and many another tart comment on Pasternak. The plain fact is that he – for all his recalcitrance, oscillations and indiscretions – was yet one of Stalinism's beneficiaries, whereas Mandelstam was one of its most pathetic victims and was to be utterly destroyed by it within a few years.

An episode from the year preceding Mandelstam's arrest sheds light on the temperamental differences between the two poets. The Mandelstams had just been granted occupancy of a new flat marginally less sordid than the squalid quarters in which they had previously lived. Pasternak called to congratulate them, and volunteered the friendly comment that Mandelstam, having at last acquired a proper apartment, would now be able to write poetry again. But Mandelstam was accustomed to compose poetry in his head – he scorned pens, paper, desks and flats along with all other material possessions – and he was incensed by the remark. It provoked him to write a vitriolic poem after Pasternak had left: a poem denouncing the new flat, proclaiming his wish to move straight out, and pronouncing the place fit only for time-serving writers willing to glorify the sufferings imposed by the regime.[29] His rage is understandable in the context, even if the poem grossly overstates its case in so far as Pasternak was its target. Still, it does serve as a reminder that there were those beside whom Pasternak seemed, however unfairly, to represent the epitome of worldly success and even of bourgeois complacency.

How greatly Mandelstam differed from himself Pasternak recognized in comments made on 10 November 1932 after one of the last poetry recitals that the other poet was permitted to deliver. 'I envy you your freedom', Pasternak told him. He then added, perhaps feeling his remark to be inadequately cryptic, that what he personally needed was 'non-freedom'.[30]

In the course of the 1930s literature was subjected to increasing regimentation as part of the general tightening of totalitarian controls. The most important step in bringing authors to heel was the abolition, by the Party Decree dated 23 April 1932, of the entire network of literary associations which had been active since the Revolution and which had expended so much effort on intriguing against each other. The decision had been taken to replace these multifarious writers' groups with a single organization, the Union of Soviet Writers.

The aim of the political authorities was to bring *belles-lettres* under more stringent control while presenting the change of policy as a relaxation. Notionally imaginative writers, many of whom had already been converted into pliant purveyors of publicity material in favour of the Stalinist system, were now to be cajoled, bribed and bullied into adopting their propagandist role with an even greater degree of commitment. With this in view substantial rewards were granted to members of the new union who were prepared to behave with propriety, and they were granted an increasing share of the substantial privileges available to the Soviet élite as a whole. These included preferential housing, earnings far exceeding those of peasants and manual workers, superior medical treatment, lavish holiday facilities and access to the special shops where food and other goods were on sale at a discount. Steps were also taken to establish a superior caste of author-officials through an intensification of the system, common in all Soviet walks of life, whereby rank-and-file members of a given profession are, in the first instance, kept in line by other members of the same profession. Such literary bureaucrat-tycoons, often consisting of mediocre or failed writers, naturally received the most munificent perquisites of all.

Conditions of publication and remuneration were such that it was no longer possible to practise the profession of letters without being a member of the Writers' Union. As an additional measure of control, a new literary method, Socialist Realism, was evolved and imposed on Union members as a matter of formal obligation. It required from these toilers on literature's production line 'a truthful, historically concrete depiction of reality in its revolutionary development'. What is truth? What, for that matter, is reality? Since the political authorities were the sole arbiters of both notions in all contexts, historically concrete or not, the formula was well devised to ensure that authors did what, through a chain of politico-literary intermediaries, the highest interpreters of Stalin's policies told them to do.

Pasternak's reaction to this development was typical: at a literary conference of 1931 he strongly protested against those who kept shouting that poets must 'do this, do that!' As for Socialist Realism, he largely ignored the concept as beneath contempt, though he once described it as masking 'everything that is pompous, pretentious, rhetorical, without substance, useless in human terms and morally suspect'. And yet, despite all his distrust of jargon and politico-literary chicanery, he by no means tried to swim against the new literary current. He actively co-operated in setting up the Georgian branch of the Writers' Union while revisiting Tiflis in November 1933 with a delegation from Moscow sent out for the purpose. When the Writers' Union of the USSR as a whole was formally established at its founding congress in Moscow in August and September 1934, he was to accept election to its Board. Well might he seem to have 'sold out' to the Soviet establishment by comparison with the disgraced Mandelstam, now exiled to Voronezh in southern Russia: while Pasternak was lording it with the literary notables of Tiflis and Moscow, the unfortunate Mandelstam was being falsely accused of trying to worm his way into the Voronezh branch of the Writers' Union as a 'Trotskyite'.[31]

Pasternak's participation in the First Congress of the Soviet Writers' Union had a characteristically ambiguous and even farcical flavour. He sat on the platform, he delivered a speech, he was praised by other speakers. All this represented the peak of his vogue as an officially accepted author, according to one observer.[32] No doubt his eccentricities were tolerated because of his high reputation as a poet. With all his defects as a potential Soviet laureate he still seemed a more promising candidate for that role than any comparably eminent rival, for Yesenin and Mayakovsky were dead and Tsvetayeva was in emigration, while Akhmatova and Mandelstam had long been politically beyond the pale.

As the Congress proceeded it became more and more evident that Pasternak had his limitations as a tool of the new literary organization. Though the doomed Bukharin acclaimed him enthusiastically, Bukharin also went out of his way to stress his remoteness from current affairs. True, Pasternak 'accepted the Revolution'; but he had also kept aloof (said Bukharin) from the struggles of his era, concentrating rather on exquisite and painstaking craftsmanship.[33]

Pasternak's deportment at the Congress included a vintage display of choreographed self-effacement. When a delegation of toilers from the Moscow Metro, currently under widely publicized construction, was paraded as part of a pageant designed to emphasize the solidarity between workers by hand and workers by brain, Pasternak stepped forward and attempted to relieve a woman navvy of some heavy construction tool which she bore as a stage property symbolic of the dignity of labour. To the amusement of the assemblage the chivalrous gesture was brushed off by the burly wench. But why did Pasternak thrust himself forward in this way? Was he inspired by pity, so often reflected in his verse, for suffering womanhood? Did he wish to symbolize the self-abasement of the intellectual before the all-conquering worker? Was he trying to mock and disrupt the ludicrous stage-managed proceedings? All that can be asserted with confidence is that the episode was characteristic of him. Also typical was his insistence, when he himself came to address the Congress, on dragging in a reference to his ill-considered and better-forgotten gesture. He attributed it to a feeling that the young woman had been 'in some momentary sense my sister'.[34] One is left reflecting once again on his talent for making himself awkwardly conspicuous. To draw attention to his ardent wish not to draw attention to himself – here was a recurrent behaviour pattern supremely characteristic of his complex nature.

Pasternak's speech to the Congress revealed further elements of non-conformity. He not only failed to adopt the liturgical patter by now almost compulsory on public occasions, but he also made his views clear, in barely veiled language, on the new policy of bribing writers to behave themselves. His advice to his colleagues was: 'Don't sacrifice your true nature to status.' He went on to identify the main temptation dangled before authors by the regime. 'Such is the warmth with which the people and the State now surround us that the danger of becoming a literary bigwig has become too great.'[35]

In April 1935 Pasternak fell seriously ill with a form of nervous breakdown of which the main symptom was insomnia. 'For a whole year I could not sleep.' He told Ivinskaya that the affliction was caused by a tour of the collective farms which he had undertaken, like so many other writers of the period, on the assumption that it would lead to a book proclaiming the triumphs of Stalin's agricultural policies. It is not clear whether he was referring to his unhappy visit (mentioned above) to the Urals of summer 1932 or to some other, otherwise undocumented, expedition. In any case what he witnessed was misery beyond description, 'a calamity so terrible that . . . the mind just couldn't take it in'.[36]

In June he was undergoing treatment at a sanatorium when instructions suddenly reached him – through a secretary of Stalin's, according to one account[37] – to leave for Paris, where an international Conference of Writers for the Defence of Culture had been organized by a group of well-known French authors anxious to challenge the advance of Fascism. A delegation from the Soviet Union – including Aleksey Tolstoy, Fyodor Panfyorov and Ilya Ehrenburg – had already left for the French capital. The last-minute attachment of Pasternak, as also of the short-story writer Izaak Babel, was the result of a request by some of the French authors.[38] They surely did not realize that Moscow would translate their polite expression of interest in the two Russians into a peremptory command to leave for Paris without delay.

On his way to France by train Pasternak enjoyed a brief reunion in Berlin with his sister Josephine, who came from Munich to meet him. She found him distraught, depressed and tearful. He complained of insomnia, bemoaned the obligation to attend the Conference and discussed his plans for writing a novel about his second wife.[39]

His appearance at the Conference provoked an ovation from the floor and compliments from the platform. A recital (by André Malraux) of a poem of Pasternak's in French translation was acclaimed, as was his own brief speech largely devoted to his health problems. But he also spoke of poetry, claiming that it would always remain a peak higher than any Alp while simultaneously wallowing in the grass beneath one's feet.[40]

In Paris he met Ida Vysotskaya, with whom he had been in love in 1912; he impressed her as eccentrically dressed, as seeming to be living through a waking nightmare, and as complaining of heart trouble. But the most significant episode of his stay was his reunion with Marina Tsvetayeva. He met her in the corridors of the conference hall, he went out to see her and her family in the suburb of Medon, and (according to an unsubstantiated assertion of Akhmatova's) he also made love to her. Love or no love, the encounter was a disappointment. With Pasternak and Tsvetayeva it was less a matter of absence making the heart grow fonder than of absence being an ingredient absolutely crucial to their friendship. Their Paris meeting did nothing to revive an intense emotional attachment which had been exclusively based on the exchange of letters and literary material, and which had already begun to decline in the 1920s. Tsvetayeva was particularly annoyed with Pasternak for having taken a beautiful young wife; she thought that a betrayal of their exalted relationship. There were other barriers to their *rapprochement* too. Pasternak believed that 'Marina combined every kind of female hysteria in concentrated form'. There was also a clash of temperament, according to Olga Ivinskaya, who has contrasted the 'mannish, brusque, peremptory' Tsvetayeva with the 'soft, feminine, complicatedly gentle' Pasternak.[41]

One aspect of the meeting was to assume considerable importance in later years. Tsvetayeva's husband and children wished to leave France for the Soviet Union, and she consulted Pasternak on the advisability of joining them in taking so drastic a step. He returned an evasive answer for which he was later to blame himself bitterly.

On his way back to the USSR by sea, Pasternak shared a cabin with an influential political figure, A. S. Shcherbakov – then Secretary of the Writers' Union and soon to become a candidate member of Stalin's Politburo. To him Pasternak addressed what he himself was later to describe as a non-stop deranged monologue. The suggestion has even been made that this helped to save him from arrest, if indeed (as has been suggested) Shcherbakov reported to higher authority that the poet was completely off his head.[42] Lunatics and village idiots have always enjoyed a special measure of tolerance in Russia.

Temporary mental derangement continued after the boat had docked at Leningrad, where the poet took up residence as a guest of his cousin Olga and seemed inclined to stay indefinitely. He was too apathetic to take the train to Moscow, or even to inform his wife of his return. But he did show initiative in another direction, if Akhmatova's witness may be credited. This was, she says, one of three occasions on which he proposed marriage to her (Akhmatova) – and with especial insistence, even though both of them were already equipped with partners in life. These aberrations ended with Pasternak's wife arriving in Leningrad and conveying the distraught poet back to Moscow under her personal escort.[43]

On 6 October 1935 Pasternak wrote to Titsian Tabidze explaining that he was still far from well, and referring vaguely to his nerves, his heart, his liver and his insomnia as the causes of his sufferings. 'I am saddened and at times frightened by the abrupt change . . . in me. . . . I want to try to do some work (for over four months I have done nothing).'[44] It is tempting to correct this statement. The fact is that he had done nothing for four years rather than four months – nothing, that is, in the way of creative literary production.

The desertion of his art does not seem to have been caused by lack of public response. Olga Ivinskaya, then a student of literature, has described a recital which he gave at Herzen House in Moscow in the early 1930s. She portrays the 'mad, young' poet (he was over forty) with ruffled, raven-black hair, as he was mobbed by his admirers – and responded with ill-humoured nervous 'mooings'. But his mumbles only whetted the fans' ardour. They ripped his handkerchief to shreds and ravished his cigarettes in their hunger for souvenirs. He was also beginning to be noticed abroad. English versions of his poetry appeared in an article by George Reavey published in a Cambridge literary review, and a correspondence between poet and translator followed. *Safe Conduct* appeared in Czech translation in 1935.[45]

If Pasternak's literary silence cannot be put down to insufficient appreciation by his admirers, still less can it be attributed to lack of official recognition as measured by the number of his writings sanctioned for publication at home. The years 1931–4 saw the appearance of numerous items by him in sundry periodicals, of two editions of *Second Birth*, and of a further eight volumes – two of prose, six of verse, all consisting of republished material. He was evidently as acceptable to those who determined publishing policy as he was to the reading public.

And yet he not only came close to abandoning poetry from 1931 onwards, but almost gave up work in imaginative prose as well. There need not necessarily be a reason for such a flight from creativity, which comes and goes without the creator necessarily being able to account for its caprices. But it does seem likely that Pasternak's hesitancy about the Stalinist order – as reflected by his urge to praise it at one moment and to decry it at another – may have helped to reduce him to silence. There was also his recurrent obsession with the need to undergo yet another literary rebirth. And so, though he was producing practically no new imaginative literature during these years, he was at least brooding on what he would like to produce. He was increasingly tormented by the urge to do something new and different, and he even indicated, in a letter to his father, that he was trying to turn himself into a second Dickens. After that he meant to become a poet in the manner of Pushkin. Further references to a 'large-scale work' indicate that the phantom of a long novel, which had pursued him for so many years, continued to haunt his fantasies.[46]

While original literary work remained in abeyance he was making enormous strides in the area of literary translation. He had been fascinated by the process for two decades, he had already published numerous translations, and he had depended on them for his livelihood in the early post-revolutionary years. But he had always retained a semi-amateur status, so to speak, and it was only in 1934 that he became a true professional. His translations of the next quarter of a century were to be voluminous, highly acclaimed and his chief source of income. He was principally a translator of verse, working extensively from English, French and German, the three languages which he knew best, but also from other tongues which he knew barely or not at all. This was made possible through the practice of providing line-by-line cribs in Russian; they were furnished by linguists who were sometimes also the original poets. He was eventually to translate over fifty poets from twelve languages, his renderings of Shakespeare and Goethe being the most widely praised.

Literary translation had features peculiar to the Soviet context. The main drawback was that the necessary contracts were dispensed at the discretion of editors or publishers dependent for their well-being on official approval. They were liable to suffer drastic penalties for channelling work to an individual who later fell into disgrace. Bureaucratic whim, bureaucratic fear, bureaucratic self-seeking – these plagues were endemic to the translation world, as they were to the newly reorganized literary world as a whole. On the other hand, translation was well remunerated in relation to the skill and effort involved, which has rarely been true of literary (as opposed to technical) translation in non-Communist societies. Translation could also offer disgraced authors a refuge. It provided Akhmatova and Mandelstam with a living at times when they could not publish original work, and the same was to be true of Pasternak himself at certain periods of his later life.

His plunge into the role of committed and fully professional translator was inspired by his contacts with Georgia. In 1934–7 scores of Georgian lyrics by a dozen of Georgia's poets, including his close friends Tabidze and Yashvili, appeared in his Russian in various periodicals; he also translated a famous long poem from the Georgian, Vazha Pshavela's *Snake-Eater*. A collection of Pasternak's versions entitled *Georgian Lyric Poets* appeared in book form in 1935, and came out in a second edition two years later. Not knowing Georgian, he relied on cribs, and naturally required metrical indications as well. This method of processing poetry can never be fully satisfactory. Nor can any other, as he himself reflected in a letter to Tabidze of 12 October 1933. 'All translations – good and bad – are to a certain extent a violation of the original.' His ignorance of Georgian was balanced by his intense sympathy for the poets of Georgia, their country and their culture. There is another, perhaps surprising, consideration too. Many Georgian poets had originally written under the influence of Russian poets, including Pasternak himself, and so he found much congenial and familiar material emanating from Tiflis. As for the operation's more pedestrian aspects, he once boasted that his Georgians could provide him with enough to live on for a year or eighteen months.[47] There is also the point that translations so extensive from Stalin's native language may well have been undertaken as part of the translator's persistent campaign to attract the Leader's attention to himself.

In 1935 the distant, largely one-sided dialogue between Poet and Leader was resumed with two letters from Pasternak to Stalin. One of them was a plea for Akhmatova's common-law husband Nikolay Punin, an art historian, who had recently been arrested by the security authorities. The letter was answered to the extent that Punin was quickly released.[48] Curiously, the episode coincided with the very period in which Pasternak was attempting to usurp Punin's position in Akhmatova's personal life, according to her own assertion.

The second letter to Stalin was provoked by the Leader's decision of late 1935 to promote Mayakovsky, nearly six years after his suicide, to the position of the Soviet Union's premier poet. Stalin had been persuaded to adopt this course by Mayakovsky's bereaved mistress, Lili Brik. She was a jealous custodian of her deceased lover's literary heritage and may well have feared that Pasternak, now at the height of his popularity with Soviet authority, might assume the status of the Soviet Union's poet laureate by default. She therefore wrote to Stalin and pressed Mayakovsky's case, to such effect that he scrawled on the margin of her letter a memorable comment. 'Comrade Brik is right: Mayakovsky was and remains the most talented poet of our Soviet epoch.' He then added a characteristic note of menace. 'Indifference to his memory and works is a crime.' This was virtually a death sentence on any individual who could be represented as failing to promote Mayakovsky within the limits available to him, and a feverish Union-wide cult was accordingly launched. Statues of Mayakovsky appeared in public places. Streets and squares were named after him. So too were tanks, tractors, trawlers and minesweepers. The new cult drew from Pasternak the ironical comment that Mayakovsky was being forcibly propagated like potatoes under Catherine the Great. But Pasternak was not displeased by this development, since he did not wish to advertise himself like a Mayakovsky – only to advertise his determination not to advertise himself. Idiosyncratic as ever, he took the risk of writing another letter to Stalin to explain that he welcomed Stalin's endorsement of Mayakovsky because it 'rescued me from the inflation of my significance to which I was first exposed in the mid-1930s at about the time of the Writers' Congress'.[49]

By now the custom of the country dictated that ecstatic allusions to Stalin's person, as well as to his political system, should figure prominently wherever the printed word appeared – not only in political statements, but also in studies of Greek vases, thermo-dynamics, Celtic philology and every other conceivable aspect of human endeavour. Obsequious references to the Leader accordingly began to appear in Pasternak's published writings, including his translations. Such poets as Yashvili and Tabidze, Stalin's fellow countrymen and Pasternak's personal friends, could not avoid the general obligation, and it would have been out of the question for Pasternak and his editors to have omitted their sycophantic material on the dictator from his translations from the Georgian. Pasternak's *Georgian Lyric Poets* of 1935 accordingly contains Yashvili's poem 'Stalin', which stresses the dictator's massive strength, and describes him as 'at one with the Party'. Stalin protects the USSR from its foes.

> The faintest whiff of enmity to Moscow
> Straightway doth spawn a strategist's reply
> In thy immeasurably lucid head.

The same volume also contains a poem to Stalin by Nikolo Mitsishvili. Here the Leader is addressed as 'forged like sword by thy homeland'. Georgia has concentrated the tears of all the masses into a single tear in Stalin's eye, a drop to which the firmness of a diamond has been imparted and which will melt the ice of slavery like the sun. The prediction was to prove as untrue as its metaphors were mixed, but Pasternak translated it regardless.[50]

What of eulogies of Stalin appearing over Pasternak's own name? Only two will be found in his verse – an exceedingly rum brace of lyrics published in the newspaper *Izvestiya* on 1 January 1936. Each celebrates the partnership of the Infinitely Great (the Dictator) and the Infinitely Small (the Poet), but only one mentions the Dictator by name.

> Eternally landsliding
> In from outside,
> Great things shall be echoed
> In poor little me,
>
> In laughter near crofts,
> In the countryman's lore,
> In Lenin, in Stalin,
> In lines such as these.[51]

In the other *Izvestiya* poem the Kremlin-based Stalin is invoked as follows.

> Within that antique stronghold
> Dwells Action Man in person –
> The essence of a doer
> Swollen to global bulk.
>
> Fate gave him as his birthright
> What history left out.
> He's what the boldest dreamt of,
> He's what none dared before.
>
> For all his fabled exploits
> The cosmos stayed intact.
> He did not rocket upwards.
> He kept his shape and glow.
>
> While mingled tales and relics
> Float Kremlin-like o'er Moscow,
> The ages have accepted
> Him like the belfry's chimes.

And he remains so human.
If he should bag a hare
In winter the woods echo
His shot like any other's.[52]

Juxtaposing the colossal figure of the Leader and the pathetically tiny figure of the Poet, Pasternak goes on to express once again an idea which seems to have obsessed him during the 1930s. This was the hope that he himself would somehow strike up a harmonious and beneficial dialogue with Stalin.

The Genius of Action
So dominates the Poet
That he is soaked sponge-heavy
With all the other's traits.

The bard, small though his role be
In contrapuntal cross-talk,
Has faith that these antipodes
Have mutual awareness.[53]

Here is an attempt by Pasternak to be reconnected to the Kremlin switchboard and to resume his interrupted telephone conversation of 1934 with Stalin. But the second voice in the fugue was still silent, and the first continued to cry out in vain.

The two *Izvestiya* poems were not written as a crude bid to curry favour, a gesture of which Pasternak was temperamentally incapable, but accurately express a current in his thinking of the period. This is confirmed in a letter from him to Olga Freydenberg of 3 April 1935. 'In spite of everything I'm more and more imbued with faith in all that's being done in this country.... Never before has such a far-sighted and praiseworthy policy been adopted, or one based on such vital, dynamic principles.' He was not writing in forgetfulness of the period's oppressions, for the same letter begins with an allusion to the mass arrests and deportations ordered by Stalin in Leningrad after the assassination of the city's Party leader Sergey Kirov on 1 December 1934.[54] It is evident that neither these horrors, nor those of collectivization, nor any other sufferings of the period were – yet – enough to deter Pasternak's wayward gusts of loyalty to the Stalinist order.

An earlier impulse favourable to Stalinism is clearly evident in a passage from Pasternak's letter of 18 October 1933 to his cousin. 'A certain truth, still nameless, is already crystallizing – whether in the Party purges, in children's consciousness and language, or as a yardstick for assessing art and life.... The world has never seen anything more aristocratic or more free than our society – poverty-stricken, vulgar, accursed and lamentable though it be.'[55] Approving references to the purges! Fully fledged Stalinism presented as offering freedom beyond compare! Here is a Pasternak different indeed from what he was later to become: the doyen of Soviet-domiciled opposition to Stalin's legacy.

Twenty years later Pasternak was to call his two poems in praise of Stalin 'a sincere endeavour, one of my most intense (and my last in that period) to live by – and in tune with – the era's ideas'.[56] Sincere the endeavour surely was; it was also typically short-lived. In February 1936, a few weeks after publishing the *Izvestiya* lyrics, Pasternak was haranguing a meeting of the Board of the Writers' Union at Minsk, and went out of his way to disparage the poems, calling them 'bad verse'. He said they had been written hastily, but added that he did not propose to revise them. To boast openly of having written about the Leader hastily! And that while flaunting a refusal to repair the matter! Pasternak might have been trying to commit suicide. But worse was to follow in the same speech. Its riskiest sentiment is an appeal for writers not to be afraid of showing signs of genius. 'I don't remember any decree banning genius in our judicial system. If there was one, some of our leaders would have had to ban themselves.'[57] Here is a transparent sneer at the bewhiskered, pockmarked eminence whose unique and many-sided talents Pasternak had so recently been advertising in his own verse and his translations.

In the same speech Pasternak went out of his way to scourge the cant phraseology of the era as 'pompous and complacent braggadocio now so ingrained that everyone thinks it compulsory'. He also denounced those who had denounced *him*, as some had, for failing to stump the country declaiming his work from platforms like a good little democratic versifier. This activity had been appropriate for Mayakovsky, said Pasternak. But then, Mayakovsky had been a superb public performer. He himself preferred to meet his readers on the printed page, as Pushkin and Tyutchev had before him. He further rebuked those who judged poetic production by bulk, as if the poet were a hydraulic pump spewing out so many gallons of water per hour. The true criterion of literary success was (he said) not volume of output, but a capacity to surprise.[58]

In an address delivered in the following month to a group of Moscow writers the unrepentant Pasternak went on to flail the official regimentation of literature. 'No demands in terms of form or content should be made of the writer. You can't tell a mother that she has to bear a girl and not a boy.' He also ridiculed two officially sponsored cultural heresy hunts of the moment, those directed against Formalism and Naturalism, sardonically claiming that such persecutions did not appear to have been inspired by a love of art. They were, said he, sponsored by bureaucrats insultingly indifferent to the fact that writers had by now 'grown out of short trousers'.[59]

Though Pasternak may give the impression of courting disaster by his various indiscretions of 1936, he was less endangered than might seem likely in view of the fact that the first six months and more of the year were a relatively easy period. This was the lull before the storm of Stalin's worst oppressions as they were to erupt from late August onwards. Far from suffering persecution in the early part of the year, Pasternak even contrived to solve what was for many the supremely intractable domestic problem of the age: that of living accommodation.

Preferential housing was the most prized of the many privileges available to favoured authors, or to anyone else, and Pasternak was now able to equip himself with a dacha – a sizeable country home – at Peredelkino, about twelve miles south-west of Moscow. It was part of a small village colony newly constructed for writers, and his next-door neighbour was the novelist Konstantin Fedin; the essayist and literary critic Korney Chukovsky and the novelist Leonid Leonov lived not far away. At the same time Boris Leonidovich also acquired a flat in a new block specially built for authors in Lavrushensky Street in central Moscow; the building was twelve stories high, and it had its own bank and barber's shop. Never having been an acquisitive person, he was guiltily aware that he had contrived to be allocated three times as much space as he really needed. But he wanted to make provision for his parents,[60] whose residence in Munich increasingly exposed them to the threat of racial persecution; in the event they were to escape from Hitlerite Germany in a different direction by moving to England in 1938. As for their elder son, he was to retain both his country house and his town flat until the end of his days, despite all the troubles of his later life and despite all the official disgrace which he was eventually to incur.

Among the perquisites of authorship available to Pasternak in the summer of 1936 was another expedition – his third – to Georgia. It yielded a small crop of lyrics, *Travel Notes*, which appeared in the October issue of the journal *Novy mir*. Georgia's roses, waterfalls, apricots, oleanders, plums, herdsmen and rivers are commemorated. So too is Georgian hospitality, as dispensed by Pasternak's favourite Tiflis hosts Yashvili and Tabidze. But Pasternak did not put his heart into these poems, and has called them fatuous bird-like twitterings. He has also condemned their 'silly' beat[61] – that of the iambic trimeter, a line apt for Russian doggerel.

The drama's next act sees Pasternak turning from equivocal support of Stalinism to passive opposition, and falling from official favour into semi-disgrace. This transformation took place soon after the onset of Stalin's harshest period of oppression, as introduced in August 1936 by the Kamenev–Zinovyev Trial (the first of the three major Moscow judicial pageants of the period). The ensuing reign of terror – known as the *Yezhovshchina* from the name of Nikolay Yezhov, head of the security forces during the period – was to rage for some two years before beginning to lose momentum. During the *Yezhovshchina* oppressions comparable in scale to those previously inflicted on the peasantry were visited on the towns as well. Vast numbers were imprisoned, exiled and executed, while many of those who remained at liberty sought to escape persecution by their zeal in denouncing others. Individuals and groups were more than ever required to make acts of public obeisance by signifying enthusiastic approval for Stalin's latest measures, especially for the show trials themselves.

In the course of the Kamenev–Zinovyev Trial, *Pravda* of 21 August 1936 published a letter from the Soviet literary fraternity demanding capital punishment for the defendants. Pasternak's name appeared in the list of signatories.[62] But he was never again to lend support to one of these recurrent campaigns.

Disillusion with the new society came over him suddenly, according to his own account. 'Everything snapped inside me in 1936 when all those terrible trials began, instead of the cruelty season ending. as I had expected in 1935. My identification of myself with the period turned into opposition which I did not conceal. I took refuge in translation. My creative work stopped.' His political disaffection owed much to exasperation with the literary establishment. In a letter of 1 October 1936 to Titsian and Nina Tabidze he mocked the Writers' Union as a hotbed of competitive timidity, also deriding *Literaturnaya gazeta* (the Union's main publication organ) as 'ridiculous'. The Union had no claim to any connection with revolution, said he. The trouble was, he believed, that Soviet society had become dominated by spiritually sterile nonentities. He forcibly expressed this idea, which was to figure prominently in *Doctor Zhivago*, in a letter to his cousin of the same date. It refers to 'miserable, utterly crushed nobodies who are compelled by the momentum of their own insignificance to equate their age's style and spirit with the dumb, quaking servility to which . . . the poverty of their intellectual resources has doomed them'.[63]

While Pasternak was attacking the Soviet literary establishment in private, its most exalted official was preparing to have a go at him in public. In December 1936 V. P. Stavsky, the current Secretary of the Writers' Union, condemned Pasternak's recently published poems about Georgia for 'slandering the Soviet people'. Here was a clear warning of danger to which a less courageous or foolhardy poet might have responded by capitulating and confessing the error of his ways. But Pasternak did not hesitate to publish a letter of self-defence in *Literaturnaya gazeta* of 5 January 1937.[64]

In April 1937 he moved further towards open defiance of the political control system by withholding his endorsement from the era's latest heresy hunt. Its target was a recent book published in Paris, *Retour de l'U.R.S.S.*, in which the French author André Gide had expressed disillusion with the Soviet Union. Pasternak was expected to append his signature to a collective statement denouncing Gide, but refused on the ground that he had not read the offending work. His excuse was an additional offence in the eyes of colleagues who had no more read the book than he, but had signed the letter because they were told to. Small wonder that they found his moral squeamishness 'provocative'.[65]

His next act of defiance was to refuse his signature to a collective letter reviling Marshal Tukhachevsky and other leading generals whose execution for treason had been announced in the press on 11 June 1937. The implications of this failure to co-operate were so serious, and not for him alone, that a posse of literary bureaucrats, headed by Secretary Stavsky in person, descended on Peredelkino to urge him to sign. But he rejected their entreaties. He also turned down the tearful pleas of his pregnant wife, who flung herself at his feet and begged him not to destroy her and their unborn child. In the end his colleagues appended his signature without his consent, thus leaving both Pasternak's honour and life intact, together with their own reputations as effective manipulators of their fellow writers. Meanwhile the poet was writing yet another letter to Stalin. It explained his refusal to endorse the generals' execution as the product of Tolstoyan convictions which prevented him from posing as an arbiter in matters of life and death.[66]

His indiscretions were piling up, and it seems astonishing that he did not disappear for ever into the archipelago of Stalin's labour camps of the late 1930s, as happened to so many other authors. Mandelstam, Babel and Pilnyak were the most prominent among those writing in Russian. Other casualties of the period included Pasternak's Georgian friends Tabidze and Yashvili, who both came to grief in August 1937.

Yashvili killed himself with a double-barrelled shot-gun at the headquarters of the Georgian Union of Writers, of which he was the secretary, on learning that his friend Tabidze had been arrested earlier in the month. After that nothing more was heard of Tabidze until 1955, when it was announced that he had been executed two months after his original arrest. Pasternak has commemorated these and other victims of the *Yezhovshchina*, without mentioning any names, in the lyric 'My Soul', which describes his own spirit as the common sepulchre, burial urn and charnel-house of all who died during the years of agony.[67]

As the year 1937 rolled on, so too did Pasternak's indiscretions. In the autumn he denounced the arrests and executions of the period in private conversation with a friend on the Gogol Boulevard in Moscow. He also wrote to commiserate with his cousin Olga over the arrest of a close relative, regretting his inability to help. 'In such cases human sympathy can't go beyond sighs and bulging eyes. For the last two years such catastrophes have been so organized that appeals from bystanders are fruitless and only make things worse.'[68]

During the years of intensified terror Pasternak had remained in touch with Mandelstam, whose term of exile expired in 1937, and when the Mandelstams returned to Moscow they went out to see Pasternak at Peredelkino. But Zinaida Pasternak refused to receive them at the dacha, no doubt fearing the drastic consequences of so thoroughly disgraced a poet's descent on her household. Pasternak was reduced to conversing with the Mandelstams on the platform of the local railway station, where his talk so fascinated them that they let train after train leave for Moscow without embarking. According to Nadezhda Mandelstam, his discourse showed him still as obsessed with Stalin's personality as ever, and it was on this occasion that he attributed his continuing inability to write original works of literature to his failure to secure a personal interview with the dictator at the time of their famous telephone conversation of 1934.[69]

In 1938 Mandelstam was arrested for the second time, and vanished for ever into the labour camp empire of the Far East. The circumstances of his death have never been fully clarified. When a confused account of it filtered through to Moscow, Pasternak was the only person to pay a visit to the widow.[70] This showed his courage and humanity. It also added to the catalogue of his indiscretions, for by now contact with such 'enemies of the people' as Nadezhda Mandelstam had become notoriously dangerous.

A glimpse of Pasternak at the height of the *Yezhovshchina* is given in the diary of the playwright Aleksandr Afinogenov. The poet is described (21 September 1937) as absorbed by his art, taking solitary walks, reading Macaulay's *History of England* and 'writing his novel'. He and his wife were beset by money worries which could only be solved by translation work. Pasternak was never idle, and he never read the newspapers.[71] In view of what the newspapers contained in these days of purges, heresy hunts and show trials, such self-denial was surely the height of wisdom.

Akhmatova has provided a more vivid account of Pasternak's professional and domestic activities of the period, though Zinaida Pasternak did her best to prevent the two poets from meeting. By 6 May 1940 Akhmatova had concluded that Boris Leonidovich was going into decline at home, where he was no longer writing original verse because he was translating other poets. Meanwhile his wife was playing cards non-stop and neglecting their baby son Leonid, who had been born on the last day of 1937. According to Akhmatova, everyone had noticed at once what a coarse, vulgar creature Zinaida Niko-layevna was – everyone except Pasternak himself. He had been too blinded by infatuation to see anything at all, and had gone into ecstasies about her scrubbing floors simply because she possessed no other attribute worthy of ecstasy. But now at last his eyes had been opened. He was dropping indiscreet comments about her, and referring to her as a complacent mediocrity. Akhmatova believed that he would certainly have left her had it not been for their infant son. Besides, he was, in Akhmatova's view, 'one of those conscientious husbands who can't face a second divorce'.[72]

Such were Akhmatova's tartly affectionate tirades about Pasternak, delivered in the style of a mother rehearsing the shortcomings of a favourite son. But she was also capable of expressing passionate devotion, grouping Pasternak and Mandelstam together in the heart-rending cry 'Akh, how I love both Osip and Boris Leonidovich!' Akhmatova also wrote an ode to Pasternak, in 1936. She has him squinting through his 'horse's eye' at a slight angle to the cosmos, and she lists some of his preferred themes as puddles, backyards, platforms, whistling locomotives, grinding surf, the Daryal Gorge in the Caucasus, Moscow, Laocoön-like smoke, thistles in cemeteries. She ends by describing him as 'sort of permanently childlike'.[73]

As Akhmatova indicated, translation continued to provide Pasternak with his main livelihood. His russianized Georgian lyrics were still appearing in quantity in 1937, but he deserted such crib-based translation in the following year to work from languages which he knew. The switch is surely significant. So long as Pasternak was making up to Stalin he continued to translate from Stalin's native language. When the futility of his efforts became apparent he turned to material with which he felt more at home. He translated German and French authors (Becher, Kleist, Verlaine), while becoming more and more attracted to English poetry. Translations of verse by Raleigh, Byron, Keats and Shakespeare followed, after which he tackled Shakespeare's *Hamlet*. His rendering was first published in complete form in the journal *Molodaya gvardiya* for May–June 1940. It is the first item in the memorable sequence of eight Shakespeare plays which he was eventually to translate into Russian.

Pasternak had lost all interest in writing original verse by late 1936. 'My mind is not set on poetry', he told a friend in October, also referring to 'the prose that would set me free'.[74] He duly brought out four short items of prose fiction in periodicals of 1937–9, which demonstrates that the publication of his original work had not fallen under a formal interdiction even at the time of greatest danger. These loosely interconnected studies are partly set in the opening years of the twentieth century and partly in the months preceding the 1917 February Revolution. Their interest lies in their significance as preliminary sketches for *Doctor Zhivago*, which they anticipate in some of the themes and episodes, and also in the names of certain characters.

The four skimpy prose passages of 1937–9, together with the score of quirky lyrics published in 1936 and discussed above – this miserable collection constitutes the sum total of the new works of original literature brought out by Pasternak in 1933–40. One reason for deserting his vocation must have been that he felt stifled by the atmosphere of Stalinism militant. Fear for his own safety and that of his family must also have deterred him from seeking publication in an age when almost anything might be used against almost anyone by almost anyone. But this supposition cannot be documented from Pasternak's own evidence, since the very fear which presumably prevented him, and many another writer, from writing also prevented them from specifying the cause of their failure to write. The same fear, too, silenced those potential memoirists who might have borne fuller witness to his doings, for which reason the source material on his life (never exactly lavish) is particularly scanty where the late 1930s are concerned.

Even when conditions eased, after Stalin's death in 1953, Pasternak did not exploit the new relaxations – such as they were – in order to quarry his own and his country's experiences of the 1930s as literary copy. Far from portraying the decade's mass atrocities, he went out of his way to avoid the topic, doing little more in *Doctor Zhivago* and

Autobiographical Sketch than indicate that the subject lay beyond the scope of his pen. It seems, then, that he chose not to describe the 1930s because he considered the 1930s indescribable. But a break in the rhythm of creativity cannot be ruled out; only a non-author could possibly regard it as easier and more natural to write than to abstain from writing.

So much for the reasons for his creative silence. What of the reasons for his personal immunity? How could so politically recalcitrant a creature escape execution, or a more lingering death in the camps, as meted out to Babel, Mandelstam, Pilnyak, Tabidze and the innumerable other literary and non-literary victims of the age?

Again, one can only speculate. As the most distinguished living Russian poet domiciled in the USSR, and as an author with at least some record of support for Stalinism behind him, Pasternak represented an asset which individual influential persons might well hesitate to squander through fear of being later called to account for cultural sabotage by rival flunkeys. Then again, Pasternak's very indiscretions, his impishness, his refusal or inability to conform – these qualities may conceivably have appealed to Stalin. The dictator is known to have displayed occasional sympathy for eccentrics; for example, he had already (however exceptionally) exempted two other aberrant writers, Bulgakov and Zamyatin, from persecution. And though Pasternak's numerous attempts to establish communication with Stalin had failed to elicit any known response, except for the single telephone call about Mandelstam, it by no means follows that these appeals had gone entirely unheeded. The poet may well have owed his safety to the dictator's protection.

He may equally well have owed his survival to sheer accident. The operation of blind chance was no more inhibited during the *Yezhovshchina* than it has been in less hectic phases of Russian and world history. Boris Leonidovich always seems to have had his share of good luck. He came within a hair's breadth of arrest in the second half of 1939, according to information which eventually leaked out of the security apparatus.[75] But for some reason he was spared; nor was that necessarily the period of his greatest peril.

To review Pasternak's activities of the 1930s as a whole is to be amazed that he went so far in two diametrically opposite directions – that of defying and that of pacifying Stalin. Perhaps the poet succeeded in puzzling contemporary political authority as much as he puzzles many later students of his development, thus mesmerizing the very apparatus of terror into immobility.

6

THE POET GOES TO WAR

After the rigours of the *Yezhovshchina* had been slightly relaxed in 1938, the Soviet Union entered an alliance with Hitlerite Germany in August of the following year; whereupon the Second World War broke out between Germany and the Western Allies. The USSR joined Germany in subduing Poland, and went to war in Finland in November 1939. But the general tenor of Soviet life remained unchanged, even though certain minor cultural relaxations were permitted.

One such concession was the publication of Akhmatova's verse in a comprehensive one-volume collection after she had been virtually excluded from the press for seventeen years. The new volume appeared in the early summer of 1940, and was called *From Six Books*. Pasternak was overjoyed to see his old friend in print again. He wrote to tell her that she was unique, like the early Pushkin, and that Blok alone rivalled her eloquence. He himself, and Mayakovsky too, were 'far more indebted to you than is usually thought'. This generous praise must have pleased her, though she doubted whether Pasternak ever read anyone's verse except his own. She believed that his invariably extravagant eulogies of other poets were no less invariably hypocritical.[1]

Hitler's victories of 1940 in Western Europe profoundly depressed Pasternak, who wrote as follows to his cousin Olga from the hospital where he was recovering from radiculitis. 'I've said goodbye in my mind to all that I loved, to all that was lovable in Western Europe's traditions and aspirations. I've wept for them and buried them, my own family along with them.'[2] His words reflect his anxiety about his father and sisters, who were now living in Oxford, his mother having died in England in 1939.

In late 1940 Akhmatova's new book of verse was suddenly withdrawn by order from on high, and she resumed her previous position as a disgraced and unpublishable poet. Pasternak was quick to console her by letter. He told her that one should never give up hope, and added a particularly significant phrase. 'As a true Christian you must know all this.'[3] The sentence comes as a shock, implying as it does considerable sympathy for the Christian faith on the part of a speaker whose adherence to Christianity is scantily documented indeed outside the pages of *Doctor Zhivago*, where it is fervently and (in the context of his record as a whole) surprisingly affirmed. By offering the comforts of Christianity to Akhmatova in 1940, Pasternak has at least contributed some substance, however meagre, to an alleged sudden religious conversion which two scholars have attributed to him in 1940 or 1941, but in each case without giving evidence. Boris Thomson refers to 'the profound spiritual experience which Pasternak *seems* to have gone through' in 1940, and 'which *probably* made him a Christian'.[4] George Katkov alludes to a 'new religious experience' which entered the poet's life through an 'illumination' dating from the first months of the Second World War, and which Katkov claims to find expressed in the lyric 'Daybreak'.[5] But surely there were enough sudden illuminations in Pasternak's life already, many of them deriving (one suspects) from his tendency to dramatize his evolution into a sequence of abrupt crises. It seems a pity to add to them without indicating any basis for the allegation. It may be surmised that Pasternak in fact drifted towards Christianity during and after the war, and that the sudden conversion of 1940 is apocryphal. Only in *Doctor Zhivago*, written in the post-war period, is his Christianity expressed comprehensibly and with evident conviction, forming one of the book's major themes.

If Pasternak was suddenly converted to anything in 1940 it was less to religion than to poetry of a new kind. Two lyrics, 'Summer Day' and 'The City', broke a poetical silence of more than four years when they appeared in the monthly *Molodaya gvardiya* in January 1941. They were later republished as part of the small verse cycle entitled *Peredelkino*. It consists largely of material describing scenes in his home village and composed there in 1940 and early 1941.

This group of poems introduces a new period in his literary evolution – the second of the two major divisions into which his work as a whole falls. The difference between these periods has already been indicated. The pre-1940 writing is complex and obscure; the post-1940 writing is simple and comprehensible. But this generalization is helpful only if the necessary riders are borne in mind. Not all the early poems are irredeemably mysterious. Nor are all the later writings crystalline in their clarity. If they were so it would not, presumably, have been found necessary for an entire book to be devoted to the interpretation – and that a highly disputable one – of a small section of them (Donald Davie's *The Poems of Doctor Zhivago*). There is also the point that a drift towards greater simplicity had set in long before 1940; for example, the collection *Second Birth*, of 1932, may be considered to represent an interim stage between the early, complex and the late, simple Pasternak.

The poet himself often pointed to the year 1940 as the most significant turning-point in his literary development, and held strong views on the comparative merits of his two periods. Too modest to claim his post-1940 work as good, he made no bones about dismissing his pre-1940 work as bad. 'I don't like my pre-1940 style.' In 1958 he said that he was now 'writing differently. It started at the beginning of the 1940s.' Alluding, on one occasion, to 'my ghastly early poems ... the very titles of which throttle my heart with pain and revulsion', he went on to renounce, 'with few exceptions, almost everything I did before the Second World War'.[6] This new simplicity involved the further development of a trend already evident in his work for nearly two decades: the admission of narrative and associated elements such as are largely absent from his verse of the 1910s. These include personal reminiscences and straightforward nature descriptions, together with references to identifiable places and events.

In cultivating intelligibility Pasternak happened to be fulfilling one of the obligations placed on writers by political authority – that literature should be understood by the average reader. This was just what he himself now wanted. Like Tolstoy in later life, he no longer wished – if ever he had – to write for an élite of hypersensitive aesthetes. From now on his work was for the common man. He had, in other words, arrived by his own independent route at the point where he was eager to do just what authority wanted him to do.

The new intelligibility is especially evident in his treatment of the Peredelkino lyrics' main theme – the seasons of the year from summer through autumn, winter and spring to a second summer. If the new cycle is compared to the earlier seasonal cycle in *Themes and Variations* (1923), an obvious contrast emerges. The disjointed, quirky, excited images of the earlier poems, with their animated and highly strung trees and buildings, have given way to greater harmony and clarity. Spring is no longer the season of wonder-struck poplars, of scared skylines, of houses that fear to slump, and of air blue as a bundle of clothing carried by a discharged hospital patient. It is, rather, the time when winter's ice begins to melt in a sequence of easily visible cascades – when

> With chilled teeth chattering an icy jet
> Pours over rim from pool to pool.[7]

'Summer Day' presents the poet as he became familiar to many visitors to his home at Peredelkino – the tiller of his garden. He toils away with streams of sweat flowing over his spade, while the sun is about to fire him like potter's clay until he is covered with a glaze. And winter finds the normally buoyant Boris Leonidovich brooding on the prospect of his own death.

> From my hall window, this and every year,
> I see my final hour's postponed approach.
> Winter has cleared its paths, and eyes my life
> From knoll through yellow leaves' abomination.[8]

The most frequently quoted lyric of the cycle is 'In Early Trains', and Pasternak himself must have considered it particularly important, since he was to adopt its title for the collection of his lyrics published in book form in 1943. The poem was written in March 1941, and commemorates its author's habit of commuting between his Peredelkino and Moscow dwellings. His boots squeak as he trudges through the pitch blackness of the local wood to catch the 6.25 a.m. train to the city. Then he plunges from the cold into the stuffy compartment, where he is seized by tenderness for his fellow passengers and – through that – by love for his country as a whole.

> Through veil of past vicissitudes,
> Through war and destitution,
> I silently took cognizance
> Of Russia's unique features.
>
> I tried to hide my ecstasy
> And worshipped as I watched
> Suburbanites and farm girls,
> Students and metalworkers.
>
> They lacked the air of deference
> That poverty imparts.
> They bore life's frets and changes
> Like masters of the earth.[9]

There is something more than a little unctuous and complacent in the tone with which Pasternak here expresses his reverence for common humanity – something which might even make some readers hanker for the overweening lines of 1936 in which the poet had, so much less democratically, hinted at the desirability of establishing exclusive two-way communication between himself and Stalin.

On 22 June 1941 the massive assault of Hitlerite Germany and its allies plunged Pasternak's motherland into four years of bloody conflict. It was to be the greatest of the many calamities inflicted on Russia by citizens of other countries. Yet many Russians welcomed the war as a blessing in disguise. It was a relief to have identifiable external enemies who could be fought, even if they were engaged in exterminating the population on a scale still more intensive than any native ruler had contrived. After the first few shattering months morale improved, and internal terror was further relaxed.

Pasternak saw the war as a cleansing storm. He told a friend that it resembled 'a breeze blowing through unventilated premises. Its disasters and sacrifices were better than the inhuman lie.'[10] In the Epilogue to *Doctor Zhivago* almost identical sentiments have been put into the mouth of a fictional character, Major Dudorov. He calls the war 'a purifying storm, a stream of fresh air, a whiff of deliverance'. All war's horrors and dangers were a blessing 'compared to the inhuman domination of fantasy'. War came as a relief because it 'limited the power of the dead letter'. Everyone without exception, at home and at the front, had taken a deep breath and 'dived into the furnace of this dire, lethal, liberating struggle with rapture and a sense of true happiness'.[11] Here, as so often in *Doctor Zhivago*, a fictional character voices views which can be shown to be Pasternak's own.

The war brought more to Pasternak than a relief from the horrors of Stalinist persecution. In him, as in Akhmatova too, the conflict stirred profound feelings of Russian patriotism such as he probably did not experience, and certainly did not publicly express, in 1914–18. He was soon writing poems designed to spur his fellow countrymen to resist the invader. But he was in no position to fling his own person into the dire, lethal, liberating struggle as wholeheartedly as he seems to have wished, being hampered by his age – he was now in his fifties – and by the old leg injury which had already disqualified him for military service in earlier conflicts. All he could do was to train with the Peredelkino home guard, performing military drill and displaying his prowess at target practice. He threw himself into these activities with enthusiasm, and when he was residing in Moscow he eagerly carried out firewatching duties on the roof of the writers' apartment block in Lavrushensky Street.

One of these vigils took place on the night of 23–4 July 1941, that of an especially severe German air raid. Pasternak spent the whole night on the roof, awed by the sight of the burning city aglow in the summer dawn. The experience is commemorated in his lyric 'Lines in Haste', which recalls

> Ordeal of bombardment;
> Sirens' raucous howl;
> Bristly, sprouting, hedgehoggish
> Streets, roofs, wall.

Another poem describes the shooting down of an enemy plane in the countryside.

> Smouldering over hamlet
> Shall plummet fuming fragment –
> Shrapnel-shattered raider.[12]

Between June and December 1941 Pasternak wrote six lyrics devoted to the war. The longest and most admired is 'The Old Park'. It describes a wounded soldier's sensations as he lies in the Peredelkino manor house, now converted into a hospital.[13] But the lines are not the author's most distinguished, and his other war poems from the first year of the conflict are even less so.

Two years before the German invasion of Russia, Marina Tsvetayeva had come back to her native land after many years in emigration, bringing her teenaged son with her. She was briefly reunited with her husband and daughter, whose return had preceded hers, but both of them were soon arrested. She was never to see them again. As for her emotional relationship with Pasternak, that had long ago collapsed. But his admiration for her poetry remained. He was also instinctively kind, and did his best to help her in the troubles which beset her after her retreat to Moscow. He introduced her to the State publishing house Goslitizdat, which offered her translation work. He interceded with Aleksandr Fadeyev, the novelist and influential literary official, in a vain attempt to find her a tolerable dwelling. He also arranged for her to meet Akhmatova, thus bringing Russia's two most outstanding women poets face to face for the first time. But Tsvetayeva was now a spent force. She was no longer writing poetry, she was more convinced than ever that she had lost her attractiveness as a woman, she was desperately poor, she found Stalin's Russia utterly alien.

Pasternak saw Tsvetayeva for the last time in July 1941, when he said goodbye to her at the port of Khimki on the Moscow River as she was evacuated from the capital to the eastern hinterland with her son. They were assigned to Yelabuga, a small town on the River Kama in the Tatar Autonomous Republic. It lies some six hundred miles east of Moscow, and in order to reach it the two evacuees had to pass through

Chistopol. This was a larger and marginally less depressing river port to which, as it happened, Pasternak's wife and child had made their way a few weeks earlier, and where he was to join them in October. A small colony of writers from the centre was now assembling at Chistopol, and Tsvetayeva would have preferred to make her base there. But this was not permitted. She reached Yelabuga on 21 August in a state of advanced demoralization. She has been described as bent, gaunt, grey-haired, a combination of a tramp and a witch in her old brown raincoat and dirty blue knitted beret.[14] No one in this dump had heard of her or her work.

On 31 August Marina Ivanovna committed suicide by hanging, and it is reported that no mourners – not even her own son – attended her burial at an unrecorded spot in the local cemetery. When Pasternak learnt of her death he blamed himself for not having done enough to help her in life. He said that, if she could only have held out for another month, he would have been in Chistopol himself; he might have found her a billet in the town and arranged for her to receive better rations. He could also have obtained employment for her, and 'She could have taken part in the literary evenings we organized.'[15] Tsvetayeva certainly would have received a measure of encouragement from such solicitude, but a study of her last years makes it seem unlikely that she would have recovered the verve of former days. Literary evenings at Chistopol were all very well in their way, but they fell considerably short of a prescription for cosmic despair.

Her end was especially tragic in view of her immense talent as a poet, of which Pasternak himself was fully conscious. He spoke of the rhythms that thrummed in her soul – of her tremendous, uniquely forceful language. Hers had been a heroic life, he claimed. Its every day had been a feat of gallantry performed out of loyalty to the only country of which she was a citizen: poetry. His obituary elegy, 'To Marina Tsvetayeva's Memory', refers to her remote resting place.

> Marina, it has long been time,
> And it won't be that much trouble,
> To bring home from Yelabuga
> Your disregarded ashes.[16]

He was to retain throughout life an unstinting admiration for Tsvetayeva's genius, combined with an intense feeling of guilt for having failed her when she most needed him.

A few weeks after Tsvetayeva's suicide Pasternak joined his family at Chistopol, where a sizeable colony of evacuated writers was already gathered. One of its members was the playwright Aleksandr Gladkov.

He had long admired Boris Leonidovich, whom he had already met in Moscow in the late 1930s, and he has left a detailed memoir of the poet's life in Chistopol and Moscow during the war.

Trudging through Chistopol's autumnal mud in their stylish overcoats and soft felt hats, the literary fugitives from the centre set standards of sophistication hitherto undreamt of in the Tatar Autonomous Republic. All lived lives of luxury by comparison with the man in Chistopol's unpaved streets, but there was wide variety in the degree of privilege enjoyed by individuals. Some of the most favoured contrived to rent entire houses. The novelist Leonid Leonov was one of the pampered few. He bought the local honey by the barrel; he even hired an armed watchman to guard his premises. These were luxuries beyond Pasternak's means or desires. He was housed in a single miserable bedsitter approached through a communal kitchen. It was ill-heated, and that in a winter of abnormal ferocity. But he bore discomfort cheerfully, hauling firewood from the banks of the frozen Kama and doggedly translating *Romeo and Juliet* in defiance of all distractions. He would lunch on cabbage stew in the local writers' canteen, working between spoonfuls after laying out his pocket edition of Shakespeare and English–Russian dictionary. By February 1942 he was reading extracts from the play at a local poetry recital in aid of a welfare fund for the troops. Gladkov has described him in his black suit, gaudy knitted tie and felt boots as he declaimed with his usual engaging incompetence in a full hall lit by two paraffin lamps.[17] By now, evidently, Chistopol was fast becoming the Athens of the Tatar Autonomous Republic.

On another of Chistopol's many literary occasions the novelist Konstantin Fedin gave a reading from his memoir of Gorky. The sprightly performance included passages in which the speaker mimicked Gorky's Nizhny Novgorod accent. Pasternak sat near the front, and demonstrated his enthusiasm by repeatedly turning round and making grimaces designed to assist those in the back rows to identify the funny bits; he was, as ever, the last man in the world to stand on his dignity. On another occasion he left his bedsitter to remonstrate with fellow lodgers for playing raucous gramophone records in the adjacent kitchen, but had barely uttered his mild protest when he was overcome with remorse at aggressively placing his own interests above others'. It so preyed on his mind that he took the opportunity of yet another literary recital, which chanced to occur on the same evening in honour of the Red Army, to offer from the stage a public apology to the collective of gramophone addicts who had provoked his protest. This interpolation led to considerable tittering and embarrassment. Gladkov was not exaggerating when he commented that 'Pasternak often provoked smiles or laughter by his general conduct and individual displays of gaucherie.'[18]

After spending a year at Chistopol with his family, Pasternak paid a two-month visit to Moscow at the end of 1942. He brought with him the text of a new volume of verse, which included the cycle *Peredelkino*, and which appeared in 1943 under the title *In Early Trains*. In February of that year the momentous Battle of Stalingrad ended, several hundred miles south-east of the capital, with the rout of the German Sixth Army. Pasternak commemorated the victory with the powerful lyric 'Fresco Come to Life', where he refers to the night sky above shattered Stalingrad 'rocking in its plaster shroud' as shells burst beneath it.[19]

When he brought his family back from Chistopol to Moscow, in early 1943, his hair had become noticeably grey, and he was soon bombarding influential persons with urgent requests to be sent to the front as a war correspondent. The opportunity eventually came during the great Battle of Kursk, which raged for fifty days in the summer of the same year. Once again, as previously before Moscow and at Stalingrad, a German offensive was first held, and then converted into a victorious Soviet counter-offensive – the prelude to eventual victory in the war. On 5 August the Red Army took Oryol, the large provincial city (about 200 miles south of Moscow) which had been seized by the Germans in October 1941. Pasternak celebrated the liberation of this key locality in verse of shattering – and, surely, deliberate – banality.

> Put sombre thoughts aside, say I!
> Bring out the good old vodka!
> There's overwhelming news today!
> Oryol has been recovered![20]

Before the end of August Pasternak was in the Oryol area himself, having embarked on a two-week tour of the front with a 'brigade' of writers. He manfully bore the rigours of the recently liberated areas, he spoke to the troops. A trite address to the soldiers from his pen has survived, and inevitably includes a ritual reference to the Leader. 'As Comrade Stalin has often repeated, a just cause was bound to triumph sooner or later.' A similar obligatory reference is also found in the article *Expedition to the Front*, contributed by the poet to the newspaper *Trud*. 'The whole people has triumphed from top to bottom, from Marshal Stalin to rank-and-file toilers and ordinary fighting men.'[21]

Pasternak drew on his experiences as a temporary war correspondent in the Epilogue to *Doctor Zhivago*, which begins with scenes from the Oryol battle front in summer 1943. The passage includes a description of Karachev, a small town in the area. It has been rased, its houses turned into rubble by bombs and mortar-shells. Splintered, charred stumps mark the sites of former orchards. Some of the inhabitants are ferreting in the still smouldering ashes, while others are excavating dug-outs and cutting turves with which to roof them. The town is still burning, and from time to time a delayed-action bomb sends brick-red clouds of smoke, flame and rubble into the sky.[22]

He had also celebrated the liberation of Oryol with three lyrics written shortly after the event. Based on despatches made available to him at Army Group headquarters, they describe tactical operations as directly experienced by troops on the ground. The weakest of the three is 'Pursuit', where his all too justifiable concern over the rape and murder of a young woman by the invader is reflected in lines sadly unequal to their poignant context.

> We've kept alive her memory –
> The child we picked up in the fields,
> One that the Boche had had their fun with.
> Her hand lay on her little face,
> The wedding ring was on her finger –
> For which her ravishers shall pay
> A hundredfold their pound of flesh.[23]

The two other operational lyrics are on a higher level. Each describes an act of military self-sacrifice. In 'Scouts' a machine-gun detail bravely penetrates enemy lines without hope of survival, simply in order to provoke the rowdy minor skirmish which will enable Soviet artillery to fix the enemy's position. 'Sapper's Death' describes the secret preparations for a Soviet mass attack – the silent mining of moonlit barbed wire entanglements protecting an enemy stronghold. One man is fatally wounded, but expires heroically while suppressing the groans which would betray his comrades' presence. Pasternak stresses the value of this small operation to the campaign as a whole. The reason why the Red Army has, today, already penetrated as far west as the city of Gomel is that

> While crawling through yon moonlit glade
> We did not stint our lives last night.

The episode brings the poet back to a theme which recurs many times in his later work: life's chief meaning lies in self-sacrifice.

Life is a guttering out. That's how
Things are, and only then will you
Cheat death when by self-sacrifice
You blaze the trail to light and glory.[24]

There has been a tendency to disparage Pasternak's war poetry,[25] and no attempt has been made here to deny that some of it is unimpressive. But the quality range is wide, and the best of the war poems generate a dynamism characteristic of their author. This is especially true of the uncompleted long poem *Nightglow*. It draws its name from the radiance in the night sky created by the massive artillery salutes with which the liberation of Oryol, and later Russian victories, came to be greeted in Moscow. The poem portrays an infantry NCO, Volodya, whose truck has broken down not far from the capital while he is returning home on leave. He is puzzled by the brightness of the horizon over the distant city, and enquires what new event has provoked these summer lightnings. In answer

They name the self-same action
That he's just been engaged in.
The pyrotechnic column
Enthrals him like a schoolboy.[26]

Through Volodya's imagined thoughts Pasternak voices the people's hope that victory over Germany may bring political relaxation at home. The poet expresses these aspirations obliquely, as was inevitable, but with great power, and he also seems inclined to renew the implied dialogue with Stalin on which he had embarked in the 1930s. When his Volodya is described as cursing like a Zaporozhian Cossack, no Russian reader could miss the point that these particular Cossacks still remained the most extreme symbol of freedom, self-assertion and anarchy, which was why they had been suppressed by the Russian State in the eighteenth century. To the cursing Volodya the glow in the sky brings a vision of a new and glorious Moscow.

Bright as the future, Moscow soars from gloaming.
Thinks he: 'I'll find things there beyond the stuff
Of dreams – what blood and victory have bought,
The vistas I've descried through vision slits.'

As the poem proceeds there is a suggestion that political relaxation is more than an aspiration – that it will be demanded as a right by the victorious people.

We shall not stop at words, but as
In some prophetic dream
We'll build on a yet grander scale,
Shine brighter than before.[27]

We shall not stop at words! There is a veiled threat in this line which makes it surprising that *Nightglow* achieved publication in a context so hypersensitive – and in the Communist Party newspaper *Pravda* (which carried the text on 15 October 1943). *Pravda* published only the Introduction, consisting of the thirteen four-line stanzas from which the above quotations are taken, but Pasternak went on to complete Canto One of what was to have been an entire novel in verse about wartime Russia. Canto One of *Nightglow* has been posthumously published; it consists of thirty-five four-line stanzas, and goes further than the Introduction to the same poem in implying a critical attitude to Stalinist authority. It begins with two sarcastic stanzas directed against the automatic optimism imposed on writers by official literary policies. Such compulsory jauntiness is contrasted with the tone – tragic, yet somehow inspiring – of pre-revolutionary Russian literature. If only the writers of the USSR could be freed from the obligation to project enthusiasm they might even come to rival their Western counterparts, among whom Pasternak singles out two particular authors as the very emblems of creative effectiveness.

> Our older Russian writers spurned the lure of creature comforts.
> Their epileptic heroes smouldered, radiant and anguished.
> Methinks, if we stopped varnishing even the dullest concepts,
> We too could write as well, perchance, as Hemingway or
>   Priestley.[28]

It is tempting to call the last line one of literature's great anticlimaxes.

A vivid contrast is drawn between the clean-living, forward-looking war hero Volodya and his slatternly wife Katya, who has become the mistress of a local black marketeer during her husband's absence at the front. Katya represents the past, but Volodya belongs to a new generation of those who,

> Transformed by cordite, gallantry and risk of death,
> Have outgrown mousy scamperings and pots with cracks in.[29]

Volodya's world is one of new horizons and broad perspectives, and the People has a new part to play in it – an implicit contradiction of the official claim that such horizons and perspectives had already been attained by pre-war Stalinism. The emphasis laid by Pasternak's NCO on what he calls 'the novelty of the People's role' is more resonant still, since (according to official doctrine) the People had played a vital role in the creation and development of the revolutionary State from the beginning. Furthermore, the very expression *narodnoy roli* ('of the people's role') is but a consonant's breadth away from *Narodnoy voli* ('of People's Will'). People's Will, as few readers of *Pravda* needed reminding, was the revolutionary terrorist group which had assassinated the Emperor Alexander II in 1881. The line can, therefore, be read as conveying the oblique threat that Stalin might face assassination if he should fail to relax the rigours of his rule once final victory has been achieved. No wonder, then, that the writer and powerful literary functionary Aleksandr Fadeyev tried to prevent Pasternak from continuing work on the verse novel of which this passage was to have been a part. The poet followed Fadeyev's advice, but was later to regret his compromise with the political system. He also commented that his unwillingness to continue *Nightglow* stemmed from its partial publication in *Pravda*, an association that rendered the work distasteful to him.[30]

These political considerations are fascinating, but must not be permitted to obscure the fact that *Nightglow* contains Pasternak's finest war poetry. Here, if anywhere, he appears as the exultant spokesman of a victorious nation in arms.

During the war Pasternak by no means abandoned the habit of making indiscreet political comments. In December 1941 he told Gladkov that Stalin was a 'Skalozub' (in effect, a 'Colonel Blimp'), who intended to regiment the country even more harshly than before. He also concluded that, if post-war Russia should revert to its pre-war level, 'my inability not to be myself may land me somewhere in the north among many old friends' – in a labour camp, that is. A few weeks later the poet offered Gladkov a pointed comment on a commonly expressed view of the period – to the effect that Stalin himself must be ignorant, and therefore innocent, of the wholesale slaughter carried out by his minions. Pasternak said that if Stalin was indeed unaware of these atrocities, then that very ignorance was not only a crime, but 'perhaps the greatest crime of which a statesman can be guilty'.[31]

These were observations made in private. But Pasternak would not have been Pasternak had he not continued to behave indiscreetly in public as well. He once spent some time holding forth in a crowded Moscow tram after learning how greatly Gladkov's brother – a prisoner in the Kolyma slave empire of the Far East – prized a tattered copy of his poems which had somehow penetrated the barbed wire. Overwhelmed by emotion, the poet proceeded to interrogate Gladkov in detail on this sensitive matter, and without troubling to lower his voice.[32] This was indeed foolish, since there were few surer routes to the concentration camps – which, officially, did not exist – than to be reported as alluding to them in conversation.

Pasternak appears to have suffered from official displeasure in only one particular during the war years – the sudden abandonment of a production of his translation of Shakespeare's *Hamlet* by the Moscow Art Theatre after rehearsals had already begun. The reason was, according to rumour, the 'perplexity' expressed by Stalin on learning that the play had been put into commission.[33] His objection was probably less to Pasternak than to Shakespeare's theme, so prominent in *Hamlet*, of supreme power attained through assassination. Stalin also disliked Shakespeare's *Macbeth* and Pushkin's *Boris Godunov*, no doubt for the same reason. There was no point in putting ideas into people's heads.

Between 1940 and 1951 Pasternak was to bring out translations of eight Shakespeare plays in the order *Hamlet*, *Romeo and Juliet*, *Antony and Cleopatra*, *Othello*, *Henry IV* (Parts One and Two), *King Lear*, *Macbeth*. This body of work has established itself in Russia 'as a kind of "official" Shakespearean text', being accepted as such by the Soviet theatre as a whole.[34]

Pasternak believed that translation was a form of artistic creativity. 'Translations should be works of art. They should stand on the level of the original through their own uniqueness.' He also claimed to hold 'the nineteenth-century view of translation as a literary activity demanding higher insights'. He maintained that the translator might be forced to take liberties with his text in order to recreate the spirit of the original. The relation of the translation to the original was that of a graft to a root stock. It must be a live shoot, not a dead copy. It must reproduce life, not literature. Vitality was all. Asserting that his version of *Hamlet* 'should be judged as an original Russian dramatic work', he even tended to prefer it to all his other writings, including his original poetry.[35] But by no means all his many references to the translator's art are on this lofty level. He was also apt to call translation 'a mere substitute for real work', and he mistrusted the activity as a threat to his professional standing. 'To translate . . . means to establish myself permanently in secondary, subordinate positions, which . . . is harmful, not to say ruinous, for me.'[36]

Pasternak idolized Shakespeare's work while also regarding it as a bundle of seemingly irreconcilable extremes. Now it was compact and pithy, now it was chaotic to a degree which had exasperated Voltaire and Tolstoy. 'Shakespeare's imagery is heterogeneous. Sometimes it's the grandest poetry . . . sometimes it's blatant rhetoric cramming a dozen empty circumlocutions together in place of a single word which was on the tip of the author's tongue, but which he was in too much haste to catch.' Pasternak said that Shakespeare's metaphors were the natural outcome of the contradiction between the brevity of man's life and the immensity of his long-term tasks. 'Given this discrepancy, he's forced to look at things with an eagle's eye and to express himself in immediately comprehensible lightning flashes. That's what poetry is. Metaphor is the shorthand of the big personality, the stenography of its spirit.'[37] Seldom has one bundle of seemingly irreconcilable extremes more admirably described another, for Pasternak's every word about Shakespeare's poetry applies with comparable force to his own.

Shakespeare's metrical practices are followed in Pasternak's translations. He renders prose as prose; he converts five-foot iambic blank verse into the same measure in Russian; he preserves rhymed couplets where these occur in the original; he follows the varied metres of Shakespeare's songs. He further follows, though with considerable freedom, the principle of linear equivalency: that is, he has set himself to convey one line of Shakespeare's verse in one line of his own. This principle hampers the translator from English into Russian to this extent, that the average Russian word contains nearly twice as many syllables as the average English word. The result is that, if an English sentence is rendered into Russian containing an identical number of syllables, much of the sense is bound to be sacrificed. To attempt an adequate rendering into Russian of all that Shakespeare says would require a Russian text containing at least half as many lines again as the original, and some earlier Russian translations of Shakespeare have provided just that. But Pasternak's policy forced him to dock the English original, and in effect to simplify it.

This simplification of Shakespeare was consistent with the officially imposed doctrine of Socialist Realism. It also conformed with the policy which Pasternak had adopted, independently of official pressure, in his lyric poetry from 1940 onwards – the cultivation of intelligibility. His decision to present a clarified, comprehensible, clear-cut Shakespeare was thus triply reinforced: by official doctrine, by his own new attitude to writing poetry and by his solution of his metrical problems.

It by no means follows that Pasternak's simplified and abbreviated Shakespeare is everywhere inferior to the original. There are places where the Russian vies with or surpasses the English. But much loss was inevitable. How serious it can be is illustrated by some of the meteorological and scenic material of *King Lear*. When Shakespeare's King exclaims 'You cataracts and hurricanoes, spout', Pasternak offers the bald *'Ley, dozhd, kak iz vedra'*: 'Pour, rain, as from bucket'. True, '*iz vedra*' preserves the same idiom as the English 'in bucketfuls', and the Russian does not sound as banal as back-translation makes it. Even so, the phrase is spectacularly ill-chosen. Then again, a line or two below, Shakespeare's 'Sulphrous and thought-executing fires, / Vaunt-couriers to oak-cleaving thunderbolts' have been reduced to 'Arrows of lightnings, swift as thought, / Tree-splintering'. Nor is this the Shakespeare of the 'Murmuring surge, / That on the un-number'd idle pebbles chafes', but he whose 'waves' feebly 'break with noise on stones'. It seems both puzzling and regrettable that the early Pasternak, whose sonorous complexities are Russia's nearest equivalent to Shakespeare at his most tortuously vociferous, was not called in as equal partner to the simplicity-cultivating late Pasternak. If so his versions, excellent as they are in many respects, might have been even more impressive.

The taming of the Bard is also extended to sexual references. It is no use seeking here the Russian for the rank sweat of an enseamed bed. Pasternak's bed is just greasy and crushed. In the same passage from *Hamlet* Shakespeare's 'reechy' kisses and 'bloat' King have both been stripped of their adjectives, as if Claudius were a Stalin whose pockmarks had to be eliminated from his photographs before he could be put before the public. So far has Pasternak's 'tendency to bowdlerize the text' been carried, according to one scholar, that it 'significantly alters the play'. His squeamishness is consistent with official Soviet practice, which abhors the indecorous; but there is evidence to suggest that he himself initiated such emasculations, and did not have them foisted upon him by authority.[38] This tendency to accentuate propriety has reduced the element of sensuality in Shakespeare's Juliet, Ophelia and Desdemona. They have not been changed out of recognition, but they have been gently nudged to make them conform more closely with Pasternak's ideal of a young woman: a pure, pliant, featureless, docile creature.

Pasternak also infuses his Shakespeare with a little of his own eagerly affirmative attitude to 'life' (his favourite word), and thus softens the English dramatist's pervasive insistence on humanity's capacity for evil. One result is too tame an Iago. The presentation of Hamlet, as a man inspired by a selfless devotion to duty, again involves an arguable divergence from the angle of the original. But Pasternak had his own designs on the Prince of Denmark, and they are incorporated in a 'Hamlet' entirely his own, the first item in the lyric cycle contained in *Doctor Zhivago*.

The defeat of Germany and Japan in 1945 did not bring internal peace to the USSR. So far, indeed, was the victorious Stalin from fulfilling the hopes expressed in Pasternak's *Nightglow* that he celebrated victory over his foreign enemies with renewed internal oppression on a massive scale. It was designed to rid his realm of the supposed contamination sustained during the war through widespread contact with aliens – by no means excluding his own allies. Newly released Soviet prisoners of war were rigorously screened, many being sent on to forced labour camps. A similar process was applied to Soviet civilians who had returned home after deportation to the West by the Germans, to Soviet prisoners of war repatriated (often forcibly) by the Western allies, and to the inhabitants of the huge areas of the USSR which had been occupied by the enemy during the war. Whole peoples were deported to Siberia from the Caucasus and elsewhere. The result of these harsh policies was a huge increase in the concentration camp intake. As Olga Ivinskaya has explained, Stalin and his security chief Beria had converted victory over an external enemy into the rout of the victorious population.[39]

Intensified oppression had surprisingly little effect on Soviet literary life in the short term. The relatively easy-going cultural policies of wartime remained in force during the fifteen months following Germany's capitulation, and censorship continued to be imposed less stringently than in the late 1930s. In 1945 Pasternak was, accordingly, able to publish a verse collection – *Earth's Expanse* – which included many of his wartime lyrics. He also brought out his translation of Shakespeare's *Othello* and some renderings of the Georgian poet Nikolos Baratashvili in the same year.

Meanwhile Stalin was preparing to pounce on the intellectual world. The chosen area for his initial assault was literature, and the weapon was the Party decree of 14 August 1946, which bore the harmless-sounding title 'On the Magazines *Zvezda* and *Leningrad*'. It denounced these periodicals for opening their columns to ideologically alien material, including the work of two Leningrad writers who were now singled out as the premier targets for abuse. One was Anna Akhmatova. The other was a comparably renowned author of prose fiction, Mikhail Zoshchenko. A week later the Party decree was reinforced by a virulent speech in which the cultural overlord Andrey Zhdanov further developed the attack. Akhmatova and Zoshchenko were both savaged for cultivating art for art's sake, for poisoning the minds of the young, for subservience to the West, for ignoring Communist ideology, for standing aloof from politics. Zoshchenko was pilloried for implying (in his sketch *Adventures of an Ape*) that the monkey house of a zoo provided a more civilized habitat than the

Soviet Union; Akhmatova was denounced as 'half nun, half whore', and as the author of personal poetry accessible only to a few. This last charge had been levelled against her for more than twenty years, and against Pasternak too.

An avalanche of intensive abuse followed in all Soviet organs of publicity, and the campaign soon fanned out to include the other arts, especially those of the cinema and theatre. The rejection of Western influence in every shape and form, real and imagined, became a dominant theme. So, too, did the promotion of extreme Russian nationalism.

This campaign, known as the *Zhdanovshchina*, plunged Soviet cultural life into a deep freeze, and was to last until Stalin's death in March 1953. It obliged professional communicators to concentrate, to a degree unparalleled even in Soviet history, on issuing blatantly propagandist advertising copy in favour of the political system. Pasternak brought out virtually no new original work at this time, though the publication of his translations was not suspended. In view of his past record he was lucky not to have been chosen as a scapegoat along with Akhmatova and Zoshchenko. Even they had been fortunate, if only in the sense that the controllers of cultural policy were more concerned to impose unprecedentedly severe restrictions on the published word than to reintroduce the execution and imprisonment of intellectuals on the scale of the 1930s. Neither Akhmatova nor Zoshchenko was shot, neither was even arrested. They were merely expelled from the Writers' Union, deprived of their ration cards and converted into social pariahs.

The choice of Akhmatova as a target may have been due in part to an episode from the last year of the war. In May 1944, while returning from evacuation in Tashkent to Leningrad, she had broken her journey in Moscow and had been persuaded to take part in a poetry recital. She was received with applause so enthusiastic that she took fright – with good reason, for this spontaneous tribute (to a poet virtually denied publication since 1923) is said to have been reported to Stalin. He is quoted as asking a suspicious question: 'Who *organized* that standing ovation?' When the remark came to Pasternak's ears, he commented that it was so typical of Stalin's style that it could not possibly have been invented. It was 'quite beyond the Boss to imagine anyone achieving popularity without the aid of an apparatus that specialized in putting over the day's idols to the masses'.[40]

These persecutions, combined with the horrors of post-war Stalinism as a whole, propelled Pasternak into the deep sense of abhorrence which makes 1946 one of the most important turning-

points in his career. Ten years later he recalled that, when victory over
Germany had been followed 'by a return to the brutal chicanery of the
darkest and most imbecile pre-war years', he had experienced 'a feeling
of shocked revulsion against the established dispensation'. The shock
was, he said, even more severe than that caused by Stalin's show trials
and other repressions of 1936 onwards, when 'everything snapped
inside me'. He put the same point still more forcibly when he said to a
close friend, 'Had we foreseen all the post-war horrors in a nightmare,
we'd have been sorry not to see the Stalinists go down with the
Hitlerites.'[41]

The poet's forthright remarks well emphasize the significance of the
shift in his attitude to the Stalinist way of life. As has been stressed
above, his political reactions had varied considerably over the years.
After virtually ignoring public affairs during his first three decades, he
had embarked in the early 1920s on the hesitant and meandering course
of one who sporadically flirted with, supported, rejected and ignored
the increasingly insistent demands put forward by authority in the
name of the new society. He had hymned Russia's revolutionary past
in some poems, and had derided it by implication in others; he had
written and translated sycophantic litanies to Stalin, and had also dared
to seek communication with Stalin as a potential equal. He had lapsed
into ambiguous silence during the *Yezhovshchina*; he had emerged to
praise the Red Army's military triumphs during the war. All these
things he had done. But never, during the whole of this period, had he
come near to achieving stability and consistency in his political
thinking.

Only in 1946 did Pasternak assume a stable political standpoint, one
of resolute opposition to the system created and bequeathed by Stalin.
He was to devote himself, during his fourteen remaining years, to
mocking and discrediting that system through such seemingly limited
means as were open to him. They excluded overt political activity – as
need hardly be said, for such was the nature of the society in which he
found himself. But the political framework which so rigorously
excluded direct participation was to turn out, if only after Stalin's
death, astonishingly vulnerable to oblique attack through the
choreography of self-effacement. Here was Pasternak's speciality. His
posture was not that of Ajax defying the lightning. It was, rather, that
of an exceptionally small sovereign state which has quietly withdrawn
diplomatic recognition from an exceptionally large one under circumstances which chance to expose the occurrence to the full glare of
international publicity.

PART THREE

ENEMY OF THE PEOPLE

1946–1960

7

ICE AGE FROLICS

It was in Moscow and in October 1946 that Pasternak first met Olga Vsevolodovna Ivinskaya, who was to become the beloved companion of his last years and who was to leave a record of her life with him in her memoir, *A Captive of Time*. They met on an occasion when he had chanced to call at the offices of the literary journal *Novy mir*. She was employed there as a junior editor, she was aged thirty-four at the time of their encounter, and she was a woman of considerable beauty. She also possessed the vitality necessary to survival in Stalin's Russia, where physical and moral toughness could be valuable aids to avoiding extermination.

A vigorous and attractive woman may leave a trail of havoc in any society, and Stalin's Russia was no exception. Ivinskaya's memoirs allude to her 'many amorous attachments and disappointments'. She also mentions, so casually as to sound complacent, that her first husband, Yemelyanov, had 'hanged himself because of me'. She had then married his rival and enemy Vinogradov, 'who died in my arms in hospital'. Olga Vsevolodovna's mother had spent three years in a concentration camp during the war, possibly as the result of being denounced by her son-in-law Vinogradov for 'slandering the Leader' in a private conversation.[1]

At the time of Ivinskaya's first meeting with Pasternak she was living in Moscow with her mother and her two children, one by each marriage – her daughter Irina Yemelyanova, aged seven, and her infant son Mitya Vinogradov.

Ivinskaya had worshipped Pasternak's poetry since adolescence, even though 'I couldn't understand half of it'. She had read his prose story *Childhood of Lyuvers*, marvelling that a male author could possess insights so profound into a young girl's secret world. As a student of literature in the early 1930s she had been taken by her first lover to a recital by Pasternak. On this occasion, to which reference has already been made in Chapter 5, he struck her as nervous, raven-locked, young and maniacal, and was greeted by an audience of 'ecstatic fanatics'. She also attended one of his few post-war recitals. When she returned home late that night her mother protested at having to open the door at such an hour. The young woman curtly asked to be left alone, and added that she had 'just been communing with God'.

When Pasternak entered Ivinskaya's office on the momentous day of their first meeting, she was introduced as 'one of your ardent admirers', and he flashed her a glance which she at once recognized as 'so imperious, so appraising, so male, that it left no room for error'. She noted his healthy tan and heavy, virile jaw, 'the jaw of a leader'. Even his 'yellowish, horsy teeth with wide gaps in the middle' struck her favourably. His amber eyes were like an eagle's, yet there was a feminine elegance about him. He made no attempt to conceal the overwhelming attraction which he felt. He also promised to give her some of his books, and straightway informed her – never having been one to conceal what lay closest to his heart – that he had just begun writing a novel. Thus, in yet another 'cloudburst of light', were united the two themes of his last and most significant double rebirth: his love for Ivinskaya, his work on *Doctor Zhivago*.

The distinguished suitor pursued his courtship openly and vigorously. He bombarded Olga Vsevolodovna with volumes of his verse; he telephoned her almost daily; he would call at *Novy mir* of an afternoon and escort her to the Potapov Street flat where she lived with her mother and children. He would often coquettishly remark that, ugly though he was, he had frequently 'been the cause of women's tears'. He also expressed his enthusiasm for the young matron in conversation with mutual friends in terms which, if she has correctly reported them, sound fatuous even for a man in love. 'She is so enchanting, so radiant, so golden. And now that this golden sun has entered my life it is so wonderful, so wonderful. I never thought I'd know such joy again.' Soon he was telling Olga Vsevolodovna that he no longer loved Zinaida Nikolayevna, his wife since the early 1930s; that he wished to leave her; and that he had already realized in the first year of their marriage how wrong he had been to marry her.

After six months of such wooing the idyll was consummated on Friday 5 April 1947, when Pasternak arrived at Ivinskaya's flat at 6 a.m. after walking the streets of Moscow all night. The other members of her family were conveniently absent on an outing to the country. And so, in the lady's narrative, 'As newly-weds spend their first night together, we now had our first day together.' A true prototype of Lara in *Doctor Zhivago*, Olga Vsevolodovna delighted in performing humble domestic services for her man, and all she will say about their love-making is that she ironed his trousers.

Meanwhile, at the offices of *Novy mir*, there were clashes between Olga Vsevolodovna and the officious deputy editor Krivitsky, who frustrated her attempts to publish certain poets while alluding menacingly to her relations with Pasternak. Hearing of this, Boris Leonidovich urged her to resign her post, and offered to take care of her himself. In early 1948, about eighteen months after their first meeting, she gave up her editorship to embark on the new career of freelance literary translator under his tuition.

The poet and his pupil made no attempt to set up house together during their first years as lovers, but opportunities for assignations frequently occurred at his flat in Lavrushensky Street and at her flat in Potapov Street. The chief drawback to the idyll was his refusal to divorce his wife and marry his mistress. Tension was increased by Ivinskaya's mother, who staged emotional scenes such as he especially detested in her efforts to persuade him to regularize his relations with her daughter. Other relatives too nagged the young woman to distraction, urging her to induce her paramour to marry her at all costs. Meanwhile she was bombarding him with tantrums so inartistically tempestuous that he would compare her to a character in a bad novel. The most embarrassing scene of all occurred when Olga Vsevolodovna suddenly found herself confronted by the second Mrs Pasternak in person. A 'heavily built, strong-minded woman', Zinaida Nikolayevna admitted that she no longer loved her husband, but declared that she would never let her family be broken up. She added that she 'spat on' the love of Boris and Olga.

Pasternak may have retained more affection for Zinaida Nikolayevna than would appear from Olga Vsevolodovna's memoirs. Whether inspired by such affection, by a natural reluctance to behave callously, or by attachment to the domestic comforts of Peredelkino, the poet never let himself be brought to the point of leaving his second wife. She was, accordingly, to retain until the end of his life the position of controller of his household, while his mistress reigned as empress of his heart. His own view of these entanglements is accurately represented, according to Olga Vsevolodovna, by the following passage in *Doctor Zhivago*: 'The notions of "free love" and of the "rights and needs of the senses" were alien to him. . . . He did not think of himself as a superman demanding special rights and privileges.' He was opposed to rules for this kind of thing, and once said so to a woman visitor. Every case was different, he told her. 'Life itself is the arbiter.'

Since most of the above information comes from Ivinskaya's memoir, an attempt must be made to assess this source as evidence. A wife or mistress may be the best witness to a man's inner life, but she also has the greatest potential for emotional bias. Possessed as she is of intimate information exclusive to herself, she is free to suppress, to invent and to colour her narrative so as to present whatever picture of events happens to suit her own interpretation. To what extent is *A Captive of Time* open to such criticism?

Though there is little scope for checking the most intimate passages against other sources, Pasternak's devotion to Ivinskaya has been well attested by witnesses as violently hostile to the liaison as Akhmatova and Chukovskaya. Ivinskaya's willingness to criticize her own actions and decisions, the regret which she expresses for the emotional scenes to which she often subjected her lover, the readiness with which she admits to having advised him wrongly on occasion – such examples of self-criticism do much to recommend the objectivity of her recollections. They offend less, it may be suggested, in terms of accuracy than in matters of taste and tone.

A general lack of intellectual distinction sharply differentiates *A Captive of Time* from Nadezhda Mandelstam's two books of memoirs, which are the premier Russian literary reminiscences of the period. In place of the austere authority of Mandelstam's widow, Olga Ivinskaya parades a preoccupation with external superficialities, and often evokes the tone of the traditional old-fashioned 'women's magazine story'. An obsession with hair styles is obtruded from the start. Perhaps it does indeed contribute an extra dimension of vividness to be told that Konstantin Simonov, editor-in-chief of *Novy mir*, sported 'a luxuriant head of hair already grey like a beaver skin', and to meet on the following pages the 'fair-haired Yevtushenko' and Zabolotsky 'with his hair slicked down and parted on the slant', not to mention the ruffled, raven-black locks of Pasternak himself in youth. Still, an excess of such picturesque details calls to mind what an English novelist has permitted one of his characters to claim – however unjustifiably – as typical of women in general: 'their concern with the surface of things, with objects and appearances, with their surroundings and how they looked and sounded in them'.[2]

There is also a measure of inelegant emotional self-indulgence. 'What bliss, horror and turmoil that man brought into my life!' Indeed yes. But Nadezhda Mandelstam cannot be imagined as writing of her husband in such a tone, even though the remark would have been just as true of her. Nor can one see Mandelstam's widow referring to her Osip in such pompous terms as the following: 'The most generous man on earth, who had been given the right to speak in the name of the clouds, the stars and the wind.'

Olga Ivinskaya also lacks Nadezhda Mandelstam's insight into literature, some of her comments on the subject being dauntingly facile. Such is the suggestion that even the most difficult of Pasternak's poems are easily comprehensible through the process of 'unravelling the magic skeins of the metaphors. You just pull a thread and they come untangled.' True though the comment indeed is of certain poems, it does not sound like the observation of someone who has ever seriously read them as a whole. Credit must, however, be given to the memoirist for the modesty with which she speaks of literary matters. Despite her considerable experience as editor and translator, her references to her own competence in these matters are refreshingly humble. Never for a moment does she pretend to professional equality with her lover. And he, for his part, would never have dreamt of condescending to her.

Ivinskaya's memoirs form a valuable comment on Pasternak's later poems, particularly those of *Doctor Zhivago*, since they often enable the reader to relate an otherwise unexplained detail to its real-life context. For example, she elucidates the lyric 'Explanation' as the echo of a quarrel over his refusal to leave his wife for her. The line 'Once more I prepare my excuses' is thus made clear, as also is 'Don't cry, don't purse your swollen lips.' Again, 'Summer in Town' refers to the joys of shared insomnia as experienced during the early days of their love, while the phrase 'woman in helmet' alludes to the memoirist at a time when she had hoisted her coiffure in some particularly note-worthy fashion with her mother's tortoiseshell comb. The 'lamp-shade's fiery skin' in 'Unnamed' is also biographical, as are the references in the same lyric to the two lovers' distorted shadows, and to the dark beads of Ivinskaya's necklace held on her lap.[3]

Another of the late poems, 'Intoxication', describes the poet and his beloved lying on an old raincoat. This too is authentic biographical detail. There was such a raincoat, they used it to make love on when a more suitable venue was not available, and the poem was actually written by Pasternak while he was kneeling on the raincoat. 'Intoxi-cation' spurred Akhmatova to lament the inappropriateness of so passionate a love affair to a man of the author's mature years. She has also objected to another lyric of the same period, 'Autumn', in which he strikes an erotic note foreign to his work as a whole.

> You shed your dress like coppice shedding leaves,
> And in silk-tasselled robe fall in my arms.

The robe too is drawn from life: when Pasternak and Ivinskaya were meeting almost daily in Moscow, she would wear a Japanese dressing-gown with a pattern of little houses. But the poem stung Akhmatova to another tart comment. 'I can't stand that tasselled dressing-gown stuff, her falling into his arms . . . and that lying down in coppice business. Those aren't subjects for a man of sixty.'[4]

Ivinskaya's commentaries on the poems, valuable though they are, must be taken with a pinch of salt. What conceivable point is there in her telling posterity that 'Autumn' is set in the city of Moscow when the very text belies her by firmly locating itself in a cottage in a deserted wood? Then again, she places the 'street lights like gauze moths' of the lyric 'White Night' in Moscow's Potapov Street, explaining that she and her lover used to watch these same lights from the window of her flat. No doubt they did. But she has evidently failed to notice that he has set this particular poem in Leningrad, four hundred miles north-west of Potapov Street, as his text makes abundantly clear.[5] She has dredged the poems for supposed references to herself, but did she (one finds oneself asking again and again) ever seriously *read* them? Another point is this – that to collate all the scattered references in her memoirs with Pasternak's later poems is to wonder whether she has not been too keen to appropriate every conceivable erotic reference to herself. Every attractive woman in his later work must inevitably be she – but with the significant exception of the Mary Magdalene of the *Zhivago* poems, whose heavily stressed status as a prostitute naturally discouraged self-identification.

No one can deny that Ivinskaya was the only great love of Pasternak's last years, or that she helped to inspire his poems, or that her comments on him and his work are of enormous value. If she seems to crave excessive attention for herself, if she appears culpably self-indulgent on occasion, it must also be remembered that she suffered appallingly through their liaison. Whatever reservations may be made about her talents as a memoirist, posterity must be grateful for the comfort which she brought to the poet in his last years, and for shedding so much light on a crucial phase of his life.

The persecution of Akhmatova and Zoshchenko seems to have been a major factor in persuading Pasternak to devote the rest of his life, as in effect he did, to challenging Stalin and Stalinism. It began with a resolute refusal to endorse the campaign launched by Zhdanov. Far from shunning Akhmatova's polluting presence along with everyone else, Pasternak made a special point of seeking her out during a visit which she paid to Moscow. He knew that she had been rendered destitute, and so he contrived to leave her a thousand roubles – which he tactfully tucked under a cushion in her room so as not to offend her by the offer of charity. When a meeting of the Writers' Union Board (to which he still belonged) was summoned to denounce her, he eluded the obligation to attend. For this offence he was expelled from the Board,[6] though not from ordinary membership of the Union.

He is also reported as uttering a deliciously astringent retort when threatened by literary bureaucrats with persecutions similar to those inflicted on Akhmatova and Zoshchenko – and on the grounds that his verse was, like theirs, 'alien to the People and cut off from the modern world'. He told them that he had already heard all that many years ago 'from your man Trotsky'.[7] *Your* man Trotsky! Pasternak was referring to his meeting of 1922 with that – then still powerful – Bolshevik leader. The jeer is a classic in view of the senior status long accorded to Trotsky, in the demonology of Stalinism, as the embodiment of evil.

Pasternak's love of taunting high literary officials is further illustrated by an episode which occurred after he had sent some new lyrics to *Novy mir* at the behest of the journal's chief editor, Konstantin Simonov. Unfortunately, Simonov's deputy Krivitsky – the power behind the throne at *Novy mir* – pounced on the items in question, and declared them unacceptable. Simonov then rang up and apologized to Pasternak, saying how glad he would have been to bring out the poems had he not been prevented from doing so. The poet replied with a parody of official jargon – he inquired what individuals had 'dared to hamper the work' of so influential a public figure as the great Simonov. 'You must go into print immediately and unmask the individual wreckers or sabotaging organizations who have dared to place obstacles in the path of a Simonov.' When Akhmatova heard this story, she described it as Pasternak's latest clash with Phariseeism, and lovingly referred to him as 'Borisik', a specially emotive diminutive form of his first name.[8] It aptly expressed her maternal tenderness towards him – a feeling often combined with extreme, no less maternal, exasperation.

Pasternak's baiting of Simonov is a reminder of his contempt for the Soviet professional classes as a whole. 'What swine they are. . . . I can't stand our intellectuals because they toady to power and sit on the fence so. They're only half human.'[9]

It was inevitable that the half-human swine would retaliate against Pasternak sooner or later, especially as Zhdanov's attacks on Akhmatova and Zoshchenko had rapidly broadened out to embrace the whole of Soviet intellectual life. In this context continued failure to revile so unrepentant a nonconformist as Pasternak might well have endangered the literary bureaucrats guilty of such dereliction of duty.

Yet he remained almost unscathed for about six months after the persecution was first launched in August 1946. Such immunity is surprising in view of his dubious political record, and of his well-known inability or unwillingness to assume the prescribed submissive postures. It could not last for ever, and in early March 1947 he duly came under attack in a speech made by the novelist and senior literary functionary Aleksandr Fadeyev at a literary conference. Fadeyev called him 'ideologically alien' and 'not one of us'. Sounding the xenophobic note characteristic of the *Zhdanovshchina*, Fadeyev also claimed that Pasternak's popularity in foreign countries was no accident; it was no accident, either, that he was 'so much to the taste of our enemies'.[10] Shortly afterwards came a further denunciation. It issued from Aleksey Surkov, another senior literary functionary and a minor poet who was soon to become Pasternak's bitterest enemy. In an article of 22 March 1947, Surkov accused Pasternak of flaunting his aloofness from the modern era, of living as a hermit alien to his own age, of being at odds with the new society, and of referring to the Revolution 'with palpable ill will and even malice'.[11]

To students of the tonality of Soviet denunciation it was immediately obvious that Pasternak's disgrace was only partial, for Fadeyev and Surkov had not spoken in the ultra-harsh terms which were being applied to the major cultural criminals Akhmatova and Zoshchenko. The fact that Surkov's article carried its author's by-line was also a favourable sign, since the most authoritative expressions of official ill will tended to be published anonymously.[12] It was clear, therefore, that Pasternak had merely been reprimanded, not anathematized. But the reprimand was sufficiently severe to put a stop to the publication of his original work. A volume of his verse entitled *Selected Lyrics*, scheduled to appear in 1948 and set up in type, was pulped after advance notice of its appearance had already been given in the press. A few copies had been printed, and survived – as was typical of instances when such sudden interdictions were imposed at the last moment – and editors have made use of the material.[13]

Pasternak was well aware of the dangers threatening him at this period, and was relieved to receive a contract (which he had feared to lose) for the translation of Goethe's *Faust*. 'At least they've decided not to let me starve.'[14]

While Pasternak lapsed into disgrace severer than that of 1937–40, more sinister dangers still threatened. It is now known that the Minister of State Security, Viktor Abakumov, was taking a keen personal interest in him. Preparations had been made, it is alleged, to 'frame' him as a British spy, and the mere fact that his sisters lived in

Oxford would have been enough to clinch the charge if the decision had been taken to go ahead.[15] Whether through good luck, or through immunity secretly conferred on the poet by Stalin's orders, the case was never set in motion.

Semi-disgrace did not prevent Pasternak from using his prestige to help Olga Ivinskaya as she embarked on her new career of freelance translator. He was able to secure publication of work which – good, bad or indifferent – she might have found difficult to market without so influential a sponsor. Some of her translations were brought out under the lovers' joint signature, and he even took pleasure in passing off versions of hers as his own. At the time of their first meeting he himself was translating the Hungarian national poet Sándor Petöfi (1823–49), on whom he had already worked in the late 1930s; eleven of Petöfi's lyrics appeared in his version in a collection of the Hungarian's work published in Russian in 1949.

Pasternak explained to Ivinskaya the basic principles on which he worked as a translator. Economy was important; one must learn to keep the sense while discarding words; the work must not be prettified. The translator must 'manoeuvre, as on a razor's edge, between ... translation and improvisation on the theme of the original'. A general fault of modern translators was to offer an excessively literal version. Primed by such advice and by her lover's practical help, Ivinskaya was soon making a good living out of her new skill. The collaboration was to continue into the late 1950s, and she has described it with commendable modesty, making it clear that she always felt like an apprentice at the feet of a genius, punctilious though her lover was in treating her as his equal.[16]

Meanwhile Pasternak's great sequence of Shakespeare plays marched on. Parts One and Two of *Henry IV* appeared in 1948, followed by *King Lear* in 1949. Nor did the text of his previously published translations of Shakespeare remain inviolate. *Hamlet* was especially vulnerable to re-editing, and in one instance close examination of the text, as published in the 1947 edition, has revealed a startling variant transcending the concerns of purely literary scholarship. The passage in question consists of five lines from the hero's well-known soliloquy 'To be or not to be'. Vladimir Markov has shown that this passage, as translated in Pasternak's 1947 rendering of the play, bears only a sketchy relationship to the text of the previous editions (the first of which had appeared in 1940), while the relationship to Shakespeare's original is sketchier still. The most important point is this: when Shakespeare's words are carefully compared with Pasternak's translation, as emended for the 1947

Russian edition, it becomes clear that the new lines were inserted in order to express the translator's view of Stalinized Russia.[17]

A fair idea of the degree of swerve imparted to the original may be obtained by collating the lines in question with a literal back-translation into English of Pasternak's version as it appeared in the 1947 edition. Shakespeare's lines (from *Hamlet*, Act Three, Scene One) are given first.

Shakespeare's Text

For who would bear the whips and scorns of time,
The oppressor's wrong, the proud man's contumely,
The pangs of dispriz'd love, the law's delay,
The insolence of office, and the spurns
That patient merit of the unworthy takes.

Back-Translation into English of Pasternak's Russian Version of the above

Who, otherwise, would tolerate the spurious grandeur
Of rulers, the ignorant rudeness of potentates,
The universal hypocrisy, the impossibility
Of pouring out one's heart, unhappy love
And the belittling of merit by nonentities.

As Markov points out, Pasternak's 1947 version has nothing in common with the original except for the unhappy love. The passage 'sounds like a precise description of Pasternak's own lot or of the situation of many Soviet artists and intellectuals'. Here is no translation, but 'a lyrical confession camouflaged as a translation' – a kind of encoded message from Pasternak to the audience who attended performances of this version of *Hamlet*. It seems astonishing that such impertinence should have escaped official notice. But it did attract attention in the end: scrutiny of the 1956 edition of Pasternak's *Hamlet* shows that steps had been taken to change the offending passage yet again, and to render it innocuous. The episode helps to explain an accusation included by Fadeyev in his denunciation of Pasternak of March 1947: he charged the poet with infusing not only his original verse but even his translations with 'pernicious ideological obfuscation'.[18]

On one occasion the conflict between Pasternak and authority led to a political demonstration which was probably unique in Stalin's postwar fief. A recital of verse by some twenty poets was to be held on 23 February 1948 at the Polytechnic Museum, in Moscow's largest auditorium, and was advertised as follows. 'A POETRY EVENING ON

THE THEME: "DOWN WITH THE WARMONGERS! FOR A LASTING PEACE AND PEOPLE'S DEMOCRACY!"' As the billing shows, it was to be a propaganda exercise claiming Soviet foreign policy to be exclusively peaceful in contrast with the newly formed NATO alliance, which was to be pilloried as a conspiracy of warmongers.

This was just routine claptrap. But the advance billing had one surprise to offer – the inclusion of the name Boris Pasternak in the list of poets scheduled to perform. He was known to be in semi-disgrace, and he was also notorious for his stubborn failure to ape the sycophantic squirmings of other members of the writing fraternity. Why had he consented to appear on such a platform? Had he, of all people, at last agreed to seek reconciliation with the authorities by lending his support to the 'peace campaign'?

It was probably due to the presence of Pasternak's name on the programme that the house was packed with an excited audience when proceedings began. But in vain did members of the public peer at the score of poets who sat on the stage awaiting their turn to declaim. Pasternak was not there, and the performance had to begin without him. The first poet to step forward was Aleksey Surkov, who read out a work of his own composition proclaiming Winston Churchill as the evil genius of the Cold War. The poem was tepidly received until, just as the reciter was launched into his last line, the audience suddenly burst into loud applause. The occasion has been described by Max Hayward, then a member of the British Embassy in Moscow, who was sitting in the front row. 'Startled at this ovation, which was clearly not for him', Surkov glanced over his shoulder and 'saw what everybody else could see: Pasternak had slipped in from the wings and was just taking his seat in the back row.' This was not calculated to endear the late arrival to his enemy Surkov. But Pasternak made imploring gestures with his outstretched palms until the crowd eventually grew quiet and the recital could proceed. As it did so poet after poet received a lukewarm reception from an audience, listless and bored with literary eunuchs, which had eyes and ears for one man alone. When his turn at last came deafening applause broke out.

Here, if ever, was a time for the choreography of self-effacement, and Pasternak's mastery of that technique was equal to the task. He disdained the microphone used by his predecessors, and further dissociated himself from them by stepping down from the stage into the body of the hall. He then muttered to the audience that he chanced not to have written any verse on the evening's topic – and it is indeed true that the warmongering machinations of the Soviet Union's alleged enemies had never figured in his writings – but he did admit to having written some verse before the war, and his offer to recite from it provoked renewed applause. The bizarre performance began, and when he forgot his lines he was immediately prompted from different parts of the hall. So much for the policy of denying him publication: members of the audience seemed to know his work by heart in spite of the ban, and everyone appeared unmindful of the danger involved in displaying so much enthusiasm for a writer who was under a cloud.

The proceedings developed along even more dangerously un-orthodox lines when members of the audience began clamouring for the 'Sixty-Sixth'. They were referring to Shakespeare's Sixty-Sixth Sonnet, which had appeared in Pasternak's translation in 1940. In this work, which begins with the line 'Tir'd with all these, for restful death I cry', the English poet records the weariness of spirit provoked in him by a long catalogue of troubles. They include

> Strength by limping sway disabled,
> And art made tongue-tied by authority,
> And folly – doctor-like – controlling skill,
> And simple truth miscall'd simplicity,
> And captive good attending captain ill.

Art made tongue-tied by authority! Shakespeare might almost have had Zhdanov's cultural policies in mind when he framed that particular line. But on the present occasion art fortunately had the sense to remain tongue-tied, for Pasternak was sufficiently prudent to abstain from reciting an item so hazardous. Enough was enough, and the time had come to call a halt. An intermission was decreed from the chair, the excitement subsided, and the incident blew over without pro-voking dire consequences.[19]

Almost anyone else would have been arrested for such a gross act of political 'provocation', according to Hayward. The same observer has also claimed that Pasternak can only have escaped arrest during this period of acute oppression because Stalin had given specific in-structions that he was to be spared. It is a plausible inference, as is the suggestion that Pasternak owed his immunity to possessing a kind of 'fool's licence'.[20] There was, indeed, more than a little of the court jester in his attitude to Soviet authority. But was this penchant for buffoonery what actually saved his skin? One can only speculate.

Moscow witnessed a very different political demonstration in autumn 1948, when Golda Meir, Foreign Minister of the newly formed State of Israel, paid an official visit to the Soviet Union. Her presence inspired displays of enthusiasm from thousands of Soviet Jews who gathered on the streets of the capital. They did so without orders from authority, and this inevitably alerted Stalin's suspicions. He was reminded of the potential dangers to his system presented by Zionism in its capacity as a creed transcending other loyalties and affiliations. He therefore decided to mix a strong lacing of anti-Semitism into the brew of political oppression. The leading Jewish actor Solomon Mikhoels was assassinated, probably at Stalin's instigation; members of the Soviet wartime Jewish Anti-Fascist Committee were arrested; publications in Yiddish and the flourishing Yiddish theatre were closed down. An article in *Pravda*, entitled *On a Certain Group of Anti-Patriotic Theatre Critics*, gave the signal for a general attack on leading Jewish cultural figures. Some were arrested, some were dismissed from their posts, and all were pilloried in the press as 'rootless cosmopolitans': a thinly disguised synonym for those of Jewish origin.

Though Pasternak was a Jew, the anti-cosmopolitan campaign was less of a threat to him than might be assumed, since his attitude to Jewish culture was far from enthusiastic. That he would never have supported the persecution of Jews, or of anyone else, need not be said. But his own culture was no more and no less permeated by Jewish tradition than might be expected of any educated gentile, and he often went out of his way to deplore what he considered Jewish cultural exclusiveness. He has forcibly expressed that point of view several times in *Doctor Zhivago*, for which reason the Zionist leader David Ben-Gurion has condemned the novel as 'one of the most despicable books about Jews ever to be written by anyone of Jewish origin'. Pasternak once told Gladkov that he believed total assimilation to be the greatest boon available to the Jews. 'Personally I only feel at home in Russian culture.' He freely admitted that he had Jewish blood in his veins, yet claimed that nothing was more alien to him than Jewish nationalism, 'except, perhaps, Russian chauvinism'.[21] The reservation puts the matter in perspective.

Ivinskaya says that Pasternak's racial origins were a sore point with him. He was not embarrassed to be a Jew, but he was at a loss what to do or say 'when it transpired that his Jewish descent was never forgotten or forgiven', despite the fact that he was 'in spirit a profoundly Russian poet'.[22] This helps to explain his immunity during the anti-cosmopolitan period. Strongly infused with generalized anti-Semitism though the campaign was, it was directed more against those Russian Jews who considered themselves Jewish than against those who considered themselves Russian.

Many details have already been given about Pasternak's submerged conflict with Stalinism from 1936 onwards, but it remains to consider the greatest act of political defiance of his life: the composition and publication of *Doctor Zhivago*. His decision to forge ahead with the work sprang directly from post-war disillusion with the Stalinist system. 'I returned to my novel when I observed the thwarting of our hopes for post-war change.' This observation helps to confirm Hayward's claim that *Doctor Zhivago* 'was deliberately conceived as a challenge to everything Stalin and his régime stood for'.[23]

To write a novel was never a punishable offence in Stalin's Russia, provided always that the work contained an acceptable infusion of suitable publicity material. *Doctor Zhivago* had nothing of the sort to offer, however, and its author never pretended that it did. Nor did he make the slightest attempt to camouflage his involvement with fiction of a type potentially uncongenial to authority. He openly told anyone who would listen that he was writing a novel. He described the work's progress. He recounted the plot. He read passages of his drafts to individuals and at private gatherings. He did not hesitate to lend parts of the manuscript to interested persons.[24]

By 1948 a substantial section of the work, consisting of its earliest chapters, was already in typescript, and the author's plans were far enough advanced for him to inform a correspondent that his narrative would begin in 1903; it would be set in Moscow and the Urals; the hero would be a doctor with a strong literary bent, 'like Chekhov'; one chapter would consist of a book of poems attributed to the hero. At about the same time Pasternak read Chapter One of *Doctor Zhivago* to Anna Akhmatova over a period of four hours. It nearly precipitated an attack of her angina, he later reported.[25]

On 30 January 1948 he gave a semi-public recital from *Doctor Zhivago* to a Moscow theatre company. He first declaimed passages from his newly completed translation of Shakespeare's *Antony and Cleopatra*. Then he spoke of his novel, explaining that its hero was a doctor who had left the manuscript of certain poems behind after his death. He was referring to the lyrics which form the novel's last chapter, and he went on to recite several of them, including some which have Christian themes and have consequently never been published in the Soviet Union. The *pièce de résistance* was 'Hamlet'.[26] In these famous lines (later to figure as the first item in the *Zhivago* cycle) Shakespeare's hero, the actor playing Shakespeare's hero, Pasternak's hero, Pasternak himself and Jesus Christ are symbolically equated because all have accepted as a matter of duty an obligation imposed upon them, by God or destiny, to sacrifice themselves for others. Irony has rarely penetrated deeper: by the very act of reciting 'Hamlet' in public its author risked setting in motion precisely the process of martyrdom which is invoked in his text. How fortunate that his 'Hamlet' is so replete with multiple oblique implications: it is difficult to imagine even the most conscientious police informer, among those who must have been present at the recital, contriving to frame a lucid summary which the security authorities could have used as a weapon against the lyric's author.

Some disgraced Russian writers have been so well-known internationally that their arrest has had to be ruled out for fear of damage to the country's reputation as a self-proclaimed humane and civilized society. In the late 1940s Akhmatova was such a person, and Pasternak was another. But what the security authorities might not venture to do to them directly could be done to the individuals closest to them with the aim of extracting public recantations from the principals, of inhibiting their politically undesirable activities, and of calling the literary world as a whole to order. In Pasternak's case there was an extra motive in the drive to suppress a specific work in progress, *Doctor Zhivago*.

Such considerations led to the arrest of Olga Ivinskaya on the evening of 6 October 1949. She was conveyed to the Lubyanka and subjected to routine procedures which included meticulous body search, periods of solitary confinement, exposure to dazzling lights and deprivation of sleep. She was also confined with the usual 'stool pigeons' – other prisoners who had been assigned to worm confidences out of her and report their findings to the authorities. It was in such gruesome circumstances that she found herself to be pregnant. But this at least meant that her exposure to hunger and sleeplessness was slightly reduced as a concession to her condition. Another sign of distinction, and an indication of the overriding importance attached to Pasternak by authority, was the fact that she came to be interrogated in person by no less a figure than Minister of State Security Abakumov.[27]

Abakumov told her that Pasternak's fate depended on her answering all questions dutifully. He accused her of planning an illegal escape from the country; he dismissed her lover's views and his novel as anti-Soviet. These themes were later taken up by a less exalted interrogator, who revealed that Pasternak too was likely to be charged with planning to escape abroad, and with spying for the British. The new interrogator also expressed surprise that a Russian woman such as Ivinskaya could have fallen in love with 'this old Jew'. As the prisoner listened to these absurdities she found herself increasingly fearing for her lover's safety. She remembered the writers of the past who had disappeared for ever after being arrested by the security police: Babel,

Mandelstam, Tabidze and many others.

Further prison adventures followed. After being falsely informed that Boris Leonidovich had just arrived at the Lubyanka to visit her, Olga Vsevolodovna found herself face to face with someone very different: her daughter's English teacher, who – in accordance with the routine of Stalinist judicial practice – had been terrorized into bearing false witness to the effect that the lovers had tried to persuade an aviator to fly them out of the Soviet Union illegally. The shock of having this grotesque confrontation substituted for the expected meeting brought on the miscarriage of Ivinskaya's child by Pasternak.

Pasternak wept when he learnt of Ivinskaya's arrest. He was sure that he would never set eyes on her again. He took to calling Stalin a murderer, even in the presence of strangers. The emotions aroused in him by her arrest, and the disorder created in his life, are also reflected in Chapter Fourteen of *Doctor Zhivago*, at the point where the hero is left alone in an abandoned country house in the depths of the Urals. The same experience helped to inspire 'Parting', one of the finest lyrics of the *Zhivago* cycle. It is a description by and of the poet Zhivago – and, through extension, by and of the poet Pasternak – arriving at a beloved woman's house, only to discover that she has unexpectedly disappeared or been abducted.

> Her departure seems like flight.
> Everywhere are signs of havoc.[28]

The lyric includes poignant references to Pasternak–Zhivago's love for Olga–Lara, and to the sufferings imposed by separation from the beloved.

When Pasternak received news of Ivinskaya's pregnancy he went round Moscow informing his friends and acquaintances that she was bearing his child, and then proceeded to the Lubyanka in full expectation of collecting the infant. He had decided that it should be cared for by his wife. But Zinaida Nikolayevna, not surprisingly, 'made a terrible scene' over the proposal that she should rear his by-blow. When informing a friend of this, the prospective father added a comment breath-takingly insensitive in the context. 'I just had to put up with it.'

Only after being admitted to the Lubyanka did the poet learn that his unborn child had perished. He at once demanded pencil and paper, and wrote to Minister Abakumov demanding to be put in prison in his mistress's place. By now the author of *Doctor Zhivago* had acquired such kudos in the security world that several Lubyanka interrogators made excuses to look into the room where he was arguing with the official chiefly responsible for the case. They had never set eyes on such a prodigy before.

Pasternak and Ivinskaya both believed that her interrogations represented a determined attempt to fabricate an indictment against him as a British spy, and that the frame-up foundered on her heroic resistance to pressure. But it may be said without prejudice to her courage that, if Stalin indeed had decided to send Pasternak to the camps, thousands of purported mistresses could have been brought in off the streets and swiftly induced to bear witness to anything whatever.

Ivinskaya was sentenced, after several months of prison and interrogation, to five years in a hard labour camp, 'for close contact with persons suspected of espionage'. The sentence came under Article 58 of the Criminal Code, and was pronounced by a judicial tribunal in her absence. The prisoner was then transported, by train and forced marches, to the concentration camp network in the Mordovian Autonomous Republic several hundred miles south-east of Moscow. She was put into a grey convict's smock marked with her number in chloride of lime, and was set with other political prisoners – that is, those also sentenced under Article 58 – to tilling the dry, hard earth of Mordovia's plains as they sweltered in the summer heat. Thoughts of Boris Leonidovich helped to maintain her morale. He sent her poems and wrote her love letters, trying to conceal their origin from the camp censors by signing them 'Mother' and referring to himself in the third person. 'He says . . . you are the most sublime expression of his own being that he could ever dream of. . . . He lives in a fantastic world, and says that it consists entirely of you.'[29]

After Ivinskaya's arrest Pasternak took to seeing more of Akhmatova, with whom he came to share a similar grief when her son was arrested on 6 November 1949. The young man was treated more severely than Ivinskaya, being beaten by his interrogator over a period of three months; he was also forced to sign a statement, very much in the period's idiom, confessing that his mother had invited him to assassinate the cultural satrap Zhdanov. Meanwhile she was doing what she could to effect his release. In particular she forced herself to make abject public obeisance by bringing out a cycle of fifteen lyrics entitled *Glory to Peace* in the weekly *Ogonyok*. They express enthusiasm, again in the idiom of the period, for the officially promoted peace campaign whereby approval of Soviet foreign policy was identified with a hatred of war and warmongers. Nor was the inspirer of the peace campaign ignored in Akhmatova's text.

> Where Stalin is, there too are freedom,
> Peace and earth's grandeur.[30]

Unfortunately this act of self-humiliation failed to secure her son's freedom.

Pasternak wrote to a friend welcoming the appearance of Akhmatova's *Glory to Peace*. His reaction was understandable in one who had her welfare at heart, since the mere acceptance of her poems for publication was a favourable sign: from those consigned to ultimate disgrace even the freedom to demean themselves by public recantation was withheld. Pasternak also noted that one effect of the publication of Akhmatova's Stalin-eulogizing poems was that everyone had begun to expect something similar from him. 'They have all started looking expectantly in my direction.' But he considered that he had already been through that phase. 'Everything she has said now I had already said twenty years ago.'[31] He must have been alluding to the material in *Second Birth* praising Stalinism, and it seems clear that no form of pressure could ever induce him to write in that manner again. Even for the person nearest to him he would not put his name to such material. He was deeply distressed by Ivinskaya's fate, as has been noted; he tried to intervene on her behalf; he sent her messages of love and copies of his poems. He also supported her two children financially in her absence. But he was not prepared to adopt the postures of servility which Akhmatova herself had so understandably – and, indeed, nobly – been willing to assume in the hope of saving her son. Above all, he was unwilling to abandon *Doctor Zhivago*. The authorities may have believed themselves able to extort that concession through the victimization of Ivinskaya. But if so they had mistaken their man.

Though Pasternak's original writings were to be denied publication during the remainder of Stalin's life, his Russian versions of foreign poets continued to appear in print, and to such effect that he arguably reached the peak of his translation career during Ivinskaya's years of durance. In this period he completed the sequence of Shakespeare plays which he had begun publishing in 1940. *King Lear* appeared in 1949, and in an impressive two-volume edition of the seven Shakespeare plays which he had so far translated. *Macbeth*, the last in the series of eight, followed in 1951. As the successive translations came off the presses so did the translator reveal a decreasing urge to impart slight swerves to Shakespeare through such practices as toning down the more explicit sexual references, rendering the young heroines more ladylike, and diluting the characteristic emphasis of the original on humanity's evil potentialities. The later a given translation stands in the succession, the less evident is any attempt on Pasternak's part to turn it into an original artistic creation, and the greater is his tendency to content himself with workmanlike fidelity.

Pasternak's versions of Shakespeare are rivalled, perhaps even eclipsed, by his next major assignment – the translation of both parts of Goethe's *Faust*. It, too, belongs to the time of Olga Ivinskaya's absence: the work was spread over the years 1949–52. *Faust* may well represent the climax of Pasternak's translating career, according to Vladimir Markov.[32] The same critic's close study of the text has thrown up a further instance of the translator impishly tampering with his original, just as he had previously doctored Hamlet's soliloquy 'To be or not to be' in order to express covert criticism of Stalin's oppressions. In *Faust* the passage in question comes from Baucis's speech about the ornamental canal which is described as being built by forced labour in Part Two, Act Five. It reads as follows in Goethe's original.

> Menschenopfer mussten bluten,
> Nachts erscholl des Jammers Qual;
> Meerab flossen Feuergluten,
> Morgens war es ein Kanal.

> Human victims had to bleed.
> Grief's lament rang out at night;
> Fiery glows flowed from the sea.
> By morning it was a canal.

Pasternak has converted this quatrain into a two-line rhetorical question demanding the answer 'no' and unmistakably referring to Stalin's notorious canal-building projects – the White Sea Canal and others – which were accomplished by convict labour with heavy loss of life from the early 1930s onwards. The couplet in question reads as follows.

> Человеческие жертвы
> Окупает ли канал?

> Those human sacrifices –
> Is a canal worth that?

The lines took this form in the first complete edition of Pasternak's *Faust*, that of 1953. But in later editions they appear in a toned-down rendering,[33] just as the offending *Hamlet* speech later resurfaced in a modified form designed to conceal the impertinences with which the translator had privily loaded it. These bowdlerizations presumably occurred through the intervention of unknown custodians of political decorum.

Pasternak's translation of *Faust* met with the degree of abuse appropriate to a semi-disgraced author. One reviewer described the work as 'decadent', while another accused the translator of distorting Goethe's ideas in order to defend the reactionary theory of 'pure art'. He was said to have spiked his text with an aesthetic and individualist flavour, while saddling Goethe with reactionary views. Writing to Tsvetayeva's daughter Ariadna Efron, now in distant exile after release from the camps, Pasternak lamented that he had been accused of 'glossing over Goethe's progressive ideas'. He added a pungent query: 'What are they?'[34]

Much as Pasternak admired Goethe, he did so this side of idolatry where the Second Part of *Faust* was concerned. In a letter of 5 December 1950 he referred to *Faust*, Part Two, as 'ridiculous', and complained that translating it was hampering his other literary activity. But he remained grateful to translation for providing his chief source of income. Shakespeare and Goethe gave him the further satisfaction of handling English and German, the two foreign languages which he knew best. He preferred working from these tongues to the very different kind of translation which had also brought him success – that made from languages of which he was ignorant. In June 1952 he wrote that he must never again translate from interlinear cribs, but only from languages that he knew. His success with Goethe and Shakespeare was acclaimed by Akhmatova. She compared his *Henry IV* with the original and pronounced it 'marvellous'. She had some reservations about *Faust*, however. While considering the Archangels' lines at the beginning of the Prologue to Part One to be an improvement on Goethe, she felt that Pasternak had failed to make Margarete adequately young and naive in the early pages of the poem.[35]

In his choice of texts for translation Pasternak must have been guided by his strong desire to speak out as a witness to his age, and reference has already been made to the potent symbolical significance which Shakespeare's Hamlet had for him as an epigone of Jesus Christ and forerunner of himself. It is perhaps significant, too, that he chose to end his series of Shakespeare translations with *Macbeth*, where the hero's advance to supreme power through a succession of blood-boltered corpses offers a striking parallel to Stalin's career. Trotsky was, perhaps, the Kremlin Highlander's Duncan, and Bukharin his Banquo? Such considerations have led one connoisseur of Pasternak to

ABOVE Rozaliya and Leonid Pasternak, Odessa, 1896.

BELOW Boris Pasternak, aged eight, sketched by his father.

LEFT Pasternak as a youth.

BELOW The Pasternak family at Molodi during the First World War. *Left to right, standing:* Leonid, Boris, Aleksandr, Josephine; *seated:* Rozaliya, Berta Kaufman (Rozaliya's mother), Lydia.

ABOVE Pasternak in 1913.

BELOW Pasternak with his first wife
Yevgeniya and their son Yevgeny,
Leningrad, 1924.

ABOVE Tsvetayeva. BELOW Mayakovsky.   ABOVE Akhmatova. BELOW Mandelstam.

LEFT Nina and Titsian Tabidze, Tiflis, 1933.

BELOW Boris and Zinaida Pasternak with Zinaida's son by her first marriage (Adrian Neygauz), 1934.

ABOVE Olga Ivinskaya, 1936.

BELOW Pasternak at Peredelkino, 1946.

ABOVE Pasternak with his wife
Zinaida (*right*) and Nina Tabidze
shortly after the Nobel Prize
announcement, October 1958.

LEFT Pasternak and Olga Ivinskaya,
1960.

Pasternak in his garden at Peredelkino shortly before his death.

claim that he 'chose for translation works which said things he could no longer publicly express in his own name'. The same authority also says that Pasternak intended *Faust* to 'speak as eloquently for himself as *Hamlet* had done'.[36] Still, however much he may have manipulated translation to make political statements, he 'was obviously not using Shakespeare's works simply as a means for topical comment', as another student of his work has usefully pointed out.[37] There could never have been a question of so dedicated an artist subordinating his art to politics to that extent.

Devoted as Pasternak was to the imprisoned Olga, he did not spend the years of her enforced absence brooding exclusively on her sufferings. He was more inclined to count his blessings, and even to number the companionship of his wife among them. On 18 November 1950 he wrote to a Georgian friend that Zinaida and he were 'one inseparable piece of existence just like the way I walk on the floor or see with my eyes'. On 5 December, even as Olga Vsevolodovna shivered in the now frozen wastes of Mordovia, Boris Leonidovich was writing to Tabidze's widow Nina that he was 'more than at any time satisfied' with his life and did not desire any changes.[38]

Again and again during the years of Ivinskaya's absence Pasternak chose to stress the buoyancy of his morale. He wrote to Nina Tabidze in early 1951 to say how grateful he was to heaven for having led so happy a life. Its fundamental bases had been 'the example of my father's work, love of music and Scriabin, two or three chords in my own writing, night in the Russian countryside, the Revolution, Georgia'. He rejoiced that fate had not spoilt him with outward success, but had treated him 'with apparent severity'. He had always lived productively, by practical work, and had advanced in his trade. These letters emphasize how unremittingly Pasternak had always indulged in hard, concentrated work. He was used, he said, to having his day 'filled with work as it is filled with the sun and the sky'.[39]

Such was his sense of mission, such were his high spirits, that he was no more daunted by serious illness than by the absence of his beloved. She has ascribed his first heart attack, which occurred in 1950, to separation from her. No doubt this excursion into medical diagnosis comforted her. But it seems to exaggerate the extent to which she was at all times the be-all and end-all of her lover's existence.

When a second, more serious, attack followed in autumn 1952 the poet was removed to a large Moscow hospital so crowded that he was detained in a reception room for five hours, and then had to spend the night in a corridor. In spite of periodical fainting and vomiting, in spite of recurrent thoughts of death, he experienced 'a wonderful feeling of calm and bliss'. He wrote to Nina Tabidze stressing the religious aspects of the experience, this being one of the few passages outside the pages of *Doctor Zhivago* in which he has directly testified to the Christian faith of his later years. He describes feeling that his last moment had arrived, and tells how he responded with a prayer. 'Lord ..., I thank you for having laid on the paints so thickly and for having made life and death the same as your language – majestic and musical.' He also thanked God for having made him a creative artist, 'and for having prepared me all my life for this night'. This moving experience made the poet weep for joy. He has expressed the gamut of his deathbed sensations in a celebrated lyric, 'In Hospital'. As a patient's personal details are being recorded on a form,

> Suddenly from the nurse's questions,
> And from the way she shook her head,
> He saw he'd little chance of getting
> Out of this rigmarole alive.

The sick man rejoices to proclaim himself and his role in life as gifts from the Almighty, and concludes as follows.

> Dying in bed in hospital,
> I feel myself warmed by your hands.
> You hold me like your artifact,
> Hide me like ring in jewel case.[40]

Reflecting on his illness in a letter to Ivinskaya's mother of 2 January 1953, Pasternak once again stressed that he had never ceased to thank Providence for the life he had led, which was the best he could have wished for. He stressed the part played in his recovery by his wife's care. 'She saved me. I owe my life to her.' His restoration to health left him with a single obsession. He must finish his novel.[41]

Happily, Pasternak emerged from this supposed deathbed to yet another rebirth. He also underwent extensive dental surgery which greatly altered his appearance. Akhmatova approved. 'The old horsy look did do something special for his face, of course, but he's far better this way – pale, handsome, a head of great nobility.' It was the end of the yellowish teeth with wide gaps in the middle which had so impressed Ivinskaya at their first meeting. The remodelling of his jaw and his new, immaculate dentures (manufactured abroad) were to render him 'more classically handsome' in his beloved's eyes.[42] They also help to emphasize the wide variety of special privileges available to élite citizens of Stalin's Russia – a category to which Pasternak continued, in effect, to belong despite his semi-disgrace. With one hand the regime removes his beloved Olga to the slavery of the labour camps; with the other it furnishes preferential dental treatment far beyond the reach of the population at large.

8

BIRTH PANGS OF A NOVELIST

Stalin's death on 5 March 1953 marked the end of a quarter of a century's particularly harsh regimentation, and his passing was welcomed for the hope of widespread relaxation which it seemed to offer. The hope was to be justified, but only in limited degree, during the four-year struggle for power between Nikita Khrushchev and his rivals which immediately followed, and also during the succeeding period – that of Khrushchev's ascendancy as the country's principal political figure from 1957 onwards. It was against this background that Pasternak lived out his last seven years of life.

The period was characterized by extreme hesitancy on the cultural front. There were alternating phases of relaxation, commonly termed 'thaws', and of renewed regimentation, commonly known as 'crack-downs' or 'freeze-ups'. The period had the advantage that conditions were never, even during the severest frosts, to revert to the harshness of fully developed Stalinism. It had the disadvantage that – even during the most benign of thaws – relaxation was never to approach what either Pasternak, or any other intelligent person uncommitted to the Kremlin's brand of Communism, would be likely to accept as a desirable degree of freedom from interference by political authority.

The release of large numbers of political prisoners from the camps was an especially welcome feature of post-Stalin policy. Though it took several years to restore freedom to many of the rank-and-file victims, the effect was almost immediate in the case which concerned Boris Leonidovich most intimately: Olga Vsevolodovna was set free in autumn 1953, only a few months after the dictator's death. This concession was probably due to the special significance attached to the Pasternak affair by the security authorities, and the poet himself liked to think that it was his name which had cut short his companion's ordeal. She had served four years altogether, including the period preceding the pronouncement of her five-year sentence. Ivinskaya has claimed that her release is commemorated in 'Folk Tale', the *Zhivago* lyric in which a knight saves a maiden from a fire-breathing dragon.[1]

Though Pasternak was naturally delighted by Ivinskaya's release, her memoirs make it clear that he was by no means singlemindedly determined to reunite his fate with hers at the first opportunity. He was still convinced that he owed his recovery from his heart attack of 1952 to the devoted care of his wife, and had decided to express his gratitude by sacrificing his personal feelings and abandoning his liaison with Ivinskaya. He also had a more mundane reason for shrinking from a reunion, according to her own frank account of the matter, since he had erroneously assumed that the appalling conditions of the camps must inevitably have turned her into 'a fearful hag'.[2]

Instead of eagerly seeking out his beloved immediately after hearing the news of her release, he accordingly took the eccentric step of asking her teenaged daughter Irina to speak to her mother on his behalf. His message was that he still loved her, but that a change might now take place in their relations. This wounding message Irina was sensible enough to leave undelivered at the time. She only disclosed it to her mother many years after Pasternak's death, prompting Ivinskaya to reflect that her lover had been 'a compound of candour, guileless charm and arrant cruelty'. In any case Pasternak seems to have thrown off his reservations fairly promptly, for the lovers soon contrived to be reunited, and without Olga Vsevolodovna having cause to suspect Boris Leonidovich's brief flirtation with perfidy. When they at last met, all his reservations were swept aside on a tidal flood of passion, according to her account. She says that they were carried away by the 'living black magic of hot embraces' invoked in his lyric 'Bacchanalia', claiming that the poem (about a sensual orgy enacted by a ballerina and an elderly voluptuary) was really about her and her lover. 'We were both gripped by a kind of desperate tenderness and a resolve to stay together for ever.'[3]

After Ivinskaya's release she and Pasternak fell into the domestic routine which they were to follow during the rest of his life: they were to remain intimate companions, but only to the limited extent permitted by his decision not to abandon his wife and the comfortable residence, with its excellent working conditions, which she maintained for him at Peredelkino. In summer 1954 Ivinskaya dispatched her two children and her mother to stay with a relative, after which the lovers had her Potapov Street flat to themselves. She was pregnant by Pasternak for the second time, but he airily brushed aside any difficulties which might be expected to arise. 'Surely the earth is big enough for your and my child.' It was not to prove so in the event: she unfortunately suffered another miscarriage at the end of August, and Pasternak wept bitterly over the loss.[4]

Olga Vsevolodovna now began to rent, in or near Peredelkino, a succession of lodgings in which she could house members of her family and receive her lover with decreasing degrees of inconvenience. She and Boris Leonidovich thus entered on the openly acknowledged arrangement of his last years, whereby a short stroll would take him into the arms of his beloved whenever he wished. Meanwhile the long-suffering Zinaida Nikolayevna retained her status as the mistress of the efficiently managed 'big house', as they took to calling the Peredelkino dacha. It was one of those compromise solutions, based on an equipoise of tension, which sometimes prove workable even though they may not be wholly satisfactory to any of the parties concerned. As the object of so much feminine concern, Pasternak may be thought to have had either the best or the worst of the bargain, since the situation had the advantage or disadvantage of exposing him to a double measure of marital exhortation. His wife was forced to tolerate the presence of his mistress a few stone's throws from her front door. Meanwhile his mistress was denouncing him for his unwillingness to obtain a divorce and to bestow on herself the protection against official harassment that she would have received by taking his name of legal right.

No serious account of Pasternak's life in the first post-Stalin years can pass over an unsavoury allegation made against Olga Ivinskaya by Lidiya Chukovskaya in her memoirs of Akhmatova. It is an accusation of meanness much at variance with the idyllic picture of Pasternak's beloved conveyed in her own memoirs, and its terms are as follows. She had become friendly, before her release from the Potma concentration camps in autumn 1953, with a fellow convict – the minor writer Nadezhda Adolf-Nadezhdina, who chanced to be a close friend of Chukovskaya's. After being released from the camps, Ivinskaya agreed to mail food parcels and sums of money provided by Chukovskaya to Adolf-Nadezhdina, who remained imprisoned at Potma, and the arrangement continued in force for two-and-a-half years, from autumn 1953 onwards. But when, in April 1956, Adolf-Nadezhdina herself was finally released, it turned out that not a single parcel or remittance had reached her. The conclusion, inescapable to Chukovskaya, was that Ivinskaya had stolen all these gifts – which, had they been delivered, could have meant the difference between life and death.[5]

The accusation is clearly put forward in good faith, but cannot be regarded as proven. Theft by postal employees, warders, camp officials, 'trusties' or other prisoners could not be ruled out by anyone familiar with the country and period. There is also the point that

Nadezhda Mandelstam, an objective judge, refused to believe in Ivinskaya's guilt. But the charge was fully credited by Chukovskaya, who cannot be accused of spitefulness, pettiness or malice where other matters are concerned. Ivinskaya's guilt was also credited by Akhmatova. She spoke most indignantly on the subject – and with reason, should the charge have been true. 'To rob someone in a concentration camp! And when she herself was at liberty! While being generously supported by Boris Leonidovich – *and not by him alone, presumably*.'[6] The waspish afterthought, here italicized, is yet another reminder that universal acceptance has not been accorded to the picture of Ivinskaya purveyed in her own memoirs. But the waspishness was clearly the product of jealousy, and the remark must not be taken as sustaining a charge of sexual promiscuity or venality.

Akhmatova told Chukovskaya that Pasternak should be informed of Ivinskaya's alleged misdeeds. But Chukovskaya flatly refused to speak to him about the matter because she could not bear to hurt him. She was also certain that he would never believe anything so damaging to his adored Olga's reputation, especially as there was no concrete evidence to back the charge. Chukovskaya, who had known Ivinskaya in the early post-war years when they had been colleagues on the staff of *Novy mir*, vented her disapproval by recalling the other as she had seemed in those days: 'slovenly, pathologically mendacious, boorish', and much given to boasting about her love affairs.[7] Nothing could be further from the heroine of *Doctor Zhivago* than this picture of her prototype painted by an observer normally shrewd and accurate in her comments.

For the phase of cultural relaxation which followed Stalin's death, and which continued into 1954, the term First Thaw is sometimes used to distinguish it from the Second Thaw of 1956. The meteorological metaphor derives from Ilya Ehrenburg's novel *The Thaw* (Part One, 1954), which was remarkable for adopting an apolitical stance such as had long been excluded from Soviet-published literature. In the same spirit and at roughly the same time certain literary articles, by V. Pomerantsev and F. Abramov, attempted to assert the right of authors and critics to reflect their individual vision of the world more freely than had been permitted for many years. These works were all published by *Novy mir*, of which the liberal poet Aleksandr Tvardovsky had become editor in succession to Simonov.

Pasternak was little impressed by the Thaw, and recorded his continuing 'general alienation from what is happening in literature and from literary circles' in a letter of September 1953.[8] Still, one of the most notable symptoms of the change of climate was that it again became possible to publish Pasternak the creative artist. Though Pasternak the translator had been publishable all along, no new, original verse or prose by him had appeared under a Soviet imprint since the collection *Earth's Expanse* of 1945. But now, after this nine-year interval, the journal *Znamya* brought out ten new poems from his pen in April 1954, having no cause to suspect that they would later figure in the greatest literary scandal of the Soviet period. They are, in fact, ten out of the twenty-five lyrics that were later to be published abroad as the verse cycle forming the last chapter of *Doctor Zhivago*. These poems were prefaced in *Znamya* by a note in which Pasternak recorded the progress of his novel, explaining that it embraced the period 1903–29, with an epilogue set in the Second World War. 'The hero is Yury Andreyevich Zhivago, a doctor, an intellectual, a seeker, a man of creative and artistic turn, who dies in 1929. He leaves behind some memoirs and amongst other papers some . . . verse, part of which is offered here and which, grouped together, will form the novel's final chapter.'[9]

Before the First Thaw had melted much ice the authorities began to fear a flash flood, and accordingly imposed a return to sub-zero conditions. In the course of 1954 Tvardovsky was removed from the editorship of *Novy mir* – he was to reassume it a few years later – and the publication of sensitive material was halted. But it was easier to control publication than composition, and Pasternak pressed on with his novel undeterred. In 1955 *Doctor Zhivago* was at last completed. Clean and carefully revised typescript copies were prepared, and the decision was taken to offer them for publication in the Soviet Union. Of the two copies submitted for serialization in journals, Pasternak sent one to *Znamya* and the other to *Novy mir*. A third was submitted to Goslitizdat with a view to publication in book form. But the author had grave doubts about the chances of the work being accepted by these or any other Soviet outlets. In the autumn he told Ivinskaya that nothing in the world would induce a Soviet editor to issue something which, as he himself now realized after completing the work, failed 'to depict the Revolution as a cream cake'.[10]

After Olga Ivinskaya's return from the camps in autumn 1953 other individuals linked to the Pasternak saga were released in slow succession: Aleksandr Gladkov in 1954, Tsvetayeva's daughter Ariadna Efron in 1955, Akhmatova's son Lev Gumilyov in 1956. Pasternak transferred to Ariadna Efron, who had suffered sixteen years of camp and exile, some of the concern that he had felt for her mother the poet. Ariadna was now made welcome at Peredelkino, where she reinforced the formidable battery of feminine advice available to Boris Leonidovich in his last years, and where she would criticize the disorderliness of his domestic arrangements with the frankness of an old friend. Another link with the past was revived when, in October 1955, the authorities at last released information on the Georgian poet Titsian Tabidze, of whom nothing had been heard since his arrest in 1937; only now was it officially disclosed that Tabidze had been executed two months after his original disappearance.[11]

The second and more extensive Thaw of the post-Stalin period was introduced by Khrushchev's celebrated oration, delivered on 24–5 February 1956 to the Twentieth Congress of the Communist Party of the Soviet Union. This so-called 'Secret Speech' has never been published in the USSR, but was leaked abroad and issued by the American State Department.

Khrushchev's denunciation of Stalin chiefly concentrated on two charges: on his failure to take proper defence measures during the period before the war, and on his slaughter of leading Communists. Almost nothing was said about the oppression of peasants under collectivization or of the population as a whole under the *Yezhov-shchina*. In the context of those widespread persecutions Khrushchev's denunciation was almost comically mild, and set the tone for the formula (soon to be adopted) whereby the mass atrocities of 1930–53 were to be chastely invoked in public as 'events associated with the cult of J. V. Stalin'. Khrushchev's motive for criticizing Stalin was by no means exclusively a concern for the public weal, since he was able to exploit the widespread revulsion against the dead leader to strengthen his own power at the expense of highly placed rivals. He was referring to the 'Anti-Party Group', consisting of Malenkov, Molotov and others whom Khrushchev was soon to overthrow – partly through his success in associating them with Stalin's misdeeds.

To disparage Stalin and Stalinism at a Party Congress, however mildly and for whatever reason, was to send a shock wave of expectancy through the country and the world. Could the Soviet Union be on the verge of radically transforming its political and social system? In 1956 anything seemed possible, particularly as Khrushchev publicly paraded such vitality and impulsiveness that he seemed capable of breaking down any barrier whatever, if only in a fit of simulated drunken rage.

Pasternak was ready to give Khrushchev due credit for denouncing Stalin. But he had not lost his dislike of public posturing, and signally failed to warm to Khrushchev's flamboyant personality. His verdict on Khrushchev and Stalin was uncompromising, and it lumped them together. 'For so long our Tsar was a maniac and a murderer; now it's a fool and a pig.' Boris Leonidovich happened to read George Orwell's *Animal Farm* at about this time, and he compared Khrushchev to the chief hog in that allegory. He was also heard to say – somewhat mysteriously – that the new Soviet leader wore his collar round the wrong part of his anatomy.[12] As for the Cult of J. V. Stalin's Personality, Pasternak found the formula ridiculous. Whatever Stalin's faults may have been, he had at least never been a nonentity such as – in Pasternak's opinion – the Soviet Union's new rulers were. He wrote a short poem, 'Cult of Personality', to point out that the change in leadership had brought no significant improvement. The cult of personality might have been dethroned, but the cults of pompous verbiage, philistinism and mediocrity had increased a hundredfold.

> While the cult of personality's been thoroughly besmirched,
> That of evil and monotony have never prospered more.

The country's new rulers are dismissed as 'group photographs of pig snouts', and the poem ends by denouncing yet another cult, that of vulgarity, for provoking the drunken suicide of those who can bear it no longer.[13]

The last detail alludes to an event of 13 May 1956, the suicide by shooting of Aleksandr Fadeyev. He had risen from humble beginnings as a novelist of talent to become the country's most powerful literary functionary and one of its most distinguished alcoholics. He was also notorious for his double standards. At one moment he would publicly abuse Pasternak (as has already been mentioned) for writing verse 'remote from life'; at another he would order a cognac in a café and declaim at length what he called 'real poetry' – the verse of Pasternak. The poet once said that Fadeyev would be fully capable 'of having me hung, drawn and quartered' before getting drunk and saying 'how sorry he was for me and what a splendid fellow I had been'. Pasternak was sure that Fadeyev must have worn on his face, even as he pulled the fatal trigger, the same guilty grin which he had retained throughout his long career of political intrigue. Pasternak also pronounced over the dead man's body, as it lay in state in Moscow's House of Unions, a wry obituary comment. 'Aleksandr Aleksandrovich has rehabilitated himself.'[14]

After Khrushchev's 'Secret Speech' Pasternak once again found himself in demand as a Soviet-published author, but only for works other than *Doctor Zhivago*. In September 1956 *Znamya* brought out a further batch of eight new lyrics from his pen; they were later to be incorporated in the cycle *When Skies Clear*. But *Znamya* had still not decided whether or not to publish *Doctor Zhivago*. Goslitizdat was also stalling about Pasternak's novel, while remaining eager to undertake an ambitious edition of his poetry. The plan was to issue a large one-volume collection of verse from all periods of his life. It was to include the entire cycle of poems from *Doctor Zhivago*, and Pasternak was also to supply a preface in the form of a sizeable autobiographical memoir. A contract was signed, a publisher's editor was appointed, and the author set to work.

These successes meant little to him so long as a question mark hung over the future of *Doctor Zhivago*. But weeks turned into months after the 'Secret Speech' without him receiving an answer from any of the three Soviet concerns to which the novel had been submitted in 1955. Then he suddenly took the fateful decision to hand over a typescript of the work for publication outside the USSR. The occasion was a visit made to Peredelkino in May 1956 by Sergio d'Angelo, a Moscow-based associate of the well-known Milan publisher Feltrinelli. The Italian publisher's interest was natural enough, since rumours of *Doctor Zhivago* were already causing considerable stir in the non-Soviet world, and the novel would clearly represent a scoop to any Western publisher fortunate enough to secure it.

Pasternak was working in his garden when d'Angelo arrived. The guest received the usual cordial welcome from the master of the house, and broached the purpose of his visit during a long talk on the verandah. When he enquired whether any objection of principle had been raised against the novel by a Soviet publisher, he was told that there had been no response to it at all, favourable or unfavourable. In the end Pasternak let himself be talked into handing over the typescript. As he said goodbye at the gate he remarked, 'You've invited me to my own execution.'[15]

Fortunately this gloomy prediction was not to be fulfilled in the literal sense. It is possible, however, that Pasternak's death, which occurred four years later, was hastened through a figurative form of 'execution' – the vicious, officially inspired harassment to which the foreign publication of *Doctor Zhivago* eventually exposed him in his native country.

Pasternak's main cause for apprehension, when he handed over the typescript, was not so much the text of his novel as the prospect of it being brought out in countries outside the Soviet orbit without official Soviet sanction. Not since the 1920s had Soviet-based writers been in a position to arrange for their work to receive its first publication abroad. Pasternak himself had done so at the time. But then, in 1929 and through the Pilnyak–Zamyatin scandal, the foreign publication of literary works by Soviet-domiciled writers had suddenly become inadmissible. Now, nearly thirty years later, the prohibition still remained in force, and the whole subject was still acutely sensitive. Since 1929 no significant new item of imaginative literature, written in the Soviet Union but denied publication there, had been brought out abroad.

It is easy to overlook the cardinal importance of *Doctor Zhivago* in reviving a procedure long discontinued. The foreign publication of writings of the type under discussion (composed in the Soviet Union but denied a Soviet outlet) has become so common an occurrence in the years following the scandal which raged round Pasternak's novel that it is now taken for granted. Works by Andrey Sinyavsky, Alexander Solzhenitsyn and numerous other famous or less famous non-conformist Russian writers, Soviet-domiciled at the time in question, have been brought out abroad in the last three decades – some pseudonymously, some under the author's true name – while remaining unpublished in their country of origin. Some of the writers concerned have been savagely denounced in the Soviet media; some have been tried and imprisoned; some have been bundled into exile. One or two have suffered all these fates. But works of this type have continued to filter through. In addition to *belles-lettres* these (in effect) contraband goods have included much valuable material on Pasternak himself: the memoirs of Nadezhda Mandelstam, Olga Ivinskaya, Lidiya Chukovskaya and Aleksandr Gladkov. But the foreign publication of this vast corpus of Russian literary contraband must not be allowed to obscure the fact that it was *Doctor Zhivago* which initiated the practice in the post-war period. Pasternak it was who blazed the trail now so well worn.

Though events were to prove Pasternak's forebodings of May 1956 not to have been unduly alarmist, there were also reasons for hoping, at the time, that he might have a chance of coming out of the affair unscathed – especially since Khrushchev's 'Secret Speech', delivered some three months before the handover of the novel, had opened up the prospect of widespread relaxation in the Soviet intellectual world. There was a cautious awareness that a new era had dawned, and that its guidelines had yet to be drawn up. Under these conditions almost anything seemed possible, even that a novel such as *Doctor Zhivago* might be brought out, uncensored, in its country of origin.

Certain it is that the heavens did not fall on Pasternak immediately after the handover. Nearly two-and-a-half years were to follow that momentous event without his being exposed to serious molestation by Soviet authority. It even seems likely that, had it not been for the offer of the Nobel Prize in October 1958, he might have lived out his last years in relative peace. However, as events were to prove in due course, *Doctor Zhivago* was a package of high explosive. The fuse was lit with the handover of May 1956.

Pasternak's wife and mistress were both quick to sense the perils involved in sending *Doctor Zhivago* abroad, and both deplored his impulsive decision to give the novel to the Italians. But he brushed their protests aside. He was ready to face all the troubles that might follow, knowing that Soviet authority would not long remain ignorant of the handover.

It is a measure of the importance attached to Pasternak by the Soviet leadership that a major role in determining the fate of his novel was assigned to an official as senior as Dmitry Polikarpov – head of the Cultural Department of the Party's Central Committee, and responsible for policy towards literature. His tactic was infinitely gentler than the strong-arm methods of the Stalin era, since he attempted to work on Pasternak through Olga Ivinskaya by playing on her influence over her beloved and on her concern for their joint welfare. He urged her to secure the immediate return of the typescript from d'Angelo. But it turned out that the fatal document was already beyond the Central Committee's reach, having been dispatched to Feltrinelli in Milan.[16]

This news caused Polikarpov to change his tactics. Since he was forced to accept foreign publication as inevitable, he decided to make the best of a bad job by promoting parallel publication at home – but in an edition carefully doctored to eliminate the material most likely to involve Kremlinite loss of face. With luck such an emasculated version might be foisted on the foreign publishers too, in the guise of last-minute author's corrections. It would not be easy, but it seemed worth trying. Polikarpov accordingly telephoned Goslitizdat, and suggested that a contract to publish *Doctor Zhivago* (with suitable cuts and changes) should be offered to the author. Suggestions from the Central Committee are not lightly turned down, and Goslitizdat – having already undertaken to bring out the comprehensive one-volume collection of Pasternak's verse mentioned above – readily took on the novel as well.[17]

Meanwhile the backwash of Khrushchev's 'Secret Speech' had by no means subsided. The release of prisoners from the camps was being stepped up, as was the official 'rehabilitation' – in many cases posthumous – of individual victims of the Stalin terror. As for literary publications, always the most sensitive barometer of Soviet political change, writers were now conceded greater freedom than had been available in 1953-4 to publish imaginative works implying disapproval of the country's administrative, political and social arrangements. The Second Thaw had begun, and Soviet books and journals were now bringing out material more critical of their system than had been permitted for a quarter of a century. The result was that 1956 became known abroad as the USSR's 'year of protest'.

The most widely discussed work of Protest Literature was Vladimir Dudintsev's novel *Not by Bread Alone*, which denounces the organization of Soviet industry with particular reference to the stifling of inventive talent. The novel was serialized in the journal *Novy mir* in the August, September and October issues of 1956. But Dudintsev was only one among many authors who availed themselves of the new freedom. Two large symposia, both entitled *Literary Moscow*, were published by a group of writers operating independently of the full range of official controls traditionally exercised over the printed word. These collections included extensive miscellaneous material comparable to Dudintsev's in 'daringly' hinting at various blemishes of Soviet society such as the mass executions and the death camps.

Only against a background of thought control rigorously imposed for nearly three decades could the Protest Literature of 1956 appear as the dawn of a new era of freedom. Some foreign analysts of Soviet affairs proclaimed it as such, but their prophetic tones were those in which a doctor might announce that a patient, totally paralysed for years, had unexpectedly proved capable of signalling with one toe. It was only to such a limited extent that the 'year of protest' marked progress in the direction of independence for the expression of individual views – independence sensational in its cramped context, but always restricted in its scope and in any case soon to be declared unacceptable by authority.

Pasternak regarded Protest Literature as a farce and a fraud, but could not escape involvement entirely. To the leaders of the movement, some of them his personal friends, he was an important 'name' – one of several comparably illustrious figures who had incurred varying measures of disgrace in the past. Now at last their work could be published again, if only to a token extent, and the very act of publishing it seemed to symbolize the change in climate. The *Literary Moscow* symposia accordingly brought out Pasternak's article *Notes on Translating Shakespeare's Tragedies* together with some lyrics by the long banned or suppressed Akhmatova and Tsvetayeva. It was also proposed to include Pasternak's *Autobiographical Sketch* in a third symposium which never appeared. But, though the new ventures might woo him, his view of them remained jaundiced. He even claimed to prefer conventional Soviet journals to such new 'co-operative' enterprises which had been launched without official sanction. He spoke of the new outlets with contempt. 'They permit themselves so little; they differ so little from the official publications. It's the familiar dodge of taking something that's been foisted on you and palming it off as if it were freely expressed: a doubly odious form of fraud.'[18] As this comment emphasizes, there is an immense gap between *Doctor Zhivago* and the Soviet-published Protest Literature of 1956.

While Goslitizdat was still nominally committed to Polikarpov's plans for publishing *Doctor Zhivago* as a book, the plan to serialize it in a Soviet periodical suffered a serious setback. In September 1956 Pasternak at last received an answer from the editorial board of *Novy mir*. The document was some ten thousand words long, and it was signed by eight members of the editorial board. It came down firmly against publication, on ideological grounds, but received no publicity until it was eventually released by the Soviet authorities as part of the campaign against Pasternak launched in response to the Nobel Prize award of October 1958.

This rejection of *Doctor Zhivago* is an index of extreme disarray in the Soviet literary world. First, the head of the Central Committee's Cultural Department personally negotiates the work's publication in book form, as already described. But now, a few months later, the trail-blazing 'liberal' journal *Novy mir* rejects it for serialization. Which, then, were the 'hawks' and which the 'doves'? A further paradox is this: at the very time when the 'liberal' editors of *Novy mir* wrote to Pasternak rejecting *Doctor Zhivago*, their journal was in the middle of publishing Dudintsev's 'daring', 'controversial', 'liberal' and scandal-provoking novel *Not by Bread Alone*. This simultaneous acceptance of the one work and rejection of the other is an indication of the gulf separating Pasternak's novel from Dudintsev's. It is the gulf between a free emanation of the human spirit and the work of one temporarily licensed to simulate protestive postures.

Now that *Doctor Zhivago* had been rejected for publication by the leading liberal journal no more was heard of the proposal to serialize it in *Znamya*. Goslitizdat's plan to publish it in book form was also dropped, despite the exalted sponsorship which it had briefly enjoyed. But this did not mean that Goslitizdat automatically abandoned its plan to publish the less controversial writings of Pasternak which it had also contracted to produce. Work on the one-volume edition of his verse, with its prefatory author's *Autobiographical Sketch*, continued well into the following year.

In revising his poems as a whole for publication in the extensive one-volume edition, Pasternak was embarking on the second of the two comprehensive re-editings of his verse undertaken in the course of his life. His previous large-scale revision – that of the late 1920s – had involved the radical reworking of much early material. Now, in 1956–7, as news of the latest revision leaked out, many of his admirers feared that something comparably drastic was afoot. This restless poet, who was constantly referring to his pre-1940 verse as worthless – what appalling mutilations might he now be inflicting on lyrics belonging to the great heritage of Russian literature? The ever-vigilant Akhmatova was aghast when she thought of him 'correcting' such early verse as 'Weeping Garden' from *My Sister Life*. She threw up her hands in despair at the mere idea, and then said quietly but emphatically that this particular lyric was Russian poetry at its best. 'It's a twentieth-century classic. Boris is off his head.'[19] But she need not have worried over that particular item, because he happened to leave it unchanged.

Pasternak's second revision of his verse did not cut as deep as the near-massacre of 1928–9. He himself has indicated the very different principles which he followed in 1956–7, also stressing that the changes were all his own and had to be fought through against the stubborn resistance of Goslitizdat. He was wise to emphasize this point since readers familiar with the context might otherwise have assumed the opposite – that the changes had been imposed on him, and from the familiar political motives. But a scrutiny of the relevant texts suggests that brevity, conciseness and clarity were the chief aims of the operation. As for political acceptability, his verse had always met the conditions for publishability in the Soviet Union – with only trifling exceptions and in strong contrast with his novel, as also with the poetry of such a contemporary as Osip Mandelstam. The new revision was accordingly confined (Pasternak claimed) to purging a few individual passages of a 'foggy obscurity' which spoilt the overall impression; it did not involve changes of substance.[20]

The result was that certain lyrics were shortened in the interests of simplicity. From the celebrated 'Marburg' (first published in *Over Barriers* and already many times reworked) four of the more difficult stanzas were removed. The comparably impressive 'Mirror' (from *My Sister Life*) lost three stanzas. Among lyrics reworked rather than docked was the splendid 'Oars at Rest', also from *My Sister Life*.

What of the inconsistency involved in Pasternak's eagerness to reissue a substantial selection from his early verse and his simultaneous eagerness to denounce the entire corpus of his pre-1940 writings as worthless? The poet confronted the dilemma head on in a passage designed as a conclusion to his *Autobiographical Sketch*. He there confesses that he would not lift a finger to rescue three-quarters of his writings from oblivion, but adds that he is reconciled to republishing the material for two reasons. There are frequent grains of vital and felicitous material among all the dross, and the lyrics in question represent the preparatory steps towards 'my main and most important work', which was of course *Doctor Zhivago*.[21]

In the first sentences of the new memoir the author explicitly dissociates it (as has already been mentioned) from *Safe Conduct* – his previous major excursion into autobiography, which he was now describing as 'unfortunately vitiated by otiose preciosity, a common sin of those years'.[22] As these words indicate, *Autobiographical Sketch* indeed is crisper and clearer than its predecessor. It is also much shorter, less discursive, and less given to philosophical and aesthetic musings. There is a shift of emphasis away from the author's experiences of summer 1912 in Marburg and Italy: in the earlier memoir they account for two score pages, whereas they are skipped through in a few paragraphs in that of 1957. But Pasternak's study of music in the 1910s, and his relations with the composer Skriabin, have been less drastically curtailed. Nor has Mayakovsky been banished from the later of the two autobiographies; he plays a far less prominent role, though, no longer being the object of enthusiasm such as he had aroused in Pasternak thirty years earlier.

Autobiographical Sketch contains a wider spread of cultural references than will be found in *Safe Conduct*, together with a fuller account of Pasternak's indebtedness to other creative artists. Among them are Aleksandr Blok and Lev Tolstoy. And the later memoir ends with a commemorative eulogy, entitled 'Three Ghosts', in which the author praises the three poets among his close contemporaries for whom he felt the greatest sympathy and admiration. They were Marina Tsvetayeva and the two Georgian bards whom he had translated and visited: Titsian Tabidze and Paolo Yashvili. All three had been victims of their age – Tabidze by execution, Yashvili and Tsvetayeva by suicide. Pasternak mourns their sad fate, in the evening of his days, as 'my greatest grief'.[23]

These three deaths occurred in the period 1937–41, and therefore fall outside the framework of *Autobiographical Sketch*, for Pasternak firmly shuts the door on the main body of his narrative when it has reached the end of the 1920s. Here is another surprising feature of the two autobiographies. The second, written nearly three decades later than the first, breaks off at almost the same point. Feeling a need to explain this, Pasternak states towards the end of *Autobiographical Sketch* that it would have been 'immeasurably difficult' to have continued his narrative into the 1930s and beyond. Without explicitly invoking the horrors of fully developed Stalinism, he asserts that the period 'would have had to be described in such a way as to make the heart miss a beat, to make people's hair stand on end'. To write about it in a lifeless, conventional manner, to use colours paler than those lavished by Gogol and Dostoyevsky on their St Petersburg descriptions – that would not only be senseless and pointless, it would be base and shameless too.[24] In any case there would have been no chance of publishing such material in the Soviet Union, despite the fluctuating relaxations of the post-Stalin era. Since Pasternak's death another Russian, Alexander Solzhenitsyn, has come nearer than anyone else – chiefly in works issued exclusively outside the Soviet Union – to carrying out the task which Pasternak described as beyond himself.

Pasternak's unwillingness to attempt a portrayal of fully fledged Stalinism in his *Autobiographical Sketch* is reflected in *Doctor Zhivago*. The narrative of all three works – the novel and the two memoirs – is cut off at the same date: the end of the 1920s. It is on a hot August day in 1929 that Yury Zhivago suffers his fatal heart attack in a Moscow tram, the event which concludes the novel's main narrative. A further link between *Autobiographical Sketch* and Pasternak's novel is stressed by Gladkov. He maintains that the memoir is misleadingly selective because it picks out from the author's life only 'that which contributed to the creation of *Doctor Zhivago*'. The result was 'to impoverish, and even to distort, the portrait of the Pasternak whom I had already known and loved for many years'.[25]

From the biographer's point of view *Autobiographical Sketch* and *Safe Conduct* both have the drawback that their author concentrates on his artistic and spiritual evolution to the exclusion of almost everything else. Yet nothing could be more misleading than to deduce from the two memoirs a rejection by their author of domestic comfort and everyday life. Far from abjuring the material trappings of ordinary existence, known in Russian by the pregnant word *byt*, Pasternak came to attach supreme importance to them, if only in his later years. Such is one of the main messages of *Doctor Zhivago* – a very hymn to *byt*. Speaking so freely of his hero's *byt* in the novel, but so little of his own in his memoirs, Pasternak confronts his reader with yet another paradox. He also faces his biographers with the embarrassment of learning far more about the domestic life of the fictional Yury Zhivago from the novel than they can ever hope to discover about Zhivago's creator from his own accounts of his own life.

The preparation of Pasternak's *Autobiographical Sketch* and revised poems proceeded apace in 1957. He received his proofs on time, and he duly corrected them. But then, late in the year, the whole project fell foul of the growing scandal surrounding the publication of *Doctor Zhivago* outside the Soviet Union. This rapidly compromised the author to the extent of making it inconceivable for any of his imaginative work whatever to appear under a Soviet imprint in the foreseeable future. The one-volume verse collection, with its accompanying *Autobiographical Sketch*, accordingly fell by the wayside.

The one-volume collection proved no exception to the tendency whereby isolated copies of Soviet publications, banned after being set up in type, are apt to survive. Both the prose and the verse found their way abroad. *Autobiographical Sketch* was snapped up by publishers. It first appeared in English translation in London and New York in 1959, and it was eventually published in the USSR too – in 1967, but only after certain cuts had been imposed. As for the collected poems, revised in proof by the poet in 1957, they were never to be published as a whole in the form prepared by him for the press. But they fortunately became available to editors, at home as well as abroad, and have been used extensively as a basis for the two most comprehensive collections of his work which have been brought out to date: the Ann Arbor (Michigan) edition of 1961 and the Moscow–Leningrad edition of 1965.

During the build-up to the Nobel Prize crisis Pasternak suffered severe ill health. After acute pains in back, leg and knee had caused him to utter screams of agony audible in his Peredelkino garden, he was admitted to hospital in early 1957, and wrote to Ivinskaya from his sickbed asking her to pray for him to be granted a speedy death. No clear diagnosis was offered. Was this a kidney complaint? Arthritis? Radiculitis? Each possibility was mooted, but the patient himself could only say that 'All my vital functions are becoming atrophied, except two: the capacity to suffer pain and the capacity not to sleep.' Another phantom was also mentioned, a tumour on the spinal cord.[26] It seems possible that the grave symptoms of 1957 may have marked the first assault of cancer, the affliction which was eventually to destroy him.

Meanwhile a further change of cultural climate was taking place in the Soviet Union. The Hungarian uprising of October 1956 against Moscow-dominated Communist rule had been suppressed by Soviet armed force, and the Soviet authorities – fearing the spread of disaffection to their own territory – understandably decided that too many concessions had been made to cultural liberalism at home. The

Second Thaw was therefore brought to an end, and a second freeze-up was decreed. This change of policy was spelled out at three meetings of writers and artists harangued by Khrushchev in mid-1957. In this new and harsher climate all prospect of bringing out *Doctor Zhivago* in the Soviet Union vanished, seemingly for ever. However, the harsher the cultural climate became inside the Soviet Union the more spectacular did the prospects become for the novel's reception outside the country's boundaries. The tantrums directed at writers by Khrushchev in Moscow were gleefully reported in the Western press, and could only whet Western readers' appetites for a work known to be flagrantly at odds with everything that Khrushchev stood for. The more the ranting bully blustered, the more the spotlight of publicity was bound to switch to Pasternak as the most outstanding by far among those who had dared to breach the conventions of Soviet cultural discipline.

Doctor Zhivago was now in production, or under negotiation for production, on a global scale. By agreement with Feltrinelli (who held the world rights) photocopies of the typescript were being translated in many countries of the world. Feltrinelli himself led the race as he pressed ahead in Milan with publication of the original Russian and an Italian translation.

Frantic attempts were made by the Kremlin to prevent Italian publication from going ahead, or at least to delay it. Togliatti, the leader of the Italian Communist Party, was persuaded to urge Feltrinelli, himself a Communist, to abandon the project; but to no avail. Then Feltrinelli received a letter from Goslitizdat claiming – mendaciously, by this time – that *Doctor Zhivago* was to be published in the Soviet Union in September 1957, and asking him to postpone his own publication date until then. But this appeal too went unheeded, as did the next attempt to disrupt publication – the arrival in Milan of a telegram bearing Pasternak's signature and instructing Feltrinelli to abandon publication pending the receipt of the author's corrections. Pasternak had signed the telegram under pressure, having previously ensured that any such communication would not be taken seriously at the Italian end. He also knew that no power on earth could prevent the appearance of his novel in the West now that preparations were under way in so many countries. In any case Feltrinelli predictably ignored the telegram and continued to forge ahead.[27]

A last attempt to put pressure on Feltrinelli was made in October 1957, when Pasternak's leading opponent Surkov attached himself to a delegation of Soviet poets which was visiting Italy and descended on Milan in person. But he was soon forced to realize that *Doctor Zhivago* would be in the bookshops within weeks, and that he could do no more than anathematize it in advance. He accordingly attended a press conference in Milan on 19 October, and announced that the forthcoming publication was contrary to its author's wishes, which it most certainly was not. Surkov claimed – with only Pasternak's mendacious telegram to back the claim – that publication had been expressly forbidden by the author, who had asked in vain for the return of the manuscript so that he could revise it. But Pasternak's wishes had been overruled. 'The Cold War thus invades literature. If this is how the West understands freedom, then I must say that we view it differently.'[28] As indeed they did.

In November 1957 the novel appeared in Milan in Italian translation, the Russian text also being published there shortly afterwards. Rapid reprintings followed, as did translations into other languages – well over a score in the next two years. The book became a best-seller.

9

DILEMMAS OF A DOCTOR

The phantom of a long novel had haunted Pasternak sporadically for at least forty years before the publication of *Doctor Zhivago*. In a lyric of 1917 he was already announcing his intention of abandoning unadulterated poetry for fiction linked with poetry, which is exactly what *Doctor Zhivago* was to be.

> *Au revoir* to you, idolized poetry.
> We shall *rendez-vous* next in a novel.

In 1918 Pasternak told Tsvetayeva that he wanted 'to write a long novel – with love, with a heroine – like Balzac'. He also went ahead and composed the substantial work of prose fiction which (as is mentioned in Chapter 3) he somehow contrived to lose irretrievably, except for the fragment surviving as the short story *Childhood of Lyuvers* (1922). That story's heroine has been identified by Olga Ivinskaya as a possible prototype of the heroine of *Doctor Zhivago*: 'Is Lyuvers the future Lara?'[1]

In the mid-1920s Pasternak was still obsessed with the idea of writing a novel, according to Nadezhda Mandelstam's sardonic account. She calls him a victim of that era's 'weird gigantomania' – in other words, of the feeling that the heroic age of revolutionary Socialism demanded to be reflected in 'large forms', and that it needed (what it never got) a *War and Peace* of its own. But he had foolishly put the cart before the horse, said she. Instead of taking an idea as the starting-point for creative activity, and only then attempting to find a suitable genre, he had first become obsessed with his genre and had then gone hunting for a theme to fit it.[2] One might add that he had succeeded to this extent: he had already published what he called a novel – *Spektorsky*, which first appeared in completed form in 1931. But this, with all its sterling virtues, remained a short, allusive piece of versified fiction. It was neither a twentieth-century *War and Peace* nor the major prose work which had so long obsessed its author. As for *Childhood of Lyuvers* and the other short stories and sketches culminating in *A Tale* (1929), they did not even begin to match the dimensions of his ambition.

His continued obsession with novel writing is reflected in the four prose fragments which he published in 1937–9, and to which reference is made in Chapter 5. Their status as preliminary sketches for *Doctor Zhivago* is confirmed by the presence of certain characters bearing names which were to recur in the novel, and by the anticipation of at least one minor incident. Still, the fact remains that the fragments are exclusively set in the pre-1917 era. They therefore do not and cannot anticipate the novel's main narrative stream, since that flows through the early post-revolutionary period. Nor, frankly, does a close study of the four prose fragments cast much illumination on *Doctor Zhivago*. Their chief value is as evidence that Pasternak was vaguely mulling over some of the novel's themes a long time before he began systematic work.

As these numerous early anticipations of *Doctor Zhivago* suggest, the novel represents the principal creative preoccupation of Pasternak's life. He considered it his supreme achievement, and he was saying so long before its appearance in print turned his name into an international household word. He called it 'my chief and most important work, the only one I am not ashamed of and for which I can answer with the utmost confidence'. So he wrote in a note (dated May–June 1956) to his *Autobiographical Sketch*, adding that the entire corpus of his pre-*Zhivago* poetry was no more than a series of preliminary steps towards the novel. He told Lidiya Chukovskaya that the novel was 'the only worthwhile thing I have ever achieved'.[3] He said much the same to his many other friends, acquaintances and visitors, including myself.

During our meetings in summer 1958 Pasternak contrasted *Doctor Zhivago* with his early writings. He claimed that they were too fragmentary, too personal and too obscure to match the great and tragic events of their age. They did not even attempt to do justice to the wars, the upheavals, the persecutions which had rendered human life far more significant – if also far more hazardous – in the twentieth century than it had ever been before. Brooding on events so cataclysmic, he had felt bitterly ashamed of all his earlier achievements, and had decided that he must attempt to justify his undeserved reputation with a new work conceived on a grander scale: something 'big and simple'. He was too modest to claim that he had achieved this aim with *Doctor Zhivago*, and he volunteered his own criticisms of the novel – of the weak beginning, of the thin characterization. But, though he would not trumpet *Doctor Zhivago*'s merits, on one point he was adamant. Good, bad or indifferent, the work eclipsed all his own previous literary efforts. When this claim was contradicted by admirers of his early poetry, the normally peaceable poet–novelist would show irritation or even fly into a rage.

Readers of *Doctor Zhivago* have by no means all accepted the claims made for it by the author. Many have embarked on it with his world-wide notoriety in mind, and the result has sometimes been to make their first acquaintance with the text puzzling or disappointing. Instead of a rousing prophetic manifesto in favour of freedom and human rights, instead of some portentous transcontinental *J'accuse* launched against the evils of totalitarianism and reeking of exotic Muscovite local colour, they have found a narrative surprisingly low-key and unassertive.

The novel chronicles a single main hero, Yury Andreyevich Zhivago, who eclipses all the other characters in importance. He is a Muscovite, a doctor and a poet – an observer rather than a man of action. He sees something of the 1905 Revolution as an adolescent; experiences the February Revolution of 1917 as a medical officer on the Russian western front; witnesses the October Revolution of 1917 in Moscow; spends the Russian Civil War as a civilian in the Urals and as a press-ganged doctor serving a group of Red partisans in Siberia. The main narrative ends with his return to Moscow in 1921, when Lenin's New Economic Plan is being introduced, and passes quickly to the hero's death from a heart attack in a Moscow tram in August 1929. The brief, still more telescoped, Epilogue shows how Zhivago lives on in the memory of his friends during the war and into Stalin's last years.

The novel reflects the hero's philosophical, social and political thinking in detail. It describes his private life, especially his relations with his wife Tonya and his mistress Lara. It conveys the impact made on him by his love for these two women, by natural beauty, by his Christian faith. Above all it portrays his dedication to the art of poetry. It shows him in action as a poet, illuminates the nature of his inspiration, and in the final chapter offers extensive specimens of his verse – the cycle of twenty-five lyrics which form an integral part of the work and should on no account be dismissed as a mere afterthought or embellishment.

The novel runs to 567 pages in its first Russian edition, as published in Milan in 1957, and consists of seventeen chapters. The first sixteen are all prose narrative, Chapter Sixteen forming the Epilogue. Chapter Seventeen, entitled 'Yury Zhivago's Poems', differs from the pre-ceding material; it offers poetry where there had previously been prose, and also a significant change of stance. Whereas the prose material of Chapters One to Sixteen consists of third-person narrative deployed as by an omniscient author, the verse of Chapter Seventeen is presented as the work of Pasternak's hero, not of Pasternak himself. The novel accordingly has an original or even eccentric structure, and one which throws particular emphasis on the poetry which concludes it. Hence one of the many paradoxes projected by the work: even in the act of seemingly abandoning poetry for prose fiction, a renowned poet yet makes that very prose fiction a vehicle for asserting the primacy of poetry.

The Soviet period had already generated much impressive Russian lyric poetry and a vast quantity of somewhat less impressive Russian narrative prose. But it had never generated anything comparable to Pasternak's hybrid product, and it had rarely equalled him in either genre.

Doctor Zhivago is intimately and multiply linked with its author's personal evolution. It seems to have been written explicitly to demonstrate what lessons he himself had learnt between childhood and advanced middle age. He expounds this material chiefly through the medium of a hero who is in some ways a self-portrait of his creator. And yet, even while painting Zhivago in his own image, Pasternak was also making strenuous efforts to dissociate himself from his hero by endowing the latter with characteristics and experiences demonstrably different from his own. It is instructive to examine the novel in an attempt to distinguish the areas in which the hero exactly mirrors the author from those in which a distorted reflection, or no reflection at all, is to be discerned.

In one respect at least Pasternak and his hero are united. Yury Zhivago is presented as a boy of ten in 1901. This means that he is exactly the same age as his creator, whose own eleventh birthday fell in that year. But Pasternak was to live out his full three score years and ten, whereas his hero perishes of a heart attack while still in his thirties.

The hero's parentage may have been chosen in order to form as strong a contrast as possible to the author's. Far from being brought up in a cultured and stable parental home such as the Pasternak family apartment at the Moscow School of Painting, the young Yury is the son of a shady and peripatetic businessman who commits suicide by throwing himself out of a train after abandoning his wife and child for a series of mistresses. This is a far cry from the author's own father, the respected artist and professor Leonid Pasternak. And the talented Roza Pasternak had little in common with Zhivago's mother, a vaguely benevolent figure who dies when her son is still in infancy.

Zhivago copies Pasternak in being a native of Moscow, and also in sojourning for prolonged periods in the Urals, except that the periods of residence are different. Pasternak was in the Urals between 1915 and 1917, when the region was somnolescent, whereas his hero is described as living there some three years later, in a period of acute dangers and upheavals. This points to another contrast between fictional doctor and real-life author: the extent of the privations suffered by each during the years of war and revolution. While Boris Pasternak is working as a civilian far back in the rear areas during the First World War, Yury Zhivago is serving at the front as an army doctor. Both suffer the perils and shortages of Moscow during the early post-revolutionary weeks, but such tribulations are far more severe as undergone by Yury in the Urals, and still more so when he is in Siberia during his spell as a kidnapped medical officer serving with the Red partisans. Yury eventually escapes, trudges back to the Urals, and then on to Moscow – where he arrives in an advanced stage of exhaustion, having become a tramp. The transformation is brilliantly described. But it is one that Pasternak himself did not undergo, despite his poverty in the Civil War years and early 1920s.

Author and hero could hardly differ more in their appearance. For instance, Yury Zhivago is described as 'that snub-nosed, utterly unremarkable person'.[4] Snub-nosed Pasternak most emphatically was not. Still less could he be called 'utterly unremarkable'. With his clean-shaven and impressively protrusive chin may be contrasted Zhivago's 'dark auburn beard'. The ordinary exterior, the snub nose, the auburn beard – these are almost all the details that the reader ever learns of the hero's appearance in a novel where physical descriptions of the major characters are dispensed most grudgingly. Indeed, the reader is not even aware that Yury Zhivago sports a dark auburn beard until he is informed that it has begun to turn grey after his return from Siberia to the Urals.[5] But numerous photographs and portraits survive of Pasternak himself in his twenties, not to mention the testimony of many who admired his style of beauty. He was, and remained until his death, a man who stood out in any company through his vitality and sheer physical presence.

Far more is known, then, about Pasternak's appearance than about his hero's. In general, however, the availability of information is balanced the other way. The author purveys considerably more intelligence about Zhivago's doings and domestic surroundings – about where, how, with whom and on what resources he lived – than he was willing to disclose in his two accounts of his own life, *Safe Conduct* and *Autobiographical Sketch*, despite the fact that they cover roughly the same historical period as the novel. Even when those two accounts are supplemented with the sparse biographical material available from other sources, it is still arguable that more is known of Yury Zhivago during his four decades of life than can be ascertained with certainty about his creator during his corresponding years.

Yury's marital arrangements mirror those of his creator in their general outlines, since he hovers between a wife and a mistress – just as Pasternak did in both his marriages, especially the second. But Zhivago is content to let both his women go, whereas his creator proved more retentive.

Yury's mistress Lara owes much to the inspiration of a real-life prototype, Olga Ivinskaya, as is attested in great detail in her memoirs. But she also shows a salutary awareness of how distant the relationship between a finished literary image and its original real-life inspiration may be. In spite of her repeated insistence on identifying herself as Lara, Ivinskaya is objective enough to point out that she was 'probably not a total Lara or he a total Yury'. The same contention is driven home by Pasternak himself on the pages of the novel, at the point where Yury is left alone at the Varykino house after parting from his mistress for the last time. He begins to commemorate her in verse, but 'The more he crossed things out and changed one word for another, the further did the Lara of his poems and jottings recede from her real-life prototype.' Though these alterations had been made in order to increase the force and accuracy of what Yury the poet wrote, 'They also reflected the promptings of inner reticence which forbade the excessively frank exposure of personal experience, of that which had occurred on the non-fictional plane.'[6]

In the light of this statement it becomes easier to understand how the images of two real women (Pasternak's wife Zinaida and his mistress Olga) flowed into the two fictional figures (Zhivago's wife Tonya and his mistress Lara) in such a way that their characteristics mingled. Ivinskaya wrote that Tonya 'had features of myself and of Zinaida Nikolayevna, just as Lara had something from both of us, and from somebody else as well'. But there was 'more of Zinaida Nikolayevna in Tonya and of me in Lara'.[7] For example, the housewifely virtues of Tonya obviously derive from the comparable skills deployed by Zinaida Nikolayevna. But Lara by no means lacks the same virtues. She too seems permanently poised to launder the hero's shirts.

Despite the affinities between Lara and Tonya, both as representatives of the eternal feminine and as darners of socks, some contrast of temperament and experience is to be observed. Lara's seduction at an early age by the villainous voluptuary Komarovsky has left her, in her own opinion, 'flawed for life',[8] just as Dostoyevsky's Nastasya Filippovna (in *The Idiot*) had felt permanently tainted by her youthful association with an elderly seducer. There is no evidence that Ivinskaya had undergone a similar experience, or been left with similar feelings of inadequacy, but Lara's relatively tempestuous emotional life (as opposed to that of the more placid Tonya) is surely a reflection of Ivinskaya's turbulent marital and amatory history, as recounted in her memoirs. The differences between the two fictional women are stressed in the letter which Tonya writes to her husband after their final separation. She says that Lara is 'the complete opposite of myself. I was born into this world to simplify life and seek the correct solution. But she was born to complicate life and to lead people astray.'[9]

One of Yury Zhivago's outstanding characteristics, both in amatory and in other contexts, is an unwillingness to assert himself, an almost complete lack of male aggressiveness. Here is a feature of Pasternak himself, as has been illustrated more than once on these pages. The trait was expressly confirmed by Ivinskaya when she contrasted her lover's 'soft, feminine' nature with that of the brusque and mannish Tsvetayeva. Yury Zhivago is similarly inclined, as is revealed by his actions, by his lack of actions, and by the comments made on him in the narrative and dialogue. There is reference to the Doctor's 'lack of character', and also to a feature quintessentially Pasternakian – his 'obscure, unreal language'. Then again, Yury's wife refers to his talent and intelligence as seeming to 'take the place of his total lack of will-power'.[10] It would be absurd to suggest that Pasternak himself totally lacked will-power. But it is also true that he did not always choose to draw on his undoubted strength of character, and that the occasions on which he did so alternated with others on which he permitted the tide of events to wash over him, just as Yury Zhivago often does in the novel.

As a qualified and – for a time – practising doctor, Zhivago has a profession other than that of writer, whereas Pasternak was a professional author throughout his life and never seriously pursued any other calling – with the possible exception of his youthful musical and philosophical activities. He and his brain child in the novel are, however, united by the most important of all their many common features, the poetic vocation. Yet crucial differences are to be noted here too. One concerns the degree of renown enjoyed by hero and author. Pasternak had been recognized as one of the most distin-guished Russian poets of his generation ever since the first publication of *My Sister Life* in 1922, whereas Yury Zhivago's case is very different. His poems are indeed described as being highly rated by a few *aficionados*, but there is no suggestion that he ever attracted a degree of recognition comparable to that enjoyed by his creator.

The other difference between Yury the poet and Boris the poet emerges when the date of their writings is collated with the literary technique employed in them. The former turns out to be considerably the more precocious of the two: in the year 1920 he is already writing in the famous 'simple' manner which Pasternak himself attained only after prolonged struggle and on the eve of the Second World War. During the very years when Pasternak was composing the difficult, impressionistic, frequently obscure lyrics of *My Sister Life* and *Themes and Variations*, the doctor–poet of his imagination is pictured as already composing in his creator's more straightforward style as it did not fully emerge until he had entered his sixth decade.

In the evolution of his philosophical and political views Pasternak's hero displays similar precocity. Almost anyone who had the privilege of talking to Pasternak in later life can confirm that Yury Zhivago is everywhere the mouthpiece for his creator's opinions. Pasternak was constantly engaged in rehearsing his world view in language fresh, brilliantly improvised and vividly original on each occasion – yet often markedly reminiscent in style and content of specific passages in the novel. Both Gladkov's and Ivinskaya's memoirs record numerous off-the-cuff pronouncements – on art, religion, love, nature, God and the like – made to them, live, by Pasternak, either before or after very similar sentiments were included in the text of *Doctor Zhivago*, where they are attributed to the main hero. These were all Pasternak's own views, then. But they are very far from the views which he was expressing in the years during which his hero is described as voicing them. In the relevant period, from roughly 1917 to 1929, Pasternak held somewhat different opinions on art and history, together with strikingly different opinions on revolution in general and on the Russian upheavals in particular. It took him nearly thirty years (1917–46) to arrive at the definitive conclusion that the society thrown up by Russia's October Revolution had taken a tragically mistaken road. But Yury Zhivago is described as reaching a comparable pitch of disillusion almost immediately after the Bolshevik take-over of 1917, and this despite the early enthusiasm for revolution which he is portrayed as sharing with his creator.

Through the main hero's comments and experiences, reinforced by those of several minor mouthpieces and by Pasternak's own observations as author, *Doctor Zhivago* forcefully conveys a comprehensive philosophy of life, differing modes of human behaviour being reviewed in such a way as to make the author's strong disapproval or approval clearly evident. This world view is obtruded on the reader in isolated explicit passages. It also permeates the novel as a whole, rendering it so strongly didactic in its fundamental character that it may almost be called a fictional sermon.

Pasternak's message has its positive and its negative aspects: he teaches humanity both how it should and how it should not behave. The positive doctrines were far more important to the author than the negative. But the latter were to play a particularly prominent part in determining the novel's fate, and in making it a source of scandal. They therefore merit detailed consideration, and will be examined first.

The main target for Pasternak's disapproval is the activity of politics, with special reference to Soviet practices and phraseology. His disparagement of these will be analysed by proceeding from the particular to the general – that is, by working inwards from short, isolated, self-contained passages alluding to specific features of the Soviet scene (passages which could easily have been cut if a Soviet edition had been published) to the core of the novel's negative message, which no degree of mutilation could have concealed. At the same time it must be emphasized yet again that the whole of this negative message, husks and core alike, was of secondary importance to the author. His main concern was to accentuate the positive.

The material most offensive to Soviet taboo, but also the most easily excisable (had Soviet censorship been applied), is that section of the Epilogue where Yury Zhivago's old friend Dudorov dismisses the whole of the Stalinist 1930s in a few curt phrases. Dudorov calls the collectivization of agriculture a failure. He adds that, since the failure could not be admitted, the most violent methods had to be employed to cover it up. Dudorov claims that 'All means of terrorization had to be applied to stop people judging and thinking, to force them to see what wasn't there, and to maintain the opposite of what stared them in the face. Hence the unprecedented cruelty of the *Yezhovshchina*.'[11] This goes far beyond the limited criticisms levelled against Stalin's policies in Khrushchev's 'Secret Speech' of 1956, and far beyond the hints at Stalinist malpractices permitted in Soviet-published Protest Literature of the post-Stalin period. These sentiments, together with the colloquial word *Yezhovshchina*, would have been unlikely to survive Soviet censorship. So too would the short, harsh references to Stalin's prison empire – to the camp where Zhivago's friend Gordon was held before being drafted from it into the army, and to the 'innumerable . . . concentration camps of the north', in one of which the heroine Lara is reported to have perished.[12] These few references could easily have been expunged. Or they could have been preserved in modified form, since guarded, carefully modulated allusions to the labour camps do occur in Protest Literature of the period. Allusions comparably outspoken to the camps and kindred sensitive topics were, incidentally, to be permitted to fiction-writers and memoirists active shortly after Pasternak's death, especially in the years 1962–5.

A reference to Lenin as 'vengeance incarnate' would have been unlikely to pass the censor, as would an oblique sneer at Stalin as a 'pockmarked Caligula'.[13] The latter phrase would not have been found unacceptable because it disparaged Stalin (this was, after all, the age of 'de-Stalinization'), but for stylistic reasons. It did not fall within the carefully delineated range of formulae licensed for use by those permitted to denounce Stalin – which Pasternak himself in any case was not.

The text includes several sacrilegious allusions to Marxism, and these would certainly have had to go as well, had Soviet publication been undertaken. They include Yury's derisive rebuttal of the contention that Marxism constitutes a science. 'It hasn't enough self-control for that. The sciences have more equilibrium. And what of Marxism's so-called objectivity? I don't know any movement further from the facts.' Other allusions to Marxism include one from Yury's uncle Nikolay, who claims loyalty to Marx as a key characteristic of mediocrities and victims of the herd instinct.[14] These comments could only have been admitted in a Soviet-published work of fiction if they had been put forward by readily identifiable villains and circum-stantially refuted by readily identifiable positive characters. As it is they are clearly made in the author's own name, and therefore constitute a downright blasphemy against Soviet doctrine.

Though the passages alluding specifically to Marxism, concen-tration camps, Lenin and Stalin could easily have been censored out, Pasternak's attitude towards the sacred concept of revolution as a whole is a very different matter. His viewpoint is expressed in his comments as narrator and through the mouths of his characters. It represents the inner core of the novel's negative message, and would have presented an insoluble problem to any literary official charged with the task of rendering *Doctor Zhivago* suitable for Soviet publication. Such an official would, it is true, have found little cause for objection in the novel's first five chapters – those set in the period preceding the October Revolution of 1917 – for they are remarkably free from ideological heresy. The hero emerges as sympathetically disposed to the abortive Revolution of 1905, as Pasternak himself had been at the time. That upheaval is pictured as favouring the interests of the oppressed and downtrodden. The Tsarist dispensation is deplored by implication – again a reflection of Pasternak's own attitude – and the Tsar-Emperor Nicholas II is portrayed, when briefly glimpsed at the war front, as a pathetic example of a weakling in power. In passages quoted from the novel in Chapter 3, the February Revolution of 1917 is hailed as a massive collective sigh of relief, while the October Revolution is applauded as an example of superb surgery which has excised all the old, stinking sores at one fell swoop; it is 'a straightforward, no-nonsense guilty verdict on age-old injustice'.[15]

So far so good. No Soviet censor could object to any of that. But the trouble is that Yury's enthusiasm for the October Revolution evaporates within a few hours of Lenin's seizure of power. For a brief moment the singlemindedness, the uncompromising nature of the upheaval had indeed been irresistible. 'But such things survive in their pristine purity only in the heads of those who have brought them about – and even then they only last through the day on which they are proclaimed. The chicanery of politics turns them inside out on the morrow.' As for the triumph of materialism supposedly achieved by the new regime based on dialectically materialist theory, Pasternak's hero sarcastically notes that its only practical effect has been to consign material objects to the realm of the notional. Once there was food and firewood. Now there is only a provision problem and a fuel shortage.[16]

No sooner has Lenin grasped power than Yury is already describing the new government as 'hostile to us'.[17] He accordingly decides that he and his family must leave revolutionary Moscow and seek to muddle through the Revolution's troubles in the wilds of the Urals. From this point onwards Yury has nothing to say in favour of the October Revolution and the new social order which it is bringing about.

It is not so much the privations, the sufferings and the general instability of post-revolutionary society which Pasternak depicts as preventing Yury from working, from practising as a doctor and from writing poetry. It is, rather, the era's intolerable verbiage which has unnerved and incapacitated him – 'the spirit of the shattering platitude that so dominates our age'. Again and again Yury expresses his disgust at the pompous phraseology of the day by deriding such locutions as Dawn of the Future, Building a New World, Mankind's Torch-Bearers.[18] He might have added the most pretentious of all these phrases and assumptions – that whereby it was proclaimed to be everyone's duty to Sacrifice his Life for this, that or the other. The solemn obligation was being invoked on all sides by individuals who obviously had no intention of sacrificing so much as the vouchers enabling them to buy food at heavily discounted prices at the special stores dispensing produce unavailable to the citizens at large.

Another such phrase is Transforming Life, on which Yury Zhivago harangues one of the Red partisan leaders in Siberia. Yury says that the only people capable of using this trite term are those who have never known life, who have never sensed its spirit and its essence. 'For them existence is a lump of coarse material which has not been ennobled by their touch and which needs to be processed by them.' But life never is a material or a substance. It is the principle of uninterrupted self-renewal. 'It keeps carrying out its own self-reform and self-transformation, and it is itself a great deal more sublime than your and my dull theories.'[19]

The novel also breaches Soviet taboo in the importance which it everywhere attributes to individual human beings, while deriding the collectivist enthusiasms that play so prominent a role in Communist speech patterns. Only individuals seek the truth, proclaims the novel, while dismissing the 'herd instinct' as the refuge of mediocrities, 'no matter whether their loyalty is to Vladimir Solovyov, Kant or Marx'. Such passages illustrate Pasternak's determination not to confine his opposition to revolution to the Russian October episode. He is so far from doing so that he expresses hostility to virtually all revolutions everywhere. Though Yury is described as initially sympathetic to the idea of revolution, he soon concludes that violence achieves nothing. Revolutions are the work of one-sided fanatics, of geniuses of self-limitation. The hurly-burly of chopping and changing is the revolutionary's 'only natural habitat', Yury tells Lara. Such people will not operate on a less than global scale. 'Building New Worlds, Transitional Periods – for them these are an end in themselves. That's all they've learnt to do, they're incapable of anything else.' And all these endless, futile preparatory operations stem from the utter sterility and incompetence of the revolutionary leaders.[20]

Such, then, are some of the points in *Doctor Zhivago* where Pasternak attacks revolution in the abstract and its manifestations on Russian soil in particular. His counter-revolutionary posture formed the basis for most of the objections raised against *Doctor Zhivago* in the important communication which reached him from *Novy mir* in September 1956.

The editors claimed that no cuts, no alterations could adequately correct a work which reflects, in its general spirit, a complete rejection of the October Revolution and insists on portraying that event as a catastrophe. The editors went on to contrast *Doctor Zhivago* with Pasternak's four long poems of the 1920s – which met with their approval – and they complained that his novel depicted the utter destruction of the Russian intelligentsia through the Revolution. And his reason for condemning the Revolution was so contemptibly selfish: just that it made people's lives uncomfortable. His approved characters spend all their time chasing after mundane irrelevancies like potatoes and firewood. They are not willing to freeze or starve for ideas; they show no wish to uphold ideas of any sort, let alone to Sacrifice their Lives for Ideas. Zhivago himself has medical qualifications, yet selfishly abandons the practice of his profession, and so turns his back on his Duty to the People. To set against these faults the editors concede one virtue only: natural scenery is portrayed with remarkable truth and poetic power. But this cannot redeem the work as a whole. It is a profoundly anti-democratic political sermon, and it cannot conceivably be accepted for publication in their journal.[21]

The *Novy mir* editors have argued their case well, and in a tone astonishingly respectful for a communication addressed to an ideological offender. But they have emphasized Pasternak's negative message so strongly as to convey a misleading impression of his novel as a whole. True, *Doctor Zhivago* does contain many polemical passages disparaging revolution, and some of these have been quoted above. But it is emphatically not what the *Novy mir* editors imply: a document anti-revolutionary in the sense of being principally devoted to the denunciation of revolution, either in its Soviet or its general historical context. Pasternak damns the Revolution far more scathingly by treating it as a side issue – a virtual irrelevance to any serious conception of human life. Throughout the novel the assumption is made that revolution, together with political activity as a whole, is too petty and insignificant a process even to be worth disparaging. Politics is portrayed as an inevitably sterile activity indulged in by despicable, limited, fanatical and even cocaine-addicted individuals such as the Antipovs (father and son), Tiverzin and the Red partisan leader Livery. Their assumptions are not seriously discussed. They are casually, not even scornfully, dismissed. Here is no great ideological battle between good and evil such as Dostoyevsky has staged in all his great novels. Here, rather, is a novel in which evil is regarded as so much beneath notice that it is not worthy of reasoned refutation, and still less of being embodied in fictional characters comparable in stature to the representatives of good.

Pasternak's greatest sin against Soviet doctrines and dispensations was this very refusal to take them seriously. Theirs was a conception of the world 'so warped and narrow that in the ordinary way of things it would have lain completely outside his vision'.[22] To Soviet authority,

and to the *Novy mir* editors as its representatives, a militantly
counter-revolutionary work would have been far less objectionable
than *Doctor Zhivago*. They would have known where they were with
that. Had not the system always conceded the existence of rabid,
hysterical, teeth-gnashing Enemies of the People? It was far less
disposed to tolerate, still less to admit the existence of, an author who
found its pretensions too boring even for hatred, and who – if he
thought about them at all – shrugged them off as beneath the attention
of anyone endowed with a spark of true creativity on however humble
a level. Despite the admitted frequency and vehemence of Pasternak's
denunciation of revolution, the theme still remained of secondary
importance, and that was what the Soviet official mind could not risk
seeming to forgive him.

It also seems likely that Pasternak's senior literary colleagues
objected to *Doctor Zhivago* at least as much through personal pique as
from political motives. He had, after all, accepted the same impressive
range of inducements as everyone else in the writing fraternity. But
here he was high-mindedly failing to deliver the kind of copy for the
sake of which the inducements had been offered in the first place. To
the average comfortable Soviet writer in good standing he must have
seemed to be 'rocking the boat' while hypocritically 'having the best of
both worlds'.

'Man is born to live, not to prepare for life.' This brief sentence, put
into the mouth of Yury Zhivago, might be taken as a motto for the
novel as a whole.[23] The revolutionaries were those who prepared for
life. The time has now come to consider those who *lived*.

Doctor Zhivago's principal aim is to convey its creator's conception
of all that is most positive and worthwhile in human existence. Natural
beauty, the love of man and woman, family life, religion, the art of
poetry – here are the major themes. They are powerfully developed in
the course of the narrative, and are closely interwoven with each other.
Again and again these great issues are seen to transcend the sterile
world of politics, even as politicians seek to pervert life's true blessings
by substituting for them the promotion of their own cheap slogans.

The nature descriptions have much in common with Pasternak's
writing as it developed from his earliest days. There are more animated
storms and suns, there are comparably vivid evocations of snow,
spring floods, trees. Some of the most impressive passages are
associated with travelling, among them being the description of Yury's
train journey with his family to the Urals shortly after the October
Revolution. The beauty of such passages has been acknowledged by

many who have condemned the novel as a whole – even the *Novy mir* editors praised the truth and power of its landscapes. Akhmatova approached *Doctor Zhivago* from a very different point of view, and she seems to have liked it still less. Yet she found its nature descriptions superior to all others in Russian literature, including those of Turgenev and Tolstoy. They revealed to her the same genius that she found in the Caucasian hazelwoods invoked in Pasternak's *Second Birth* – an eloquent indication of what was, to her, the pinnacle of literary praise.[24]

The novel has been acclaimed as 'one of the most beautifully orchestrated love duets in all of Russian fiction', and as containing 'one of the most profound descriptions of love in the whole range of modern literature'. Here too the scenic background forms part of the mixture. The hero and heroine 'loved each other because everything around them willed it – the earth underfoot, the sky above, the clouds, the trees'. Their passion for each other, and for natural beauty, is vividly contrasted with the sterile and pretentious world of politics. 'The exaltation of Man above the rest of nature, the modish coddling of Man, the worship of Man did not attract them. The principles of spurious public-spiritedness served up as politics seemed pathetically shoddy to them.' Lara makes the point again in her lament over the dead Yury at the end of Chapter Fifteen. 'The riddle of life, the riddle of death, the beauty of genius, the beauty of nakedness: those things we perhaps understood. But trivial, earth-shaking squabbles about reshaping the globe – well, they're just not our line, I'm sorry.'[25]

The reference to 'nakedness' is exceptional, for Pasternak typically confines his evocations of love's sensual aspects to such brief hints. Another is found at the point where he describes Lara as 'so powerfully charged with all conceivable femininity' that to touch her is to risk summary electrocution. A further hint at sensuality establishes a characteristic linkage by invoking Pasternak's religious theme in the context of love. He has Yury reflecting, as he looks forward to his meeting with Lara in Yuryatin, that he will there 'receive her white beauty, God's creation, as a gift from the Creator's hands'.[26] Such are the novel's most erotic moments – a consideration which vividly emphasizes the extent to which the composer of the beautifully orchestrated love duet has chosen to focus on the spiritual. But he also focuses on the mundane details of ordinary domestic life as a context in which the love of men and women blossoms to perfection.

One of Yury's greatest pleasures is 'to work from dawn to dusk for himself and his family' – as opposed to working for Mankind, the People, the Future. He naturally assigns a prime role in this domestic idyll to Woman, reflecting as follows while he observes Lara at her domestic chores. 'With her prosaic and workaday appearance, dishevelled, with rolled-up sleeves and tucked-up apron, she almost terrified him with her majestic, breath-taking allure' – more than if he had found her dressing for a ball. Loving his mistress Lara, Yury loves his wife Tonya no less. Her housewifely virtues are equally commended, and she is praised for deploying her home-making skills with economy of effort.[27]

Though the women of *Doctor Zhivago* are highly prized for their domestic virtues, and for their willingness to launder the hero's shirts and mend his trousers whenever such services are required, the novel also projects the passionate idealization of woman in the abstract to which the author had been prone since childhood. Tonya is 'the most inaccessible and complicated object that Yury could imagine, a woman'. Motherhood is woman's greatest glory; every mother is a Madonna, and 'Every conception is immaculate'.[28]

In thus linking love and domesticity with a Christian symbol, Pasternak is stressing what he regards as some of the chief Gospel lessons, while once again touching on the religious theme which is crucial to the novel as a whole. Zhivago's uncle Nikolay, one among several author's mouthpieces in the work, argues that Christianity's true essence does not lie in moral precepts and regulations, but in Christ's habit of speaking in parables from everyday life, and of illuminating the truth with the light of the everyday world. The bestial savageries of ancient Rome had been transformed (says Uncle Nikolay) by the coming of Christ with his 'deliberate human quality, his deliberate Galilean provincialism'. The result had been an important historical change. From that moment 'Gods and peoples ended, and man began.'[29]

Christianity differs from the stagnant world of politics and revolution by concentrating on the freedom of the individual personality. This message is preached by the eccentric Urals evangelist Sima Tuntseva, another of the author's mouthpieces. Her sentiments echo the teaching of Uncle Nikolay – that history in the modern sense began with Christ, with the idea of the free personality, with the concept of life as sacrifice for others. These attitudes have replaced the bloody brutality of cruel, pockmarked Caligulas who did not suspect how sterile every enslaver is. 'Only after Christ did people breathe freely.' Ancient Rome with its rulers and collectivist psychology gave way to the individual, to the doctrine of freedom. 'Individual human life became the story of God and filled the universe with its presence.'[30]

This interpretation of Christianity lays much emphasis on the doctrine of immortality. History, in the new sense imparted to it by Christ in the Gospel according to Pasternak, is a second universe constructed by humanity as a means of conquering death. When Yury is called upon to console a dying woman, he tells her that life is constantly renewing itself. She need not worry about her own resurrection since she has already been resurrected once – at the moment of her birth. 'Man in other people – that *is* man's soul. . . . You've already existed in others, and you'll continue to do so.'[31] There are passages, and this is one of them, in which the novel's positive message seems to have worn a little thin, however splendidly it may be expressed elsewhere.

The idea of life as repeated self-renewal, as a succession of rebirths, had long been a familiar element in Pasternak's thinking. It permeates his novel in evocations of fresh springtime vegetation and of Christ's Resurrection at the same season. The link between life and death is further linked with another of the author's chief concerns – the contribution made to human life by art, and particularly by his own art of poetry. During a visit to his mother's grave, Yury reflects that 'Art is always uninterruptedly concerned with two things. It is constantly brooding on death, and it is thereby constantly creating life.'[32]

The author of *Doctor Zhivago* did not confine himself to creating life. He was also keenly concerned to interpret it. He cared little whether he entertained his readers; his chief aim was to instruct them. In this respect he continued the great tradition of nineteenth-century Russian fiction as represented by its novelist–prophets Gogol, Dostoyevsky and Tolstoy among others. Each of them had used, or attempted to use, his art to promote a philosophy of life. That tradition had been revived in the Soviet period – but with this important difference, that fiction-writers were no longer free to choose what way of life they would recommend, but were obliged to advocate that imposed by the State.

Doctor Zhivago reasserted the tradition in its Russian pre-Soviet form – that whereby the writer propagated his own view of the world, not one imposed from outside. As has already been indicated, Pasternak did this far more singlemindedly than Dostoyevsky, who had a view of good as ultimately more potent than evil, but who went to great lengths to present evil as powerfully as possible. That was not Pasternak's way in *Doctor Zhivago*, where evil is given no comparable opportunity to put its case, but is repeatedly, authoritatively, wittily and offhandedly dismissed.

While lacking the vibrant dialectical equilibrium of Dostoyevsky, Pasternak nevertheless appears to have contracted an obsession common to Dostoyevsky, to the Russian nineteenth-century literary tradition as a whole, and even to the practitioners of Socialist Realism in Stalin's era – the urge to create a so-called positive hero. Such a hero is conceived as furnishing a model for the reader to emulate, whether it be some tough Communist labour boss in one of the Five-Year-Plan novels of the 1930s or figures so very different as Sonya, the heroine of Dostoyevsky's *Crime and Punishment*, and Prince Myshkin, the hero of Dostoyevsky's *The Idiot*.

It is known that Dostoyevsky specifically set out to present his Myshkin as a 'positively good man'. But Dostoyevsky was far less successful in infusing positive characteristics into that harmless blunderer than in creating a vague atmosphere of combined saintliness and absurdity. Myshkin, as he emerges in the novel, is a negatively rather than a positively good man. He *is* good, certainly. But what good does he *do*? The same question may be asked of Yury Zhivago, who is almost equally inept at coping with his surroundings. Yury does indeed prize art, love, nature, woman, family life and religion above everything. But he eventually abandons all or most of these blessings without making the slightest attempt to defend and retain them. He saveth others, himself he cannot save. Such ineffectualness no more constitutes a defect in Pasternak's novel than it does in Dostoyevsky's. But it does raise the question of the extent to which both Yury Zhivago and his creator may conform with the concept of a saintly buffoon or holy fool.

Many a Russian novelist has set himself to teach his readers how to live. But none, perhaps, has been more successful in achieving this aim than Pasternak, who has so harmoniously fused his negative and positive elements that it is hard to say which is the more effectively presented. *Doctor Zhivago* is a radiantly affirmative work in which the affirmative element neither mars the impact of the whole (as is often the case with Tolstoy) nor suffers eclipse through the prominence given to glamorized evil (as so frequently in Dostoyevsky).

Doctor Zhivago may not be the best of all Russia's many didactic novels. But it is surely one of the most persuasive.

In the prose narrative of *Doctor Zhivago* Pasternak goes to some pains to present the cycle of twenty-five lyrics which end the novel as the product of his hero's brain, rather than of his own. He further emphasizes the point by giving the cycle a chapter to itself with the title 'The Poems of Yury Zhivago'. Still, however insistently Pasternak may attribute the *Zhivago* lyrics to Zhivago, nothing can conceal the fact that they are the work of a real poet and not of a fictional doctor.

Nor can there be any doubt that they represent, in every particular, Pasternak's own responses and attitudes to the world around him. Zhivago's philosophy is that of Pasternak's maturity. As such it is fully consistent with the view of life projected by the novel as a whole, whether expressed in prose or verse. It embodies, in effect, what Pasternak himself had learnt during half a century and more of living.

The twenty-five lyrics put forward a distilled version of this credo, concentrating heavily on its positive, affirmative aspects. They are, therefore, partly significant for what they do not contain – that is, for their marked failure to refer to the squalid world of fanatical, sterile revolutionary mediocrities with its collectivist philosophy and its shrill, cliché-ridden verbiage. In the lyric 'March', which contains a vivid description of the earth's rebirth after winter through the agency of dung, one critic has detected a possible allusion to an important event of March 1953: the death of Stalin.[33] The suggestion is ingenious, and well worth recording as a curio. But it is unlikely that the poet wished to invoke, however distantly, an episode so insignificant to a philosophy based less on a dislike – however intense – of politicians than on the love of nature, woman, God and art. It is these four key topics that Pasternak the poet emphasizes as he speaks through the mouth of Zhivago the poet in the lyrical cycle which ends the novel.

Pasternak's perception of nature, to which so many superlative prose passages of the novel are devoted, is also memorably expressed in the *Zhivago* lyrics. Once again he takes his reader through a twelve-month seasonal cycle, as he already had in *Themes and Variations* in his days of 'modernist' obscurity, and again in the cycle *Peredelkino* with which he had inaugurated his later, simpler, period in 1941. The *Zhivago* cycle reflects the poet's lifelong preoccupation with the concept of rebirth by relating this to the advent of spring, and by linking the theme to Christ's Passion and Resurrection at Easter. The cycle accordingly begins and ends with spring, most of the individual lyrics being firmly fixed at a specific season or month of the year. This is evident from some of their titles: 'March', 'In Holy Week', 'Spring Floods', 'Summer in Town', 'Indian Summer', 'Autumn', 'August', 'Winter Night', 'Christmas Star', 'Gethsemane'.

Resembling the *Peredelkino* cycle in the attention paid to the successive seasons of the year, the *Zhivago* cycle differs from it in stressing the theme of love. In 'Explanation' the poet again pays tribute – in somewhat bathetic style – to the eternal feminine which still calls to him in the evening of his days.

> The miracle of woman's arms, back, shoulders, neck
> I have revered subserviently all my life.

To the Yury Zhivago of these poems, as to the Yury Zhivago of the prose narrative, love is as much a spur to separation as to fulfilment. 'Explanation' ends as follows.

> Tightly though night may hold me clamped in hoop of yearning,
> Another tug – the lust for ruptures – pulls yet stronger.[34]

One is reminded that Yury had allowed both his great loves, Tonya and Lara, to vanish from his life without making any serious effort to retain them – perhaps because this would have meant emigrating from Russia and thus cutting himself off from the mainspring of his art, to which he is ready to sacrifice everything.

In 'Parting' the poet evokes the symbol of the sea to express his love.

> She was as dear and close to him in all her features
> As are the breakers to the beach along the shore line.

The heroine of 'Parting' resembles both Lara and Olga Ivinskaya in the link created between her and her lover by the sufferings characteristic of the age.

> In years of ordeal, in that mind-unhinging epoch,
> Fate's tide had swept her in to him from ocean's bosom.[35]

As in the prose narrative, a few delicately erotic allusions are permitted. In 'Explanation' the poet refers to himself and his mistress as 'high-tension wires', an echo of the prose passage in which Lara is described as carrying a lethal charge of electricity. The cycle also includes the two lyrics 'Intoxication' and 'Autumn', which (as has been noted above) Akhmatova once denounced for indulging in a degree of sensuality inappropriate, on her interpretation, to a man in his sixties.

It was Pasternak's habit to link his major themes together, and just as love is often fused with the perception of nature, so too it is sometimes combined with the religious theme. This is particularly true of 'Magdalene One', which has been interpreted as a work of 'passion and ruthless directness', owing to the stress on Mary Magdalene's role as a harlot – especially as she is one whose most exalted customer, 'undoubtedly at one level of apprehension', is Christ himself. Mary's 'cradling and comforting the body of Christ as it is brought down from the cross' cannot help but carry 'a defiantly erotic meaning; and this means that there may even be deliberate phallic overtones to the reference to the shaft of the cross'.[36]

With or without phallic overtones, the Christian motif receives more exposure in the *Zhivago* verses than in any of Pasternak's other lyrical cycles. It also assumes far more importance in the verse section of *Doctor Zhivago* than in the preceding prose narrative, being prominent in the last eight items in the twenty-five lyric cycle, while also figuring in two of its earlier poems, 'Hamlet' and 'In Holy Week'. The religious poems are not only linked with the theme of love through the figure of Mary Magdalene, but they are also intimately fused with the major theme of nature through the coincidence of Christ's Resurrection with the spring season and associated rebirth of the vegetational year.

'Daybreak' is the only one of the eight concluding religious lyrics which fails to invoke the Gospels, and it is also anomalous in expressing a personal confession of faith. Is the confession Yury Zhivago's or Boris Pasternak's? The lyric is addressed to Christ, and records its author's religious belief as having gone through a long period of suspension.

> You were the meaning of my life.
> But then came war and devastation,
> And for a long, long time there was
> No rumour of you, not one word.

In the second stanza of the lyric Pasternak alludes to his reconversion to Christianity after a long interval – a reconversion which otherwise remains scantily documented.

> Now, after many, many years
> Your voice has troubled me anew.
> All night I read your testament,
> And seemed to wake out of my swoon.[37]

The lyric thus alludes to three phases in the evolution of Pasternak's religious belief: the brief, intensely Christian phase of 1910–12 (assuming that there actually was one); a long interval of indifference; the revival of his faith in his last years.

Nowhere in Pasternak's writings is the Christian faith more movingly expressed than in the concluding eight lyrics of *Doctor Zhivago*. The sequence culminates with 'Gethsemane', which commemorates Christ's Passion and triumph. The lyric itself, the entire cycle of twenty-five lyrics, *Doctor Zhivago* as a whole – all end with the superb lines in which Pasternak affirms his Christian faith through words attributed to Christ himself.

> On the third day shall I arise.
> Into the tomb shall I descend.

And, riverborne, the rafts of time
Shall stream toward me to be judged –
Barges in convoy, out of darkness.[38]

Out of darkness! These last words of *Doctor Zhivago* are the affirmation of a great poet's optimistic view of human destiny, and echo the last words of the prose narrative. Here Zhivago's two friends, Gordon and Dudorov, in whom the dead doctor–poet survives through their love for his poems and their memory of him, are standing by an open window high up in Moscow. The period is that of Stalin's post-war rule. Even so, they seem to sense in the air a 'foretaste of freedom' and are 'overwhelmed by the silent music of happiness'. The book of Zhivago's poems in their hands 'seemed to know all this and to support and confirm what they felt'.[39] Pasternak may have been uncertain in his technique when he came to begin his novel. But he certainly had a way with him when it came to ending it.

While so richly reflecting Zhivago–Pasternak's love of nature, woman and God, the *Zhivago* poems have little to say on a no less fundamental preoccupation of their dual author – artistic creativity. It was to art that Yury Zhivago and Boris Pasternak both arguably sacrificed everything else in life; and the theme figures in many other poems of Pasternak, besides also being prominent in the prose narrative of *Doctor Zhivago*. But though art, especially the art of poetry, might have been expected to occupy a comparable position in the *Zhivago* lyrics, this is perhaps rendered superfluous by the fact that they themselves are actual specimens of the poetic art. As such they might be thought to pre-empt consideration of the theme in the text.

Though the cycle as a whole does indeed neglect the theme of art, this is not true of the opening lyric, 'Hamlet'. This sixteen-line poem reflects the dislike of public prominence that had characterized Pasternak since the long-past days when he had first begun to dissociate himself from the flamboyant Mayakovsky. It further reflects his reluctance – yet willingness – to accept the role, which he believed to have been thrust upon him, of witness to his age. This was the witness that he had felt compelled to bear by publishing *Doctor Zhivago* as a whole.

The biblical prayer 'Abba, Father, let but this cup pass from me', which occupies a line and a half of 'Hamlet', has a multiple resonance, and it forces the reader to speculate on the identity of the poem's 'I', who appears in each stanza. Is it Pasternak himself? Is it Pasternak's hero Yury Zhivago? Is it Shakespeare's hero Hamlet? Is it an actor playing Hamlet? Or is it the original author of the cry 'Abba, Father' –

Jesus Christ? The 'I' of the poem looms as a composite portrait, in which all these elements are fused, as the phantom figure describes itself emerging on to a stage and trying to catch a distant echo of the events which will take place in its time. Night's darkness is focused through a thousand opera glasses on this figure, which reconciles itself to acting out its destined role even as it prays to be relieved of that duty. The poem also stresses the central figure's loneliness in a world of spurious values and the supreme difficulty of that supremely difficult task – living life, whether ordinary or extraordinary, as it should be lived.

> But the acts' pattern's foreordained,
> And journey's ending can't be bypassed.
> I am alone. All drowns in cant.
> To live a life's no easy task.[40]

The prayer 'Abba, Father', as voiced in the cycle's opening lyric by its composite hero, is repeated in its more familiar historico-religious context in the mouth of Christ in the twenty-fifth and last lyric, 'Gethsemane'. This feature emphasizes the cyclical structure of the *Zhivago* lyrics, contributing to the unity and harmony of the sequence as a whole. The repetition also helps to reinforce the equation made between Pasternak himself and the figure of Christ through four intermediaries: Shakespeare, Hamlet, the actor who plays Hamlet and Yury Zhivago. It is for such reasons that one critic can speak of Pasternak as having taken on himself a mission of 'apostolic service', while another says that 'his motherland was his Golgotha'.[41]

Of all the possible equivalents for the 'I' of 'Hamlet', Yury Zhivago is the candidate who least aptly fits the first person singular of what purports to be his own poem. The lyric's composite hero is, after all, a man very much in the public eye. Pasternak himself was certainly that. And so, too, in their different ways, were Shakespeare, Hamlet, the actor playing Hamlet and Jesus Christ. But Yury Zhivago lives and dies in relative obscurity. Never in the novel does he appear on a metaphorical stage to bear public witness. It is perhaps a measure of Pasternak's genius that the inconsistency, if it is one, does not impair the force and originality of the conception that inspired 'Hamlet', the lyric cycle and the novel as a whole.

The mysterious 'I' of 'Daybreak' and 'Hamlet' prompts consideration of a problem posed by the lyric cycle as a whole. Did Pasternak intend these twenty-five poems to reflect his hero's life and thinking as described in the novel's preceding sixteen parts? Or are they a writer's comment on his own life and thinking? In other words, is the reader to take the lyrics as Zhivago's work? Or as Pasternak's? What is to be made, for example, of the woman portrayed in 'August' as 'throwing her challenge at an abyss of humiliations'? Is this Zhivago's Lara? Or is it Pasternak's Olga, as Olga Vsevolodovna herself would have it? Is Olga indeed, as she also maintains, the damsel in distress rescued from a dragon by a knight errant, as described in 'Folk Tale'? Are the maiden's sufferings, as Olga Vsevolodovna again maintains, an allegorical reflection of her own martyrdom in the concentration camps?[42]

Critics have offered conflicting interpretations of this tantalizing identity crisis. An extreme view is Donald Davie's. He argues – in his book *The Poems of Doctor Zhivago* – that Pasternak most emphatically intended his reader to identify the twenty-five lyrics as the work of his fictional hero, and to distinguish them sharply from the poems published in his own name. The argument is forcefully put, but is unlikely to have made many converts. The claim, made by another authority, that some of the connections established in Davie's commentary 'seem to be rather farfetched' is if anything an understatement. And this contention is directly contradicted by Katkov, who claims that the *Zhivago* lyrics have 'an even closer relation to the life of Pasternak himself and to his spiritual development' than they have to the episodes of the novel.[43]

Attempts to equate the *Zhivago* poems with their original inspiration, whether in Yury Zhivago's fictional life or in Pasternak's real life, are best clarified by recalling the key passage in which the genesis of the hero's love poetry is described in the prose narrative of the novel. 'The more he crossed things out and changed one word for another, the further did the Lara of his poems and jottings recede from her real-life prototype.'[44]

Such 'growing away' from a living prototype is well illustrated in 'Parting'. It describes a man who visits his beloved, only to make the unexpected and horrifying discovery that she has disappeared from her home, which has been left in a state of extreme disarray. The poem clearly reflects the emotions aroused in Yury by his separation from Lara, as described in Chapter Fourteen of *Doctor Zhivago*. But it most certainly fails to reflect the specific circumstances of that separation. Lara's departure had come as no surprise to Yury, since he had engineered it himself for reasons of his own. Is 'Parting', then, closer to real life than to the novel? Katkov says that it is a description of Pasternak's 'own feelings when he learnt of the . . . arrest of Ivinskaya' in 1948. He adds that few of Pasternak's fellow citizens 'can have failed to appreciate the situation described or to have recognized the reference to an unexpected arrest and the disorder of a room after a police search'.[45] Very possibly. But there is no evidence to show that the real-life Pasternak in fact became aware of Ivinskaya's arrest under conditions comparable to those described in the poem, or that those conditions are any more faithfully reflected in the poem than are the circumstances of Yury's reactions to Lara's absence. Rather has the woman of the poem 'grown away' from both her fictional and her living prototype in accordance with Zhivago–Pasternak's creative technique.

Doctor Zhivago is certainly one of the most important literary documents of its century. But what of its qualities as a literary work? Is it indeed a masterpiece? Or do its aesthetic qualities fall short of its historical significance? Is it yet another example of Russian didactic fiction making an impact out of all proportion to its literary merit, as had Chernyshevsky's *What is to be Done* in the previous century?

Widely differing opinions have been expressed on the merits of *Doctor Zhivago*. Many Western reviewers and critics have voiced admiration bordering on ecstasy. 'One of the great novels of the last fifty years, and the most important work of literature that has appeared since the war' – this judgement, offered by Stuart (now Sir Stuart) Hampshire in 1958 would still find many supporters. But so too perhaps might Isaac Deutscher's dismissal of the novel, in an article of 1959, as essentially 'flat, clumsy, labored, and embarrassingly crude', despite some impressive and polished lyrical passages.[46]

Among Soviet-published Russians Ilya Ehrenburg has taken a comparatively mild view when complaining in his memoirs that too many pages of *Doctor Zhivago* are 'devoted to what the author has not seen or heard'.[47] Other Soviet-published assessments have been far harsher, but have little consequence since they do little more than reflect official policy on what critics are permitted to write on a hypersensitive matter. But it so happens that adverse opinions have been expressed by certain Soviet-based writers and critics of 'dissident' persuasion, who – lacking any outlet for voicing their findings publicly at home – have reported them in detail in material spirited out of the Soviet Union. They happen to be the four individuals who have done most, in memoirs published exclusively outside the USSR, to illuminate Pasternak's later life: Nadezhda Mandelstam, Anna Akhmatova, Lidiya Chukovskaya and Aleksandr Gladkov. They have all commented on *Doctor Zhivago* as friends and well-wishers of Pasternak, and as admirers of his work in general, who nevertheless do not admire the novel, and who therefore tend to speak of its alleged defects more in sorrow than in anger. All four commentators are wholly independent of Kremlin-inspired thought control, and yet they have been apt to refer to *Doctor Zhivago* almost as disparagingly as did its Soviet-published detractors during the phase of its most acute condemnation by official Russia.

The most amusing of these condemnations came, as might be expected, from Akhmatova in conversation with Chukovskaya. After finishing *Doctor Zhivago*, Akhmatova said that it contained some 'wholly unprofessional pages' which made her want to cross them out one after the other with an editor's pencil. So poor was this material that – Akhmatova claimed in all seriousness – it could not possibly have been written by Pasternak himself. It must be the work of the detested (by Akhmatova) Olga Ivinskaya! Nadezhda Mandelstam is almost equally scathing. She will agree to call *Doctor Zhivago* a 'novel' only because she happens to associate the term with 'light reading'; she would never think of Tolstoy's *War and Peace* or Dostoyevsky's *Idiot* as novels.[48]

A more extensive criticism comes from Gladkov, whose claim to write of Pasternak with sympathy, and even with reverence, is borne out by the tone of his memoir as a whole. Gladkov was an unstinting admirer of Boris Leonidovich's poetry and personality, but he found himself unable to regard *Doctor Zhivago* as his friend's major achievement. Pasternak would have done better to write an extensive memoir of his times, suggests Gladkov. He had been mistaken in trying to dress up something of this sort as a novel, for everything novelistic in the book was so weak.[49]

The characterization of *Doctor Zhivago* has been judged particularly harshly. The characters 'lack vitality, they are contrived', according to Akhmatova. Doctor Zhivago himself is neither a Zhivago nor a doctor: that is, he has done nothing to earn his surname (a variation of the Russian adjective *zhivoy*, 'alive') because he is so lifeless, while his failure to practise medicine during most of the narrative invalidates his professional pretensions. Akhmatova's amanuensis Chukovskaya agrees on the weakness of the characterization. 'You're right. The main figures aren't alive; they're made of cardboard, and the most cardboardy of the lot is Doctor Zhivago himself.' Gladkov is equally dissatisfied on this score, complaining that the characters are mere mouthpieces of the author; their dialogue consists either of naïve expressions of Pasternak's own views, or else of 'maladroit impersonations'.[50]

A parallel criticism is voiced by Fyodor Stepun in an article published by a Russian *émigré* magazine. He claims that the novel's chief characters suffer from a certain diffuseness of imagery, but adds that the secondary characters 'are drawn very vividly indeed'. Stepun goes on to instance Komarovsky, the somewhat melodramatic villain, who is indeed memorable, but also two other minor figures (Khudoleyev, Yusupka) whom few readers will easily recall.[51]

Gladkov also criticizes Pasternak's attempts to reproduce popular or substandard Russian speech, claiming that the conversation of 'ordinary people' – for example, in the train journey to the Urals and in the Siberian partisan camp – strikes a false note because the author had no ear for that sort of thing. Here Chukovskaya comes to Pasternak's rescue, saying that the speech of workers, of the common people, is rendered 'with genius', and invoking the similar success with which Pasternak had reproduced popular speech in parts of *Lieutenant Shmidt*.[52]

Pasternak's narrative technique has also been impugned. Gladkov calls it sketchy and inadequate, as might be expected from one whose creative skills had previously been deployed in an entirely different genre. Hampshire, otherwise one of *Doctor Zhivago*'s most persuasive admirers, has admitted the 'lack of a firm narrative' in the novel's first fifty pages.[53] Other criticisms have focused on the excessive and irritating part played by unconvincing coincidences. Over the length and breadth of Russia characters keep running into each other again and again. This may be plausible as a typical feature of an unstable age. But Pasternak seems to protest about coincidence too much, as in the scene of Gimazetdin's death at the front. 'The mutilated dead man was Private Gimazetdin, the officer screaming in the wood was his son, Second Lieutenant Galiullin, the medical sister was Lara, Gordon and Zhivago were witnesses. They were all together, side by side, and they did not recognize each other.' So what? This passage also contains a sentence so excruciatingly clumsy that it aroused Akhmatova's acute indignation. 'On elevation to the porch the mutilated one screamed, shuddered all over and gave up the ghost.' Akhmatova's comment: 'And the author of "August" ' (one of the finest *Zhivago* lyrics) 'could write that!'[54]

Some weight should perhaps be given to a recurrent anachronistic urge noted by Deutscher.[55] While describing the years 1917 to 1921, in which the main action is set, Pasternak often seems to be unconsciously betrayed into speaking of Soviet society as it was some two decades later in the worst years of Stalin's excesses. The suicide of the revolutionary warlord Antipov-Strelnikov, the consignment of Lara to the concentration camps – these were more characteristic of 1937 than of the early 1920s, when they are described as occurring.

Almost all the harsher critics of *Doctor Zhivago* make an exception for the passages of landscape description, to which tribute is universally paid. The passages in question are undeniably impressive, but repeated reference to them rings like damning by faint praise; it recalls Sonya's remark in Act Three of Chekhov's *Uncle Vanya*: 'When a woman isn't beautiful, people always say, "You have lovely eyes, you have lovely hair." '

Max Hayward, who translated both Gladkov's memoirs and *Doctor Zhivago*, has replied at length to Gladkov's criticism of the novel. Hayward claims that Pasternak himself contributed to the misinterpretation of *Doctor Zhivago* by his insistence on calling it a novel, when it is less a novel in the usual sense than a 'lyrical kaleidoscope'. Since Pasternak never aimed to construct a novel such as Tolstoy's *War and Peace*, there is no point (says Hayward) in criticizing him for his failure to do so. On the other hand, Pasternak was wise not to offer a comprehensive memoir of his period, as Gladkov would have had him do. Such a genre would have hampered him, confining him to the events of his own life. He would have been unable to write, however distantly, of his love for Ivinskaya. And he would have been unable to pass the typescript around or give readings, since the material would have been too flagrantly compromising both personally and politically. Hayward regards Pasternak's decision to cut short his narrative in the year 1929, with the death of his hero, as a masterstroke. He refers to the decision to pass over the 1930s in silence as a 'devastatingly simple device (perhaps unprecedented of its kind in literature). . . . The unspeakable cannot, by definition, be spoken of.'[56]

Perhaps it would be better to stop seeking excuses for Pasternak's particular method of handling the novel form, and to admit frankly that some of the strictures retailed above are only too well founded. The thinness of the characterization, especially – can this really be justified by insisting, however justifiably, that *Doctor Zhivago* is not a novel in the usual sense, and therefore does not require characters in the usual sense? The same argument could be employed to explain away any defect whatever. As for the narrative technique, though its faults may have been exaggerated by some, it is certainly uneven and at its worst irritating, with its habit of treating the reader as if he were already informed of what he cannot possibly know, its inept handling of exposition and its parading of gratuitous obscurities without the compensations with which the obscurities of Pasternak's verse so often reward the patient student. The narrative is particularly clumsy in the first hundred pages of the novel, as if the author were serving his apprenticeship at his reader's expense. It improves greatly as the work proceeds, and there are sustained passages in which it is superb.

It happens that I myself was given a special opportunity to judge Pasternak's workmanship in a context entirely free from the preconceptions which most other readers have been unable to avoid. About a year before the novel appeared I was asked to pronounce on a chapter of a Russian work of fiction which was submitted to me in English translation in typescript for an opinon – but without any indication of the author's identity. It was in fact the first chapter of *Doctor Zhivago*, but I neither knew nor remotely suspected this. I read it carefully, and replied in all honesty and innocence with what may, unintentionally, have been the cruellest remark ever made about Pasternak's novel: that these unattributed pages could only be the work of Konstantin Fedin. Re-reading the chapter in Russian, I can still understand how I was betrayed into forming such an opinion. But there is a ripple behind this lame, tame, early narrative which I had not earlier detected. Who but Pasternak could have perpetrated the splendid poet's pun on the first page, in the form of a brief dialogue exchanged at the funeral of the hero's mother? ' "*Kogo khoronyat?*" "*Zhivago.*" ' (' "Who's dead?" "Quick." ') Fedin could never have written that.

The early pages of Pasternak's narrative suffer abominably from the introduction of far more characters, identified by little more than their names, than most readers could either wish or expect to assimilate in the course of a dozen novels. This is, notoriously, a feature of Russian fiction in general, and one which appeals to some foreigners for its exotic quality, but it is doubtful whether any other novelist has so abused the practice as Pasternak. He brings in an average of one new named character per page in the opening chapters of *Doctor Zhivago*. Some of this material reads like an inept parody of a Russian novel. 'Nikolay Nikolayevich . . . brought Yury to Moscow and the family circle of the Vedenyapins, the Ostromyslenskys, the Selyavins, the Mikhaelises, the Sventitskys and the Gromekos. At first Yury was installed with the slovenly old windbag Ostromyslensky, dubbed "Fedka" by his clan. Fedka lived in sin with his ward Motya.' A few pages later the reader learns of guests assembling for a party. 'There arrived: Adelaida Filippovna, Gints, the Fufkovs, Mr and Mrs Basurman, the Verzhitskys, Colonel Kavkaztsev.' True, the sequence has a certain ring to it in Russian, not unlike the 'Uncle Tom Cobbleigh' catalogue in the song 'Widdicombe Fair'. But Pasternak's English translators cannot have thought much of the sentence, since they chose to omit it *in toto*.[57] It is an understandable decision.

The plethora of named but otherwise undistinguished characters exceeds the bounds of what is tolerable to all except addicts of pseudo-Russian exoticism, and there is no point in trying to excuse it or explain it away. Far better to admit that Pasternak's novel has grave flaws, but that it is nevertheless a masterpiece. So too is Homer's *Iliad*, where the Catalogue of Ships in Book Two out-Pasternaks even Pasternak the compulsive name-dropper. The *Iliad* too is a loosely constructed chronicle rather than an example of the narrator's art at its most taut and concentrated. The artistic level is uneven, swinging from the sublime to the more than occasionally ridiculous. Yet who can doubt its status as a masterpiece? Or that of Dante's architecturally impeccable *Divina Commedia*, where far more characters are invoked by name than is the case with Pasternak, and perhaps with Homer too?

One aspect common to great works of art in general is indicated by a telling passage from *Doctor Zhivago* itself. It comes from the point, in Yury's Varykino diary, where he speaks of art – primeval, Egyptian, Greek, our own – as 'a sort of life-affirming force' which has remained unchanged throughout the millennia. 'When a granule of this dynamism enters a more complex brew, the tincture of art dwarfs all else into insignificance. It emerges as the core, the essence, the very fibre of that which is depicted.'[58] This is more than an apologia for shoddy craftsmanship. It is an artistic confession of faith which emphasizes that Pasternak's work as a whole puts him, on however inferior a level, in the same camp as the sublime blunderers Homer and Shakespeare, rather than with the Horaces, the Dantes and the Racines.

Pasternak's virtues as a novelist go far beyond the passages of landscape description so often praised, for these are only one element in the creation of a special atmosphere, that of tragic impending doom, which forms one of *Doctor Zhivago*'s most signal achievements. Atmospheric doom reaches its peak in Chapter Fourteen ('In Varykino Again') with its description of Yury's parting from Lara and of the experience of writing poetry about her in that desolate landscape with its baying, powerfully symbolic wolves. Few chapters of fiction by other twentieth-century Russian writers can bear comparison with this sustained evocation of looming catastrophe.

Even if the novel's tragic intensity is ignored, it can be appreciated on a humbler level as a documentary account of its age. Pasternak's contemporary Sergey Spassky, a minor poet, wrote to him as follows. 'Probably anyone of our generation who reads your novel will recall a good deal of his own life and will take it as an account of something he has lived through himself.' Spassky congratulated Pasternak on having the courage to show 'life at the ordinary everyday level: sealing windows with putty ... fetching firewood ..., the delirium brought on by typhus'.[59] Where, in the literature of this bizarre period, have these mundane matters been more fully, more convincingly and more evocatively portrayed?

Above all, *Doctor Zhivago* triumphs as a hymn to man in his creative capacity, no matter whether he is a poet or a tiller of the soil – and the hero is both, as was his creator. Pasternak's championship of family life, of love, nature, God and art, which shines through his pages increasingly as the work gathers way, reaching its climax in the lyrical sequence at the end, is balanced by his destructive criticism of political manipulation as the embodiment of tedium and stagnation. Pasternak has championed life in all its aspects against the sterile interference of collectivist busybodies, and he has written a noble tribute to the human spirit. Flaws or no flaws, one wonders where so central and vital a point, or one so crucial to his own age and that of his successors, has ever been better presented. One could wish that it had been more heeded, and not only in the author's own country.

10

PRIZEWINNER

With the publication of *Doctor Zhivago* in Italian and Russian in November 1957, soon followed by versions in English, French, German and many other languages, Pasternak found himself playing the role of international celebrity in which he had reluctantly and fearfully consented to be cast as a matter of duty. The novel's vogue was based not only on what it was, but on what its author seemed to stand for in a world dominated by the tension between the inscrutable East and the baffled West. Had the Russian poet–novelist become a kind of extra-territorial moderator between these opposing forces? Might he even be the point at which the twain were, in some mysterious fashion, destined to meet in concord? Such a possibility seemed to hover over a world torn by strife and in sore need of a messiah, even one who sported wellington boots and an old mackintosh, to proclaim a solution to its problems.

In spite of the many changes that had taken place since Stalin's death, the USSR still remained a land of mystery, authority and menace to the world outside. It was hard to gauge Soviet potential, but Soviet power and size made it vital to do so. Each tremor of aberrant Muscovite activity was, accordingly, recorded on international seismographs, particularly close attention being paid to the ebullient Khrushchev's many oscillations: to his sponsorship of the erratic yet carefully modulated relaxations of Stalinism; to his suppression of the Hungarian uprising; to his success in ousting senior Party colleagues; to his denunciations of erring writers; to his Falstaffian outbursts. The difficulty, from the foreign observer's point of view, was that most of these notionally significant episodes, including both the tentative thaws and the cautious freezes, seemed – like everything else which occurred in Russia – to emanate almost exclusively from the highest authority. They seemed to reflect differences of opinion within the Party leadership, or conflicting impulses of Khrushchev's mind, rather than the spontaneous workings of independent forces. When, in heaven's name, would a Russian voice be heard other than that of the loutish supreme leader and his myriad echoing satellites, including so many tenth-rate writers licensed to simulate independent postures which could be promptly abandoned at the first breath of official displeasure?

In this context *Doctor Zhivago* had a multiple appeal to the world outside the Kremlin's orbit. It unmistakably represented the voice of an individual Russian citizen, not of someone – however dissident, protestive and notionally 'daring' – who was in effect operating with official sanction. Then again, the Protest Literature of Dudintsev and others tended to be as shrill in tone as the Soviet official voice which these authors sought or pretended, within the narrow limits open to them, to contradict. But who wanted to read an inverted *Pravda*? The equable tone, the absence of stridency, in *Doctor Zhivago* gave the novel a special appeal. So too did the general approach of an author who was not inhibited by domicile in the USSR from finding his themes in such fundamentals of human existence as love, death and God, rather than in devices for improving pipe-laying procedures. The novel's artistic merits were also a potent factor in enhancing its international appeal. However severely the blemishes of *Doctor Zhivago* may be judged, it still remains what it was called by a Western scholar shortly after publication, 'the only contemporary Russian novel that can be said to have appealed to Western readers on literary grounds'.[1] And yet, perhaps, none of these considerations so effect-ively commended *Doctor Zhivago* to the world at large as the fact that the work was denied publication in its country of origin. Here was a political system loudly claiming to have pioneered new dimensions of freedom, and to have abolished censorship. But the most famous author living under this endlessly self-congratulating dispensation had been unable to secure the publication of his most celebrated work in his native land. No wonder that the scent of forbidden fruit seemed to pervade the universe.

While *Doctor Zhivago* was beginning to enter the best-seller lists in the world at large, its impact within the USSR remained largely confined to rumour. Since the novel's foreign publication was so embarrassing to the Kremlin's controllers of public opinion, refer-ences to it were avoided in Soviet publicity organs during the eleven months between its first appearance in November 1957 and the offer of the Nobel Prize to its author in the following October. Knowledge of the text was at first restricted to the few Soviet readers who had access to the author or his typescripts. It later embraced those who were able to lay hands on a copy smuggled into the country from abroad. Some came to know the novel through the extensive extracts broadcast by the BBC's Russian Service. Otherwise the average Soviet citizen's acquaintance with Pasternak's text was to be limited to the violent denunciations put out by the country's official publicity machine.

It would be misleading to picture Pasternak as hanging with bated breath on every twist and turn of the international scandal which was beginning to develop around *Doctor Zhivago*, for he also had other serious preoccupations. In early 1958 he again fell grievously ill. Again he screamed with pain, again he longed for death. Consultants attended him at Peredelkino, but no authoritative diagnosis or effective palliative measures emerged. A distressing symptom of the previous year was repeated when the patient found himself incapable of urinating. No catheter was to be had in Peredelkino, but his friends scoured Moscow and its environs until they were eventually able to locate one and provide relief. On this occasion it proved particularly difficult to place the sufferer in a suitable hospital bed. His friend and neighbour Korney Chukovsky spent five days pulling strings; he appealed to the Writers' Union headquarters and to that organization's Literary Fund; he even rang up the All-Union Central Council of Trade Unions. But all was in vain until a hospital bed was eventually found through a secretary of Mikoyan, one of the top Party leaders. By means of this exalted agency Pasternak was admitted to a private ward in the country's most exclusive clinic, that of the Central Committee of the Communist Party. As the delinquent novelist was carried off in a kind of melancholy triumph by stretcher down his garden path to the vehicle waiting to convey him to this medical Valhalla, he was seen blowing kisses to the friends who had gathered to see him off.[2] Even in disgrace, it turned out, the Soviet Union preserved a proper sense of hierarchy: the top nonconformist was to receive top treatment.

On learning that hospitalization on so sublime a level had been granted to a supposedly disgraced writer, Akhmatova remembered her own past sufferings in the sordid common wards of less privileged lazarets, and fired off a characteristically corrosive comment. She said that someone who had written as Pasternak had written 'shouldn't expect a private ward in the hospital of the Party's Central Committee'. But there is no evidence that he ever *had* expected it – a point which Chukovskaya has stressed. This was not what he had asked for, but what his friends had managed to arrange for him by sheer persistence.[3]

Among the ordeals inflicted on Pasternak in the Central Committee's clinic was a bluff proposal which reached him from a fellow novelist, Fyodor Panfyorov, who had for many years zealously purveyed by pen and mouth the officially prescribed enthusiasms for increased industrial and agricultural output. Panfyorov now had the effrontery to advise the sick man to take himself off to Baku in a car, which Panfyorov was prepared to provide, and to study the construction of oil rigs in the Caspian with a view to celebrating this economic miracle in fiction better suited to Soviet requirements than *Doctor Zhivago*.[4] Here was a fatuous attempt, which can hardly have assisted Pasternak's recovery, to enlist the creator of *Doctor Zhivago* as one more literary copy writer assigned to recommend current economic 'achievements' to the public.

During Pasternak's confinement in hospital of early 1958 he was again rumoured to be suffering from cancer. But again no authoritative diagnosis was communicated, and again the poet threw off ill health for the time being. In the months preceding the Nobel Prize crisis his morale and physical condition combined the pathetic and the triumphant. There is the lonely, defenceless figure in cap, wellingtons and old mackintosh of Ivinskaya's memoirs, with his evening strolls to the Peredelkino Writers' Club, where he was accustomed to make relays of telephone calls. But there is also Ivinskaya's beloved as he still appeared to her – young, radiant, handsome. Chukovskaya recorded a similar double impression after meeting him in April 1958. He looked weary, doomed, isolated. Yet she also found him 'sunburnt, wide-eyed . . . , youthful-looking, animated and talkative'. When she called on him he was in full verbal cascade like a tumultuous human waterfall. 'Verbal masterpieces, born in boiling and rumbling, followed one another, one destroying the other . . . like clouds which no sooner conjure up the spectacle of a ridge of cliffs than they change in a second into an elephant or snake.' The poet Yevgeny Yevtushenko has also expressed admiration for the youthful vigour of Pasternak at this period. He looked like a man in his forties. 'His whole appearance breathed a sort of amazing, sparkling freshness like a newly cut bunch of lilac with garden dew still iridescent on its leaves.'[5]

This description agrees in substance, if not in tone, with my own reactions on meeting Pasternak in the summer of 1958, when I was privileged to have several long discussions with him after first calling with messages from the English translators of his novel. He was a strongly built, vigorous man, white-haired and sunburnt. Despite his recent illness, no one could have imagined him to be approaching three score years and ten. His conversation fully lived up to Chukovskaya's images of waterfall and clouds, and his voice – rich, rough, throaty, unmistakably Muscovite in lilt and texture – was captivating. The memory of it has often betrayed me into compulsive sympathetic mimicry when I speak Russian myself.

So emotionally involved was Pasternak with *Doctor Zhivago* that he had burst into tears, he told me, on first seeing a copy of it in book form – the French translation. He was, in general, a man who wept frequently, as many witnesses have confirmed, and as might be inferred from his writings. But one could not conceivably guess from his writings how readily he laughed or how witty, how engagingly humorous was his conversation. He was particularly amusing in discussing his attitude to his country's political system, as he uninhibitedly did – and without seeming to worry about the almost inevitable concealed microphones. He criticized Soviet propaganda for pontificating away as if the Revolution had occurred only the day before yesterday, and as if its 'achievements' were still so precarious as to require defending in some never-ending desperate last-ditch stand. But he was not in the least anti-Communist in any vulgar sense. He did not attack Communism; he simply implied, as he so often implies in the text of *Doctor Zhivago*, that the assumptions of the creed were not worth discussing. He several times referred to the Soviet way of life, with a grin and an airy wave in the direction of his windows, as *vsyo eto*: 'all that'. His attitude to 'all that' was further illustrated when I chanced to tell him that I was to give a lecture to the Philological Faculty of Moscow University on the next day, and added that I felt somewhat shy of addressing this coven of professors for two hours in what was their – but not my – native language. These forebodings he impatiently dismissed. 'Never mind that; let them look at a free man.'

From Pasternak's upstairs study we could occasionally observe the stately passing of a black limousine, of the type associated with the security authorities, along the lane outside the poet's house. It would slow down at his gate as if to stop; and though it never actually did so, the tactic was an effective form of nerve warfare, if indeed (as seems likely) it was devised as such. Pasternak did not appear to take the slightest notice, except for an occasional stiffening. And yet, for all he knew, such a limousine might arrive at any moment and remove him for ever. He was brave enough to face the prospect. But I am sure that he was unable to dismiss it from his mind.

During part of a lunch which lasted most of the day Pasternak's wife Zinaida Nikolayevna was present. She presided silently, and I felt uncomfortably aware that neither I, nor the numerous other foreign visitors of these years, would have crossed her threshold if she could have prevented us. But she was willing to fulfil punctiliously and courteously her function as mistress of a household simultaneously threatened and protected by the master's international contacts.

Meanwhile, in his second home, Olga Ivinskaya reigned supreme as the mistress of his heart. I was already vaguely conscious of this triangular tension pattern at the time of my visits, during which Ivinskaya's name was not mentioned. But Pasternak did allude, in his wife's absence, to someone near to him whose past sufferings had been incurred through her association with him.

It is hard not to feel sympathy for Zinaida Pasternak during her quarter of a century's attempts to palliate the disaster of being married to a major Russian poet. By now, inevitably, she was no longer the enchanting youthful apparition immortalized by her husband in a lyric written nearly thirty years earlier. No one could have taken the elderly, black-garbed Zinaida Nikolayevna of 1958 for the radiant young woman who had appeared, in a previously quoted lyric of 1931,

> In something white and simple
> Cut straight from the material
> They use to tailor snowflakes.[6]

Vigorous and energetic though he seemed, Pasternak must already have been suffering, at the time of our meeting, from the illness that was to kill him within two years. He showed his own awareness of such a possibility in a letter of 3 August 1958 to Jacqueline de Proyart. 'If only I could tell you, Jacqueline, how marvellous everything is, and how saturated with the future, even at this advanced hour, a few paces away from the probable end.'[7] The passage well illustrates how little he permitted intimations of mortality to blunt his natural love of life in what would have been his declining years, had he been capable of going into a decline.

Meanwhile, despite official efforts to conceal the existence of *Doctor Zhivago* from the Soviet public, at least one attempt was made to call its author to account before his professional colleagues. Ivinskaya writes of an occasion in the summer of 1958 when a special session of the Writers' Union Secretariat convened under Surkov's chairmanship in order to discuss Pasternak's 'unseemly conduct' behind closed doors. He himself was summoned or invited to attend, but was persuaded to stay away by Ivinskaya, who took his place and represented his interests. She arrived at the meeting with a note granting her the authority to speak in his name, only to find herself under attack for permitting the crisis to occur in the first place. As Pasternak's 'good angel' she should have been in a position to restrain him. Desultory hints at his 'treachery' followed, combined with the complaint that he had laid himself open to the accusation of being actuated by political and mercenary motives.[8]

These rumblings behind closed doors were soon followed by the first occasion on which Pasternak was publicly accused of conduct unbecoming in a member of the Writers' Union. It occurred at a recital of Italian poetry held in Moscow on 13 September 1958, and the moving spirit in condemning him was – once again – his old enemy Surkov, who was chairing the meeting. Someone in the hall asked why Pasternak was not present, and Surkov replied that Pasternak had written an 'anti-Soviet novel directed against the essence of the Russian Revolution', and had sent it abroad for publication.[9]

The stage was now set for the eruption of the Nobel Prize affair in October 1958, some two-and-a-half years after the original handover of *Doctor Zhivago* to Feltrinelli, and about eleven months after the novel's first publication in Italian and Russian.

By 1958 Pasternak had been canvassed for more than a decade as a possible recipient for the Nobel Prize for Literature, and rumours of his candidature had naturally increased in the months following the publication of *Doctor Zhivago*. He was appalled by the prospect of so high an honour and could think only of the trouble that it would cause him, but expected that the Italian novelist Alberto Moravia might be preferred to himself.[10] This was not to be, for the Swedish Academy announced the offer of the prize to Pasternak on Thursday 23 October 1958. In the official citation emphasis was laid on the adjudicators' intention to make the award for his work as a whole, not for *Doctor Zhivago* alone. The key phrase was: 'for his significant contribution to modern lyric poetry, as well as to the great traditions of the Russian prose-writers'.[11]

Pasternak forgot his previous forebodings in his delight at receiving so signal a distinction, and at once telegraphed his acceptance to the Swedish Academy. 'INFINITELY GRATEFUL, TOUCHED, PROUD, SURPRISED, OVERWHELMED.' The offer of the award was swiftly announced by the media outside the Kremlin's orbit; congratulations poured in from all sides; foreign correspondents swooped on Peredelkino to photograph and interview the honorand. But Radio Moscow, and the Soviet publicity machine as a whole, maintained an ominous silence. Even Peredelkino did not lack its spectre at the feast. Pasternak's next-door neighbour, the novelist and future exalted literary official Konstantin Fedin, strode over from his dacha in no mood to offer felicitations. He bluntly informed Pasternak that he would have to repudiate both the prize and the novel. Pasternak rushed off, greatly agitated, to consult Ivinskaya in the 'little house' which they shared near the village.[12]

Fedin had quickly realized, as the world at large soon realized, that the award was one of the greatest blows ever inflicted on Soviet prestige. No longer could the USSR's publicity organs pretend that Pasternak and his novel did not exist, as had been attempted during the eleven months following the work's first publication. The Stockholm announcement made it necessary to counterattack, and the Soviet media accordingly braced themselves to anathematize the prize, the adjudicators, the novel, its author and the 'capitalist' world in general. The ensuing hate campaign was to be discussed by the non-Soviet world in such exhaustive detail as to confer on *Doctor Zhivago*, in one hectic fortnight, a volume of publicity unprecedented in the history of the novel as an art form. But the lucky author was so far from basking in this sudden notoriety that he was brought to the brink of suicide.

On Saturday 25 October the first huge salvo was fired when the Moscow newspaper *Literaturnaya gazeta*, official organ of the Writers' Union, came out with a two-page spread consisting of attacks on Pasternak. They included an editorial article, *Provocative Sally of International Reaction*, in which the award of the prize to a 'decadent' poet was stigmatized as a dirty trick. *Doctor Zhivago* was dismissed as 'an artistically poverty-stricken and malicious work . . . full of hatred of Socialism'. The novel was said to constitute a hostile political act directed against the Soviet Union and calculated to intensify the Cold War. *Doctor Zhivago* was a 'carefully thought out ideological diversion' containing the life story of a malicious Philistine and enemy of the Revolution – its hero, Yury Zhivago. The work revealed its author's contempt for 'ordinary people' and his open hatred of his fellow Russians. It was a slander on Soviet partisans and on the Red Army. As for the novel's hero, whom Pasternak presented as a 'great martyr', he was a mere internal emigrant – pusillanimous, base, trivial and alien to the Soviet People. Pasternak himself is invoked as a 'Judas' who has shut his eyes to the transformation of his country by victorious Socialism. He has put a weapon into the hands of the ideological enemy while spitting at the Russian people and its great Revolution. His novel is bait transfixed on the rusty hook of anti-Soviet propaganda. But Judas–Pasternak should remember that bait is thrown away when it goes rotten. An ignominious end awaits him.[13]

The same issue of *Literaturnaya gazeta* also carried the letter which has been mentioned above as having been sent to Pasternak by the editorial board of the journal *Novy mir* back in September 1956. It was now published for the first time after a two-year delay. The letter itself contains a reasoned and tolerably equable analysis of the novel, and of the board's reasons for deciding to reject it for publication in *Novy mir*. But this document was accompanied on the pages of *Literaturnaya gazeta* by a shorter covering letter which the *Novy mir* editors had newly concocted in the light of the Nobel Prize award, and which was couched in language less temperate. Many of the points made in the *Literaturnaya gazeta* editorial are repeated, and Pasternak is charged with bringing discredit on the honourable calling of Soviet writer. For his 'libel on the October Revolution', for contributing a weapon to the arsenal of international reaction, for his shameful and unpatriotic attitude, he is pilloried as meriting only disgust and contempt.[14]

On the same day, 25 October, attempts were made to dragoon the students of the Moscow literary institute at which Ivinskaya's daughter Irina was enrolled into mounting a 'spontaneous' demonstration against Pasternak. A few of them were persuaded to parade the streets with placards showing him reaching with grasping fingers for a sack of dollars. Another had the caption 'THROW JUDAS OUT OF THE USSR'. Attempts were made to persuade the students to sign a collective letter of protest against *Doctor Zhivago*, and this duly appeared in the press a few days later along with all the other abusive material. But it seems that only a third of the pupils could be persuaded to put their names to the document.[15]

On Sunday 26 October the press campaign against Pasternak was stepped up. The *Zhivago* scandal now invaded the pages of *Pravda*, the official organ of the Communist Party of the Soviet Union – a sign of the overriding importance attributed to the issue by the top leadership. Here an article, *Reactionary Uproar over a Literary Weed*, appeared over the signature of D. Zaslavsky, who was already notorious for his virulent attacks on the victims of previous press campaigns. Zaslavsky denounced Pasternak's literary career as a whole, going back to the days when he had joined a pack of Decadents, Symbolists and Futurists engaged in trying to poison Russian literature. Pasternak's early verse had 'had nothing in common with the Life of the People'. True, he had at least tried to become a Fellow Traveller for a time, and had written *Nineteen Hundred and Five* and *Lieutenant Shmidt*. But he had stopped short at that point, and had become increasingly hostile to the Revolution. He was a self-infatuated Narcissus marooned in a literary backwater, and he had been hostile to Soviet society and Soviet literature for forty years. Falsely portrayed abroad as a martyr, he lived off the fat of the land in his large country house. Pasternak did possess a modicum of talent, granted. But he had never been a writer of the front rank. Now he was trying to avenge himself on Soviet society for being an outsider and a weed on Soviet soil. The Nobel Prize had been conferred for political motives, not in respect of literary achievement. If Pasternak had any 'spark of Soviet dignity' in him he would reject so tainted an award.[16]

Alerted by the signal given in *Pravda*, the rest of the Soviet media struck up an orchestrated campaign of abuse, repeating the points already made with minor flourishes and cadenzas of their own. Leading articles in *Literaturnaya gazeta* and *Pravda* and broadcast denunciations were reinforced by letters from 'ordinary Soviet workers' – a traditional feature of all such hate campaigns. Ivinskaya's daughter Irina says that Pasternak fortunately 'did not read the newspapers', and that he just plodded around in his usual cap, mackintosh and wellington boots looking heart-rendingly lonely and ignoring the abuse hurled at him on all sides.[17] But there are ample indications that he was fully aware of what was going on. Much though he despised the drill of massed ritual posturings, and inclined though he was to laugh helplessly at the absurdity of it all, he was an acutely sensitive man, deeply worried even as he vainly tried to shut the whole affair out of his consciousness. Unlike the victims of previous literary witch-hunts – Pilnyak, Zamyatin, Akhmatova and Zoshchenko among them – Pasternak had deliberately brought the avalanche upon himself by calculated activity spread over more than ten years. He had known all along what writing *Doctor Zhivago* might imply. He had even written poems predicting this great triumph or disaster: 'Had I but Known the Way of it' and 'Hamlet'. Had he been right to tread his road to Calvary? Misgivings must have crossed his mind, especially as those near to him were bound to suffer as well. All he had needed to do in order to pass his last years in peace and comfort was to confine himself to translating and pottering in his garden. Zinaida Nikolayevna must have told him so thousands of times.

Practical measures designed to deprive Pasternak and his closest ally of their livelihood were soon added to the verbal assaults ringing out on all sides. Even before the Nobel Prize scandal had erupted Olga Ivinskaya had lost all her translation contracts, and so had Pasternak too, with the possible exception of one for the play *Marja Stuart* by the Polish poet Juliusz Slowacki.[18] Then, at noon on Monday 27 October, four days after the Nobel Prize announcement, the Presidium of the Board of the Writers' Union of the USSR met in conclave with various august ancillary bodies of which the mere names illustrate the degree to which literary affairs had become bureaucratized: the Bureau of the Organizing Committee of the RSFSR Branch of the Writers' Union, the Presidium of the Board of the Moscow Section of the RSFSR

Branch of the Writers' Union. Pasternak was summoned to this ecclesiastical court so that anathema might be pronounced on him in person. He chose not to appear, but sent a letter in which he asserted that the writing of *Doctor Zhivago* was not incompatible with the calling of Soviet Writer, and proclaiming (inaccurately, as it was to turn out) that nothing would induce him to give up the honour of the Nobel Prize.[19]

In Pasternak's absence the assembled inquisitors of the central, RSFSR and Muscovite Writers' Union organizations passed a resolution repeating variants of abuse already familiar from press and radio, while adding a tangible disciplinary measure. The culprit was formally divested of the title of Soviet Writer and expelled from the Soviet Writers' Union. This posed a serious threat to a livelihood wholly dependent on literary earnings. It also marked a signal escalation of what Ivinskaya called the campaign 'to starve us into submission',[20] since it now seemed likely that the outcast would never be able to place any work in a Soviet publication again.

The Writers' Union resolution was duly published in the press on 28 October. On the same day Pasternak took the step of rejecting the Nobel Prize. Without consulting Ivinskaya, the person most closely concerned, or (it appears) anyone else, he wired the Swedish Academy as follows. 'IN VIEW OF THE MEANING GIVEN TO YOUR AWARD BY THE SOCIETY TO WHICH I BELONG I MUST RENOUNCE THIS UNDESERVED DISTINCTION WHICH HAS BEEN CONFERRED UPON ME. PLEASE DO NOT TAKE MY VOLUNTARY RENUNCIATION AMISS.' At the same time Pasternak also dispatched a telegram to the Party Central Committee. 'HAVE RENOUNCED NOBEL PRIZE. LET OLGA IVINSKAYA WORK AGAIN.'[21]

On the following day, 29 October, Moscow Radio carried a speech by V. Semichastny, head of the Komsomol (Young Communist League). It contained the most venomous passage to be found in all the many attacks on Pasternak. After calling him a 'scabby sheep' the speaker varied his zoological comparisons and went on to compare him, unfavourably, with the pig – that relatively clean animal which is not accustomed to pollute the place where it eats. Let Pasternak go and sniff the air of the foreign capitalist paradise which he so much admires. No obstacle will be placed in his way, and Soviet air will become purer to breathe.[22] Semichastny was articulating the threat which Pasternak feared more than any other, that of exile from his native land. No matter how badly the Soviet Union might treat him, he passionately desired to remain a Soviet resident. After briefly considering emigration, he firmly dismissed the idea, fearing for those whom he might have to leave behind him, and unable to face abandoning Russia, its familiar birch trees and its no less familiar trials and tribulations. He also believed, as he caused Yury Zhivago to reflect in the novel, that 'A grown man must grit his teeth and share his country's destiny.'[23]

Further pressure was applied to Pasternak and Ivinskaya at this stage through coarse surveillance of their activities by KGB operatives who obtrusively observed and otherwise discommoded them with ostentatiously paraded hooliganism. For instance, groups including men dressed as women would hold rowdy 'parties' on the landing outside Ivinskaya's flat in Potapov Street. It also turned out, as the lovers had long suspected, that concealed microphones had been installed in their various dwellings by the security authorities. Indeed, it was Boris Leonidovich's practice to greet these devices with a low bow and a 'Good day, Mike.'[24]

At one point, as the pressure mounted, Pasternak proposed to Ivinskaya in all seriousness that they should both commit suicide. He told her that he happened to have twenty-two tablets of Nembutal, which should be enough to dispose of them both. Such was their distress that they permitted this desperate discussion to take place in the presence of Ivinskaya's small son by her second marriage, the 'chubby, curly-haired Mitya'. Fortunately Ivinskaya persuaded Pasternak to call off his desperate plan, and she rushed next door in the hope of enlisting the help of the influential Fedin.[25]

When Fedin learnt that his next-door neighbour was on the verge of suicide, he dourly remarked that Boris Leonidovich had 'dug an abyss between himself and us'. All Fedin could offer in the way of help was to arrange a meeting between Ivinskaya and Polikarpov, who was still the senior official responsible for dealing with the Pasternak case. Polikarpov responded by giving Ivinskaya clear instructions that she must at all costs prevent Pasternak from committing suicide, for that would be 'a second stab in the back for Russia'. She must help him, instead, to 'find his way back to his People'. It was not enough that he had rejected the Nobel Prize. It was also necessary, Polikarpov vaguely indicated, for him to express some kind of public contrition.[26]

During the next few days Pasternak was persuaded to sign two letters of recantation through pressures ultimately applied by Polikarpov. The first was engineered through the intermediary of one Grimgolts, a young lawyer attached to the Writers' Union Department for Authors' Rights. Grimgolts conveniently made Ivinskaya's acquaintance at this time, posing as an ardent admirer of Pasternak and his work. As such he was able to persuade Ivinskaya (in accordance with his instructions from Polikarpov) that a suitable letter addressed to Khrushchev personally was the only possible way for Pasternak to avoid expulsion from the USSR. Grimgolts was already primed with suggestions for the wording of the kind of letter that would be found acceptable, and his rough draft was worked over by an informal committee which included Ivinskaya, Ariadna Efron and Ivinskaya's daughter Irina. That young woman, who seems to have had more sense than all Pasternak's other well-wishers combined, stoutly maintained that no such missive should be sent; but she was overruled by her mother, who feared for Pasternak's life. After discussion by the ladies the Grimgolts draft was reworded in parts to make it sound less unlike something that could have emanated from Pasternak. He signed it at once, stipulating only one minor change: that the land of his birth should be described as 'Russia', not as the Soviet Union. He also went out of his way to dissociate himself from the proceedings by signing several blank sheets of paper. In this way he made it possible for his advisers, had they wished, to undertake further revisions, and to send in whatever text they chose without putting him to the embarrassment of having to know what was in it.[27] It is a measure of his weariness of spirit and contempt for the proceedings.

Before long Irina Yemelyanova was able to take the finalized text of the letter to the Central Committee. It was broadcast on Moscow Radio on 1 November, and appeared in *Pravda* on the following day. It consisted chiefly of a personal appeal to Khrushchev not to enforce exile from the Soviet Union, as recently threatened in Semichastny's speech. Pasternak is described as tied to Russia 'by my birth, by my life, by my work', and his departure from his native country is described as being, for him, the equivalent of death. The letter ended as follows. 'With my hand on my heart, I can say that I have done a thing or two for Soviet literature, and may yet be of service to it.'[28]

From the authorities' point of view the letter represented a step forward. But though its pleading tone was satisfactorily abject, the wording did not have the proper ring to it. Even the cliché at the end, which is also the sentence which must have been the most humiliating to its signator's *amour propre*, was not couched in the prescribed liturgical diction. There was no reference in the entire missive to the glorious future, to sacrificing one's life, to the achievements of the Soviet people, or to anything of that kind, while the allusion to 'Russia' rather than to the Land of Socialism or the Soviet Motherland could not but grate on connoisseurs of the approved style.

Meanwhile further pressure was being put on Pasternak at a meeting of the Moscow branch of the Writers' Union held on Friday 31 October. Over a dozen members rose to voice their righteous indignation. The delinquent was denounced as having been a secret enemy of the State for the last forty years, and the hope was expressed that he might be deprived of his Soviet citizenship. To this resolution the customary unanimous agreement was recorded, but another custom of the period was also observed: a number of the writers corralled in order to sanctify these proceedings found it convenient to be 'accidentally' absent at the buffet or in the washroom when the vote was taken. Those present had acted either out of fear or in order to further their careers, Ivinskaya explains – unnecessarily, for rarely was any member of the Writers' Union in a position to act otherwise on public occasions.[29] There was also, no doubt, some genuine indignation with Pasternak. *They* had kept their contract with the State, whereby – in return for a whole array of very tangible privileges – they periodically assumed certain required public postures and mouthed certain sanctified formulae. Pasternak had long enjoyed the same range of privileges as they. He too (from their point of view) had sold out; but *he* would not stay sold.

On the same day, 31 October, farce intruded even more blatantly when Pasternak and Ivinskaya were suddenly whipped off from Peredelkino at no notice, and in the traditional black official limousine, as the result of a summons from Central Committee headquarters. Arriving there, and required by the guard at the entrance to produce his papers, Pasternak could only offer 'this membership card of the Writers' Union that you've just thrown me out of'. He further informed the uniformed representative of the People, in equally characteristic style, that the reason why he was wearing such an old pair of trousers was that he had not been given time to change them. Fortified by valerian drops, that traditional Russian tranquillizer, Pasternak then entered the august premises of the Central Committee, fully expecting – he who had long sought a dialogue with Stalin – to be confronted at least with Khrushchev. It was, however, merely the departmental head Polikarpov who greeted him, and who told him that he must now find a way to allay the people's wrath. The use of this hoary cliché triggered Pasternak's resentment, and he accused Polikarpov of glibly producing the trite word 'people' like something taken out of his trouser pocket. Then Polikarpov made the mistake of patting Pasternak patronizingly on the shoulder with the remark 'Dear me, old chap, you really have landed us in a mess.'

This was too much for Pasternak, who could be irascible on occasion and who was by no means overawed by any official, whether low or – in this case – of some eminence. 'Kindly drop that tone', the poet told the country's chief cultural satrap. 'You can't talk to me like that.' When Polikarpov responded with another cliché to the effect that Pasternak had stabbed the country in the back, Pasternak insisted on his withdrawing the remark. Polikarpov did so at once, and Pasternak terminated the conversation by walking out. But Polikarpov detained Ivinskaya and explained that it would now be necessary to draft a second, more acceptable, letter of recantation to be published in Pasternak's name.[30]

By now the Wrath of the People was swamping the media. Excavator operators, collective farm chairmen, pianists, geologists, oil workers, old age pensioners and various other self-characterized honest toilers wrote in from outlying republics of the USSR to express their anger and indignation over Pasternak's effrontery in publishing a novel which few of them can possibly have set eyes on.[31]

Meanwhile Ivinskaya and Polikarpov had extracted the draft of a second letter of recantation from Pasternak, and were soon working on it 'like arrant counterfeiters'. When their version was presented to the poet he made a dismissive gesture and signed it with as little objection as he had voiced over the first.[32] It was published in *Pravda* on 6 November.

The letter is addressed to *Pravda*'s editors, and is somewhat longer than its predecessor. So heavily and repeatedly is the free and voluntary nature of the statement stressed in the text that this very emphasis could only arouse suspicion. The document records Pasternak's present, belated realization that the award of the Nobel Prize had all along been a political move. It also records his regret at not having heeded the warning of *Novy mir*'s editors when they had told him, in their letter rejecting his novel for publication, that *Doctor Zhivago* might be interpreted as directed against the October Revolution and the basis of the Soviet system. Pasternak is further presented as admitting that his novel appeared to challenge the historical validity of every revolution in history. The text continues with the one phrase in which its manufacturers appear to have admitted a measure of ambiguity. 'It is quite clear that I cannot put my name to assertions so inane.' Hence the renunciation of the prize. The statement concludes with yet another assurance that it has not been extracted under pressure, and even shows Pasternak offering unconditional phraseological surrender as he speaks of his radiant faith in the future and of his pride in the age he lives in.[33]

For all its more abject and subservient tone this second letter of recantation still did not have quite the proper ring. It lacked the full ritualistic polish. But it was good enough for Khrushchev's era, though it would never have done for Stalin's. In return the public campaign against Pasternak was at once moderated. It was to smoulder on, sputtering into flame from time to time, but there was to be no repetition of the hate orgy of 23 October to 6 November. Rather was the attempt made to remove Pasternak from the public gaze.

Ivinskaya has apologized in her memoirs for her part in concocting Pasternak's two letters of recantation, and for collaborating with the authorities by extracting his signature to both documents. She admits that neither letter should ever have been sent. At the time when her memoirs were written hindsight had brought her round to agree with her daughter, who had been against public recantation all along.[34]

When, shortly after Pasternak's death, the *Zhivago* scandal was succeeded by the sequence of Solzhenitsyn scandals, the posture adopted by Pasternak in October–November 1958 began to seem pitifully feeble. Solzhenitsyn never made such concessions, and his record seems to show how unnecessary they were. But Solzhenitsyn possessed a fighting temperament almost unequalled in historical record: he had fought off cancer, he had survived years in the camps, and he was a far younger, tougher man than Pasternak. Ailing, and in his sixty-ninth year at the time of the Nobel Prize crisis, Pasternak could not anticipate Solzhenitsyn's later achievement. There is also the point that Pasternak's readiness to make concessions did, presumably, help to achieve his aim of avoiding expulsion from Russia – a form of punishment (if it was one) which the uncompromising Solzhenitsyn did not succeed in eluding.

Only the most insensitive observer could dream of reproaching Pasternak with lack of courage. As for lack of tactical finesse, that is another matter. After choosing to take on the Soviet authorities in unequal combat, and after winning the decisive battle against all the odds, he seemed – for the time being at least – to have thrown away the fruits of victory at the last moment in a fit of despair or absent-mindedness. It is tempting to comment that all he had needed to do during the two-week crisis had been, quite simply, nothing at all.

Pasternak paid the price for his letters of recantation in terms of personal suffering. During the rest of his life the false statements to which he had put his signature preyed on his mind. 'The main point was that he could not do such violence to his own nature with impunity.' His principal lie had been the repeated assertion that he had not been acting under duress, compounded by the boast (contained in the second letter) that nothing in the world could compel him to 'behave with duplicity' (*pokrivit dushoy*) or go against his conscience. He had never done so previously, perhaps, but he was certainly doing so now. Or rather, to be more precise, he would have been doing so had he been the actual author of the text and had he signed it in all seriousness. Ivinskaya, who knew him better than anyone else, has claimed that the violence done to him during the fifteen days of the Nobel Prize crisis 'broke and then killed him'.[35]

Pasternak entered a phase of relative stability with the publication of his letter of recantation in *Pravda* on 6 November 1958. Though the campaign of public abuse was to be revived sporadically, the Soviet media were henceforward to treat the poet–novelist more as an unperson than as an enemy of the people. No less important was the restoration of his livelihood through renewed access to translation contracts, which had shown signs of drying up entirely after the consignment of *Doctor Zhivago* to a foreign publisher. This concession came through the deal which Ivinskaya made with the authorities during the Nobel Prize crisis. In return for a suitable document bearing Pasternak's signature – the *Pravda* letter – the high Party official Polikarpov firmly and explicitly promised that the ban on the publication of translations by both Pasternak and Ivinskaya would be lifted, and that his version of Goethe's *Faust* would be cleared for re-issue in a new edition (the fourth). When it duly appeared, in 1960, it contained the original preface by one N. Vilmont – but in a significantly bowdlerized form. The translator's very name, along with Vilmont's numerous flattering references to his work, had been expunged.[36]

Further translation contracts were also made available to Pasternak after the crisis had blown over. But his original writings were another matter. Publication of those in the Soviet Union ceased in 1958, and it was not to be resumed until he was safely dead.

So far as the Soviet authorities were concerned, the less said about Pasternak the better once he had gone on record with an act of public submission. But the fascination aroused in the world at large by his personality, his posture and his novel were undiminished, and he remained a potential source of global banner headlines. This helped to protect him from harassment at home, and he came to enjoy an enhanced special – almost extra-territorial – status in his own country. True, there were still no practical obstacles to indicting him on some trumped-up charge, to prosecuting him, to imprisoning him, or to harrying him severely in all manner of ways. But the authorities confined themselves to inflicting minor irritations. They feared the renewed international scandal which would burst forth if the persecution of the world's most newsworthy poet–novelist were once more permitted to assume journalistically exploitable dimensions. And so Pasternak sat out his last years at Peredelkino in a posture like that of Tolstoy at Yasnaya Polyana many years earlier. Both sages were the targets for pilgrimage from far and wide, being renowned alike for their writings and for their prestige as acknowledged opponents of an authoritarian State which dared not touch them for fear of exposing itself to ridicule and contempt. The parallel was once ironically stressed by Pasternak himself in conversation with me. He spoke of his Peredelkino home as Neyasnaya Polyana ('Blurred Glade') – a punning distortion of Tolstoy's Yasnaya Polyana ('Clear Glade').

The authorities did little or nothing to interfere with the vast correspondence addressed to Pasternak from all parts of the globe after the Nobel Prize award, and he is believed to have received from twenty to thirty thousand letters between the award of the Nobel Prize and his death. A whimsical lyric of January 1959, 'Wide World', expresses his appreciation of this correspondence, often handed to him in a package by the local postwoman on a woodland path near his home. The poem concludes with a wry comment: how lucky any philatelist would feel if he could change places with its author.[37]

Foreign admirers also came to see him in person at Peredelkino, in spite of a clumsy attempt by authority to prevent such visits. One day Pasternak was virtually kidnapped by officials at his country home, and whisked off in the usual large car to an office in Moscow, where he found himself confronted by R. A. Rudenko, the Soviet Union's Public Prosecutor. This august official, who chiefly impressed Pasternak by lacking any semblance of a neck, presented for his signature a prepared statement. It was an undertaking to have nothing more to do with foreigners, but Pasternak replied that he was only prepared to sign a statement to the effect that he had seen this document; he was not prepared to sign it, or to give the required guarantee. The authorities also urged Ivinskaya to give a similar undertaking, but were no more successful with her than with him. He did go so far as to display on the front door of his dacha a notice in English, French and German. 'PASTERNAK DOES NOT RECEIVE. HE IS FORBIDDEN TO RECEIVE FOREIGNERS.' But received the foreigners still were.[38] They included several who have since published books about him: Jacqueline de Proyart (Professor of Russian at the University of Poitiers), and the West German journalists Gerd Ruge and Heinz Schewe.

In December 1958 Pasternak was subjected to a squall of renewed abuse in the Soviet press. The occasion was the founding congress of a new branch of the Writers' Union: that of the Russian Republic (RSFSR), an organ dominated to an even greater extent than the All-Union apparatus by literature's hard-liners and 'heavies'. Pasternak's misdemeanours formed a natural target for this moot of diehards, among whom the literary functionary and author of bluff seafaring yarns Leonid Sobolev was prominent. He denounced the perpetrator of *Doctor Zhivago* on 7 December, in language long ago familiar, for giving a weapon to the Soviet Union's enemies, and for playing into the hands of Cold War agents. Sobolev also accused Pasternak of carrying self-obsession 'to extreme pathological lengths'. It was only one of several attacks mounted against Boris Leonidovich at the same congress. Other speakers fulminated against the Pasternak cult which had allegedly sprung up among certain young Soviet authors. Then Aleksey Surkov spoke. He was still the First Secretary of the All-Union Writers' Union, he was still Pasternak's arch-enemy among Soviet literary officials, and he now rose to mock that 'putrid internal *émigré*' as a treacherous apostate driven from the honourable family of Soviet writers by our righteous wrath.[39]

Well might Surkov bluster, for his own position as literature's top official was far from safe. He was fast developing into one of the *Zhivago* scandal's major casualties, discredited as he was by his persistent advocacy of a strategy which had brought nothing but trouble to the Kremlin. Surkov had advised against the publication of *Doctor Zhivago* in the Soviet Union, and had been prominent in promoting the vicious campaign launched against Pasternak by the Soviet publicity machine after the Nobel Prize announcement. This was the combination of policies which had blown up the *Zhivago* affair into a major international scandal, and now Surkov had to pay the price. He was soon to be dismissed from his First Secretaryship. He is even said to have been summoned by the enraged Khrushchev who 'grabbed him by the collar, shook him fiercely and gave him a terrible dressing-down for failing to mention that Pasternak was a world-famous author'.[40]

This story is consistent with the opinion on the handling of the *Zhivago* scandal which was to be expressed in Khrushchev's memoirs as published in 1974, ten years after his removal from office. The ousted statesman and scourge of literary flunkeys here maintains that Soviet publication of Pasternak's novel should have been permitted, and that readers should have been given the opportunity to make up their own minds about it. Such was Khrushchev's considered view; but he himself had still not read the novel at the time when he offered this comment.[41]

January 1959 was a busy month for Pasternak. He had at last agreed to make a final break with his wife and to go away with Ivinskaya. Their intention was to elope to Tarusa, a small provincial town south of Moscow, where they had been offered a refuge by the elderly memoirist and short-story writer Konstantin Paustovsky. Once established at Tarusa, Pasternak was to seek a divorce from Zinaida Nikolayevna and marry Olga Vsevolodovna as his third wife.[42]

While occupied with these private plans, he reverted to activity in the public arena by granting an interview to a British journalist, Alan Moray Williams. The result was an article published in the London *News Chronicle* on 19 January 1959. It sounded like, and indeed was, a defiant public challenge to Soviet authority. Pasternak criticizes the efforts of 'technocrats' to exploit writers for social purposes 'like so many radioactive isotopes'. But the author's true function is a very different one. 'The writer is the Faust of modern society, the only surviving individualist in a mass age. To his orthodox contemporaries he seems a semi-madman.' Pasternak also declared that the Soviet Writers' Union 'would like me to go on my knees to them – but they will never make me'.[43] To give publicity to such views in a foreign periodical was to make an open breach in the informal concordat made with the Soviet authorities in November 1958, and trouble was bound to follow.

It happened that Pasternak's departure for Tarusa with Ivinskaya was scheduled to take place on the day following the publication of the *News Chronicle* interview. But on that very day, at the very last moment and before the Soviet authorities had had time to react to Pasternak's public challenge, he suddenly confronted his beloved with the announcement that he had decided to call off their proposed elopement altogether. He said that he did not want to 'hurt people who were not at fault' – his wife, in other words. The predictable result of what seemed a callous betrayal was a violent tantrum by Olga Vsevolodovna. She had always wanted him for herself, she had served four years in prison and labour camp as a direct consequence of her association with him, and she now understandably feared for her own and her children's future. What would become of them after his death, which – in view of his recent severe illnesses – might be only too imminent? To bear the name of Pasternak would have afforded her considerable protection. Can it be wondered that she made him feel the full fury of a woman simultaneously scorned and exposed to serious risks that she had been counting on minimizing through wedlock? Or that she stormed off from Peredelkino to Moscow with threats of abandoning her lover for ever?[44]

At her Moscow flat on the next day Ivinskaya received an urgent telephone call from the Party Central Committee. The cultural chieftain Dmitry Polikarpov was on the line yet again to protest vigorously against Pasternak's latest indiscretion, the *News Chronicle* interview. It was too late, now, to do anything about that, but Polikarpov feared that Pasternak might be about to embark on 'new insanities'. He wanted Ivinskaya to go back to Peredelkino and stop them.[45]

It need not be said that the estranged lovers were more concerned with each other than with Polikarpov and his troubles. A passionate reunion ended their quarrel, and Olga promised that she would never leave Boris again. As for the 'new insanities' feared by Polikarpov, one had already been committed. When Ivinskaya had flounced out of Peredelkino on the previous day, after losing all patience with her lover, Pasternak had immediately sat down and written a poem pouring out his agony of spirit at the combination of acute personal and public sufferings which now assailed him.[46] This lyric, 'Nobel Prize', has become one of his most famous, and though it is not one of his best it does comment touchingly on his personal predicament. He describes himself as a beast at bay with the hunt at his heels and all escape cut off. Yet what, he asks, was his crime? Was he a villain or a monster of depravity? All he had done was 'To make the whole world weep / At my homeland's beauty'. He alludes to his mistress's departure for Moscow after their quarrel as follows.

> No longer is my right hand with me.
> My darling's here with me no more.

In the last stanza Pasternak refers to feeling a noose round his throat, speaks of the hour of his death being nigh, and longs for the presence of 'My right hand / To wipe away my tears'.[47]

As if to show that the *News Chronicle* interview was no isolated accident, Pasternak conveyed the text of 'Nobel Prize' to a second British journalist, Antony Brown. It was published in the London *Daily Mail* on 11 February, but without the two final stanzas in which the poet alludes to his temporary estrangement from Ivinskaya. Still, even a truncated version of so outspoken a poem could only feed the flames rekindled by the *News Chronicle* interview of three weeks earlier. Further protests from the Soviet authorities followed, and the poet yielded to their pressure to the extent of making a conciliatory statement. It was published in the New York *Herald Tribune* of 14–15 February. Pasternak now denounced Antony Brown for publishing 'Nobel Prize' without authorization, also declaring that he would receive no more foreign correspondents. 'They only hinder my work and cause harm.'[48]

This disavowal was a mere tactical manoeuvre, and did nothing to redeem matters in the eyes of Soviet authority. With the *News Chronicle* interview and the 'Nobel Prize' lyric Pasternak had doubly repudiated his earlier public recantations. 'With his poem he cancelled all his persecutors' efforts to hoodwink posterity into believing that his renunciation of the prize had been completely "voluntary", and that he had publicly "repented".' Here was his revenge for being harried into signing his two letters of submission in the previous November.[49]

In February 1959 the spectre of further public scandal loomed as the time approached for the British Prime Minister, Harold Macmillan, to make an official visit to Moscow. What if Mr Macmillan, or some member of his entourage, should express a wish to meet the world's most notorious literary outlaw? It would be impossible to turn down such a request without loss of face, in which case heaven only knew what tactless remarks Pasternak might blurt out for instant dissemination over the ether. And so the decision was taken in the Central Committee's Cultural Department to have him tactfully spirited away from the Moscow area. Polikarpov urged Olga Ivinskaya to use her influence in her lover's own best interests lest he harm himself by giving another 'reckless interview'. Then an invitation conveniently arrived – or was privily elicited by the authorities – from Nina Tabidze, widow of the executed poet Titsian Tabidze, for Pasternak and his wife to stay with her in Tbilisi. Pasternak readily agreed to visit so old a family friend. But this decision to accompany his wife on a holiday in the far south naturally provoked further outbursts from his mistress, whom he now accused – not for the first time – of talking like a character in a bad novel.[50] Nor could Olga Vsevolodovna's intervention prevent Zinaida Nikolayevna from bearing her husband off to Tbilisi, where they arrived not a day too soon: on 20 February, the very eve of the dreaded Macmillan's arrival in Moscow.

Pasternak was on friendly terms with many of the Georgian Republic's surviving writers, as was natural for so distinguished a translator from their language, and for one who had so often visited their country in the past. But the local literary fraternity had been advised not to make too ostentatious a fuss over a visitor notoriously liable to provoke public scandal. And so his two weeks in Tbilisi developed as a period of pleasant rest in congenial surroundings, and not as some traditional Georgian orgy of hospitality. It was now that he at last finished reading Marcel Proust's great cycle of novels, which had occupied his attention for some time. In Tbilisi, Pasternak also conceived the intention – never to be carried out – of writing a new novel of his own, some sort of sequel to *Doctor Zhivago*.[51] Another *Doctor Zhivago*! The Kremlin's very masonry might have crumbled before a second such battering. How fortunate for the stability of Moscow and its Empire that a threat so dire was to remain unimplemented.

THE LAST REBIRTH

The lyrics written by Pasternak from 1956 onwards have remarkable unity as reflections of his mood, and it is not surprising that he wished to publish them as a collection. He transcribed them in an exercise book, gave them the title *When Skies Clear* and launched them on the world like *Doctor Zhivago* by permitting them to be spirited abroad. The volume was eagerly received in the non-Soviet world, being rapidly published both in Russian and translation. It contains forty-four lyrics.

When Skies Clear was not as offensive to Soviet orthodoxy as *Doctor Zhivago*. Nearly half the lyrics in the collection had appeared in Soviet publications shortly after they were written, and most of the rest would presumably have done so too if the poet's disgrace had not intervened. Indeed, the collection as a whole eventually did come out in Moscow as part of the 1965 one-volume edition of his verse. But four especially sensitive items were omitted from that edition on what can only have been political grounds, and do not appear ever to have been published in the USSR. The lyric 'Nobel Prize' was inevitably one of them. The others were 'Change', 'My Soul' and 'After Storm'.

'Change' offends by denouncing the facile enthusiasm which members of the Writers' Union were required to cultivate in their works; grief itself is said to be robbed of dignity by 'the writhing of vulgarians and optimists' who have corrupted their whole age, the poet himself with it. 'My Soul' was even less suited for Soviet publication, being a dirge for the victims of Stalin's persecutions. Finally, 'After Storm' was probably the most politically unacceptable of all the lyrics of the collection, but is perhaps the most successful as poetry. The poet describes nature brightly reviving after a thunderstorm, but claims that the artist's power to transform the world is even greater than nature's. That the storm symbolizes the disasters of recent Russian history is made clear in the last two quatrains, where individual creative inspiration – as opposed to revolutionary change – is shown to hold the secret of the future. Here is one of the main contentions of *Doctor*

Zhivago, and eight lines of the poem have already been quoted as the epigraph to the present study.

> Fifty years' memories recede.
> The tumult of their thunder dies.
> This century has come of age.
> It's time to let the future happen.
>
> Catastrophes and revolutions
> Don't clear the path to life's renewal
> As do the insights, squalls and bounties
> In one man's incandescent soul.[1]

Pasternak's favourite theme of art and the artist, hinted at in 'After Storm', is extensively invoked in *When Skies Clear* as a whole. An especially celebrated lyric devoted to this topic begins with a terse opening quatrain.

> I want to probe in everything
> Its inmost core:
> In work, in seeking out my path,
> In heart's confusions.

The poet goes on to wish that he could concentrate all the properties of passion in a mere eight lines of verse.[2]

It is in the following, no less renowned, item (already quoted in the Introduction) that Pasternak switches the discussion of his art to the area, so important to him personally, of the artist's fame and its undesirability.

> There's ugliness in being famous.
> That's not what elevates a man.
> No need to institute an archive
> Or dither over manuscripts.
> The aim of creativity is giving.
> It's not publicity or fame.

The artist must above all be true to himself, and leave it to others to worry about the details of his life.

> Let others, hot upon your trail,
> Pace out your life's span inch by inch.
> But *you* your failures from your triumphs
> Must never differentiate.[3]

Several other poems of *When Skies Clear* expose aspects of art and creativity. There is the cycle of four lyrics on Aleksandr Blok, whose work Pasternak had admired for half a century. There is a final tribute,

'Music', to the art whic.. Pasternak himself had cultivated in youth. And there is 'Night', in which the insomniac poet's reflections on his vocation are inspired by visions of a lonely aeroplane crossing the sky overhead. The lyric ends with Pasternak's famous address to the artist, who is urged to remain awake, to work uninterruptedly, to fight drowsiness 'like airman, like star'. The final quatrain revives an idea which the poet had begun to express many years earlier. Art is eternal, and it transcends the age in which it is created.

> Sleep not, sleep not, O artist.
> Yield not to slumber's grasp –
> You hostage from eternity,
> Held captive by your time.[4]

Besides making these memorable statements on art the Pasternak of *When Skies Clear* has also revived another lifelong obsession – woman. 'Eve' pays tribute to abstract womanhood with comments prompted by the sight of five or six lady bathers wringing out their swimming costumes on a beach.

> O woman, sight and glance of you
> No whit abash me.
> O essence of my breathlessness
> When passion chokes me.[5]

In 'Unnamed' the poet goes on to portray a specific anonymous woman. She is shy yet passionate, owns a fiery-skinned lampshade, and is identified by Ivinskaya as herself. After threatening to imprison this seductress in the dark seraglio of his verse, he offers to rename the trite word 'love', along with everything else in the world, just for her. In 'Women in Childhood' he contrasts his present devotion to the eternal feminine with the unedifying spectacle of females quarrelling in his presence long ago in his boyhood.

> I had to bow my sullen head,
> Bear women's twitter like a lash,
> Before I learnt the lore of lust
> And scaled infatuation's peak.

Ever ready to descend into the banal, Pasternak concludes by expressing his debt to womankind as follows.

> To all who've passed my way, my thanks.
> I am in debt to all.[6]

In this last collection of his verse Pasternak also rehearses, as so often in the past, the spectacle of the changing seasons. Three quarters of the year are pictured in the thirteen-lyric sequence which begins with 'Woodland Spring' and ends with 'Foul Weather'. Among the finest poems in this group is the lyric which has given its title to the collection as a whole, 'When Skies Clear'. It is serene in tone, describes the onset of fine weather after a period of prolonged rain, and compares the whole earth to a great cathedral. There is also the five-lyric sequence on winter in which intimations of the poet's own death – that rare but recurrent theme of his late years – may be discerned. Winter appears in person in his garden and peers through his windows as he is preparing to write.

> While she whispered 'Hurry!'
> With frost-blanched lips,
> I was sharpening my pencils
> As I made my clumsy jokes.[7]

In 'Unique Days', the last lyric in the collection, the poet reflects on the winter solstice as it has recurred annually from time immemorial. Time itself has stood still.

> And drowsy hands can't bother
> To flounder over dial.
> One day outlasts the century.
> The kissing never stops.[8]

With 'Unique Days', composed in January 1959, Pasternak completed nearly two decades of verse written in the new, simple manner which he had first begun to evolve in 1940 for the cycle *Peredelkino*; had continued with his wartime verse; and had then brought to its peak with the *Zhivago* cycle and *When Skies Clear*. His lyrics of these two decades add up to some five score individual items, and they form about a quarter of his overall lyrical output.

Akhmatova has made some trenchant comments on *When Skies Clear*. At one of their rare meetings Pasternak gave her seven or eight of the lyrics from the collection to read. Her verdict: 'Four are splendid, but the others stink.' Which items she so disliked on this occasion is unknown, but the verses which she rated superb were 'In Hospital', 'Foul Weather', 'Night' and the lyric from which the collection as a whole takes its title:'When Skies Clear'.[9] As is suggested by these and other comments which came from Akhmatova during Pasternak's last years, her attitude to him was still the same old potent blend of love, jealousy, resentment, condescension and concern.

Akhmatova's terse observations on *When Skies Clear* show her fully aware of the unevenness of Pasternak's writing, in strong contrast with those judges who are apt to plaster the whole of it with indiscriminate praise. His habit of soaring into the heights did not blind her to his capacity for occasional excruciating lapses. Her own off-the-cuff criticism of him shows the same characteristics. Many of her comments are sensitive and penetrating, and most of them are witty. But some seem based on mere prejudice. Just as she had once objected to certain mildly amorous passages in the *Zhivago* verses, so too she went on to deplore such whiffs of eroticism as are detectable in *When Skies Clear*. She mocked 'Eve', in which Pasternak ruminates on woman's sensual potentialities. She also dismissed 'Bacchanalia' as 'revolting' and 'shameful' – the poem which contains an allusion, outspoken by its author's chaste standards, to a love affair between an elderly man and a ballerina.

Ivinskaya has claimed to identify the hero of 'Bacchanalia' with Pasternak himself and the heroine – on the strength of the line 'prison's vaults have not broken her' – with herself. Other details include the lover kneeling before his mistress, the 'vivid black magic in their hot arms', and the fact that 'a short second together' means more to them than the whole universe. Of all this Ivinskaya wrote: 'Yes – it's all us, all about us.'[10] But much of it could have been about any lovers in the world, which helps to explain why it so exasperated Akhmatova. She had written much more love poetry than Pasternak, and her own love affairs had once been far, far more turbulent than his. But they had decently subsided with the passing of the years, and she still thought that it would only have been proper for him to undergo the same evolution.

Another factor prejudicing Akhmatova against 'Bacchanalia' was what she felt to be its sympathetic portrayal of the Soviet artistic élite. Having belonged to that élite ever since it had first emerged, Pasternak still did belong to it – despite all his misdemeanours, despite all the disgrace that he had so courageously incurred. But Akhmatova remained the outsider she had so long been.

For decades Pasternak had resided comfortably in his country villa and Moscow apartment, while Akhmatova had been ill-housed in shabby bedsitters in disorderly communal flats. Pasternak's translation contracts had brought him a far larger income than she had earned from the same activity. He moved easily and of right in the world of leading Russian actors, musicians and writers – a milieu over which Akhmatova had once reigned unchallenged as the empress of the country's artistic Bohemia. Now, however, she was excluded as too poor, too unfashionable, too compromised by a long record of non-cooperation with the political system. It was, consequently, the emphasis on privilege and luxury in 'Bacchanalia' that most offended her – the lavish ball, the scenes of drunkenness, the atmosphere of conspicuous consumption.[11]

Akhmatova heartily disliked the whole tone of Pasternak's life at Peredelkino, as is evident from her comments on a visit of September 1956. It had been a glittering social and cultural occasion, with one piano performance by Svyatoslav Richter before dinner and another by Mariya Yudina after dinner, followed by a poetry recital from the host. A brilliant scene indeed – but it was uncongenial to Akhmatova. There was also the problem of Pasternak's relations with his wife, whom he insisted on addressing in public by the embarrassing endearment *mamochka* ('mother'). This could only have been acceptable to Akhmatova had it been a sign that Pasternak had broken with Ivinskaya; alas, it was not. The mere air of wealth and privilege was wearying, and it was impossible (Akhmatova all too pertinently adds) to guess which particular individuals in the dazzling assembly were the police informers;[12] given the thoroughness of Soviet security precautions they may well have formed the majority.

On one occasion the striking contrast between the outcast Akhmatova and Pasternak the darling of the Soviet cultural élite was expressed by his wife Zinaida Nikolayevna in devastatingly frank terms which help to explain her unpopularity among her husband's well-wishers. She said that her Boris was a modern man, 'Soviet through and through', whereas Akhmatova 'smelt of moth-balls'.[13]

Akhmatova was to carry her resentment of Pasternak beyond the grave. Shortly after his death she exploded with indignation on hearing one of his admirers describe him as a martyr to persecution. This was stuff and nonsense, she told Chukovskaya. Far from being a sacrificial victim, Boris Leonidovich had been extraordinarily lucky. His temperament had ensured that he always enjoyed himself in any circumstances whatever. Almost all his writings had achieved publication in the Soviet Union or abroad, and the rest had been eagerly passed from hand to hand in manuscript. Pasternak had always had money; Akhmatova had long been desperately poor. Neither of Pasternak's sons had ever been arrested; Akhmatova's son had served long terms in labour camps. One had only to compare Pasternak's fate with Mandelstam's and Tsvetayeva's to see how fortunate he had been. And Chukovskaya could not help reflecting that Pasternak's sufferings over the Nobel Prize affair had been a mere 'butterflies' duel' in comparison with the persecution of Akhmatova and of Zoshchenko from 1946 onwards.[14]

Chukovskaya was quick to challenge Akhmatova's criticisms of

Pasternak, pointing out that he was highly sensitive to the persecution of others, even if he had not suffered severely in his own person. He was comparatively well off, yes. But he had worked hard for his income; and had been generous to the less fortunate, including Akhmatova. Even Akhmatova was better off than those (Chukovskaya did not mention that she herself was one of them) whose menfolk had never returned from the camps at all.[15]

Akhmatova listened to this impassioned defence in contemptuous silence, her nostrils quivering, 'like a countess in a bad novel'. How could she forgive a man who had been so repeatedly and excruciatingly tactless in his dealings with her? Boris Leonidovich was always promising to visit her and always failing to turn up. He kept trying to persuade her to receive his mistress, refusing to sense that Akhmatova cordially detested the woman. He had included long, eloquent laments for the deceased Marina Tsvetayeva in his *Autobiographical Sketch*, while sparing only a few scant words for Akhmatova herself. He had thus implied that he thought her a poet of infinitely less consequence (all the more wounding because that is what she surely is). His praise of her work might be warm, but it was suspiciously so. It was also casual, tastelessly expressed and insincere. When he briefly alluded to her writings in print, he could not even get her titles right. For this she called him a 'divine hypocrite',[16] and felt as deeply wounded as if he had been her own son, which, in her mind, perhaps he was.

On at least one occasion Pasternak made a direct assault on Akhmatova's maternal instincts. 'He rushed in here yesterday to explain that he is a nonentity', she drily informed Chukovskaya on 20 January 1954. Akhmatova explained that she had comforted him by saying that, even if he had written nothing in the last ten years, he would still remain one of the twentieth century's greatest poets. 'I adore the man', she added. 'But he's intolerable.'[17]

The episode once again calls to mind the issue of Pasternak's habit of demeaning himself on every possible occasion. Modesty this may indeed have been; still, it was closely bound up with 'an exceptional sense of his own worth', according to G. O. Vinokur, an acute observer who knew Pasternak well and was very fond of him. 'Where the humility ends and where the sublime conceit begins I don't know', the same observer went on to confess. His comment reminds one of the remark which has been quoted in Chapter 1 as having been addressed to the youthful Boris Leonidovich by his cousin Olga. 'Your fondness for disparaging yourself – I call it vanity disguised as modesty.'[18]

These observations astounded me when I first came across them.

When myself talking to Pasternak I was profoundly impressed by something very different – by the total absence of that casual arrogance which so often seems to emanate from individuals of considerably less distinction who chance to have caught the world's eye. I rarely met a man who seemed less concerned with establishing a 'pecking order'. Did this proceed from genuine egalitarianism? Or from an assumption of superiority so profound that the question of giving it expression simply could not arise? Perhaps the world will never discover. Nadezhda Mandelstam has suggested that he neither wanted relations with equals nor so much as suspected that anyone could *be* his equal. 'He always felt that he was special and stood apart.' On his fondness for exercising his own voice even his devoted admirer Gladkov has commented that 'Conversation with Pasternak was rarely a dialogue.'[19] But in my own, admittedly limited, experience discourse with him at no point ceased to be two-way communication. This was all the more remarkable since it is certainly true that the extended monologue was his preferred conversational mode.

Modest or conceited? Perhaps the best verdict is that which Gladkov gave when discussing this crux in Pasternak's character. 'It is not very easy to make sense of a person as complicated as Boris Leonidovich.'[20]

The contrast between the early, complex Pasternak and the later, less complex Pasternak was stressed by the poet himself again and again on the many occasions when he chose to disparage his earlier product. 'I don't like my pre-1940 style', a phrase occurring in *Autobiographical Sketch*, is only the best-known and one of the mildest of many such assertions. And yet the later Pasternak was not entirely consistent in dissociating himself from his early achievements. Andrey Sinyavsky has recorded the 'youthful ardour' with which the poet could still speak of *My Sister Life* when discussing that famous collection at Peredelkino forty years after it had been written.[21] In 1956–7 he was still perfectly willing to reissue *My Sister Life*, together with other extensive examples of his supposedly rejected early period, in the one-volume selection abortively scheduled for publication by Goslitizdat.

Do the later poems represent the summit of Pasternak's poetical achievement? Or do they mark a decline from the splendours of his youth? Helpful judgements have been made by Vladimir Weidlé and Angela Livingstone. Their views on the relative merits of the early and the late Pasternak are almost diametrically opposed, but both have argued their case with conviction and eloquence.

Weidlé speaks of Pasternak's outstanding early collection, *My*

Sister Life, as 'more promise than fulfilment', and as the natural outcome of what the poet himself later called his 'extrinsic piquancy' of the period. After that Pasternak had gone on (the critic maintains) to spend the rest of his career extricating himself from that phase. The process is described in a telling sentence of *Doctor Zhivago*. 'All his life he had struggled to elaborate a style so restrained and unpretentious that the reader or hearer grasps the meaning without being conscious of the process of assimilation.' Here, says Weidlé, was the goal at which the poet was aiming all his life, and which he triumphantly attained in the end while yet preserving the best from his past. He always retained his flair for the striking image, but eventually managed to bring such imagery under control. The verbal texture still dazzles, but the dazzle is no longer an end in itself. It is subordinated to content. Now at last Pasternak has something to say. He has conquered modernism, but he has not said goodbye to poetry.[22]

According to Angela Livingstone's very different verdict, Pasternak's later work suffers in comparison with that of his earlier, more dynamic period. For example, the attempted humour of the lyric 'Wide World' is trivial, just as the faith in the future expressed at the end of 'Nobel Prize' is disturbingly vague. Generally speaking, the immediacy and tension – the fight – has gone out of his work. It has become more an exposition of faith than an urgent experience. Not for nothing did the new, tamer Pasternak proclaim, in the first lyric of *When Skies Clear*, his intention

> Of planting out my verse like garden,
> With lime trees blooming in a row,
> In single file, their veins aquiver.[23]

How depressingly orderly, and what a contrast with the old casual splendour his new 'rows of rather general and simple abstractions' represent. There are also, the critic claims, far too many facile catalogues of words listed in bald sequence, an irritating trick exemplified in such lines as 'Roads, milestones, trees, ditches', and 'Mountains, lakes, islands, continents'. Angela Livingstone might also have mentioned generalized womankind's 'arms, back, shoulders, neck', as so fatuously invoked in one of the *Zhivago* lyrics. In portraying himself poised to 'Think, feel, love, live', the poet falls (she suggests) far short of achieving the purpose so masterfully asserted in one of these same lyrics, 'To probe in everything / Its inmost core'. It is all too slack, too abstract, too dull. Here is a bard reduced to confessing his inability to muster a few effective lines, however crude, on 'the properties of passion'. But he had already mustered many such lines forty years earlier – for example, in his cycle *The Breach* (1918). In sum, 'The wish – indeed the sense of compulsion – to be simple and general is accompanied by a loss and a renunciation.' In her conclusion Angela Livingstone well contrasts Pasternak's superb achievement of appearing to see the world anew – as in the early lyric 'Urals for the First Time' – with the very different vision of his maturity. 'Now the poet is seeing the world for the last time.'[24]

This opinion of the comparative merits of Pasternak's early and late periods is shared by Nadezhda Mandelstam among Soviet-domiciled connoisseurs of Russian poetry who have contrived to publish their views abroad. She takes as her text the well-known passage in *My Sister Life* where poetry is described as 'tautly bulging whistle', as 'crushed ice-floes' crunch', and as

> All that night's keen to trap
> In pool's deep crannies,
> And bring to creel as star
> On trembling wet palms.

How different from these superb images of 1917 is the line of 1956 in which Pasternak flatly asserts that

> The aim of creativity is giving.

What pomposity (Nadezhda Mandelstam continues) for any artist to go round talking about 'creativity'! The line might easily 'come from an official report'. Such gnomic utterances can indeed be embarrassing, and one might also instance

> To be a woman is a feat.
> Driving men mad's an exploit.[25]

This sounds like the sort of seductress whom age could all too easily wither, and whose claims to infinite variety might prove somewhat slender.

My own views on the comparative merits of the early and the late Pasternak are further from those of Vladimir Weidlé than from those of Nadezhda Mandelstam and Angela Livingstone. But, while accepting some of their adverse comments on certain items in the last collection of poems, I would set against such strictures the many superb lyrics of the later period which are worthy to stand alongside the poet's finest earlier achievements – such poems as 'Hamlet', 'Parting', 'After Storm', 'Woodland Spring' and many others. The assessment of Pasternak's poetry as a whole has perhaps suffered from individual critics' reluctance to recognize the unevenness of quality which Akhmatova was quick to spot, and which was so salient a feature in his writing of all periods. He can indeed be disappointing at his worst. But how startling, forceful and enchanting he is at his best. He repeatedly showed himself the unique, original and dazzling poet who is so splendidly represented in almost all his numerous phases, as in the many passages in which the virtues of the various phases are fused. To this it may be added that Pasternak always was, and remained, an outstandingly life-affirming writer. Chukovskaya has called him 'the only non-tragic Russian poet', and has pointed out that 'His voice always sounded in the major key.' Effervescent joy on the slightest pretext, or on no pretext at all, was (she claims) an abiding feature in the poetry of one who 'each year contrived to marvel at the four seasons all over again'.[26]

So much for a tentative attempt to weigh Pasternak's early verse against his late verse and to sum up his overall record as a poet. But how do his consolidated achievements as a poet compare to his consolidated achievements as a prose writer?

Pasternak's verse and prose always tended towards fairly close symbiosis. He began writing prose fiction (and also literary articles) at almost the same time as he began writing poetry, and he continued to practise the two genres side by side. The interpenetration of his prose and his verse always remained intimate, while his scattered critical articles are often fundamental to the understanding of both. This fusion of verse and prose is particularly close in *Doctor Zhivago*. All the same, Pasternak is more justly summed up as a poet who was also a prose writer than as one whose attainments in the two areas are of comparable importance.

His superiority in verse derives in part from the wayward and impulsive nature of his genius. Both in the creative and the performing arts supreme effectiveness greatly depends on the tension between an artist's power on the one hand, and his ability to control that power on the other. It is in the first of these areas that Pasternak's strength as a writer clearly lies. He has already been quoted, in Chapter 3, as claiming that his collection *My Sister Life* was written by a mysterious outside 'force'.[27] Mysterious that force may indeed have been; but it resided within the poet, not outside him. What he perhaps possessed in less ample measure was the considerable aptitude and determination required to harness his own immense innate dynamism. It was in this aspect of creativity that prosody came to his aid. His metres, rhymes and stanzaic dispositions are fundamentally regular and conventional. True, he repeatedly took inspired liberties with all three. Yet their very regularity and conventionality furnished him with a firm – though by no means rigid – framework from which his darting intellect could display its pyrotechnics to full effect.

Pasternak's temperament did not permit him to be comparably successful as a creator of imaginative prose, where – in effect – anything goes, and the writer has no curb and snaffle provided for him. It is not so much that his prose lacks the bite, the resonance, the resilience, the effervescence and the sheer impudence of his verse, as that it deploys these same admirable qualities much less imperiously and piercingly. The laxer form has yielded a comparatively flaccid result.

If one now turns from the issue of poetry versus prose to consider Pasternak's prose fiction in isolation, while seeking to establish the relative merits of the pre-1940 and the post-1940 periods, his greater strength seems to be displayed in the second. Admittedly, the early short stories and fictional sketches have their admirers and their numerous virtues. They echo, they complement, they intertwine with the verse contemporary to them, and close acquaintance with them is indispensable to a full understanding of their author's evolution. All the same, it is hard to feel that the early fiction, subtly evocative though so much of it is, outweighs the achievement of *Doctor Zhivago*. As for prose of the non-fictional variety, *Safe Conduct* is the more impressive of his two accounts of his own life, despite the many merits of the later *Autobiographical Sketch*. And when it comes to Pasternak's literary and kindred articles, his brief *Notes on Translating Shakespeare's Tragedies* (from his later period) are surely worth more on their own than all his turgid and obscure early aesthetic and cultural essays from *Wassermann Reaction* and *Black Goblet* onwards, valuable though those documents are as pointers to the workings of his mind.

After writing his last verse in January 1959, Pasternak remained as eagerly poised for artistic and personal self-renewal as ever. In his final year of life he accordingly plunged into yet another untried area of creativity by making his only serious attempt to write a full-length play. This work, *Blind Beauty*, was never to be completed. But enough of it was written, and survives, to cover more than a hundred pages of print. The text represents what would have been the beginning of the completed play, and has been estimated to form between a half and two-thirds of the projected finished article.[28] Like *Doctor Zhivago* and *When Skies Clear* before it, the fragmentary but substantial *Blind Beauty* was spirited abroad and published in the West, both in Russian and in translation. It has never been published in the Soviet Union.

Blind Beauty was conceived as a chronicle of mid-nineteenth-century Russian social history. Its proposed scope may be gauged from the extensive surviving section, supplemented by Pasternak's own comments on his unfulfilled intentions. The completed text consists of four scenes set in the years indicated in brackets: Prologue, Scene One (1835) and Scene Two (1850); Act One, Scenes One and Two (about 1860). The surviving text accordingly portrays Russia during the quarter of a century preceding the Emancipation of the Serfs in 1861. The setting is an estate called Pyatibratskoye.

Any digest of the plot, as it first develops, is bound to suggest a libretto from light opera. Count Maksimilian Norovtsev, the wicked squire of Pyatibratskoye, has frittered away the extensive dowry of his charming Countess Yelena – with the sole exception of her jewels, which he is making every effort to extort from her. But so far is she from complying with his every wish that she has taken one of their house-serfs, the Count's valet Platon, as her lover.

Serfs and their tribulations are Pasternak's chief preoccupation in the play's early pages. Every attempt is made to convey both the quaintness of their Russian speech and the appalling conditions imposed by the odious form of slavery under which they suffered. Floggings at the whim of the master or bailiff are repeatedly and eloquently invoked, as is the appalling institution of conscription whereby male serfs designated by their masters were torn from wife and family to serve twenty-five years with the colours. Another theme is peasant unrest, as provoked by these conditions. Runaway serfs have become bandits in the nearby forests, forming a constant threat to life and property.

While these matters are ventilated in pages of lively below-stairs dialogue, Count and Countess Norovtsev are still absent from Pyatibratskoye, after leaving in order to avoid the assault on their ears of serf-women keening over menfolk recently drafted into the army. When they suddenly return home two melodramatic clashes ensue. The Count fires a revolver at his cuckolding valet Platon, but misses in a manner doubly pregnant with impending doom. His bullet strikes the plaster cast of some unidentified ancestor, while also contriving to blind the pregnant housemaid Lusha – the Beauty of the title. Pasternak himself said that Lusha symbolized Russia;[29] she was eventually to have recovered her sight in a part of the play that has remained unwritten. Another melodramatic scene follows as the wicked Count is shot, but not fatally, by a disguised assassin – one of the local brigands.

From the doomed atmosphere of these first episodes the three succeeding extant scenes continue the saga in a style suggesting that Pasternak was unrolling a triumphant progressive transition from the utter hopelessness of Russia in the middle of the nineteenth century to a Russia presented as successful, happy and prosperous in the later decades of the same century. This is confirmed by what is known of the author's intentions for the unfinished part of the play.

One powerfully symbolic figure is the serf Prokhor, who begins the play as Count Maksimilian's butler. He is falsely accused of the Count's attempted assassination, flogged with atrocious brutality and sent to Siberian hard labour. But he emerges from these ordeals many years later as an idealized commercial entrepreneur, the sort of man who holds the secret to Russia's economic development in his calloused hands. Another theme, barely sketched in as the text stands, is the troupe of serf-actors whose training in Paris to the highest professional standards Count Iriney Norovtsev (the wicked Maksimilian's benevolent successor) has sponsored. The chief among these serf-actors, one Agafonov, was to have symbolized the artist, whose significance for society still transcended that of all non-artists in Pasternak's conception. In the text as it stands the theme of Agafonov the artist is as little developed as that of Lusha the spirit of Russia. But Pasternak is known to have proposed portraying Agafonov as a successful Thespian of the 1880s, by which time he would of course long have turned his back on serfdom. Agafonov was also to have linked the themes of Art and Russia by bringing an eminent European doctor to Russia to cure Lusha of her blindness. These intentions confirm the play's general line of evolution from an atmosphere of gloom, doom and obscurity to one of buoyancy, optimism and national pride.

Had the play been completed it would probably have resembled a conventional stage drama as little as *Doctor Zhivago* resembles a conventional novel. *Blind Beauty* is akin to *Doctor Zhivago* in being a pageant or chronicle, and in lacking any closely knit plot. One disquieting feature is the inordinate space given to exposition. Not only is this inevitably dominant in Scene One of the Prologue, as at the beginning of almost any play, but it also swamps the three later extant scenes. In each the author is chiefly concerned, after engineering a chronological shift of some years or months, to tell the audience what has happened in the intervening period. The paradoxical result is that this work, which was apparently designed to project an optimistic view of the future, yet bears a marked retrospective orientation throughout most of its evolution. This seems a structural fault, but it might have been redeemed to some extent if Pasternak had gone on to finish the play.

While writing *Blind Beauty* Pasternak freely offered comments on work in progress, as he had on *Doctor Zhivago*. He told the Swedish publisher of his novel that the play was designed to describe Russia of the emancipation period in 'realistic verisimilitude' – a quality somewhat impaired by the operetta-like atmosphere of many of the completed pages. But what the work may lose in verisimilitude it certainly gains in lucidity. Nowhere else in Pasternak's writing is the reader so clear about the story line. As for the play's inner meaning, Pasternak told his Swedish publisher that the main aim was exactly the same as that of *Doctor Zhivago* – to 'give a conception of life in general, of life as such, of historical being or existence'. In December 1959 Pasternak wrote to Jacqueline de Proyart that *Blind Beauty* would be just as vast in its sweep, and in the number of its characters, as *Doctor Zhivago*. It was his purpose 'to leap forward . . . from the present, to seize a small part of that obscure and magic thing called destiny, the future'.[30]

What of the potential acceptability of *Blind Beauty*, had it been finished, for Soviet publication? The sombre picture of serf conditions in the Prologue fully conforms with the officially sanctified Soviet picture of Tsarist Russia as an unrelieved hell on earth. But Pasternak would certainly have found himself in difficulties with editors and censors if he had completed the text in the manner intended, by portraying the Emancipation of the Serfs of 1861 as the dawn of bright perspectives for Russia's future. In the official Soviet view the emancipation was a fraud and a failure. Another latent message might have worried the Soviet censors still more. It is hard to believe that Pasternak did not also conceive his drama as a paradigm of events in his own time. The appalling serf-based tyranny of Nicholas 1, which forms the background of *Blind Beauty*'s Prologue, must at some level of the author's consciousness have been equated with the still more appalling slave state instituted by Stalin and only partially demolished under Stalin's successors. Such broad shifting of historical frameworks was a natural habit of Pasternak's mind.

How effectively Pasternak's message to mankind, whether hopeful or not, might have been incorporated in a completed *Blind Beauty* can only be a matter for speculation. On the basis of the play as it stands Nadezhda Mandelstam censured him for trying to write 'a traditional melodrama' in his old age. She went on to say that *Blind Beauty* was composed in ignorance of the stage. And she scouted his 'sudden craving for the footlights' as senile folly.[31] To say this of an unfinished work was, perhaps, to be excessively caustic. But it must be admitted that the extensive completed sections of *Blind Beauty* do little to substantiate the somewhat extravagant claims which their author made for its potential.

Pasternak's theatrical involvements during his last year of life included translating Calderón, the Spanish playwright, and Juliusz Slowacki, the Polish poet–dramatist. In December 1959 Boris Leonidovich was reminded of another, German work translated into Russian by himself when the touring Hamburg Drama Theatre played Goethe's *Faust* in Moscow in the original tongue. He took Ivinskaya to see it. When the show was over they were both fêted by the cast at a party which continued well into the small hours of the morning.[32]

Boris Leonidovich celebrated his seventieth birthday at Peredelkino on 10 February 1960. He is reported as looking young and fit, while continuing to regret his capitulation to the Soviet authorities over the *Zhivago* affair. But the coming of spring saw an alarming deterioration in his health. Though he was still able to stroll round the nearby woods with Ivinskaya, there was something sallow and corpse-like in his appearance, and he was complaining of pains in his chest and leg. He saw his beloved for the last time on 23 April, when he handed her a manuscript of *Blind Beauty*.[33] Then he suffered a succession of severe collapses and was confined to the bed from which he was not to rise again. Doctors and nurses from the Writers' Union Literary Fund and the Kremlin Hospital arrived. The patient was variously rumoured as suffering from angina, and as having had a succession of heart attacks, but no official medical bulletin was made public either during his last illness or after his death. The cause of that appears to have been lung cancer of at least two years' duration, which had now spread to the heart.[34]

The poet remained conscious until the end. Was it his wish to summon Olga Ivinskaya for a last farewell? There is disagreement on the point among those who have described his last days. Akhmatova has sternly criticized his family for keeping Olga Vsevolodovna away, 'whatever her faults may have been'. But it seems that Akhmatova was mistaken. Others have testified that those around the dying man repeatedly asked him if there was anyone he particularly wished to see, and that he steadfastly refrained from mentioning any desire to summon Ivinskaya. According to her own testimony, he expressly sought to prevent her visiting him on grounds of vanity. His false teeth had been removed on doctor's orders, and he had decided that he looked too pathetically ludicrous for her to remain in love with him.[35]

If the report is true it shows that he was as determined to conform with the choreography of self-effacement *in extremis* as he had been in his prime. It does nothing to detract from the evidence of those near him that he met pain and death with great fortitude.

After taking leave of his two sons and his wife, Pasternak died at 11.20 p.m. on 30 May 1960.

Olga Ivinskaya learnt of his death early on the following morning. She rushed over to his home and burst in unchallenged; no one was so unkind as to prevent her from taking a last farewell of her lover. Within a few months she was to suffer a further term of imprisonment in the camps after she and her daughter Irina had been sentenced for alleged currency offences. Their real crime was, of course, their close association with Pasternak.

In the days immediately following the death of the great poet and political criminal these disagreeable prospects still lay in the future. His body had been laid out in modest state in accordance with Russian custom, being displayed in an open coffin in his house. Mariya Yudina and Svyatoslav Richter took turns to play suitable music on his piano while friends, relatives and admirers arrived to pay their last respects. They did so, and later attended the funeral, in impressive numbers, even though this display of homage was bound to incur official disfavour. Others made themselves still more conspicuous by their failure to attend Pasternak's obsequies: such writers and neighbours as Leonid Leonov, Valentin Katayev, Nikolay Aseyev and, the most notable absentee of all, Konstantin Fedin. No doubt Fedin felt that his attendance would have compromised his new high office, in which he had recently succeeded the discredited Surkov, of First Secretary of the Writers' Union. He judged it prudent to ignore Pasternak's death and funeral, drawing the blinds in his own dacha less (it was felt) as a sign of mourning than in order to dissociate himself from the whole embarrassing and unseemly affair.[36]

Fedin had been Pasternak's next-door neighbour at Peredelkino for twenty-three years, and the two men were at least close acquaintances, if not friends. But Fedin was part of official Russia, and official Russia was bound to ignore the great nonconformist's death. *Literaturnaya gazeta*, the leading organ of the Writers' Union, did at least publish a brief obituary notice on 2 June. But the announcement was so bald that it was widely interpreted as a deliberate insult. It was made in the name of the Union's Literary Fund, of which Pasternak had remained a member despite his expulsion from the Union itself in autumn 1958. The notice read as follows. 'The Board of the Literary Fund of the USSR announces the death of Pasternak, Boris Leonidovich, writer and member of the Literary Fund, which took place on 30 May in the seventy-first year of his life after a severe and lengthy illness, and expresses its condolences to the deceased's family.'[37] This was the only obituary of Pasternak to appear in the Soviet press.

Unofficial Russia mourned the premier poet's death more ceremoniously. On 1 June a requiem mass, in the Orthodox rite, was celebrated at his house and on the following day the burial took place at Peredelkino in accordance with an improvised civil ceremony.

There could be no question of widely advertising an event so inauspicious. But the death of a great writer had long been a traditional occasion for spontaneous reactions – and even for political demonstrations – by the Russian populace, and this tradition had survived into Soviet times. News of the funeral spread by word of mouth, and handwritten notices giving the details were posted at the Kiev Station in Moscow, the terminus of the line to Peredelkino. These notices – to the effect that the interment would take place at Peredelkino at 3 p.m. on Thursday 2 June – were naturally removed by activists and busybodies. But new copies promptly appeared. The result was that a large crowd, estimated at several thousand, began to congregate at the approaches to the village cemetery. It was also part of the national heritage that policemen of various kinds should grace a Russian author's funeral in quantity, and this tradition too was fully respected on the present occasion. Uniformed militiamen and plainclothes KGB operatives – the latter easily recognizable, according to ill-wishers, from their low brows – mingled with the crowd, directed car-parking, noted names, took photographs. Foreign journalists too were present in large numbers.

The gardens and countryside near Pasternak's home were a riot of apple and lilac blossom as the coffin was borne in slow procession for half a mile along the country lanes and paths leading from his house to the cemetery.

At the graveside Valentin Asmus, a philosopher and an old friend of Pasternak's, gave a short, informal address. He spoke of Boris Leonidovich as one of the glories of Russian literature. He had set an example of unswerving honesty and of an incorruptible conscience, and had taken a heroic view of his duty as a writer. He might have made mistakes, but these could not prevent his being recognized as the great poet that he was. Asmus concluded as follows. 'The deceased was a very modest man, and he did not like being talked about too much. And so I hereby end my address.'[38]

Two of Pasternak's lyrics – perhaps the best-known of all – were then recited: 'Had I but Known the Way of It' and 'Hamlet'. Shouts of

'Glory to Pasternak' rang out. The scene was moving almost beyond endurance; tension mounted, tears fell, the phantom of a political demonstration hovered. But before long the plainclothes security men moved in and managed to terminate the proceedings without open scandal.

As the coffin lid was lowered into position the bells of the local Church of the Transfiguration suddenly began pealing, perhaps by coincidence. The coffin lid was closed. Clods of earth began to thud down. The mourners slowly dispersed, but many of them are still there in spirit.

REFERENCE NOTES

References are by authors' or editors' surnames, and occasionally by titles, as listed in alphabetical order in the Bibliography.

The following abbreviations have been employed, and are repeated in the relevant entries of the Bibliography, where the titles concerned are quoted in fuller detail. The abbreviations 'Gl.', 'Iv.' and 'P.dz' always refer to the Russian originals of the relevant works; on the rare occasions when reference is made to the editions of these works in English translation the English titles are indicated, and are preceded by the unabbreviated author's surname.

Ch.   Chukovskaya, Lidiya, *Zapiski ob Anne Akhmatovoy* (Paris, 1974, 1980)
Gl.   Gladkov, Aleksandr, *Vstrechi s Pasternakom* (Paris, 1973)
Iv.   Ivinskaya, Olga, *V plenu vremeni* (Paris, 1978)
N., 1   Mandelstam, Nadezhda, *Vospominaniya* (New York, 1970)
N., 2   Mandelstam, Nadezhda, *Vtoraya kniga* (Paris, 1972)
P.   Pasternak, Boris
P.bp   Pasternak, Boris, *Stikhotvoreniya i poemy* (Leningrad, 1965)
P.dz   Pasternak, Boris, *Doktor Zhivago* (Milan, 1957)
P.fr   Pasternak, Boris, *Perepiska s Olgoy Freydenberg* (New York, 1981)
P.geo   Pasternak, Boris, *Letters to Georgian Friends* (London, 1968)
P.s, 1 Pasternak, Boris, *Stikhi i poemy, 1912–1932* (Ann Arbor, Mich., 1961)
P.s, 2 Pasternak, Boris, *Proza, 1915–1958* (Ann Arbor, Mich., 1961)
P.s, 3 Pasternak, Boris, *Stikhi, 1936–1959* (Ann Arbor, Mich., 1961)

INTRODUCTION (pages 1–9)

1 H. Bowman, in Brown, E., *Major Soviet Writers*, 139; 2 Fleishman (1980), 7; 3 Ibid.; 4 P.fr, 335; 5 P.bp, 447–8; 6 P.s, 2:1, 213–14; 7 P.s, 3:194; Gifford, 59; 8 P.bp, 125.

PART ONE: MAZE OF MELODIES (1890–1923)
1. *Inspiration in Search of a Poet* (pages 13–29)

1 N., 1:161; 2 P.s, 2:2; 3 P.s, 1:xi; 4 L. Pasternak Slater, cited in Mallac, 5; 5 *Die Familie . . .* , 64; P.s, 2:2–3; 6 P.bp, 178–9; P.s, 2:11–12; 7 N., 2:92–3; 8 P.s, 2:3–4; 9 Mallac, 31; 10 *Die Familie . . .* , 7; 11 P.s, 2:213; 12 P.s, 2:6–7; 13 P.s, 2:203; 14 P.s, 2:204–5; 15 J. de Proyart, in *Boris Pasternak*, 517; 16

Mallac, 14; P.s, 2:207; **17** P.s, 2:10, 205; **18** P.s, 2:205; **19** P.s, 2:9, 205–6; **20** P.s, 2:267; **21** P.bp, 253–4; **22** P.s, 2:19; **23** P.s, 2:18; **24** P.s, 2:15; **25** Barnes (1972), 62; P.s, 2:22; **26** P.s, 2:24, 212; **27** P.s, 2:210; **28** P.s, 2:11; **29** P.s, 2:27; **30** P.s, 1:xi; **31** Tsvetayeva (1979), 1:136; **32** P.fr, 8–9, 34; **33** P.dz, 40; **34** Mallac, 139; **35** J. de Proyart, in *Boris Pasternak*, 517–18; **36** P.fr, 47; **37** P.s, 2:234; **38** P.s, 2:219, 239; **39** P.s, 2:222; **40** Barnes (1969), 35; P.fr, 51; **41** P.s, 2:236; **42** P.bp, 107–9, 593–5; **43** P., in *Voprosy literatury* (Moscow), No. 9, September 1972, 142–3; P.dz, 418 **44** P.s, 2:244; P.fr, 53; **45** P.s, 2:262–3; Hughes (1974), 55–6.

2. *Poet in Search of a Voice* (pages 30–49)

1 P.s, 2:214, 219; **2** Barnes (1972), 63–5; **3** Barnes (1969), 104, 113–14; **4** P. (1977), 4; **5** P.bp, 65, 491, 622; **6** P.s, 2:31–2; **7** P.s, 2:31–3; **8** P.bp, 68, 496; **9** Barnes (1969), 135; **10** Barnes (1969); **11** P.bp, 70, 581; **12** P.bp, 579–80; **13** P.s, 2:32; **14** P.bp, 583–4; **15** P.bp, 578–9; **16** P.bp, 578, 581, 584; **17** P.bp, 494–5; **18** Markov (1969), 236–7; **19** Fleishman (1977), 65–6; **20** P.bp, 125; **21** Barnes (1969), 255–64; **22** Ibid., 224–35; **23** Hughes (1974), 25, 124; **24** Barnes (1969), 224, 452; **25** Fleishman (1977), 68–9; **26** P.s, 2:269; **27** P.s, 2:269–72; **28** P.s, 2:273; **29** Ibid.; **30** P.s, 2:273; P., *Okhrannaya gramota*, 150; **31** P.s, 2:34; **32** P.bp, 503–4, 698; **33** P.bp, 586; **34** Markov (1969), 261; C. Barnes, in *Boris Pasternak*, 315; **35** Barnes (1969), 334 ff.; **36** V. Shklovsky, cited ibid., 295; **37** P.s, 2:41; **38** P.bp, 86, 103; **39** P.bp, 94; **40** P.bp, 584–5; **41** P.bp, 83; **42** P.bp, 587; **43** P.bp, 88, 626; **44** P.fr, 120; Barnes (1969), Introduction, 2; **45** Markov (1969), 268; Barnes (1969), 449.

3. *Cloudburst of Light* (pages 50–70)

1 P.bp, 242; **2** Barnes (1969), 403–4; P.s, 2:35–6; **3** P.s, 2:324; G. Katkov, in *Boris Pasternak*, 329 ff.; C. Barnes, ibid., 325; **4** Fleishman (1980), 164; **5** P.bp, 631; P. dz, 148; **6** P. dz, 147–8; **7** I. Ehrenburg, cited in Barnes (1969), 78; **8** P.bp, 633–8; J. de Proyart, in *Boris Pasternak*, 519; **9** Tsvetayeva (1979), 1:146; Ch., 1:129; **10** A. Sinyavsky, in P.bp, 20; **11** P.bp, 111; **12** P.bp, 133; **13** V. Bryusov, cited in Fleishman (1980), 14; **14** P.bp, 11, 631–2; **15** Tsvetayeva (1979), 1:142–3 **16** Ch., 2:70; P.bp, 113–14; **17** P.s, 2:283; **18** I. Ehrenburg, cited in Fleishman (1980), 13; Thomson, 263; **19** Mandelstam, O., 2:264, 350–1; **20** Tsvetayeva (1979), 1:137–9; P.bp, 113; **21** A. Sinyavsky, in P.bp, 54; J. Cohen, cited in Barnes (1969), 2; **22** P.bp, 131; **23** P.bp, 65, 126, 621; **24** Barnes (1969), 4–5; P.bp, 187; **25** Barnes (1969), 6; **26** I. Ehrenburg, in Davie (1969), 40; **27** P.geo, 166–7; **28** A. Sinyavsky, in *Boris Pasternak*, 13; **29** P.s, 2:282; **30** P.bp, 655; **31** P.dz, 198–9, 247; **32** Fleishman (1980), 15; **33** P.dz, 186–7, 199; **34** Tsvetayeva (1972), 267; P.bp, 171; **35** Fleishman (1980), 59; Mallac, 99; **36** Blok, 6:468–9; P.s, 2:18; **37** Tsvetayeva (1972), 266; **38** P.s, 2:77; M. Aucouturier, in Davie (1969), 228; **39** A. Sinyavsky, in *Boris Pasternak*, 13; **40** Tsvetayeva (1972), 277–9; P.bp, 158; **41** Tsvetayeva (1972), 279; **42** N. Aseyev, in Davie (1969), 81; D. Mirsky, cited ibid., 25; **43** N., 2:664; P.bp, 162; **44** M. Gorky, in *Literaturnoye nasledstvo*, No. 70 (Moscow, 1963), 306; **45** P.bp, 193; **46** P.bp, 243–4; **47** Fleishman (1980), 14–15; **48** P.bp, 539; **49** P.s, 3:152; **50** J. de Proyart, in *Boris Pasternak*, 519; P., *Okhrannaya gramota*, 120–1; Z. Arbatov, cited in Fleishman (1980), 19; **51** P.dz, 173.

PART TWO: FLIRTING WITH HISTORY (1923–1946)
4. *Keeping Step with Revolution* (pages 73–103)

1 Fleishman (1980), 39; **2** P.fr, 127; **3** P.fr, 96 ff., 356, 361; **4** P.fr, 134; Ch., 2:358; **5** P.fr, 103, 116; **6** Iv., 95; **7** Fleishman (1980), 170; **8** N., 2:232–3; **9** Fleishman (1980), 40; P.fr, 76; **10** P.bp, 304–6; **11** Fleishman (1980), 29; **12** P.bp, 540–1; **13** Fleishman (1980), 29; **14** P.s, 3:134; **15** Iv., 72–3; **16** N., 2:180–1; **17** P.s, 3:157–9; **18** Barnes (1972), 68–9; **19** P.s, 3:215–16; **20** V. Weidlé, in Davie (1969), 120; A. Sinyavsky, ibid., 192; Gifford, 102; **21** P.bp, 236; **22** P.bp, 239–40; **23** P.bp, 239 **24** P.bp, 652; **25** P.bp, 244; **26** P.bp, 245; **27** P.bp, 248; **28** V. Weidlé, in Davie (1969), 124; **29** Ibid., 121; Thomson, 265; **30** Tsvetayeva (1972), 307; **31** P.bp, 277–8; **32** P.bp, 302; **33** P.bp, 661; **34** P.s, 2:151; Fleishman (1980), 136; **35** P.s, 2:155; **36** P.bp, 306; **37** P.bp, 671; Fleishman (1980), 141; **38** P.bp, 311, 596–7; **39** P.bp, 318; **40** P.bp, 342; **41** P.bp, 327, 333; **42** V. Weidlé, in Davie (1969), 113; Fleishman (1980), 28; **43** P.s, 3:217; P.bp, 199–200; **44** P.bp, 87; **45** Fleishman (1980), 92–7; **46** Ibid., 95; **47** Ibid., 92; **48** P.s, 2:285; Fleishman (1980), 82; **49** Efron, 107; **50** Tsvetayeva (1972), 266–8; **51** Ibid., 267–8; **52** Ibid., 273; Tsvetayeva (1979), 1:135; **53** Efron, 108; Tsvetayeva (1972), 310–13; **54** M. Tsvetayeva, cited in Hughes (1971), 285–6; **55** Tsvetayeva (1928), 129–30; **56** P.bp, 200–1; **57** *Literaturnoye nasledstvo*, No. 70 (Moscow, 1963), 300; **58** Efron, 109; **59** Barnes (1972), 66–71; **60** Ibid., 71, 74; **61** P.s, 2:1; **62** Gl., 15; **63** P.s, 2:289, 293 **64** P.s, 2:291; P.bp, 356; **65** M. Aucouturier, in *Boris Pasternak*, 345–6; **66** Ibid., 347.

5. *Duet for One* (pages 104–136)

1 P.fr, 132; **2** P.fr, 136; **3** P.bp, 352–4, 357, 676; **4** P.fr, 138; P.bp, 674; **5** P.s, 2:49, 51; **6** P.bp, 344–8; **7** P.bp, 370; **8** P.bp, 359; **9** P.bp, 365; **10** P.fr, 140–1; **11** P.fr, 140–2; Iv., 35; **12** P.fr, 141, 144; Iv., 28; **13** Ch., 1:134; 2:358; **14** P.bp, 349–50, 371–2; **15** P.bp, 199; **16** P. bp, 349, 376; **17** P.bp, 379; **18** P.bp, 371; **19** P.bp, 351; **20** P.fr, 131; **21** P.fr, 143; G. Nivat, in *Boris Pasternak*, 521–2; Yu. Krotkov, in *Grani* (Frankfurt), No. 60 (1966), 69–70; **22** P.bp, 377; **23** Conquest, 20; M. Hayward, in Gladkov, *Meetings . . .*, 15; **24** Mandelstam, O., 1:202; **25** N., 1:88; Iv., 76–7; **26** Akhmatova (1968), 182; N., 1:152 ff.; Iv., 75 ff.; **27** N., 1:318; **28** N., 1:155; **29** N., 1:157–8; Mandelstam, O., 1:196; **30** N. Khardzhiyev, cited in Brown, C., 129; **31** P.s, 3:262; Gl., 48; Mandelstam, O., 3:286; **32** K. Bogatyryov, cited in Döring, xx; **33** N. Bukharin, cited in Davie (1969), 30; **34** P.s, 3:217; **35** P.s, 3:217–18; **36** Iv., 86; **37** M. Tsvetayeva, cited in Iv., 85; **38** G. Struve, in *Sbornik statey . . .*,

10; **39** *Die Familie* . . . , 127–9; **40** Iv., 86; Mallac, 149; **41** J. de Proyart, in *Boris Pasternak*, 519; Ch., 2:358; Iv., 181–2; **42** Berlin, 172; **43** Ch., 2:358; P.fr, 364; **44** P.geo, 61–2; **45** Iv., 16; Ivinskaya, *Captive of Time*, 433; Döring, 1; **46** Döring, 9; P.fr, 153; **47** P.geo, 44–5; Gl., 32; **48** Iv., 138; **49** Charters, 365–7; Brown, E., *Mayakovsky*, 370; P.s, 2:44; **50** P., *Gruzinskiye liriki*, 93, 129; **51** P.s, 3:138; **52** P.s, 3:241; **53** Ibid.; **54** P.fr, 153; **55** P.fr, 151; **56** Iv., 95; **57** P.s, 2:223; Barnes (1979), 299; **58** P.s, 3:219–22; **59** P.s, 3:262; **60** P.fr, 160; **61** P.geo, 68; **62** Hughes (1974), 150; **63** Iv., 95; P.geo, 68; P.fr, 161–2; **64** P. fr, 365; **65** Gl., 11; **66** Iv., 145–6; **67** P.geo, 22; P.s, 3:63–4; **68** Gl., 10; P.fr, 178; **69** N., 1:318; **70** Ibid.; **71** A. Afinogenov, cited in Davie (1969), 31; **72** Ch., 1:19, 89; **73** Ch., 1:91; Akhmatova (1976), 188; **74** P.geo, 67; **75** Gl., 136.

6. *The Poet Goes to War* (pages 137–155)

1 Haight, 111; Ch., 1:90–1; **2** P.fr, 185; **3** Haight, 113; **4** Thomson, 272, my italics; **5** G. Katkov, in P. (1962), 237; **6** P.s, 1:xxxvi, 2:34; Döring, 3; **7** P.bp, 187, 406; **8** P.bp, 395–6, 398; **9** P.bp, 405; **10** Gl., 114; **11** P.dz, 519; **12** Gl., 47; P.bp, 410, 559; **13** P.bp, 412–14; **14** Iv., 187; **15** Tsvetayeva (1972), 646; P.geo, 90; **16** Gl., 52–3; P.bp, 567; **17** Gl., 55–6; **18** Gl., 20–1, 28; **19** P.bp, 423; **20** P.bp, 559; **21** Iv., 88–9; P.s, 3:162; **22** P.dz, 522; **23** P.bp, 418; **24** P.bp, 415–21; **25** Thomson, 274; **26** P.bp, 561; **27** P.bp, 561–2; **28** P.bp, 562; **29** P.bp, 564; **30** Iv., 153; Gl., 91–3; **31** Gl., 32, 54; **32** Gl., 100; **33** Gl., 81; **34** France, 146; **35** P.s, 3:183–4, 191; Iv., 39; Gl., 32; **36** Gl., 86; P.geo, 93; **37** P.s, 3:194; **38** France, 33–4; **39** Iv., 90; **40** N., 2:422; **41** Iv., 94–5.

PART THREE: ENEMY OF THE PEOPLE (1946–1960)
7. *Ice Age Frolics* (pages 159–181)

1 Details of Pasternak's early relations with Ivinskaya (pp. 159–61) are based on Iv., 13–37; **2** Kingsley Amis, *Jake's Thing* (Harmondsworth, 1979), 286; **3** Iv., 31, 33–4, 54–5; **4** Iv., 31, 55–6; P.bp, 436; Ch., 2:123; **5** Iv., 29; P.bp, 427–8; **6** Iv., 135; N., 2:421–2; **7** A. Sinyavsky, in *Boris Pasternak*, 353; **8** Ch., 2:336–9; **9** Iv., 136; **10** Ch., 2:336; **11** Iv., 91; **12** Gladkov, *Meetings* . . . , 188; **13** Gl., 110; P.bp, 619; **14** Gl., 111; **15** Gladkov, *Meetings* . . . , 14; **16** Iv., 38–9, 43; **17** Markov (1961), 503–8; **18** Ibid., 505–6; Ch., 2:336; **19** M. Hayward, in Gladkov, *Meetings* . . . , 20–4; **20** Ibid., 13–14; **21** D. Ben-Gurion, cited in Mallac, 330; Gl., 49, 112; **22** Iv., 151; **23** Iv., 94; M. Hayward, in Gladkov, *Meetings* . . . , 7–8; **24** Ibid., 14; **25** Iv., 197; Gl., 120–1; **26** Gl., 118–19; **27** Details of Ivinskaya's arrest and imprisonment (pp. 173–5) are based on Iv., 97–131; **28** P.bp, 440; **29** Iv., 131; **30** Iv., 115; Akhmatova (1968), 151; **31** P.geo, 126; **32** Markov (1961), 504; **33** Ibid., 507–8; **34** Ibid., 504; Iv., 93; **35** P. geo, 131, 142; Ch., 2:14; **36** M. Hayward, in Gladkov, *Meetings* . . . , 19–20; **37** France, 13; **38** P. geo, 131; **39** P. geo, 134–5, 147; **40** P.geo, 149–50; P.bp, 467–8; **41** Iv., 132–4; **42** Ch., 2:14; Iv., 17.

8. *Birth Pangs of a Novelist* (pages 182–199)

1 Ch., 2:551; Iv., 36; **2** Iv., 35; **3** Ibid.; P.bp, 480; **4** Iv., 48–9; **5** Ch., 2:551–2; **6** Ch., 2:154, 383, 391; **7** Ch., 2:154–5; **8** P.geo, 153; **9** Iv., 211; **10** Iv., 213–14; **11** Iv., 138, 143; **12** Iv., 155–6; **13** Iv., 156; **14** Iv., 154; Gl., 50; **15** Iv., 215–18; **16** Iv., 221–2; **17** Iv., 222–3; **18** Iv., 230; Ivinskaya, *Captive of Time*, 429; **19** Ch., 2:70; **20** P.bp, 617–18; **21** P.s, 2:352; **22** P.s, 2:1; **23** P.s, 2:50; **24** P.s, 2:52; **25** Gl., 129–30; **26** Iv., 393–6; **27** Iv., 227–31; **28** Iv., 231–2.

9. *Dilemmas of a Doctor* (pages 200–230)

1 P.bp, 196; Tsvetayeva (1972), 266; Iv., 201; **2** N., 2:387–8; **3** H. Bowman, in Brown, E., *Major Soviet Writers*, 138; P.s, 2:352; Ch., 2:255; **4** P. dz, 149; **5** P. dz, 387; **6** Iv., 198; P. dz, 464–5; **7** Iv., 198–9; **8** P. dz, 409; **9** P. dz, 428; **10** Iv., 181; P. dz, 427; **11** P. dz, 519; **12** P. dz, 515; **13** P. dz, 10, 473; **14** P. dz, 9, 267–8; **15** P. dz, 198; **16** P. dz, 186–7, 247; **17** P. dz, 247; **18** P.dz, 294; **19** P.dz, 347–8; **20** P.dz, 9, 270, 306–7, 466; **21** Conquest, 136–63; **22** M. Hayward, in Gladkov, *Meetings . . .* , 9–10; **23** P.dz, 307; **24** Ch., 2:213; **25** V. Erlich, in Erlich, 134; S. Hampshire, ibid., 130; P. dz, 513–14; **26** P.dz, 314, 437; **27** P.dz, 286, 290, 416; **28** P.dz, 80, 290; **29** P.dz, 42, 44; **30** P.dz, 10, 423; **31** P.dz, 68; **32** P.dz, 91; **33** G. Katkov, in P. (1962), 226; **34** P.bp, 431; **35** P.bp, 441; **36** Davie (1965), 144; **37** P.bp, 443; **38** P.dz, 566; **39** P. dz, 530–1; **40** P.dz, 532; **41** G. Katkov, in P. (1962), 247; A. Gayev, in *Sbornik statey . . .* , 43; **42** P.dz, 549; Iv., 36; **43** Hughes (1974), 74; G. Katkov, in P. (1962), 224; **44** P. dz, 464; **45** G. Katkov, in P. (1962), 235; **46** S. Hampshire, in Erlich, 126; I. Deutscher, in Davie (1969), 251; **47** I. Ehrenburg, in *Sbornik statey . . .* , 43; **48** Ch., 2:213; N., 2:388; **49** Gl., 139–40; **50** Ch., 2:215, 220; Gl., 137; **51** F. Stepun, in Erlich, 119; **52** Gl., 137; Ch. 2:213; **53** Gl., 139; S. Hampshire, in Erlich, 128; **54** P.dz, 121; Ch., 2:220; **55** I. Deutscher, in Davie (1969), 253; **56** M. Hayward, in Gladkov, *Meetings . . .* , 25–30; **57** P.dz, 40, 55; P., *Doctor Zhivago* (in English), 59; **58** P.dz, 291; **59** S. Spassky, in Ivinskaya, *Captive of Time*, 419.

10. *Prizewinner* (pages 231–253)

1 McLean, 3; **2** Ch., 2:574–6; **3** Ch., 2:218; **4** Iv., 235; **5** Ch., 2: 246–7: Ye. Yevtushenko, cited in Iv., 162; **6** P.bp, 365; **7** P.s, 1:xv; **8** Iv., 236–7; **9** Iv., 240; **10** Iv., 240–1; **11** Iv., 242; **12** Ibid.; **13** Conquest, 127–35; **14** Ibid., 136–7 **15** Iv., 244; **16** Conquest, 164–72; **17** Iv., 245–6; **18** Iv., 252; **19** Iv., 248; **20** Conquest, 175; Iv., 252; **21** Iv., 252–3; **22** 'Delo Pasternaka', 30–2; **23** P.dz, 173; **24** Iv., 253; **25** Iv., 254–5; **26** Iv., 255–7; **27** Iv., 258–60; **28** 'Delo Pasternaka', 32–3; **29** Iv., 271–9; **30** Iv., 281–7; **31** Iv., 288–91; **32** Iv., 298–9; **33** 'Delo Pasternaka', 34–6; **34** Iv., 260; **35** Iv., 307; 'Delo Pasternaka', 36; **36** Iv., 299; *Sbornik statey . . .* , 42; **37** Iv., 295; P.s, 3:108–9; **38** Iv., 313–14; **39** *Sbornik statey . . .* , 41; Conquest, 95; **40** Dewhirst, 13; **41** Ivinskaya, *Captive of Time*, 430–1; **42** Iv., 317–18; **43** Conquest, 96; **44** Iv., 317–18; **45**

Iv., 318–19; **46** Iv., 319 **47** P.s, 3:107–8; **48** Ivinskaya, *Captive of Time*, 432–3; **49** Iv., 320; **50** Iv., 320–1; **51** Iv., 404.

11. *The Last Rebirth* (pages 254–272)

1 P.s, 3:63–4, 66–7, 105–6; **2** P.bp, 446; **3** P.bp, 447–8; **4** P.bp, 462–3; **5** P.bp, 448–9; **6** Iv., 55; P.bp, 449, 485; **7** P.bp, 455–6, 470; **8** P.bp, 487–8; **9** Ch., 2:201; **10** Ch., 2:210, 567; P.bp, 476, 480; Iv., 45; **11** Ch., 2:210; **12** Ch., 2:177; **13** Ch., 2:340; **14** Ch., 2:275, 334; **15** Ch., 2:334–5; **16** Ch., 2:335; Ivinskaya, *Captive of Time*, 158, footnote; **17** Ch., 2:43; **18** Gl., 98; P.fr, 47; **19** N., 2:260; Gl., 116; **20** Gl., 98; **21** P.s, 2:34; A. Sinyavsky, in *Boris Pasternak* . . . , 13; **22** P.dz, 452; V. Weidlé, in P.s, 3: vii–xv; **23** A. Livingstone, in Erlich, 166–75; P.bp, 447; **24** A. Livingstone, loc. cit.; P.bp, 446; **25** P.bp, 126, 431, 447; N., 2:373; **26** Ch., 2:333; **27** P.s, 2:282; **28** M. Hayward, in P., *Blind Beauty*, 6; **29** Ibid., 7; **30** Ibid., 5–6; **31** N., 2:408; **32** Iv., 335–6; **33** Iv., 336–40; **34** Mallac, 46; **35** Ch., 2:319, 326–7; Iv., 342; **36** Iv., 347; **37** Iv., 348; **38** Iv., 352.

BIBLIOGRAPHY

The bibliography consists of works cited in the Reference Notes, in certain cases by the abbreviations given below to the left of the relevant title.

Cited as

AKHMATOVA, ANNA, *Sochineniya*, 2 vols., ed. G. P. Struve and B. A. Filipoff (Washington, D.C.: vol. 1, 2nd ed., revised and enlarged, 1967; vol. 2, 1968)

———*Stikhotvoreniya i poemy*, ed. V. M. Zhirmunsky (Leningrad, 1976)

BARNES, CHRISTOPHER J., 'The Poetry of Boris Pasternak, 1913–1917', unpublished D. Phil. thesis, University of Cambridge, 1969

———'Boris Pasternak and Rainer Maria Rilke: Some Missing Links', *Forum for Modern Language Studies*, No. 8 (January 1972), pp. 61–78

———'The Original Text of "O skromnosti i smelosti" ', *Slavica Hierosolymitana*, No. 4 (1979), pp. 294–303

BERLIN, ISAIAH, *Personal Impressions* (London, 1980)

BLOK, ALEKSANDR, *Sobraniye sochineniy v vosmi tomakh* (Moscow-Leningrad, 1960–3)

Boris Pasternak, 1890–1960: Colloque de Cerisy-la-Salle, 11–14 septembre 1975 (Paris, 1979)

BROWN, CLARENCE, *Mandelstam* (Cambridge, 1973)

BROWN, EDWARD J. (ED.), *Major Soviet Writers: Essays in Criticism* (London, 1973)

BROWN, EDWARD J., *Mayakovsky: A Poet in the Revolution* (Princeton, N.J., 1973)

CHARTERS, ANN and SAMUEL, *I Love: The Story of Vladimir Mayakovsky and Lili Brik* (London, 1979)

Ch.   CHUKOVSKAYA, LIDIYA, *Zapiski ob Anne Akhmatovoy*, 2 vols.: vol. 1, in *Pamyati Anny Akhmatovoy* (Paris, 1974), pp. 43–198; vol. 2 (Paris, 1980)

CONQUEST, ROBERT, *Courage of Genius: The Pasternak Affair* (London, 1961)

DAVIE, DONALD, *The Poems of Dr. Zhivago* (New York, 1965)

DAVIE, DONALD and ANGELA LIVINGSTONE (EDS.), *Pasternak: Modern Judgements* (London, 1969)

'*Delo Pasternaka*' (Munich, 1958)

DEWHIRST, MARTIN and ROBERT FARRELL (EDS.), *The Soviet Censorship* (Metuchen, N.J., 1973)

Die Familie – La famille – The Family Pasternak: Erinnerungen, Berichte – Mémoires, Rapports – Reminiscences, Reports (Geneva, 1975)

DÖRING, JOHANNA RENATE, *Die Lyrik Pasternaks in den Jahren 1928–1934* (Munich, 1973)

EFRON, ARIADNA, *Stranitsy vospominaniy* (Paris, 1979)

ERLICH, VICTOR (ED.), *Pasternak: A Collection of Critical Essays* (Englewood Cliffs, N.J., 1978)

FLEISHMAN, LAZAR, *Statyi o Pasternake* (Bremen, 1977)

——*Boris Pasternak v dvadtsatyye gody* (Munich, 1980)

FRANCE, ANNA KAY, *Boris Pasternak's Translations of Shakespeare* (Berkeley, 1978)

GIFFORD, HENRY, *Pasternak: A Critical Study* (Cambridge, 1977)

Gl.   GLADKOV, ALEKSANDR, *Vstrechi s Pasternakom* (Paris, 1973)

——(the same) *Meetings with Pasternak: A Memoir by Alexander Gladkov*, tr. into English and ed., with introduction and notes, by Max Hayward (London, 1977)

HAIGHT, AMANDA, *Anna Akhmatova: A Poetic Pilgrimage* (New York, 1976)

HUGHES, OLGA R., '*Boris Pasternak i Marina Tsvetayeva (k istorii druzhby)*', *Vestnik russkogo studencheskogo khristianskogo dvizheniya*, No. 100 (1971), pp. 281–305

——*The Poetic World of Boris Pasternak* (Princeton, N.J., 1974)

Iv.   IVINSKAYA, OLGA, *V plenu vremeni: gody s Borisom Pasternakom* (Paris, 1978)

——(the same) *A Captive of Time*, tr. into English, with introduction and notes, by Max Hayward (London, 1978)

MALLAC, GUY DE, *Boris Pasternak: His Life and Art* (Norman, Okla., 1981)

N., 1   MANDELSTAM, NADEZHDA, *Vospominaniya* (New York, 1970)

N., 2   ——*Vtoraya kniga* (Paris, 1972)

MANDELSTAM, OSIP, *Sobraniye sochineniy*, 3 vols., ed. G. P. Struve and B. A. Filipoff: vol. 1, 2nd ed. (Washington, D.C., 1967); vol. 2, 2nd ed. (New York, 1971); vol. 3 (New York, 1969)

MARKOV, VLADIMIR, 'An Unnoticed Aspect of Pasternak's Translations', *Slavic Review*, vol. xx, No. 3 (October 1961), pp. 503–8

——*Russian Futurism: A History* (London, 1969)

McLEAN, HUGH and WALTER N. VICKERY (EDS), *The Year of Protest 1956: An Anthology of Soviet Literary Materials* (New York, 1961)

P.   PASTERNAK, BORIS

——*Gruzinskiye liriki* (Moscow, 1935)

——*Vilyam Shekspir v perevode Borisa Pasternaka*, 2 vols. (Moscow-Leningrad, 1949)

——*Okhrannaya gramota*, in *Opalnyye povesti*, ed. V. A. Aleksandrova (New York, 1955)

P.dz   ——*Doktor Zhivago* (Milan, 1957)

——(the same) *Doctor Zhivago*, tr. into English by Max Hayward and Manya Harari (London, 1958)

P.s, 1   ——*Stikhi i poemy, 1912–1932*, ed. G. P. Struve and B. A. Filipoff (Ann Arbor, Mich., 1961)

P.s, 2   ——*Proza, 1915–1958: Povesti, rasskazy, avtobiograficheskiye proizvedeniya*, ed. G. P. Struve and B. A. Filipoff (Ann Arbor, Mich., 1961)

P.s, 3   ——*Stikhi, 1936–1959. Stikhi dlya detey. Stikhi, 1912–1957, ne sobrannyye v knigi avtora. Statyi i vystupleniya*, ed. G. P. Struve and B. A. Filipoff (Ann Arbor, Mich., 1961)

——*In the Interlude: Poems, 1945–1960*, tr. into English by Henry Kamen, with a foreword by Sir Maurice Bowra and notes by George Katkov (London, 1962)

P.bp   ——*Stikhotvoreniya i poemy*, ed. L. A. Ozerov, with introduction by A. D. Sinyavsky (Biblioteka poeta, bolshaya seriya, Moscow-Leningrad, 1965)

P.geo   ——*Letters to Georgian Friends*, tr. into English, with introduction and notes, by David Magarshack (London, 1968)

————*The Blind Beauty*, tr. into English by Max Hayward and Manya Harari, with foreword by Max Hayward (New York, 1969)

————*Collected Short Prose*, ed. with introduction by Christopher Barnes (New York, 1977)

P.fr   ————*Perepiska s Olgoy Freydenberg*, ed. with commentaries by Elliott Mossman (New York, 1981)

Sbornik statey, posvyashchonnykh tvorchestvu Borisa Leonidovicha Pasternaka (Munich, 1962)

THOMSON, BORIS, *The Premature Revolution: Russian Literature and Society, 1917–1946* (London, 1972)

TROITSKY, N. A., *Boris Leonidovich Pasternak, 1890–1960: A Bibliography* (Ithaca, N.Y., 1969)

TSVETAYEVA, MARINA, *Posle Rossii* (Paris, 1928)

————*Neizdannyye pisma* (Paris, 1972)

————*Izbrannaya proza v dvukh tomakh*, ed. A. Sumerkin (New York, 1979)

INDEX OF
PASTERNAK'S WORKS

2 Russian titles (lyrics only)

An entry is followed by its bracketed English translation only when this appears in the text. The untranslated entries refer to lyrics cited in the text without attribution by title, or by opening phrase in lieu of title. To assist identification, key phrases from certain lyrics are appended, and are preceded by a double asterisk.

GENERAL INDEX

P. stands for Pasternak.

A NOTE ON THE TYPE

The text of this book was set in a film version of
Garamond, a modern rendering of the type first cut by
Claude Garamond (c. 1480–1561). Garamond was a pupil
of Geoffroy Tory and is believed to have based his letters
on the Venetian models, although he introduced a number
of important differences, and it is to him we owe
the letter which we know as "old style." He gave to
his letters a certain elegance and a feeling of movement
that won for their creator an immediate reputation
and the patronage of Francis I of France.

Composed by Deltatype,
Ellesmere Port, Great Britain.

Printed and bound by R. R. Donnelley & Sons,
Harrisonburg, Virginia.